The Internet For Dumm... 11th Edition

W9-AWK-661

Firefox, the world's best Web browser

- **Download it for free** from www.mozilla.org. After that, it can update itself automagically.
- **Go directly to a Web site:** Type an address into the Address box and press Enter. (You can leave off the http://.) Press F6 to move the cursor into the Address box.
- **Reload the current page:** Press Ctrl+R or click Reload.
- **Open a new tab in the Firefox window:** Press Ctrl+T. Or, Ctrl+click a link to open it in a new tab. To close the current tab, press Ctrl+W. To display the next tab, press Ctrl+Tab.
- **Add the current page to your bookmarks:** Press Ctrl+D.
- **Edit your bookmarks:** Press Ctrl+B.
- **Set your browsing preferences:** Choose Tools⇨Options.
- **Set the current page (or pages) to be your start page:** Choose Tools⇨Options, click Main, and select Use Current Pages in the Startup section. If you have multiple tabs open, Firefox remembers them all.
- **Enter or exit Full Screen mode:** Press F11.
- **Erase cookies, or the history of which Web sites you've viewed:** Choose Tools⇨Options, click Privacy, click Clean Now in the Private Data section, choose which information to delete, and click Clear Private Data Now.
- **Block popup windows:** Choose Tools⇨Options, click Content, and make sure that Block Popup Windows is selected. Click Exceptions (to its right) to specify sites that can or can't open popups.

Internet Explorer (IE), Microsoft's browser

- It comes with Windows. Download and install new versions from www.microsoft.com/ie. Beware of Internet Explorer's many security holes, for which Microsoft issues frequent updates to patch. Check for updates at windowsupdate.microsoft.com.
- **Go directly to a Web site:** Type its address in the Address box and press Enter. (You can leave off the http://.)
- **Refresh the current page:** Press Ctrl+R or click Refresh or press F5.
- **Add the current page to your favorites:** Click the Add to Favorites icon or press Alt+Z.
- **Edit your favorites:** Click the Favorites icon or press Alt+C.
- **Set your browsing preferences:** Choose Tools⇨Internet Options.
- **Set the current page to be your start page:** Choose Tools⇨Internet Options, click the General tab, and click Use Current in the Home Page section.
- **Enter or exit Full Screen mode:** Press F11.
- **Erase the history of which Web sites you've viewed:** Choose Tools⇨Internet Options, click the General tab, and click the Delete button in the Browsing History section (or Clear History in IE6).
- **Control cookies on your computer:** Choose Tools⇨Internet Options, click the Privacy tab, click Advanced, select Override Automatic Cookie Handling (in IE7 only), set First-party Cookies to Accept and Third-party Cookies to Block.
- **Block pop-up windows:** Choose Tools⇨Options, click the Privacy tab, select Turn On Pop-up Blocker, and click Settings to specify exceptions.

For Dummies: Bestselling Book Series for Beginners

The Internet For Dummies, 11th Edition

Cheat Sheet

Thunderbird, an excellent e-mail program

- The latest e-mail program from the open-source Mozilla project. Download it for free from www.mozilla.org.
- **Set up an e-mail account:** Choose Tools⇨Account Settings.
- **Set your e-mail preferences:** Choose Tools⇨Options.
- **Compose a new message:** Press Ctrl+M or click the Write button.
- **Attach a file:** Click the Attach button or choose File⇨Attach.
- **Check spelling before sending messages:** Choose Tools⇨Options, click the Composition category, and select Check Spelling Before Sending.
- **Send and receive messages:** Press Ctrl+Shift+T or choose File⇨Get New Messages For⇨Get All New Messages.
- **Block JavaScript and images:** Choose Tools⇨Options, click the Advanced category, and de-select the Enable JavaScript In Mail Messages option. Also, select the Block Loading of Remote Images in Mail Messages option.
- **Delete the current message:** Press Delete or click the Delete button.
- **Reply to the current message:** Press Ctrl+R or click the Reply button.
- **Forward the current message:** Press Ctrl+L or click the Forward button.
- **Display your Address Book:** Press Ctrl+2 or click the Address Book button.
- **Create a new mail folder:** Choose File⇨New⇨New Folder, type a name, and set the Create As a Subfolder Of box to the folder name in which you want the new folder to live.
- **Configure junk mail filtering:** Choose Tools⇨Junk Mail Controls.
- **Create mail filters:** Choose Tools⇨Message Filters from the menu to display the Message Filters window, where you can see, create, edit, and delete filters.

Windows Mail and Outlook Express (e-mail programs that come with Windows)

- Beware of security holes, for which Microsoft issues frequent security updates. Download new versions from http://www.microsoft.com/windows/oe/. Check for updates at windowsupdate.microsoft.com.
- **Set up an e-mail account:** Choose Tools⇨Accounts, click the Mail tab, and click Add.
- **Set your e-mail preferences:** Choose Tools⇨Options.
- **Compose a new message:** Press Ctrl+N or click the Create button.
- **Check spelling before sending messages:** Choose Tools⇨Options, click the Spelling tab, and select the Always Check Spelling Before Sending setting.
- **Send and receive messages:** Press Ctrl+M or click the Send/Recv button.
- **Block images (OE 6):** Choose Tools⇨Options, click the Security tab, and select Block Images and Other External Content in HTML E-mail.
- **Delete the current message:** Press Ctrl+D or click the Delete button.
- **Reply to the current message:** Press Ctrl+R or click the Reply button.
- **Forward the current message:** Press Ctrl+F or click the Forward button.
- **Display your Address Book:** Click the Addresses button.
- **Create a new mail folder:** Choose File⇨Folder⇨New or File⇨New⇨Folder from the menu, give the folder a name, and choose which folder to put this new folder in.
- **Attach a file:** Click the Insert⇨File Attachment from the menu or click the Attach button.
- **Create mail filters:** Choose Tools⇨Message Rules⇨Mail.

For Dummies: Bestselling Book Series for Beginners

The Internet

FOR

DUMMIES®

11TH EDITION

by John R. Levine
Margaret Levine Young
Carol Baroudi

BICENTENNIAL
1807
⊛WILEY
2007
BICENTENNIAL

Wiley Publishing, Inc.

The Internet For Dummies,® 11th Edition

Published by
Wiley Publishing, Inc.
111 River Street
Hoboken, NJ 07030-5774

www.wiley.com

Copyright © 2007 by Wiley Publishing, Inc., Indianapolis, Indiana

Published by Wiley Publishing, Inc., Indianapolis, Indiana

Published simultaneously in Canada

For general information on our other products and services, please contact our Customer Care Department within the U.S. at 800-762-2974, outside the U.S. at 317-572-3993, or fax 317-572-4002.

For technical support, please visit www.wiley.com/techsupport.

Wiley also publishes its books in a variety of electronic formats. Some content that appears in print may not be available in electronic books.

Library of Congress Control Number: 2007934453

ISBN: 978-0-470-12174-0

Manufactured in the United States of America

10 9 8 7 6 5 4 3 2 1

WILEY

About the Authors

Please visit all three authors online at net.gurus.com.

John R. Levine was a member of a computer club in high school — before high school students, or even high schools, had computers — where he met Theodor H. Nelson, the author of *Computer Lib/Dream Machines* and the inventor of hypertext, who reminded us that computers should not be taken seriously and that everyone can and should understand and use computers.

John wrote his first program in 1967 on an IBM 1130 (a computer somewhat less powerful than your typical modern digital wristwatch, only more difficult to use). He became an official system administrator of a networked computer at Yale in 1975. He began working part-time — for a computer company, of course — in 1977 and has been in and out of the computer and network biz ever since. He got his company on Usenet (the Internet's worldwide bulletin-board system) early enough that it appears in a 1982 *Byte* magazine article on a map of Usenet, which then was so small that the map fit on half a page.

Although John used to spend most of his time writing software, now he mostly writes books (including *UNIX For Dummies* and *Internet Secrets,* both published by Wiley, and *Windows Vista: The Complete Reference,* published by Osborne/McGraw-Hill) because it's more fun and he can do so at home in the tiny village of Trumansburg, New York, where in his spare time he was the mayor for several years (yes, really, see www.Trumansburg.ny.us) and can play with his small daughter when he's supposed to be writing. John also does a fair amount of public speaking. (Go to www.johnlevine.com to see where he'll be.) He holds a BA and a PhD in computer science from Yale University, but please don't hold that against him.

In high school, **Margaret Levine Young** was in the same computer club as her big brother John. She stayed in the field throughout college against her better judgment and despite John's presence as a graduate student in the computer science department. Margy graduated from Yale and went on to become one of the first PC managers in the early 1980s at Columbia Pictures, where she rode the elevator with big stars whose names she wouldn't dream of dropping here.

Since then, Margy has co-authored more than 25 computer books about topics that include the Internet, UNIX, WordPerfect, Microsoft Access, and (stab from the past) PC-File and Javelin, including *The Internet For Dummies Quick Reference* and *UNIX For Dummies* (both published by Wiley), *Windows Vista: The Complete Reference,* and *Internet: The Complete Reference* (both published by Osborne/McGraw-Hill). She met her future husband, Jordan, in the R.E.S.I.S.T.O.R.S. (that computer club we mentioned). Her other passion is her children, along with music, Unitarian Universalism, reading, knitting, and anything to do with eating. She lives in Vermont (see www.gurus.com/margy for some scenery) and works as a software engineer for the Unitarian Universalist Association (www.uua.org).

Carol Baroudi first began playing with computers in 1971 at Colgate University, where two things were new: the PDP-10 and women. She was lucky to have unlimited access to the state-of-the-art PDP-10, on which she learned to program, operate the machine, and talk to Eliza (a computer-based shrink). She taught ALGOL and helped to design the curricula for computer science and women's studies. She majored in Spanish and studied French, which, thanks to the Internet, she can now use every day.

Carol has been working in the computer industry since 1975. Today she's an industry analyst, consulting for emerging technology companies.

Carol loves Europe and is always looking for reasons to go. She believes that we are living in a very interesting time when technology is changing faster than people can imagine. Carol hopes that as we learn to use the new technologies, we don't lose sight of our humanity. She feels that computers can be useful and fun, but are no substitute for real life.

Dedication

John dedicates his part of the book (the particularly lame jokes) to Sarah Willow, who surprises and delights him every day, and to Tonia, now and always.

Margy dedicates this book to Jordan, Meg, and Zac, who make life worth living, to her dad, to her wonderful parents-in-law, and to Susan, the world's best cousin.

Carol dedicates her part of the book to Joshua, with all her love, and to her friends, who remind her that there's more to life than writing books — or business, for that matter.

Authors' Acknowledgments

Orion Anderson, who's younger and cooler than we are, did most of the research and writing on virtual worlds in Chapter 19. Meg Young and Angus Barstow provided a reality check (or whatever the equivalent is in cyber-space) in Chapters 9 and 17. Ernie Longey took the picture that appears on the Maiden Vermont Web site in Chapter 7.

Mark Enochs hustled us through the editorial process despite our attempts to drag it out while (no doubt at great personal cost) making us look like better writers than we are. Rebecca Whitney is the editor who can look at our scribbles and, without fail, make them say what we meant to say, only clearer. Steve Hayes gets us organized, which is no easy task. Thanks also to the rest of the gang at Wiley Publishing, especially those listed on the Publisher's Acknowledgments page.

Margy thanks Jordan for holding everything together when she broke her foot during the writing of this book (no, she wasn't kicking her computer). Carol thanks Patrick, Arnold, Suzanne, and Laura, the wonderful folks at Kesher, and her family and friends for their unending help and support. We all thank Bill Gladstone at Waterside Productions for encouragement. The entire contents of this book were edited and submitted to the publisher using the Web — practicing what we preach. We thank our Internet providers: Finger Lakes Technologies Group (Trumansburg, N.Y. Hi, Paul!), Lightlink (Ithaca, N.Y. Hi, Homer!), and Shoreham.net (Shoreham, Vermont. Hi, Don and Jim!).

Finally, thanks to all the smarties (we wouldn't say wiseacres) who sent us comments on the previous editions and helped make this one better. If you have ideas, comments, or complaints about the book, whisk them to us at internet11@gurus.com.

Visit our Web site at net.gurus.com for updates and more information about the topics in this book.

Publisher's Acknowledgments

We're proud of this book; please send us your comments through our online registration form located at www.dummies.com/register/.

Some of the people who helped bring this book to market include the following:

Acquisitions, Editorial, and Media Development

Sr. Project Editor: Mark Enochs

Executive Editor: Steven Hayes

Copy Editor: Rebecca Whitney

Technical Editor: Lee Musick

Editorial Manager: Leah Cameron

Media Development and Quality Assurance: Angela Denny, Kate Jenkins, Steven Kudirka, Kit Malone

Media Development Coordinator: Jenny Swisher

Media Project Supervisor: Laura Moss-Hollister

Editorial Assistant: Amanda Foxworth

Sr. Editorial Assistant: Cherie Case

Cartoons: Rich Tennant (www.the5thwave.com)

Composition Services

Project Coordinators: Heather Kolter, Patrick Redmond

Layout and Graphics: Carl Byers, Stephanie D. Jumper, Alicia B. South, Ronald Terry, Christine Williams, Erin Zeltner

Proofreaders: Dwight Ramsey, Shannon Ramsey

Indexer: Potomac Indexing LLC

Anniversary Logo Design: Richard Pacifico

Publishing and Editorial for Technology Dummies

Richard Swadley, Vice President and Executive Group Publisher

Andy Cummings, Vice President and Publisher

Mary Bednarek, Executive Acquisitions Director

Mary C. Corder, Editorial Director

Publishing for Consumer Dummies

Diane Graves Steele, Vice President and Publisher

Joyce Pepple, Acquisitions Director

Composition Services

Gerry Fahey, Vice President of Production Services

Debbie Stailey, Director of Composition Services

Contents at a Glance

Table of Contents

Introduction

. . . .

*W*elcome to *The Internet For Dummies,* 11th Edition. Although lots of books about the Internet are available, most assume that you have a degree in computer science, would love to know about every strange and useless wart of the Internet, and enjoy memorizing unpronounceable commands and options. This book is different.

Instead, this book describes what you do to become an *Internaut* (someone who navigates the Internet with skill) — how to get started, what you really need to know, and where to go for help. And we describe it in plain old English.

When we first wrote *The Internet For Dummies* 14 years ago (yikes!), a typical Internet user was a student who connected from college or a technical worker who had access through work. The World Wide Web was so new that it had only a few hundred pages. Now, over a decade later, the Net has grown like crazy to include a billion (dare we say it?) normal people, connecting from computers at home or work, along with students ranging from elementary school to adult education. This 11th Edition focuses on the parts of the Net that are of the most interest to typical users — how to find things on the World Wide Web, use Firefox and Internet Explorer (the most popular and useful Web programs), download interesting things from the Net, send and receive electronic mail (e-mail), and shop online, invest online, chat online, and play games online.

About This Book

We don't flatter ourselves to think you're interested enough in the Internet to sit down and read the entire book (although it should be a fine book for the bathroom). When you run into a problem using the Internet ("Hmm, I *thought* that I knew how to find somebody on the Net, but I don't seem to remember"), just dip into the book long enough to solve your problem.

Pertinent sections include

- So, What Is the Internet?
- Safety First
- The Types of Internet Connections
- Web Surfing with Your Browser
- Search, Ho!
- Finding Programs to Download
- Pick an E-Mail Program, Any Program
- Look Who's Chatting

How to Use This Book

To begin, please read the first two chapters. They give you an overview of the Internet and some important tips and terminology. (Besides, we think they're interesting.) If you have children or grandchildren, read Chapter 3, too. When you're ready to get yourself on the Internet, turn to Part II and read Chapter 4. Parts III through VI egg you on and provide extra support — they describe the Web, e-mail, and other stuff you can do on the Internet.

Although we try hard not to introduce a technical term without defining it, sometimes we slip. Sometimes, too, you may read a section out of order and find a term that we define a few chapters before that. To fill in the gaps, we include a glossary at the end of this book.

Because the Internet is ever-changing, we have additional information online, which we can update more often than this book can be republished. The *Internet For Dummies* authors have a Web site with updates, history, and other interesting articles, at http://net.gurus.com.

When you have to follow a complicated procedure, we spell it out step by step wherever possible. We then tell you what happens in response and what your options are. When you have to type something, it appears in the book in **boldface**. Type it just as it appears. Use the same capitalization we do — a few systems care deeply about CAPITAL and small letters. Then press the Enter key. The book tells you what should happen when you give each command and what your options are.

When you have to choose commands from menus, we write File⇨Exit when we want you to choose the File command from the menu bar and then choose the Exit command from the menu that appears.

Who Are You?

In writing this book, we made a few assumptions about you:

- ✔ You have or would like to have access to the Internet.

- ✔ You want to get some work done with it. (We consider the term *work* to include the concept *play*.)

- ✔ You are not interested in becoming the world's next great Internet expert, at least not this week.

How This Book Is Organized

This book has six parts. The parts stand on their own — although you can begin reading wherever you like, you should at least skim Parts I and II first to get acquainted with some unavoidable Internet jargon and find out how to get your computer on the Net.

Here are the parts of the book and what they contain:

In Part I, "Welcome to the Internet," you find out what the Internet is and why it's interesting (at least why we think it's interesting). Also, this part has stuff about vital Internet terminology and concepts that help you as you read through the later parts of the book. Part I discusses security and privacy issues and gives some thoughts about children's use of the Net.

For the nuts and bolts of getting on the Net, read Part II, "Internet, Here I Come!" For most users, by far the most difficult part of using the Net is getting to that first connection, with software loaded, configuration configured, and modem modeming or broadband banding broadly. After that, it's (relatively) smooth sailing.

Part III, "Web Mania," dives into the World Wide Web, the part of the Internet that has powered the Net's leap from obscurity to fame. We discuss how to get around on the Web, how to find stuff (which is not as easy as it should be), and how to shop online on the Web. We also wrote chapters on downloading music and video and managing your finances on the Internet.

Part IV, "E-Mail, Chat, and Other Ways to Hang Out Online," looks at the important Net communication services: sending and receiving e-mail, swapping instant messages, and chatting. You find out how to exchange e-mail with people down the hall or on other continents, how to use Internet-based phone and video conferencing programs, how to use instant messaging programs to chat with your online pals, and how to use e-mail mailing lists to keep in touch with people of similar interests. You also get a briefing on avoiding and blocking online hazards, like viruses and spam.

Part V, "Putting Your Own Stuff on the Net," talks about how to post all kinds of material on the Internet. Putting your writing, photos, and videos online is easier than ever because of the range of free Web services you can use, including Weblogs, which let anyone be an online journalist. If you want complete control over your Web site, we also give you an overview of how to create a Web site with your own domain name. Then we talk about virtual worlds — games and simulations where many people (sometimes very, very many people) can share the experience.

Part VI, "The Part of Tens," comprises a compendium of ready references and useful facts (which, we suppose, suggests that the rest of the book is full of useless facts).

We stuck the glossary at the end of the book so that it's easy to find.

Icons Used in This Book

 Lets you know that some particularly nerdy, technoid information is coming up so that you can skip it, if you want. (On the other hand, you may want to read it.)

 Explains a nifty little shortcut or timesaver.

 Gaack! We found out about this the hard way! Don't let it happen to you!

 Indicates something to file away in your memory archive.

 Points out a resource on the World Wide Web.

What Now?

That's all you need to know to get started. Whenever you hit a snag using the Internet, just look up the problem in the table of contents or index in this book. You'll either have the problem solved in a flash or know where you need to go to find some expert help.

Because the Internet has been evolving for over 30 years, largely under the influence of some extremely nerdy people, it wasn't designed to be particularly easy for normal people to use. Don't feel bad if you have to look up a number of topics before you feel comfortable using the Internet. Until recently, most computer users never had to face anything as complex as the Internet.

Feedback, Please

We love to hear from our readers. If you want to contact us, please feel free to send us Internet e-mail at `internet11@gurus.com` (our friendly robot will answer immediately; the human authors read all the e-mail and answer as much as we can), or visit this book's Web home page, at `http://net.gurus.com`. These e-mail addresses put you in contact with the authors of this book; to contact the publisher or authors of other *For Dummies* books, visit the publisher's Web site, at `www.dummies.com`.

Part I
Welcome to the Internet

The 5th Wave   By Rich Tennant

In this part . . .

The Internet is an amazing place. But because it's full of computers, everything is more complicated than it should be. We start with a look at what the Internet is and how it got that way. We tell you what's happening, what people are doing, and why you should care. We give special attention to security problems, privacy issues, and family concerns — particularly the knotty question of what's the best way for kids to work with the Internet.

Chapter 1

What's So Great about the Internet, Anyway?

*I*t's huge, it's sprawling, it's globe spanning, and it has become part of our lives. It must be . . . the Internet. We all know something about it, and most of us have tried to use it, with more or less success. (If you've had less, you've come to the right place.) In this chapter, we look at what the Internet is and can do, before we dive into details in the rest of this book.

If you're new to the Internet, and especially if you don't have much computer experience, *be patient with yourself.* Many of the ideas here are completely new. Allow yourself some time to read and reread. The Internet is a different world with its own language, and it takes some getting used to.

Even experienced computer users can find using the Internet more complex than things they've tackled before. The Internet is not a single software package and doesn't easily lend itself to the kind of step-by-step instructions we'd provide for a single, fixed program. This book is as step-by-step as we can make it, but the Internet resembles a living organism mutating at an astonishing rate more than it resembles Microsoft Word and Excel, which sit quietly on your computer. After you get set up and practice a little, using the Internet seems like second nature; in the beginning, however, it can be daunting.

So, What Is the Internet?

The Internet — also known as the *Net* — is the world's largest computer network. "What is a network?" you may ask. Even if you already know, you may want to read the next couple of paragraphs to make sure that we're speaking the same language.

A computer *network* is a bunch of computers that communicate with each other. It's sort of like a radio or TV network that connects a bunch of radio or TV stations so that they can share the latest episode of *American Idol*.

Don't take the analogy too far. TV networks send the same information to all the stations at the same time (it's called *broadcast* networking); in computer networks, each particular message is routed to a particular computer, so different computers can display different things. Unlike TV networks, computer networks are two-way: When computer A sends a message to computer B, B can send a reply back to A.

Some computer networks consist of a central computer and a bunch of remote stations that report to it (for example, a central airline-reservation computer with thousands of screens and keyboards in airports and travel agencies). Other networks, including the Internet, are more egalitarian and permit any computer on the network to communicate with any other computer. Many new wireless devices — mobile phones, Palm handhelds, BlackBerries, and their ilk — expand the reach of the Internet right into our pockets. (Hands off our wallets!)

The Internet isn't really one network — it's a network of networks, all freely exchanging information. The networks range from the big, corporate networks to tiny ones (such as the one in John's back bedroom, made from a couple of old PCs bought at an electronics parts store) and everything in between. College and university networks have long been part of the Internet, and now high schools and elementary schools are joining in. Lately, the Internet has become so popular that many households have more than one computer and are creating their own little networks that they connect to the Internet.

What's All the Hoopla?

Everywhere you turn, you can find traces of the Internet. Household products, business cards, radio shows, and movie credits list their Web site addresses (usually starting with "www" and ending with "dot com") and their e-mail addresses. New people you meet would rather give you an e-mail address than a phone number. Everyone seems to be "going online" and "Googling it."

The Internet affects our lives on a scale as significant as the telephone and television. When it comes to disseminating information, the Internet is the most significant invention since the printing press. If you use a telephone, write letters, read a newspaper or magazine, or do business or any kind of research, the Internet can radically alter your worldview.

With networks, size counts a great deal: The larger a network is, the more stuff it has to offer. Because the Internet is the world's largest interconnected group of computer networks, it has an amazing array of information to offer.

When people talk about the Internet, they usually talk about what they can do, what they have found, and whom they have met. The number of available services is too huge to list in this chapter, but here are the Big Three:

- **Electronic mail (e-mail):** This service is certainly the most widely used — you can exchange e-mail with millions of people all over the world. People use e-mail for anything that they might use paper (mail, faxes, special delivery of documents) or the telephone (gossip, recipes, love letters) to communicate — you name it. (We hear that some people even use it for stuff related to work.) Electronic *mailing lists* enable you to join group discussions with people who have similar interests and to meet people over the Net. Part IV of this book has all the details.

- **The World Wide Web:** When people talk these days about surfing the Net, they often mean checking out sites on this (buzzword alert) global multimedia hyperlinked database. In fact, people are talking more about the Web and less about the Net. Are they the same thing? Technically, the answer is "No." But practically speaking, the answer for many people is "Pretty close." We tell you the truth, the whole truth, and nothing but the truth in Part III of this book.

  Web sites can provide you with information ranging from travel information to how to raise chickens. You can also look at videos, listen to music, buy stuff, sell stuff, and play video games.

  The software used to navigate the Web is a *browser*. The most popular browsers now are Firefox and Internet Explorer. We tell you all about them in Chapter 6.

- **Instant Messaging (IM'ing):** Programs such as Windows Messenger, Yahoo Messenger, and AOL Instant Messenger let you send messages that "pop up" on the recipient's screen. We hear tales of nimble-fingered youth carrying on upward of 13 IM sessions simultaneously. Some Web sites also provide messaging services. We tell you about IM programs in Chapter 16.

Why Is This Medium Different from Any Other Medium?

The Internet is unlike all the other communications media we've ever encountered. People of all ages, colors, creeds, and countries freely share ideas, stories, data, opinions, and products.

Anybody can access it

One great thing about the Internet is that it's the most open network in the world. Thousands of computers provide facilities that are available to anyone who has Internet access. Although pay services exist (and more are added every day), most Internet services are free for the taking after you're online. If you don't already have access to the Internet through your company, your school, your library, or a friend, you can pay for access by using an Internet service provider (ISP). We talk about some ISPs in Chapter 4.

It's politically, socially, and religiously correct

Another great thing about the Internet is that it is what one may call "socially unstratified." That is, one computer is no better than any other, and no person is any better than any other. Who you are on the Internet depends solely on how you present yourself through your computer. If what you say makes you sound like an intelligent, interesting person, that's who you are. It doesn't matter how old you are or what you look like or whether you're a student, business executive, or construction worker. Physical disabilities don't matter — we correspond with deaf and blind people. If they hadn't felt like telling us, we never would have known. People become famous (and infamous) in the Internet community through their own efforts.

The Net advantage

The Internet has become totally mainstream, and you're falling further behind the curve — and at a faster rate — if you haven't yet gotten started. Increasingly, news gets out on the Internet before it's available any other way, and the cyber-deprived are losing ground.

Here are some of the ways people use the Internet:

- **Find information:** Many Web sites have information free for the taking. Information ranges from IRS tax forms that you can print and use to help-wanted ads, real estate listings, and recipes. From U.S. Supreme Court decisions and library card catalogs to the text of old books, digitized pictures (many suitable for family audiences), and an enormous variety of software — from games to operating systems — you can find virtually anything on the Net. You can check the weather forecast, view movie listings, find your childhood sweetheart, browse catalogs, and see school closings for anywhere in the world, from anywhere in the world.

Does the Internet really reach every continent?

Some skeptical readers, after reading the claim that the Internet spans every continent, may point out that Antarctica is a continent, even though its population consists largely of penguins. Does the Internet go there? It does. A few machines at the Scott Base on McMurdo Sound in Antarctica are on the Internet, connected by radio link to New Zealand. See the polar webcam at www.usap.gov.

At the time of this writing, the largest Internet-free land mass in the world is probably one of the uninhabited islands in the Canadian arctic — Melville Island, perhaps. (You can look it up on the Internet.) We used to say New Guinea, a large jungle island north of Australia, until a reader there sent us e-mail in 1997 telling us about his new Internet provider.

Special tools known as *search engines* and *directories* help you find information (and people) on the Web. See Chapter 8 for how to search for the information you need.

✔ **Get an education:** Schoolteachers coordinate projects with classrooms all over the globe. College students and their families exchange e-mail to facilitate letter writing and keep down the cost of phone calls. Students do research from their home computers. The latest encyclopedias are online.

✔ **Buy and sell stuff:** On the Internet, you can buy anything from books about beer making to stock in microbreweries. And, you can make some cash by cleaning out your closets and selling your old junk on eBay. Software companies sell software and provide updates on the Net. Most software distribution is migrating to the Internet, where a customer can download and install programs without waiting for a CD to arrive. We talk about the relevant issues in Chapter 10.

✔ **Travel:** Cities, towns, states, and countries are using the Web to put up (or *post*) tourist and event information. Travelers find weather information; maps; plane, train, and bus schedules and tickets; and museum hours online. While you're at it, you can buy your airplane tickets, rent a car, and make your hotel reservations.

✔ **Use intranets:** Wouldn't ya know? Businesses have figured out that this Internet stuff is really useful, and they create their own, private networks — like mini-Internets. On these *intranets,* companies use Web pages for company information like corporate benefits, for filing expense reports and time sheets, and for ordering supplies. An intranet provides a way for an organization to provide stuff you can see from inside a company that folks on the outside can't see, including manuals, forms, videos of boring meetings, and, of course, endless memos. In some organizations, e-mail and intranets reduce the amount of paper wasted on this stuff.

Where did the Internet come from?

The ancestor of the Internet was the *ARPANET,* a project funded by the Department of Defense (DOD) in 1969, both as an experiment in reliable networking and to link DOD and military research contractors, including the large number of universities doing military-funded research. (*ARPA* stands for Advanced Research Projects Administration, the branch of the DOD in charge of handing out grant money. For enhanced confusion, the agency is now known as *DARPA* — the added *D* is for *Defense,* in case anyone had doubts about where the money was coming from.) Although the ARPANET started small — connecting three computers in California with one in Utah — it quickly grew to span the continent.

In the early 1980s, the ARPANET grew into the early Internet, a group of interlinked networks connecting many educational and research sites funded by the National Science Foundation (NSF), along with the original military sites. By 1990, it was clear that the Internet was here to stay, and DARPA and the NSF bowed out in favor of the commercially run networks that make up today's Internet. (And, yes, although Al Gore didn't invent the Internet, he was instrumental in keeping it funded so that it could turn into the Internet we know now.) For more information, read our Web page at `http://net.gurus.com/history`.

✔ **Play games:** Internet-based multiuser games can easily absorb all your waking hours and an alarming number of what would otherwise be your sleeping hours. You can challenge other players who can be anywhere in the world. Many kinds of games are available on the Web, including such traditionally addictive games as bridge, hearts, chess, checkers, and go. In Chapter 19, we tell where to find these games.

✔ **Find love:** People are finding romance on the Net. Singles ads and matchmaking sites vie for users. The Internet long ago stopped consisting solely of a bunch of socially challenged 22-year-old nerdy guys and now has turned into the world's biggest matchmaker, for people of all ages, genders, preferences, and life situations.

✔ **Heal:** Patients and doctors keep up-to-date with the latest medical findings, share treatment experience, and give one another support during medical problems. We even know of some practitioners who exchange e-mail directly with their patients.

✔ **Invest:** People do financial research, buy stock, and invest money online. Some online companies trade their own shares. Investors are finding new ventures, and new ventures are finding capital.

✔ **Participate in nonprofits:** Churches, synagogues, mosques, and other community organizations put up pages telling Web users about themselves and inviting new people. The online church newsletter *always* comes before Sunday.

Chapter 2

Is the Internet Safe? Viruses, Spyware, Spam, and Other Yucky Stuff

*W*e like the Internet. It has been part of our lives — and livelihoods — for years. We'd love to tell you that all the stuff you may have read about the dangers of connecting a computer to the Internet is hype. We can't. The success of the Internet has attracted unsavory people who view you as a money tree ready to be plucked. (Nothing personal. They see everybody that way.) In a few countries, perpetrating Internet fraud is now a major part of the national economy.

Even if no one steals your money, information about your online activities can be gathered and result in a real loss of privacy. And, some people are trying to take over your computer so that they can use it for nefarious purposes. When a new computer is hooked up to the Internet, it's not a question of *whether* it will come under cyberattack, but when. And, the answer is measured not in months or days — but in hours or minutes.

Relax — the Internet doesn't have to be a dangerous place. Using the Internet is like walking around a big city. Yes, you need to be careful, use some protection, and stay out of dangerous areas, but you can also safely take advantage of the wonders that the Net has to offer.

This chapter describes the types of issues that abound on the Internet:

- **Privacy issues** involve how much people can find out about you over the Internet.
- **Security issues** have to do with keeping control over which programs are running on your computer.
- Just plain **annoyance issues** include ending up with a mailbox full of *spam* (junk e-mail) or Web browser windows popping up with advertisements.

Throughout the rest of this book, we include instructions for staying safe by using a firewall, a virus checker, a spyware scanner, and some common sense. Chapter 3 talks about rules for letting kids use the Internet, and most of the suggestions make sense for grown-ups, too.

Who's Who and What They Can Tell about You

Advances in technology are eroding the privacy that most of us take for granted. Innovations we use every day — credit cards, cellphones, electronic key cards, and automobile tollway transponders — allow our every purchase and movement to be tracked. The Internet is an extension of this trend. Much of what you do online may be watched and recorded — sometimes for innocent reasons and sometimes not.

All this is further compounded by the amount of publicly available information that is now conveniently available to a far *greater* public over the Internet. When paper records were kept by government officials and people had to visit the office and dig through the files for the specific information they wanted, a lot less information abuse was possible. Now the potential exists for anyone anywhere to access information about people hitherto unknown, and to gather information from various sources, including online directories. No longer are geography or time deterrents enough.

Some people worry that snoops on the Net will intercept their private e-mail or Web pages. That's quite unlikely, actually. The more serious problem is advertisers who build profiles of the sites you visit and the stuff you buy. Most Web ads are provided through a handful of companies like DoubleClick.com and Advertising.com, who can use their ads to determine that the same person (you) is visiting a lot of different Web sites and create a profile. They say they don't create these personal profiles, but they don't say they won't in the future.

Several techniques for gathering information about you as you use the Internet, or tricking you into providing information, are described in the next few sections.

Who is the party to whom I am speaking?

Although the Internet seems completely anonymous, it's not. People used to have Internet usernames that bore some resemblance to their true identities — their names or initials or some such combination in conjunction with their university or corporation names gave a fairly traceable route to real people. Creating a new e-mail address now takes just a few minutes, so revealing your identity is definitely optional.

Depending on who you are and what you want to do on the Net, you may, in fact, want different names and different accounts. Here are some legitimate reasons for wanting them:

- ✔ You're a professional — a physician, for example — and you want to participate in a mailing list or newsgroup without being asked for your professional opinion.
- ✔ You want help with an area of concern that you feel is private and you don't want your problem known to people close to you who may find out if your name is associated with it.
- ✔ You do business on the Internet, and you socialize on the Net. You may want to keep those activities separate.

Most Net activities can be traced. If you start to abuse the anonymous nature of the Net, you find that you're not so anonymous after all.

Safety first

The anonymous, faceless nature of the Internet has its downside, too. To protect you and your family, take the following simple precautions:

- ✔ In chat rooms and other getting-to-know-you situations, don't use your full name.

- ✔ Never provide your name, address, or phone number to someone you don't know.

- ✔ Never believe anyone who says that he's from "AOL Tech Support," "eBay Fraud Prevention," "PayPal Administration," or some such authority and asks you for your password. No legitimate entity will ever ask you for your password.

- ✔ Be especially careful about disclosing information about kids. Don't fill out profiles in chat rooms that ask for a kid's name, hometown, school, age, address, or phone number, because they're invariably used for "targeted marketing" (also known as junk mail).

Although relatively rare, horrible things have happened to a few people who have taken their Internet encounters into real life. Many wonderful things have happened, too. We've met some of our best friends over the Net, and some people have met and subsequently married. We just want to encourage you to use common sense when you set up a meeting with a Net friend. A person you e-mail or swap instant messages with is still largely a stranger, and if you want to meet in person, take the same precautions you would on a first date with someone you don't know: Meet in a public place, perhaps with a friend along, and be sure that your family knows where you are and when you're planning to be back.

The Net is a wonderful place, and meeting new people and making new friends is one of the big attractions. We just want to make sure that you're as careful as you would be in the rest of your life.

Phishing for inphormation

Phishing is the fastest-growing Internet crime, and you're the target. The good news is that protecting yourself is easy when you and your family know how to spot the phish-hook.

Identify what phishing looks like. After you start using the Internet and receiving e-mail (as described in Chapter 13), there's an excellent chance that you'll get a message like this:

```
Subject: Ebay Important Warning

From: eBay Billing Department! <Service@eBay.com>
```

eBay Fraud Mediation Request

```
You have recieved this email because you or someone
had used your account to make fake bids at eBay. For
security purposes, we are required to open an
investigation into this matter.

THE FRAUD ALERT ID CODE CONTAINED IN THIS MESSAGE
WILL BE ATTACHED IN OUR FRAUD MEDIATION REQUEST FORM,
IN ORDER TO VERIFY YOUR EBAY ACCOUNT REGISTRATION
INFORMATIONS.

Fraud Alert ID CODE: 00937614

Please access the following form to complete the
verification of your eBay account registration
informations:
```

http://www.eBay.com/cgi bin/secure/Fraud Alert ID CODE: 00937614

```
If we do not receive the appropriate verification within
48 hours, then we will assume this eBay account is
fraudulent and will be suspended.

Regards, Safeharbor Department (Trust and Safety
Department), eBay Inc.
```

Sounds authentic and scary. Think you had better deal with this message right away? Better think again. You are the phish, and this message is the bait. That underlined text in the middle is the hook. Click it and soon an official-looking page appears that looks just like an eBay sign-in page. After you enter your username and password, another official-looking page asks for your credit card number, PIN, billing address, checking account details (complete with a helpful graphic so that you can find the right numbers on your personal checks), Social Security number, date of birth, mother's maiden name, and driver's license number. The page is smart enough to reject an invalid credit card number. If you fill in all the information and press Continue, you see a valid eBay page that says you've logged out. Then, who knows? You're wide open for anything from a small purchase paid for by your credit card to full-scale identity theft that can take months or years to straighten out.

This message did not come from eBay. Millions of these types of messages are sent over the Internet every day.

Some clues might alert you. The misspelled words *recieved* and *informations* suggest that the author is someone whose English skills are limited. And, if you take the trouble to save the e-mail to a file and then print it, the underlined link in the middle of the message looks like this:

```
<http://192.168.45.67/cgi_bin>http://www.eBay.com/cgi_bin/
              secure/Fraud Alert ID CODE: 00937614
```

The text between the angle brackets (< and >) is where the link really goes, to a Web site with a numeric address. (When we tried clicking the link two days after we got the mail, the Web site had already been shut down. Those eBay security folks are on the ball.)

Don't take the bait

Sooner or later the phishers will find good editors or learn how to use a spell checker, so you can't rely on spelling and grammar mistakes, although they're dead giveaways when you spot them. Here are a few additional tips:

- ✔ Assume that every e-mail that leads you to a page seeking passwords or credit card numbers or other personal information is a phishing expedition.

- ✔ If the e-mail purports to be from a company you've never heard of, ignore it.

- ✔ If the message says that it's from a company with whom you have an account, go to the company's Web site by typing the company's URL into your browser (see Chapter 7), *not* by clicking a link in the e-mail. When you get to the company's Web site, look for a My Account link. When you log in there, if there's a problem, you should see a notice. If there's no way to log in and you're still concerned, forward a copy of the e-mail to the customer service department.

One trick phishers use to fool Internet users is *Web site spoofing* — tricking your browser into displaying one address when you're actually at another site. Some browsers allow a Web site to show only its main address so that it doesn't look so geeky. Phishers take advantage of this ability. Better browsers, like Firefox (see Chapter 7), offer protection against Web site spoofing — they always show the actual Web address of the page you're on.

To summarize, make sure that your family knows this rule well: Never, *never,* **never** enter passwords, credit card numbers, or other personal information at a Web page you got to by clicking a link in an e-mail.

Web bugs track where you browse

Ever since the World Wide Web became a household word (okay, three words), companies have increasingly viewed their Internet presence as a vital way to advertise their goods and services and conduct their business. They spend millions of dollars on their Web sites — and want very much to know just how people use them. Small wonder that when you visit a site, companies can keep track of your actions as you go from link to link within the site. But they *really* want to know what you were doing before you entered their sites — and what you do after you leave. To gather this intelligence, they insert special pieces of code that they call *Web beacons* and everyone else calls *Web bugs* that report your actions to a central site, often run by a separate company that places ads on Web sites. By piecing together the information from many Web sites, these tracking companies get a pretty clear picture of where you go online — and what you look at when you get there. Many are careful to provide only statistical information to their clients, but the potential for abuse is there. It's worth noting that U.S. courts set a lower standard of protection for "business records" gathered in this way than they do for personal papers stored in our homes.

Cookies aren't so bad

When you browse the Web (as described in Chapter 6), the Web server needs to know who you are if you want to do things that require logging in or putting items in a virtual shopping cart or completing any other process that requires that the Web site remember information about you as you move from page to page. The most commonly used trick that allows Web sites to keep track of what you're doing is called *setting cookies*. A *cookie* is a tiny little file that's stored on your computer. It contains the address of the Web site and codes that your browser sends back to the Web site each time you visit a page there. Cookies don't usually contain personal information or anything dangerous; they're usually innocuous and useful.

If you plan to shop on the Web (described in Chapter 10) or use other Web services, cookies make it all possible. When you're using an airline reservation site, for example, the site uses cookies to keep the flights you're reserving separate from the ones that other users are reserving at the same time. On the other hand, you might use your credit card to purchase something on a Web site and the site uses a cookie to remember the account with your credit card number. Suppose that you provide this information from a computer at work and the next person to visit that site uses the same computer. That person could, possibly, make purchases on your credit card. Oops.

Internet users have various feelings about cookies. Some of us don't care about them, and some of us view them as an unconscionable invasion of privacy. You get to decide for yourself. Contrary to rumor, cookie files cannot get other information from your hard disk, give you a bad haircut, or otherwise mess up your life. They collect only information that the browser tells them about. Internet Explorer and Firefox let you control whether and when cookies are stored on your computer. See Chapter 7 to find out how to tell your Web browser whether and when to allow a Web site to set a cookie.

Google yourself

One of the big attractions of the Internet is *all that data out there* that is now so easy to access. Some of that data is about you. If you have a personal Web site or have your own blog (see Chapters 17 and 18), you expect that all the information you put up there is available for everyone to see, usually forever. (We find stuff about ourselves from more than 25 years ago.) Other people put up information as well — newsletters, event listings, pictures from events, and other pictures, for example. Your electronic data trail on the Internet may be longer than you think. If you haven't done it before, try Googling yourself. Enter your name in quotes in the Google search box and click Google Search. If you have a common name, you may need to throw in your middle initial or add the name of your town or school. (If you do this very often, it's called *ego surfing*.)

How People Can Take Over Your PC

You can download and install software right over the Internet, which is a wonderful feature. It's wonderful when you need a viewer program to display and print a tax form or when you want to install a free upgrade to a program that you purchased earlier. How convenient! We tell you all about it in Chapter 12.

However, other people can also install programs on your computer without your permission. Hey, wait a minute — whose computer is it, anyway? These programs can arrive in a number of ways, mainly by e-mail or your Web browser.

Viruses arrive by e-mail

Computer *viruses* are programs that jump from computer to computer, just as real viruses jump from person to person. Computer viruses can spread using any mechanism that computers use to talk to each other, like networks, data CDs, DVDs, and even infrared beaming. Viruses have been around computers for a long time. Originally, they lived in program files that people downloaded using a file transfer program or their Web browsers. Now, most viruses are spread through files that are sent by e-mail, as attachments to mail messages, although instant messaging (IM'ing; see Chapter 16) is a popular alternative.

There was a time when people in the know (like we thought we were) laughed at newcomers to the Internet who worried about getting viruses by e-mail. E-mail messages back then were just text files and could not contain programs. Then e-mail attachments were introduced. People could then send computer software — including those sneaky viruses — by e-mail. Isn't progress wonderful?

What viruses do

When a virus lands on your computer, it has to somehow manage to get executed. *Getting executed* in computer jargon means being brought to life; a virus is a program, and programs have to be run — they have to be "turned on," "launched," or "started." After a virus is running, it does two things:

1. The virus looks around and tries to find your address book, which it uses to courteously send copies of itself to all your friends and acquaintances, often wrapped up in very convincing-sounding messages ("Hey, enjoyed the other night, thought this file would amuse you!").

2. Then the virus executes its payload, the reason the virus writer went through all that trouble and risk. (They do occasionally end up in jail.)

The *payload* is the illegal activity that the virus is running from your machine. A payload can record your every keystroke (including your passwords). It can launch an attack at specific or random targets over the Internet. It frequently sends spam from your computer. Whatever it's doing, you don't want it to do. Trust us. If your computer starts to act quirky or really sluggish, chances are, you've contracted a virus or 20.

In the good old days, virus writers were content just to see their viruses spread, but like everything else about the Internet, virus writing is now a big business, in many cases controlled by organized crime syndicates.

What you can do about viruses

Don't worry *too* much about viruses — excellent virus-checking programs are available that check all incoming mail before the viruses can attack. In Chapter 4, which describes getting connected to the Internet, we recommend installing a virus checker After you install your virus checker, be sure to update it regularly so that you're always protected against the latest viruses.

Worms come right over the Net

A *worm* is like a virus, except that it doesn't need a vector, like e-mail. A worm just jumps directly from one computer to another over the Net, entering your computer via security flaws in its network software. Unfortunately, the most popular kind of network software on the Net, the kind in Microsoft Windows, is riddled with security holes, so many that if you attach a nice, fresh Windows machine to a broadband Net connection, the machine gets overrun with worms in less than a minute.

If you rigorously apply all the security updates from Microsoft, they fix most of the known security flaws, but it takes a lot longer than a minute to apply them all. Hence, we strongly encourage anyone using a broadband connection to use a hardware *firewall,* a box that sits between the Net and your computer and keeps the worms out. If you have a broadband connection, you probably want to use an inexpensive device called a *router* to hook up your computers, anyway, and routers all include a firewall as a standard feature. See Chapter 4 for more information.

Spyware arrives via Web sites

Spyware (which includes adware) is like a virus, except that your computer catches it in a different way. Rather than arrive by e-mail, *spyware* gets downloaded by your browser. Generally, you need to click something on a Web page to download and install spyware, but many people have been easily misled into installing spyware that purports to be a graphics viewer or some other program you think you might want.

Know what spyware does

Spyware is called that because it's frequently used for nefarious purposes, like spying on what you're typing. Some spyware gathers information about you and sends it off to some other site without your knowledge or consent. A common use for spyware is finding out which sites you're visiting so that advertisers can display pop-up ads (described later in this chapter) that are targeted to your interests.

Targeted advertising isn't inherently evil. The Google AdSense program places ads on participating Web pages based on the contents of those pages. Targeted ads are worth more to advertisers because you're more likely to respond to an ad about something you're already reading about.

Spyware can also send spam from your computer, capture every keystroke you type and send it to a malefactor over the Net, and do all the other Bad Things that worms and viruses do.

Adware: Just another kind of spyware

Adware is a controversial type of software that many people consider to be spyware. Adware is installed as part of some programs that are distributed for free. It watches what you do on your computer and displays targeted ads — even when you run other programs. We think that no users in their right minds would knowingly install a program that peppers them with ads — and they want laws to ban the practice, pointing out that adware often behaves like a parasite, by obscuring or replacing ads from competing Web sites.

Before downloading a free program, make sure that you understand what the deal is. If you aren't sure, don't download it. Make sure that your kids know not to download free games, song lyrics, and the like — most are infested with adware. If you don't, before you know it, you'll have so many pop-up ads that you'll have to unplug your computer to shut it up.

Don't voluntarily install spyware

Lots of cute little free programs are available for download, but don't install them unless you're convinced that they're safe *and* useful. Most free toolbars, screen savers, news tickers, and other utilities are spyware in disguise. Besides, the more programs you run on your computer, the slower all your other programs run. Check with friends before downloading the latest program. Or, search the Web for the program's name (see Chapter 8) to find positive or negative reviews. Download programs only from reputable Web sites.

Protect your computer from spyware

Spyware programs are often designed to be hard to remove — which can mess up your operating system. Rather than wait until you contract a bad case of spyware and then try to uninstall it, a better idea is to inoculate your computer against spyware. To block spyware, be careful about what you click. Install a spyware checking program that can scan your system periodically, such as Microsoft's free Windows Defender. See Chapter 4 for details.

Pop-up browser windows pop up all over the place

One of the worst innovations in recent decades is the *pop-up* window that appears on your screen unbidden (by you) when you visit some Web sites. Some pop-ups appear immediately, and others are *pop-unders,* which are hidden under your main window until you close the main window. The pop-ups you're most likely to see are ads for mortgages and airline tickets. (No, we don't give their names here; they have plenty of publicity already.)

Several mechanisms can make pop-ups appear on your computer:

- ✔ A Web site can open a new browser window. Sometimes this new window displays an ad or some other annoying information. But sometimes the new window has useful information — some Web sites use pop-up windows as a sort of Help system for using the site.
- ✔ Spyware or other programs can display pop-up windows.

Luckily, Web browsers now can prevent Web sites from opening unwanted new browser windows. See Chapter 7 to find out how to tell your browser to display fewer pop-ups.

Spam, Bacon, Spam, Eggs, and Spam

Pink tender morsel,
Glistening with salty gel.
What the hell is it?

— SPAM haiku, found on the Internet

More and more often, we get unsolicited bulk e-mail (abbreviated UBE but usually called *spam*) from some organization or person we don't know. Spam is the online version of junk mail. Offline, junk mailers have to pay postage. Unfortunately, online, the cost of sending out a bazillion pieces of junk mail is virtually zilch.

E-mail spam (not to be confused with SPAM, a meat-related product from Minnesota and very popular in Hawaii) means that thousands of copies of an unwanted message are sent to e-mail accounts and even instant message programs. The message usually consists of unsavory advertising for get-rich-quick schemes or pornographic offers — something you might not want to see and something you definitely don't want your children to see. Many spam messages tout worthless stocks that the spammers have bought and hope you'll buy at inflated prices. The message is *spam,* the practice is *spamming,* and the person sending the spam is a *spammer.* A lot of spam is phishing, too.

Spam, unfortunately, is a major problem on the Internet because it's really cheap for the sleazy advertisers to send. We get hundreds or thousands of pieces of spam a day, and the number continues to increase. Spam doesn't have to be commercial (we've gotten religious and political spam), but it has to be unsolicited; if you asked for it, it's not spam.

Why it's called spam

The meat? Nobody knows. Oh, you mean the unwanted e-mail? It came from the Monty Python skit in which a group of Vikings sing the word *spam* repeatedly in a march tempo, drowning out all other discourse. (Google for **Monty Python spam** and you'll find plenty of sites where you can listen to it.) Spam can drown out all other mail, because some people get so much spam that they stop using e-mail entirely.

Why it's so bad

You may think that spam, like postal junk mail, is just a nuisance we have to live with. But it's worse than junk mail, in several ways. Spam costs you money. E-mail recipients pay much more than the sender does to deliver a message.

Sending e-mail is cheap: A spammer can send thousands of messages an hour from a PC. After that, it costs you time to download, read (at least the subject line), and dispose of the mail. The amount of spam has surpassed the amount of real e-mail, and if spam volume continues to grow at its alarming pace, pretty soon e-mail will prove to be useless because the real e-mail is buried under the junk. Another problem is that spam filters, which are supposed to discard only spam, can throw away good messages by mistake.

Not only do spam recipients have to bear a cost, but all this volume of e-mail also strains the resources of the e-mail servers and the entire Internet. ISPs have to pass along the added costs to their users. Spam volume has doubled or tripled each of the past few years. America Online has been reported to estimate that more than 90 percent of its incoming e-mail is spam, and many ISPs have told us that as much as $2 of the $20 monthly fee goes to handling and cleaning up after spam. Spammers send 100 *billion* spam messages *every day.* And, as ISPs try harder to filter out spam, more and more legitimate mail is being mistaken for spam and bounced.

The perils of free WiFi

WiFi, the wireless way that your laptop can con-nect to Internet, is available in many public places, including airports and coffee shops. Chapter 4 explains how your computer can con-nect to the Internet by using WiFi — you locate the network, click Connect, and then start using the Internet. One of the first things you'll proba-bly do is use your Web browser to check your e-mail or connect to your company's network, And, in the process, you type a password or two.

Can you trust the WiFi network? How do you know that the WiFi network isn't listening to what you type, including your passwords? Well, you don't.

WiFi spoofing is surprisingly easy. A thief sets up a computer in an airport lounge or coffee shop by using the same WiFi system identifier, and you connect to her WiFi rather than to the real one. She monitors what you type and uses your passwords to send spam, empty your bank account, or perform other nefarious deeds.

What's a traveling Internet user to do? Answer: Don't use free WiFi unless you know for *sure* that it's legit. (For example, your kids' school or your company may provide free WiFi on the school or company grounds.) If you absolutely must use public WiFi to check your e-mail while you're on the road, here's what to do (advice courtesy of our friend Mark Steinwinter):

1. Before you leave on your trip, change your e-mail password (and any other password you plan to use).

2. While on your trip, limit your public WiFi use to accounts whose passwords you just changed. Go ahead and use Web sites that don't require a password.

3. As soon as you get home, change your e-mail password again. You can change it back to what it was before your trip, or to another password. Just assume that a Bad Guy has the password you used on your trip, and never use this password again.

Many spam messages include a line that instructs you how to get off their lists, something like "Send us a message with the word REMOVE in it." Don't bother — this is usually a method for verifying that your address is real, and you will likely receive *more* spam. Reply to messages or click links to unsubscribe *only* if the messages are from lists that you remember subscribing to or from companies you have done business with.

What you can do about it

You don't have to put up with a lot of spam. Spam filters can weed out most of the spam you receive. See Chapter 14 for how to use the spam filter that may already be built into your e-mail program or how to install a separate spam filtering program.

What's the Secret Word, Mr. Potter?

Everywhere you go these days, someone wants you to enter a password or passcode. Even Harry Potter has to tell his password to a magic portrait just to enter the Gryffindor dormitory (although there's apparently no security between the boys' and girls' wings). Security experts are pretty unanimous in telling us how we should protect all our passwords:

✔ Pick passwords that are long and complex enough that no one can guess them.

Never use a word that occurs in the dictionary as a password. Consider sticking a number or two into your password.

✔ Never use the same password for different accounts.

✔ Memorize your passwords and never write them down.

✔ Change your passwords frequently.

This is very sound advice for everyone — except ordinary human beings. Most of us have far too many passwords to keep track of and too little brain to keep them in.

One common-sense approach is to use a single password for accounts where there's little risk of loss, such as the one you need in order to read an online newspaper. Use separate, stronger passwords for the accounts that really matter (such as your online banking). If you feel you can't remember them all, write them down and keep them in a safe place, not on a sticky note on your monitor.

Be careful with password hints

Web site operators are tired of dealing with customers who forget their passwords, so a new computer tool has emerged in the last few years — the password hint. When you create a new account, the friendly identity manager software asks for your user name and new password. It then makes you select and answer a couple of security questions, like "What's your favorite color?" or "What's your pet's name?"

Sometime in the future, you try to log in to that account — and find that you forgot that pesky password. No problemo! You're asked the security questions you picked; if you type the right answer, you're in. The problem is, a thief pretending to be you will get the same challenge. Rather than guess your password, all he has to

guess is your favorite color (blue, maybe?) and figure out your pet's name (and did your kid post captioned photos of Rover on the school Web site as part of his third grade computer-literacy project?).

If you encounter one of these password hints when you sign up for an important account, pick questions whose answers an attacker can't glean by researching you. And, there's no rule that says you have to answer the security questions truthfully. You can pick a friend's pet, for example, or a color you detest, or you can say that your favorite color is Rover and your pet's name is Purple. You just have to remember your less-than-truthful answers to these questions.

Our warning about not using a password that's in the dictionary — take that one seriously! Hackers managed to find a hole in our firewall one day, and we had stupidly left one password set to a normal English word (*weather,* if you must know). It took the hackers less than two hours to break into our computer, by simply having their computer type every English word until they got to one that worked.

When making up a password, stick numbers and punctuation into words or glue two words together with some numbers or spell things backward. Use both capital and lowercase letters, too. If your kids are Fred and Susie and your house number is 426, how about Fred426susiE? Or Susie426dreF? Using the first letters of each word in a phrase is a good method, too. If your favorite song is "I Wanna Hold Your Hand," it wouldn't be that hard to remember a password like Iwhyh1963. You get the idea!

How to Keep Yourself and Your Family Safe

Viruses, spyware, phishing, pop-ups, spam — is the Internet worth all this trouble? No, you don't have to give up on the Internet in despair or disgust. You just have to put in a little extra effort to use it safely. In addition to the technological fixes we suggest (virus checkers, spyware scanners, and pop-up blockers), you need to develop some smarts about online security. Here's a quick checklist:

- **Develop healthy skepticism.** If it sounds too good to be true, it probably isn't true. No one in Africa has $25 million they will share with you if you help them get it out of the country. As the old saying goes, there's a sucker born every minute. Today's fool doesn't have to be you.

- **Keep your computer's software up-to-date.** Both Microsoft and Apple have features that do this more or less painlessly. Use them. The latest software updates usually fix exploitable security flaws.

- **Use a firewall and keep it updated.** Your computer probably has firewall software built in. Make sure that your firewall is turned on. Some malware programs know how to turn off protective software, so check it every week or so. We recommend using a router — a device that lets you share Internet connections among several computers (whether wired or wireless) — because routers include built-in firewall programs that malware programs cannot disable or bypass. These units are so cheap that you should get one even if you only have one computer. (See Chapter 5 for details.)

- **Install virus-protection and spyware-protection software and keep it current.** Virus protection costs $25 per year or so. Pay it. Chapter 4 tells you how to install virus checkers and spyware scanners.

You must keep the virus-description files in your antivirus software updated — automatically if possible, and every week at least. (New viruses are launched every day.) The maker of your antivirus software should have a Web site from which you can download the updates; check your documentation.

- **Don't open an e-mail attachment unless it's from someone you know *and* you're expecting it.** Contact the sender if you aren't sure.

- **Don't click any links in e-mail messages unless you're sure that you know where they lead.** If you click one and the site you end up at wants your password or credit card number or dog's name, close your browser window. Don't even think about giving out any information.

- **Pick passwords that are hard to guess, and never give them to anyone else.** Not to the nice lady who says she's from the help desk and not to the bogus FBI special agent who claims to need it for tracking down a kidnapped child. No one.

- **Be consistent.** If you share your computer with several family members or housemates, make sure that each person understands these rules and agrees to follow them.

Are Macs the solution?

We hear you Apple Macintosh users gloating as you read this chapter: "We don't have these problems. Why don't people just use Macs?" Mac users still have to put up with phishing and other forms of junk e-mail. But to date, almost none of the viruses, worms, or spyware affects Macs. Although this situation could change, we think that Mac users will always have an easier time on the Net. First, Macs are so scarce (compared to Windows machines) that it's not worth a virus writer's time to attack them — partly because this scarcity also makes it hard to spread Mac viruses. Most e-mail addresses in a Mac user's address book belong to Windows users anyway, so if a Mac virus makes copies of itself, the copies it mails out don't find nice, vulnerable homes. (Designing a virus that will run on *both* Windows and Macs is hard, even today.) Finally, Apple's Mac OS X is designed to be more secure than Windows and is harder to infect.

Current Intel-based Macs can run Windows programs, or can even be set up to run native Windows, for applications that are Windows-only. We know of companies whose support staffs run *everything* on Macs — because they don't get infected. When employees need to run something on a PC, they do it in a window on the Mac screen. Cool.

Chapter 3

Kids and the Net

*F*ace it: Most kids are way more comfortable on the Internet than their parents (and grandparents) are. Schools assign kids to do research on the Web and e-mail information to other students or their teachers. Online games are designed for kids of all ages. Forbidding your kids from using the Net altogether is hopeless (unless they're younger than about 6), but you want to keep your kids safe. This chapter talks about what's great — and what's scary — about children and youth using the Internet.

With millions of kids online, a discussion about family Internet use is critical. (Obviously, if this isn't your concern, just skip this chapter and go to the next.)

Really Cool Ways Kids Use the Net

The Net is amazing. It can help kids with what they have to do as well as with what they want to do:

✔ **Research homework assignments:** The Internet is an incredible way to expand the walls of a school. The Net can connect kids to other schools, libraries, research resources, museums, and other people. Kids can visit the American Museum of Natural History for information about dinosaurs (at www.amnh.org, as shown in Figure 3-1) and the Sistine Chapel (www.vatican.va — click English, and then Vatican Museums, and then Online Tours); they can watch spotted newts in their native habitat; they can hear new music and make new friends. These days, many schools assume that kids have access to the Web, so parents had better be ready.

Figure 3-1:
Many
museums
have useful
information
online.

✔ **Find out how to evaluate the stuff your kids read:** When you or your kids search for a topic, you may get pages written by the world's greatest authority on that topic, some crackpot pushing a harebrained theory, some college kid's term paper, or some guy on a bulletin board who thinks he's an expert. Some Web sites are maintained by hate groups and push really nasty venom. Finding out how to identify all those types of information is one of the most valuable skills that children (and anyone) can acquire.

✔ **Make e-friends in other countries:** School projects such as the Global Schoolhouse connect kids around the world by working collaboratively on all types of projects. Its annual cyberfairs have brought together more than 500,000 students from hundreds of schools in at least 37 countries! Kids can find out more at the Global Schoolhouse Web site, www.globalschoolnet.org/GSH, where they can also subscribe to lots of mailing lists. (We explain in Chapter 6 how to get to these locations, so you can come back here later and help your kids follow up on them.)

✔ **Practice foreign languages:** Kids can visit online chat rooms, where they can try out their French or Spanish or Portuguese or Russian or Japanese or even Esperanto.

✔ **Pay for music you download:** Kids love music, and they can buy music over the Internet in several ways. (Adults can, too, as it turns out.) Apple's iTunes music store, www.apple.com/itunes, sells songs for 99 cents. Other sites, like www.napster.com, let you download as many songs as you like for a monthly fee. See Chapter 9 for details.

✔ **Write an encyclopedia article:** Wikipedia, www.wikipedia.org, is a free online encyclopedia that anyone can contribute to. It's a great research tool, but, even better, kids can add the material they found while researching those term papers to make Wikipedia even better. A worldwide team of volunteer writers and editors updates the material continually, and you — or your child! — can be one of them. (See Chapter 17 to find out what wikis are.)

✔ **Discover how to make Web sites:** A Web site can be as clever or as stupid as you like. You and your kids can put your stories or artwork up for family and friends to admire. We explain how to do these things in Chapter 17.

So-so Ways Kids Use the Net

Here are some ideas that adults might consider a waste of time, but hey, we can't be serious all the time:

✔ **Play games:** Many popular games (both traditional — like chess, bridge, hearts, and go — and video) have options that let kids compete against other players on the Internet.

✔ **IM friends:** Instant messaging (IM'ing) is a cool way to get in touch — *instantly*. Wireless options are already happening in many parts of the world. We reveal all in Chapter 16.

✔ **Talk on a videophone:** Thanks to software such as Yahoo Messenger, kids can see their friends while talking to them (not recommended on bad hair days). Chapter 16 talks about free video programs.

✔ **Create an online profile on a social networking site.** Web sites like MySpace and Facebook enable people to create pages about themselves and then link to their friends. We have privacy and safety concerns about kids using these sites. See Chapter 17.

✔ **Shop:** What can we say? Internet shopping is like shopping at the mall, but the Internet is always open and you don't have to hunt for a parking place. Kids can sell stuff too. Get started in Chapter 10.

✔ **Role-play:** Any number of Internet sites let players pretend to be a character in their favorite science-fiction or fantasy book.

Not-So-Good Ways Kids Use the Net

Make sure that your kids or grandkids stay away from the following ideas, which will just get them into trouble, some of it pretty serious:

✔ **Plagiarizing:** That's the fancy word for passing off other people's work as your own. Plagiarizing from the Internet is just as wrong as plagiarizing from a book — and (for that matter) a lot easier for teachers to catch, because teachers can Google for stuff just like kids can.

- ✔ **Cheating:** Using translating software to do language homework is also no good. Besides, automated translations are still no substitute for the real thing.

- ✔ **Revealing too much about yourself:** When chatting on the Net with people your kids don't know, they might be tempted to give out identifying information about themselves or your family, but this is dangerous — it can get them stalked, ripped off, or worse. Even revealing their e-mail addresses can get them unwanted junk mail. Some seemingly innocent questions that strangers ask online aren't so innocent, so we go into more detail later in this chapter about what to watch for.

- ✔ **Sharing copyrighted music and videos:** Now that it's easy to buy music online for a reasonable price, kids don't have much excuse for using file-sharing software to trade copyrighted music or videos without permission. The music and movie industries are getting better at finding people who do that — and are taking legal action against them. It could cost you a lot of money.

- ✔ **Visiting porn and hate sites:** This is between you and your kids. Parents should make clear rules about what Web sites are acceptable, post them near the computer, and stick to them.

- ✔ **Pretending to be someone else online:** Kids should go ahead and make up a pseudonym so that they don't have to use a real name (that can be one way to limit how much any stranger finds out). But, pretending that you're a talent agent for *American Idol* or the latest reality show looking for a date is a bad idea.

- ✔ **Hanging out in adult chat rooms:** If kids pretend to be older than they are, they can get both themselves and the chat room hosts into trouble.

- ✔ **Letting the Internet take over your life:** If the only thing your kids want to do after school is get online, maybe you should talk to someone about it.

Truly Brain-Dead Things Kids Should Never Do

Here are some ideas that kids should *never* consider because they can lead right into major trouble:

- ✔ **Meet online friends in person without telling a parent:** If a child or youth meets someone great online and wants to meet him or her in person, fine — maybe. But parents need to take precautions! First, make sure that your kid tells you about it so that you can decide together how to proceed. Second, no one (child, youth, or adult) should ever meet an online friend in a private place: Always arrange to meet in a public place, such as a restaurant. Finally, go to the meeting with your child, in case she has been completely misled. (You can lurk discreetly nearby, so bring a book.)

✔ **Do anything illegal — online or off:** The Internet feels totally anonymous, but it's not. If kids or adults commit a crime, the police can get the Internet connection records from your Internet service provider (ISP) and find out who was connected over which modem on what day and at what time with what numeric Internet (IP) address, and they'll find you.

✔ **Break into other computers or create viruses:** This little escapade might have been considered a prank back in the 1980s, but the authorities have long since lost their sense of humor about it. Kids *are* going to jail for it these days.

The Internet and Little Kids

We are strong advocates of allowing kids to be kids, and we believe that humans are better teachers than computers are. Now that you know our predisposition, maybe you can guess what we're going to say next: We are not in favor of sticking a young child in front of a screen. How young is too young? We believe that younger than age 5 is too young. At young ages, kids benefit more from playing with trees, balls, clay, crayons, paint, mud, monkey bars, bicycles, other kids, and especially older sibs. Computers make lousy babysitters. If your young children use computers, choose their programs and Web sites carefully, limit their screen time, and, most importantly, sit with them and talk about what they're doing.

We think that Internet access is more appropriate for somewhat older kids (fourth or fifth grade and older), but your mileage may vary. Even so, we think it's a good idea to limit the amount of time that anyone, especially kids, spends online. We (despite our good looks) have been playing with computers for 35 years (each), and we know what happens to kids who are allowed to stay glued to their computers for unlimited lengths of time — trust us, *it is not good.* Remember those old sayings "You are what you eat?" and "Garbage in, garbage out?" What your brain devours all the time makes a difference.

As human beings (what a concept), kids need to be able to communicate with other human beings. Too often, kids who have difficulty doing that prefer to get absorbed in computers — which doesn't help develop their social skills. Existing problems in that department get worse, leading to more isolation. If you're starting to feel like your child is out of touch and you want to put the machine in its place (and maybe even encourage your child to get her life back), here are some quick self-defense tips:

- ✔ Keep a private log of all the time your child spends in front of the screen during one week. Then ask your child whether this is really how she wants to spend her life.

- ✔ Help your child find a hobby that doesn't involve a screen. Encourage him to join a team, form a band, or create some kind of art.

- ✔ Have your child set aside one computer-free day each week.

- ✔ Make your child have meals and conversations with live human beings (you and the rest of your family), face to face, in real time.

Surf Safe

Make sure your kids or grandkids know the safety rules for using the Net. Here are some basic guidelines for your kids to start with:

- ✔ **Never reveal exactly who you are.** Your child should use only his first name, and shouldn't provide a last name, address, phone number, or the name of his school.

- ✔ **Never, ever, tell anyone your password.** No honest person will ever ask your kid for it.

- ✔ **Be suspicious of strangers who seem to know a lot about you.** Maybe they say they're a friend of yours (the parent) who is supposed to pick up your kid after school or to pick up a package from your house. Make sure that your kid knows to never go with a stranger or let him or her into the house without asking a trusted (offline) adult first.

Most kids don't have a clue about these rules. They reveal who they are without even meaning to do so. They may mention the name of their hometown ball team. They may talk about a teacher they dislike at school. They may say what their parents do for a living. They may say which church, mosque, or synagogue they attend. Such information may be revealed over the course of many messages spread over weeks or months. These seemingly harmless bits of information can help a determined person "triangulate" to home in on your kid. It all boils down to a simple rule: Your child must be very careful about what he says online — in a chat room or instant message or e-mail.

Here are a few more guidelines to help kids sidestep online trouble:

✔ **Think before you give your e-mail address to anybody.** Many Web sites ask users to register, and many require you to provide a working e-mail address that they verify by sending you a message. Before you let your child register with a Web site, make sure that it's run by a reputable company from which you won't mind getting junk mail.

✔ **Never agree to talk to someone on the phone or meet someone in person without checking it out with you (the parent) first.** Most people a kid can meet online are okay, but a few creepy types out there have made the Internet their hunting ground.

✔ **Don't assume that people are telling you the truth.** That "kid" who says he's your kid's age and gender and seems to share your child's interests and hobbies may actually be a lonely, disturbed 40-year-old. And for kids who have younger siblings, impress on them how important it is to watch out for the safety of their younger siblings. They may not understand what a stranger is and believe that everything people tell them online is always true.

✔ **If someone is scaring you or making you uncomfortable — especially if the person says not to tell your parents —** *tell* **your parents.** If something bothers your child, make sure she knows to ask you to talk to your Internet service provider. Remind your kid that she can always turn off the computer.

Sell, Sell, Sell!

If you spend a lot of time online, you will soon notice that everyone seems to be trying to sell you something. Kids, particularly those from middle- and upper-income families, are a lucrative target market, and the Net is being viewed as another way to capture this market.

Targeting kids for selling isn't new. Remember Joe Camel of the Camel cigarette campaign that many people claimed was aimed at kids? Some schools make students watch Channel One, a system that brings advertising directly to the classroom. If you watch TV, you know how TV programs for kids push their own lines of toys and action figures.

Kids should know that big company marketing departments have designed kid-friendly, fascinating, captivating software to help them better market to you. Delightful, familiar cartoon characters deftly elicit strategic marketing information directly from the keyboard in your home.

You should be aware of this situation and know what to do when someone on the Web is asking your kids for information. Keep in mind that if your kids have access to your credit cards, they can spend big bucks over the Internet.

Beware of online stores where you have configured your Web browser to remember your passwords, because your kids will be able to waltz right in and start buying. And your kids should be aware that if they spend your money online without permission, they're going to get into big trouble for it.

The Children's Online Privacy Protection Act (COPPA) limits the information that companies can collect from children under 13 (or at least, children who *admit* they're under 13) without explicit parental consent — which, by the way, we think parents should rarely give. We heard of one marketer who said he wanted to use the Net to create a personal relationship with all the kids who use his product. Ugh. We have names for guys who want relationships that get things from kids, and they're not very nice names.

The FTC's Kidz Privacy site (`www.ftc.gov/bcp/conline/edcams/kidzprivacy`) has more useful information for both kids and parents about COPPA and online privacy.

Who's Online?

Lots of kids — and grown-ups — are putting up Web sites about themselves and their families. Social networking sites, like MySpace and Facebook, make this easy. We think that this is really cool, but we strongly encourage families who use the Net for personal reasons (distinct from businesspeople who use the Net for business purposes) *not* to use their full or real names. We also advise you and your children never to disclose your address, phone number, Social Security number, or account passwords in online social situations to anyone who asks for this kind of information — online or off. This advice applies especially when you receive information requests from people who claim to be in positions of authority — for example, instant messages from people claiming that they're from America Online (AOL) tech support. They're not, as we detail in Chapter 2.

People with real authority *never* ask those types of questions. (For one thing, Internet service providers don't handle member accounts by using instant messages, and never ask for credit card info by e-mail. It all makes a great case for knowing how your Internet service provider *does* work.)

More than ever, children need to develop critical thinking skills. They have to be able to evaluate what they read and see — especially on the Web.

Regrettably, almost anyone with an e-mail address receives their share of trash e-mail *(spam)*. This situation is likely to get worse until we have effective laws — as well as technology — against unsolicited e-mail. In the meantime, one important rule to remember is this: If an e-mail offers sounds too good to be true, assume that it isn't true — and if an ad for it showed up from someone you don't know, that's also pretty good evidence that it's not true. See Chapter 14 for weapons on the war against spam.

Checking out colleges on the Net

Most colleges and universities have sites on the Web. You can find a directory of online campus tours at www.campustours.com, with links to lots more info about the colleges and universities.

After you're a little more adept at using the Net, you can use it to take a closer look at classes and professors to get a better idea of what colleges have to offer.

The Internet in Schools

Some schools and libraries use software to filter Internet access for kids. A variety of filtering systems are available, at a range of costs and installation hassles, that promise to filter out inappropriate and harmful Web sites. Sounds good, but many kids are smart enough to find ways around rules, and really smart kids can find ways around software systems designed to "protect" them.

We believe that Internet filtering in schools is not a good approach. Kids are quicker and more highly motivated and have more time to spend breaking into and out of systems than most adults we know, and this method doesn't encourage them to do something more productive than electronic lock-picking.

Many institutions rely successfully on students' signed contracts that detail explicitly what is appropriate and what is inappropriate to use. Students who violate these contracts lose their Internet or computer privileges. We recommend the approach of contracts and consequences, from which kids can really learn.

For more information on the Children's Internet Protection Act (CIPA), a law upheld by the Supreme Court that mandates filtering software in U.S. schools and libraries, see the American Library Association's page about it at www.ala.org/cipa.

A Few Useful Web Sites

Here are a few sites that may be useful for kids and parents (and grandparents).

These sites focus on education and parenting:

✔ **The Global Schoolhouse**, at www.globalschoolnet.org/GSH: An online meeting place for teachers, students, and parents.

- **Great Web Sites for Kids**, from the American Library Association, at `www.ala.org/ala/alsc` (and then click Great Web Sites for Kids).
- **KidPub**, at `www.kidpub.com`: Book reviews by kids.
- **FunBrain**, at `www.funbrain.com`: Educational games for K-8.

These sites are just plain fun:

- **Yahoo Kids**, at `http://kids.yahoo.com`: Yahoo's Web portal design for kids.
- **Kids World**, at `http://northvalley.net/kids`: Links to fun and interesting sites.
- **The Yuckiest Site on the Internet** at `www.yucky.com`: Just what it sounds like — the yuckier, the better!
- **The CIA Homepage for Kids**, at `https://www.cia.gov/kids-page/index.html`: You have to type the `https://` part because it's a secure site!
- **Net-Mom** at `www.netmom.com`: It's run by our friend Jean Polly, who has been looking for online resources for kids even longer than we have.
- **Sports Illustrated for Kids**, at `www.sikids.com`

Not just for kids: School on the Net

Your child's education (as well as your own) isn't over when you finish high school or college or (for those of us seriously dedicated to avoiding real life) graduate school. There's always more to learn. Nothing's quite like learning directly from a first-rate teacher in a classroom, but learning over the Net can be the next best thing to being there — particularly for students who live far from school or have irregular schedules. You can now take everything online from high-school-equivalency exams to professional continuing education to college and graduate courses leading to degrees. Some courses are strictly online; others use a combination of classroom, lab, and online instruction.

A few schools, like the University of Phoenix (`www.phoenix.edu`), specialize in online education, but schools all over the world now offer online instruction, and some (such as MIT at `http://web.mit.edu`) make all their course material available online for free. If the course is on the Net, it doesn't matter whether the school is across the street or across the ocean. You can find thousands of schools and courses in directories such as `www.petersons.com/distancelearning` and `www.online-colleges-courses-degrees-classes.org`.

Part II
Internet, Here I Come!

The 5th Wave   By Rich Tennant

©RICHTENNANT

"Since we got it, he hasn't moved from that spot for
eleven straight days. Oddly enough they call this
'getting up and running' on the Internet."

In this part . . .

After you're ready to get started, where do you start? Probably the hardest part of using the Internet is getting connected. We help you figure out which kind of Internet service is right for you and help you get connected, with plenty of advice for broadband (fast) and WiFi (wireless) users.

Chapter 4

Climbing onto the Net: What Do You Need to Go Online?

"*G*reat," you say, "How do I get connected to the Internet?" The answer is "It depends." (You'll be hearing that answer perhaps more often than you'd like.) The Internet isn't one network — it's 100,000 separate networks hooked together, each with its own rules and procedures, and you can get to the Net from any one of them. Readers of previous editions of this book pleaded (they said other things too, but this is a family-oriented book) for step-by-step directions on how to get on, so we made ours as one-size-fits-all as possible.

Here (drumroll, please) are those basic steps:

1. **Figure out which type of computer you have or can use.**

2. **Figure out which types of Internet connections are available where you are.**

3. **Sign up for your connection.**

4. **Set up your computer to use your new connection, and decide whether you like it.**

5. **Install the software you need to protect your computer from viruses and spyware. (See Chapter 2 for scary descriptions of the types of Internet dangers that you need to protect yourself from.)**

You need four things to connect to the Internet:

- ✔ A computer, even a little tiny computer, like a Palm or other handheld device
- ✔ A modem (a piece of computer equipment, which may be right inside the computer) to hook your computer to the phone line or cable system
- ✔ An account with an Internet service provider (ISP) or online service, to give your modem somewhere to connect to
- ✔ Software to run on your computer

We look at each of these items in turn.

If you've got more than one computer to connect to the Internet, see Chapter 5. If your computer is a laptop, see the section "Using Your Laptop at Home and Away" in Chapter 5.

Internet accounts are easy to use, but they can be tricky to set up. In fact, connecting for the first time can be the most difficult part of your Internet experience. Installing and setting up Internet connection software used to require that you type lots of scary-looking numerical Internet addresses, hostnames, communications-port numbers — you name it. These days, making the connection is much easier, partly because Internet software can now figure out most of the numbers itself, but mostly because Windows XP, Window Vista, and Macs include setup software that can step you through the process.

What Kind of Computer Do You Need?

Because the Internet is a computer network, the only way to hook up to it is by using a computer. But computers are starting to appear in all sorts of disguises, and they may well already be in your home, whether you know it or not.

Hey, I don't even have a computer!

If you don't have a computer and aren't ready or able to buy one, you still have some options.

A likely place to find Internet access is in your public library. Most libraries have added Internet access centers, with clusters of Internet-connected computers among the bookshelves. These computers tend to be popular, so call ahead to reserve time or find out which hours are less crowded.

WiFi plus Starbucks and other hotspots

If you have a laptop computer, you can use public wireless (WiFi) Internet connections, which are available at many cafes, libraries, airports, and hotels. Your laptop needs a WiFi adapter to connect. Some of these connections cost anywhere from $6 per hour to $10 per day; others are free (if you don't include the cost of the latte). Some handheld devices have WiFi, too. See Chapter 5 for details.

Another option is your local cybercafe. You can surf the Net while sipping your favorite beverage and sharing your cyberexperience. If you want to check out the Internet, a cybercafe is a great place to try before you buy. Some have computers ready for you to use, whereas others require you to bring your own laptop (see the sidebar "WiFi plus Starbucks and other hotspots").

If you want to use the Internet from your very own home, you're stuck getting some kind of computer. Luckily, almost any newish computer can connect to the Internet, and you can get quite decent ones for under $500.

Yup, I have this old, beige box in the closet

Almost any personal computer made since 1980 is adequate for *some* type of connection to the Internet. But unless you have a really good friend who is a computer geek and wants to spend a lot of time at your house helping you get online, it isn't worth fooling with that old clunker — unless, of course, you're looking for a reason for the geek to spend a lot of time at your house, but that's your business.

If you can afford it, we strongly encourage you to buy a new computer or at least one that's not more than two years old. New computers come with Internet software already installed and are configured for the latest in Web technology. If you already own an older computer, you will spend more time and energy, and ultimately just as much money, just trying to get the thing to work the way you want. We think that you're best off buying a brand-new computer.

One problem with old computers is that they tend to run old versions of software. Any version of Windows older than Windows XP or any Mac system older that OS X is more hassle than it's worth to try to use.

Yup, I got a brand new Thunderstick 2008

Ah, you *do* have a computer. (Or maybe you're thinking about buying one.) Most Internet users connect via a broadband connection, or in areas where broadband isn't available, by the computer dialing over the phone line to an Internet service provider (ISP). When you first turn on your new computer, or when you run one of the Internet programs that come installed, your computer offers to call an ISP and set up an account right then and there. Don't dial (or let your computer dial) until you read the rest of this chapter. We have some warnings and some options we think you ought to consider first.

Yup, I got this little BlackBerry, Palm, or iPhone

Modern mobile phones have little bitty screens and little bitty keypads, so industry groups devised a way to show little bitty Web pages on those screens and navigate around them. The mobile Internet is quite popular in Japan (where teenage girls use it to get updates on Hello Kitty), but it's catching on much slower in the U.S. Unlike on your PC, it doesn't require special setup beyond what your mobile phone company does when it sells you the phone.

At this point, we advise against paying a lot for a Web-enabled phone unless you have a specific use in mind and you've tried it out on someone else's phone to see if you can stand using its teeny screen. Most new phones have basic Web features, which are plenty for casual fooling around.

On the other hand, lots of other devices work okay with the Internet. Palm Treos, BlackBerries, and many other handhelds are designed to display text messages, e-mail, and simple Web pages on their small screens. Go to a store that sells phones or electronics and ask to see a demonstration. Don't forget to check out the Apple iPhone, if you might want a large set of cool features for a large amount of money.

On a mobile Internet connection, you pay by the amount of data you transfer, which can be several dollars per download. If you plan to do much browsing from your phone, call your carrier and get a monthly data plan that includes data access, such as AT&T's SmartPhone Connect or Verizon's CoreChoice.

The Types of Internet Connections

If you use a computer at a library, at work, at a cybercafe, or at someone else's house, you don't need to worry about how it connects to the Internet, because someone else has already done the work. But if you have your own computer, you have several options:

- ✔ Connect via a fast phone line (DSL line) and Internet account.
- ✔ Connect via your cable TV company, which provides an Internet account.
- ✔ Connect via AOL (America Online); AOL isn't the Internet, but it connects to the Internet.
- ✔ Dial in to the Internet by using a regular phone line and an Internet account.

A word about usernames and passwords

More than a billion people are on the Internet. Because only one of them is you, it would be nice if the rest of them couldn't go snooping through your files and e-mail messages. For that reason — no matter which type of Internet account you have — your account has a username and a secret password associated with it.

Your *username* (or *user ID, login name, logon name,* or *screen name*) is unique among all the names assigned to your provider's users. It's usually also your e-mail address, so don't pick a name like *snickerdoodle* unless that's what you want to tell your friends and put on your business cards.

Your password is secret and is the main thing that keeps bad guys from borrowing an account. Don't use a real word or a name. A good way to make up a password is to invent a somewhat memorable phrase and turn each word in the phrase into a single letter or digit. "Computers cost too much money for me" turns into Cc2m$4m, for example. *Never tell anyone else your password.* Particularly don't tell people who claim to be from your ISP — they're not.

Here are the details about each method.

Speedy Connections: DSL and Cable Internet

The most popular way to connect, now available almost but not quite everywhere, is a *broadband* (high-speed) connection. Broadband connections can provide greater *bandwidth* — that is, more data transferred in a specific amount of time — than a connection over a regular phone line. Such connections can be really fast, nominally 1.4 million bits per second, with downloads (in practice) often exceeding 140,000 bytes per second.

The good news is that broadband connections are now available and affordable for mere mortals in all but the most rural locations in the U.S. and Canada.

After you get used to having a broadband connection, you will never be able to tolerate an old-fashioned dialup connection again. It's that good.

What is broadband, anyway?

There are two types of broadband Internet connections — DSL and cable.

- ✔ A *Digital Subscriber Line* (*DSL*) is a special phone line that you or your ISP orders from your local telephone company, usually shared with the same line that connects your regular phones.

- ✔ A cable Internet account is provided by your local cable TV company, using the same cable connection that brings you 250 brain-numbing TV channels.

DSL and cable Internet accounts have a lot in common: They're fast, they don't tie up your regular phone line, and they don't use a dialup modem. Some broadband accounts have a permanent connection that works a lot like a connection to a local network in an office. Others require you to log on, just as you would with a dialup connection. The good news about both DSL and cable accounts is that the ISP usually provides most of the equipment — for example, the modem — and often sends an installer to set it up with your computer. Ask your cable company whether it offers Internet access — or ask your phone company whether it offers DSL. If you get a yes to either question, get one or the other.

High-speed cable and DSL may cost more than dialup accounts (discussed later in this chapter), usually $30 to $50 per month, plus installation and the cost of the special modem you need, minus whatever discount they give you for buying a package of broadband and the other services you get from them. However, neither cable nor DSL ties up your phone while you're online. Many people who use ordinary modems end up paying for a second phone line. When you add the cost of a second phone line to the cost of your ISP, broadband is usually about the same price. Cable and DSL connections are always available — there's usually no calling-in process, and they're significantly faster (and, we think, more fun).

A hidden cost in getting either cable or DSL Internet access is having to take a day off from work to wait for the installer, unless you feel brave enough to install it yourself. Sometimes it takes the installer two trips to get things working. Try to get the first appointment in the morning. Also, the cable company or phone company is usually also your ISP unless you pay extra, so you don't have a choice of ISPs. In theory, the phone company provides DSL access on equal terms to all ISPs — but in practice, its own ISP somehow always seems to be more equal than the others.

Cable and DSL modems

To connect to a DSL or cable account, you use a DSL or a cable modem, but keep the following in mind:

- ✔ **If you have a cable Internet account, you need a cable modem.** Your cable company generally provides the modem as part of the service.

- ✔ **DSL modems are for connecting to high-speed DSL phone lines.** Don't buy one yourself — you need to make sure that the modem you use is compatible with your DSL line, so smart Internauts get their DSL modems from the ISP that provides their DSL service.

The moral of the story: Don't buy a DSL or cable modem yourself. Get your cable or phone company to provide and install it.

You may need a network adapter

DSL and cable modems connect to your computer in one of two-and-a-half ways:

- ✔ **Network adapter:** A *network adapter* (or *LAN adapter* or *Ethernet adapter* or *network interface card*) was originally designed for connecting computers together into networks. If you have more than one computer in your home or office, you can use network adapters to connect the computers into a *local-area network* (*LAN*), as described in Chapter 5. A network adapter has an RJ-45 jack, which looks like a regular phone jack but a little bigger, into which you plug your modem or network cable. Check the back and sides of your computer for holes that look like overgrown phone jacks. Most PCs (and all Macs) have a network adapter built in.

✔ **Wireless network adapter:** If your computer isn't located close to a phone or cable outlet or you have a laptop you carry around the house, you can use a wireless network, often called WiFi. It works pretty much the same as a wired network, only without the wires (duh!). Most laptops built in the past five years have built-in WiFi. We cover the ins and outs of WiFi in Chapter 5.

✔ **USB:** Most computers come with one or more *USB* (Universal Serial Bus, if you care) connectors, which are used for connecting all kinds of stuff to your computer, from mice to cameras to printers. A USB port looks like a small, narrow, rectangular hole. Ancient (pre-1998) computers don't have USB connectors.

Most DSL and cable modems connect to a network adapter with a cable that plugs into an RJ-45 jack. If you want a DSL or cable modem with a USB connector, ask your provider whether it offers one.

If your cable or DSL modem installer reports that your computer doesn't have the network adapter or USB port that's needed to connect your high-speed modem, don't panic. If the installer can't provide the needed adapter, contact a local computer store about adding a network card — it shouldn't cost more than $20. Desktop computers need PCI card network adapters, which are printed circuit boards that you install by turning off the computer, opening the case, finding an empty slot, sliding the card in, screwing down the card, and closing up the computer. Laptops use various sorts of PC Card network adapters, which look like fat credit cards and just slide into a slot on the side of the laptop. (There are several different kinds of PC Card slots; if you buy a card, be sure it fits the kind of slot your laptop has.)

Getting your DSL hooked up

DSL service is supposed to use your existing phone line and in-house wiring. But DSL often works better if the phone company runs a new wire from outside your building to where you use your computer. (Phone companies call this a *home run.*) For most kinds of DSL to work, you have to live within a couple of miles of your telephone central office, so DSL is unavailable in many rural areas.

DSL is available at different speeds. The higher speeds cost more (surprise, surprise!). The lowest speed, usually 640 Kbps, is fast enough for most users.

If DSL service is available in your area, call either your phone company or an ISP to arrange for DSL service. Either it ships you the equipment to install yourself, or a phone installer comes with a network connection box (a glorified modem) that you or the installer hook up to your computer. DSL modems connect to a network card (which you may need to add to your computer) or to a USB port (which most new computers already have).

Getting your cable Internet hooked up

To sign up for a cable account, call your local cable company to open one. Unless you decide to install it yourself (which isn't all that hard), a technician comes and installs a network-connection doozus (technical term) where your TV cable comes into your house, installs a network card in your computer if it doesn't already have one, brings a special modem (which can look like a junior laptop computer with a spike hairdo), and hooks them together. Magic.

If you have cable television, the cable is split, and one segment goes to your computer. If you don't have cable television, the cable company may have to install the actual cable before it can wire up your computer. When the technician goes away, however, you have a permanent, high-speed connection to the Internet (as long as you pay your bill, about $40 to $50 a month). It's usually cheaper if you also get the company's TV channels as well.

Do-it-yourself DSL

Hooking up your DSL modem shouldn't be so tough. One side plugs into the phone line, the other side into your computer. How hard can that be? Well, there are a few little details.

We assume that you have a DSL modem that connects to a LAN or USB connector. If you have a LAN connector, you need a *crossover LAN cable* that should have come with the DSL modem. (Regular, noncrossover cables plug into a router or network hub, not directly from a modem to a computer.) If you're using USB, you should have a USB cable with a flat connector on one end and a squarish connector on the other. Turn off and unplug both your computer and the modem from the wall socket, plug in the LAN or USB cable, and then plug everything back in. The modem also connects to the phone line with a regular phone cord. The phone and LAN jacks on the modem are similar, but the LAN connector is the bigger one.

Now skip ahead to the section "After the DSL or cable Internet installer." And be sure to read the nearby sidebar "Avoiding the DSL buzz."

Avoiding the DSL buzz

One of the clever things about DSL is that the DSL connection shares the same phone wires with your phone without tying up the phone line. You can tell that this is the case because on all the phones on the line with DSL, you may hear a loud buzz of Data Hornets swarming up and down your phone line. (Well, not really, but it sounds like it.)

To get rid of the buzz, you may need to install a *DSL filter* (which filters out the buzz) between the phone line and all your phones, but of course not between the phone line and your DSL modem. Filters are available from your DSL ISP, but you can probably find them cheaper at stores like RadioShack. The ideal way to install a filter is to run a separate wire from the box where the phone line enters your house to the DSL modem, and to install one DSL filter in that box into which you plug the wire leading to all the phones. But life is rarely ideal, so most of us install a filter for each phone.

For the phone plug where your DSL modem is connected, you want a *splitter* filter with a filtered jack into which you plug a phone (the one you use to call tech support when your computer doesn't work) and an unfiltered jack for the DSL modem. For all the other phones, the filter just plugs into the phone jack, and the phone cord plugs into the filter. For that tidy look, you can also get wall-phone filters (which fit between the phone and the wall plate that the phone's mounted on) and baseboard phone jacks with filters built in.

Do-it-yourself cable modems

Connecting a cable modem is not unlike connecting a DSL modem, except that you connect it to your TV cable rather than to your phone line. If a TV is already attached to the cable, unscrew the cable from the TV and throw away the TV because you'll be having much too much fun with your Internet connection to waste time watching TV. (If you're not yet ready to throw away your TV, move it to another cable outlet, or get a cable splitter, available at any store that sells cable accessories.) Screw the cable into the cable modem and plug the LAN or USB cable from the modem to the computer, just as we describe for a DSL modem in the previous section.

After the DSL or cable Internet installer

The installer (which is you, if you installed the modem yourself) configures your computer to communicate with the Internet. Most DSL and cable modems come with a software CD. If you're using a Mac or a version of Windows older than XP, run the software on the CD to install the necessary stuff to set up your connection.

Fast, fibrous FiOS

Cable and DSL network speeds are limited by the old-fashioned copper wire they use. Fiber optics are much faster, and large telephone companies have been making and breaking promises to wire us up with fiber for about 20 years. According to Teletruth, a phone consumers' advocate, if Verizon had kept the promises that its predecessor Bell of Pennsylvania made in 1994, most Pennsylvania homes would be wired with 45-megabit fiber by now.

Verizon is finally sort of making good on its promises with *FiOS,* a fiber optic package that combines fairly fast Internet (not 45 megabits, though) with home WiFi, phone, and TV. If you want fast Internet and high-definition TV and you're willing to sign up for at least a full year, it's not a bad deal. But you might want to consider a few things before signing up:

✔ Verizon has some odd rules about what it supports; in particular, it doesn't support wireless connections to Macs, only wired.

✔ There's no going back. The person who hooks up the fiber will physically rip out your old copper phone line so that you can't switch back without paying for a full new installation.

✔ It depends on your house power. Regular phone service powers your phone from the central office, so the phone company's large batteries and professionally maintained backup generators keep the phones working if the power fails. FiOS uses your house power to run your phones as well as your Internet and TV connections. It provides a battery that's supposed to keep your phone going for four hours if the power fails, but the battery lasts only two or three years, and if you don't remember to replace it (Verizon won't), you'll have an unpleasant surprise when the power fails.

If you're running Windows XP, you can either use the CD or set up the connection by using the built-in New Connection Wizard in Windows XP. Windows Vista has a similar wizard but calls it Connect to a Network. We recommend the wizard because the CD usually has a pile of software that isn't of much use to you. To set up your connection using the Windows XP wizard, follow these steps:

1. **Choose Start⇨All Programs⇨Accessories⇨Communications⇨ New Connection Wizard.**

   (They sure don't make it easy to find.)

2. **For the Network Connection Type, choose Connect to the Internet and click Next.**

3. **Select Set Up My Connection Manually.**

   You can choose either Connect Using a Broadband Connection That Requires a User Name and Password (if your ISP gave you a username and password) or Connect Using a Broadband Connection That Is Always On. A connection that is always on means that your computer is more vulnerable to hackers because it's never disconnected, but it's nice to be able to saunter up to your computer at any time and not have to wait for it to connect.

   If you're worried about your computer being connected to the Internet all the time, you can shut down your computer — when it's turned off, it's definitely hackerproof! See the section "Essential Software to Keep Your System Safe," later in this chapter.

4. **Enter the required information in the boxes and accept the suggested check boxes, particularly the Internet firewall.**

Windows Vista makes it slightly easier. If your network connects with a wired LAN connection and doesn't require a login or password (this includes most cable modems), Vista normally configures itself automagically, so you don't have to do any of this. For connections that do require a login, follow these steps:

1. **Choose Start⇨Connect To, and then click the little Set Up a Connection or Network link.**

   They still don't make it easy to find.

2. **For the Network Connection Type, choose Connect to the Internet and click Next.**

3. **Select Broadband (PPPoE).**

   We cover some of the other options for dialup and wireless later in this chapter and in Chapter 5.

4. **Enter the required information in the boxes.**

   In particular, enter the login name and password that your ISP gave you.

After your connection is installed, you should be able to start up a Web browser like Internet Explorer and type the name of a Web site into the address box at the top (try our `http://net.gurus.com`). The Web page should appear momentarily. If you have a connection with a username, it may ask you whether to connect. (Well, yeah, that's the idea, but sarcasm is lost on machinery.)

Your PC communicates with the Internet by using the TCP/IP protocol, and you should see it listed in the Properties dialog box for the connection (in Windows XP). Don't fool with these settings unless you're sure that you know what you're doing!

On the other side of the pond

The ISP situation in the United Kingdom is a little different from the one in North America. For broadband, British Telecom (BT) provides DSL service with (by American standards) high speeds at a low price as long as you sign up for at least a year at a time. Cable modem service is also widely available, typically faster than BT and more expensive.

Traditionally, all phone calls in the U.K. have been charged by the minute, including even local calls, which can make long dialup online sessions mighty pricey. As a result, the U.K. now has three different kinds of dialup ISPs:

✔ **Traditional:** These ISPs charge a modest monthly fee and provide access via either local numbers or national rate numbers. Unless you're sure that you won't spend much time online or your ISP provides another service you're using, such as Web hosting, this type is probably not what you want.

✔ **Free:** These ISPs charge no monthly fee; they support themselves by splitting the per-minute charges with BT. (BT would rather not, but OFTEL, the regulatory agency

for the telecom industry in Britain, insists.) If you just want to try out the Net, free ISPs are a good way to start. We don't recommend them for long-term use because the per-minute split is less lucrative than the ISPs hoped, and free ISPs have a disconcerting habit of going out of business on short notice. The tech support also tends to be pretty weak. (It's free — what do you want, your money back?)

✔ **Flat-rate:** These ISPs charge a monthly fee of about £20 but provide an 0800 or other number you can call without per-minute fees. Most dialup users find this the best choice because it makes the bill predictable. The largest flat-rate ISPs are AOL (yes, *that* AOL) and BT. Be warned that even though access is nominally unlimited, if you "camp" on the phone 20 hours a day, your ISP will invoke small print you never noticed and cancel your account.

Depending on where you are and where your ISP is, your phone connection may be anywhere from wonderful to dreadful. If you try one ISP and keep getting slow or unreliable connections, try another.

Checking your DSL or cable connection

After you're connected, you can check the status of your connection:

✔ **Windows Vista:** Display the Network Connections box by choosing Start➪Control Panel➪Network and Sharing Center. Broadband connections appear in the upper part of the window.

✔ **Windows XP:** Display the Network Connections box by choosing Start➪Control Panel➪Network And Internet Connections➪Network Connections — broadband connections appear in the LAN or High-Speed Internet section.

> ✔ **Macs:** Use the TCP/IP Control Panel in OS 8 and OS 9. For OS X, choose System Preferences under the Apple menu and click the Network icon. Then select the TCP/IP tab.

Dialing — the Old-Fashioned Way

A *dialup modem* connects to a normal, everyday phone line — using the same little plug (a RJ-11 jack) and phone wire. You can unplug a phone and plug in a dialup modem in its place.

Most computers sold in recent years come with built-in dialup modems. If you already have a modem, use it — just examine your computer carefully for a phone jack and if you find one, plug a phone wire into it. Otherwise, you'll have to take your computer to the store and have them install one.

Note to laptop computer owners: If your computer has credit-card-size PC Card slots but no built-in modem, get a PC Card modem that fits in a slot so that you don't have to carry around a separate modem when you take your computer on the road. See Chapter 5.

Beware of phone charges

If you're not careful, you can end up paying more for the phone call than you do for your Internet account. One thing you do when you sign up for an ISP is determine the phone number to call. *Use an ISP whose number is a free or untimed local call* (so that you're not paying by the minute). Nearly the entire continent is now within a local call of an ISP; if you're one of the unlucky few, see whether your phone company has a $20 unlimited long-distance plan.

Names, passwords, and prices

To use a dialup Internet connection, you sign up with an ISP for an Internet account. The account gives you the username and password that you need when your computer's modem dials into the ISP.

The features and services that one ISP offers are much like those of another, with important differences such as price, service, and reliability. Think of it as the difference between a Ford and a Buick, where the differences between your local dealers are at least as important in the purchase decision as the differences between the cars. Most ISP accounts come with

✔ **That all-important username and password:** You have to be able to connect, after all.

✔ **One or more e-mail addresses, each with its own mailbox:** Most accounts come with from one to five e-mail addresses. If you have a family, each family member can have a separate address.

✔ **Web mail — that is, a Web site where you can read your mail:** Web mail is useful when you want to check your mail and you're not at your own computer with your own e-mail program. You can use a Web browser to display your messages from any computer.

If you don't know what your local ISPs are, check the phone book or ads in the business section of your local paper.

If you or your kids become regular online users, you will find that time stands still while you're online and that you use much more online time than you think you do. Even if you think that you will be online for only a few minutes a day, if you don't have a flat-rate plan, you may be surprised when your bill arrives at the end of the month.

Your ISP should give you a short list of items to set up your account: your username and password, its dialup phone number, and your e-mail address if it's different from the username.

Connecting to dialup accounts for Windows Vista users

Windows Vista has built-in dialup networking as well as Windows Mail and the Internet Explorer Web browser. To set up Windows Vista so that it can use an existing Internet account, follow these steps:

1. **Choose Start⇨Connect To. In the window that opens, click the little Set Up a Connection or Network link.**

   You see a window with a list of connection options.

2. **Click Set Up a Dial-Up Connection and then the Next button at the bottom of the window.**

   You see the Set Up a Dial-Up Connection window, shown in Figure 4-1.

3. **Enter the phone number, username, and password your Internet provider gave you.**

   Enter the phone number as you would dial it on your phone, as 7, 10, or 11 digits. Unless you share your computer with someone you don't trust, check the box to remember this password.

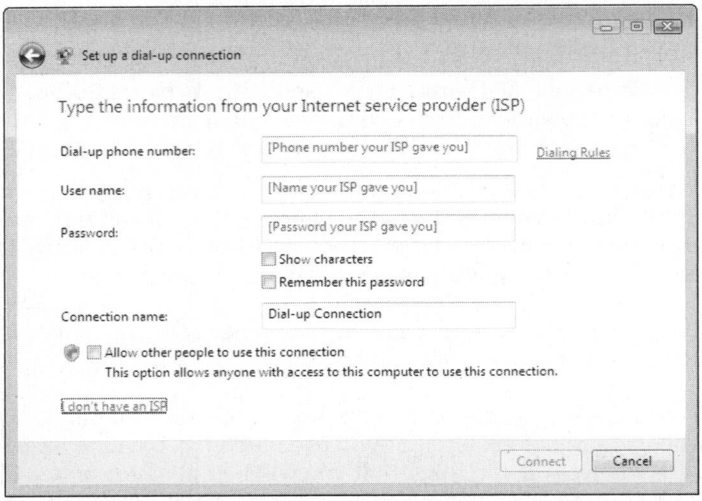

Figure 4-1:
Prepare
to tell
Windows
Vista about
your dialup
connection.

4. **Click Connect.**

   Vista should dial your ISP and connect. If it doesn't work, Vista offers some options to diagnose the problem. We've found that the most common problem is that the phone cord isn't properly connected (unplug it from the computer and plug it into a phone to check) or that you mistyped something.

After your dialup account is set up, you can connect or disconnect by choosing Start➪Connect To and then clicking the dialup connection and the Connect or Disconnect button.

Windows normally dials out automatically when you run a program that needs to use the Internet. If that's not what you want, choose Start➪Control Panel, open the Internet Options window, and then click the Connections tab to see the options never to dial, or to dial whenever a network connection is not present.

Connecting to dialup accounts for Windows XP users

Windows XP comes with an Internet dialup connection program, along with a New Connection Wizard for setting up your computer to use your Internet account. It also comes with Outlook Express for e-mail and Internet Explorer for Web browsing. To set up Windows XP so that it can use an existing Internet account, follow these steps:

1. **Double-click the Connect to the Internet icon on your desktop.**

   If you don't see it, click the Start button and choose All Programs⇨ Accessories⇨Communications⇨New Connection Wizard.

2. **Click Next on its opening screen.**

3. **Click Connect to the Internet and then click Next.**

4. **If you don't have an Internet account yet, click the top button on the screen that appears (Choose from a List of Internet Service Providers) and click Next.**

   The wizard leaves you with two options: Sign up with MSN, Microsoft's own ISP, or dial the Microsoft Internet Referral Service (a toll-free call in the U.S.) to display a list of ISPs near you. The list is usually pretty short because it includes only big ISPs that have paid Microsoft enough to be included in the service. You may find terrific local ISPs (not on the list) that you can use instead.

   If you choose an ISP from Microsoft's list, you can sign up on the spot — just check with your phone company to make sure that the phone number it gives you is really a local call.

   Skip Microsoft's referral service and do your own shopping.

5. **If you already have an Internet account, click the middle button (Set Up My Connection Manually) and then click Next.**

   Setting up your account manually isn't as scary as it sounds; it mostly means that you have to type in the ISP's name and phone number and your logon and password yourself. (Wow, it makes our fingers hurt just to think about it! Not.)

   The wizard asks how you connect to the Internet (over a regular, dialup phone line? a broadband DSL or cable Internet connection that requires a password? broadband DSL or cable Internet connection that doesn't require a password?), your ISP's name, the phone number to dial, your username, and your password. See the section "Speedy Connections: DSL and Cable Internet," earlier in this chapter, for information about broadband connections.

   The wizard also offers these check boxes (they're usually selected for you, but you can click them to deselect them):

   • **Use This Account Name and Password When Anyone Connects to the Internet from This Computer:** If your Windows computer is set up for multiple users, choosing this option enables all users to connect with this account. Unless you have some users on your computer whom you severely distrust, leave this option selected.

   • **Make This the Default Internet Connection:** If you have several Internet accounts, one is the *default* (the connection that Windows uses unless you specify otherwise). If you have only one Internet account (like most normal nongeeks), leave this one selected, too.

6. **When you click Next and then Finish, the New Connection Wizard creates a dialup connection for your account.**

   The wizard also configures Windows to dial that number automagically whenever you try to browse the Web or send or receive e-mail.

Signing on and off with Windows XP

To connect to the Internet, run your browser and request a Web page, or run your e-mail program and tell it to check your mail. When Windows sees you requesting information from the Internet, it dials the phone for you. If you see a dialog box that asks for your username and password, type them and then click Connect.

You can tell when you're connected because a two-computer-screen icon appears in the lower-right corner of the screen (just to the left of the digital clock). Double-click this icon to check the speed of your Internet connection — or, if you want to hang up, click the Disconnect button in the dialog box that appears.

Connecting to dialup accounts for Mac users

Newer Macs already have all the software you need to connect to the Internet. (Very old Macs — pre-System 8 — need a Mac TCP/IP modem program, such as FreePPP, which your ISP should be able to give you.) The only things you usually need to set are the ISP's phone number, your account name, and your password.

AOL Isn't Exactly the Internet, But Close Enough

America Online (AOL) the world's largest online service, provides access to both the Internet and its own, proprietary services. AOL has more than 20 million subscribers worldwide. To use AOL, you use software it provides. (Windows and Mac versions are available.) You can also use other software with your AOL account, such as Firefox and Internet Explorer. Like most ISPs, AOL started as a dialup service and has since added DSL and cable connections — or you can use its "bring your own access" version with any other dialup or broadband Internet account.

Note: America Online, despite its name, is available outside America. AOL has access numbers in major Canadian cities and throughout the U.K., at no extra charge, as well as versions for several other countries. If you travel internationally with your computer, AOL has more international phone numbers than anyone else, although some involve a high per-minute surcharge.

If you want to sign up for an AOL account, if your PC didn't come with the AOL access program already installed, go to any post office and pick up one of the zillion AOL signup CDs lying around. Or, call 1-800-827-3338 and ask for a trial membership. The introductory package has instructions and (surprise!) a disc containing the AOL access program. Follow the instructions on its cover to install the program and sign up for an account. You need a credit card to sign up.

For more information about how to use AOL, get *AOL For Dummies*, 2nd Edition, by John Kaufeld and Ted Leonsis (Wiley).

Essential Software to Keep Your System Safe

Okay, you're connected. Before you start surfing the Web, e-mailing, and instant messaging, you need to protect your computer from the Terrors of the Internet: viruses and spyware. Chapter 2 describes them in gory detail, and now is the time to use protection.

Walling out the bad guys

A *firewall* is a barrier between your computer (or computers) and the Internet. In big companies, the firewall may consist of a computer that does nothing but monitor the incoming and outgoing traffic, checking for bad stuff. At your home or office, you have two good options:

✔ **Use firewall software built into Windows XP or Vista.** In Windows Vista, click the little Security Center shield in the notification area at the bottom of the screen and then Windows Firewall. In Windows XP SP2, choose Start ➪Control Panel➪Security Center. In original Windows XP, choose Start➪Control Panel➪Network and Internet Connections ➪ Network Connections. (If you use the "Classic" Control Panel, choose Start➪Control Panel➪Network Connections.) Right-click the icon for your Internet account, choose Properties from the menu that appears, click the Advanced tab, and look for the Internet Connection Firewall or

Windows Firewall section. If it's not already selected, select the check box to turn on Internet Connection Firewall. When that's done, your computers have basic protection from hackers.

✔ **Use a *router*, a small box that sits between your computer (or computers) and your broadband modem.** A router has one plug for a cable to your DSL or cable modem, several plugs (usually four) to which you can connect computers, and usually an antenna for wireless WiFi connections. The router has firewall software running all the time. See Chapter 5 for how to use a router to connect more than one computer to one Internet account.

We recommend using a router because they cost only about $40 and we're sure that you'll want to hook up a second computer to the Internet before long. The firewall programs included in Windows Vista and XP work fine, too. Hey, why not use both?

A router is a particularly good idea if you have a broadband connection that is always on (that is, always connected). The router is always on, too.

No viruses need apply

Viruses are sneaky programs that arrive via e-mail or in downloaded programs, and immediately get up to no good. (See Chapter 2 for details.) You need to run a virus checker program all the time, and you need to update its list of viruses regularly so that the program can detect the latest viruses.

Many virus checkers are available. The free AVG from `http://free.grisoft.com` isn't bad, particularly at the price. Two popular commercial programs are McAfee VirusScan, which you can download from `www.mcafee.com`, and Norton AntiVirus, at `www.symantec.com`. If you have more than one computer on the Internet, consider F-Prot, at `www.f-prot.com`, because you have to pay for only one license to run the program on all the computers in your house.

The commercial programs require that you pay annually for a subscription to updates. Do it — without updates to the list of viruses that it's looking for, your program doesn't spot and block the latest viruses. Some bundle the virus checker with other security packages so that you can get all the protection you need with one purchase.

Don't think that you're saving money if you don't subscribe to a virus-checking service. New viruses come out every day (well, every week, anyway). Your virus checker can check for only the viruses it knows about. You need a service that updates your list of viruses to check for. It's like the FBI sending out new Wanted posters to the local police.

A good virus checker automatically connects to its home base over the Internet at least once a week and downloads updates to its virus lists. You may see a dialog box on your screen when this is happening. Your subscription usually lasts a year, and you should see warnings to update your subscription (that is, pay again) when your year is almost up.

For help with downloading and installing a virus program, see Chapter 12.

Detecting spyware

Spyware is a class of programs that sneaks onto your computer, usually when you're browsing the Web, and runs unbeknownst to you, doing God-knows-what. (See Chapter 2 for details.) A number of anti-spyware programs are available for free, although no single program seems to spot all types of spyware. We recommend that you run several anti-spyware programs from time to time, to sweep your hard disk and look for bad stuff.

The programs we use are

- ✔ **Spybot Search & Destroy**, at `www.spybot.info` (shareware; donations appreciated). Note that several unscrupulous programs have started using the word *spybot* in their names, so don't just Google to find the program. Go to the official Web site at `www.spybot.info` to download the program.

- ✔ **Ad-Aware Personal Edition**, at `www.lavasoftusa.com`. It's also free, although the developer wants you to buy the fancier paid version).

These programs (and many others) are also available for free download from `www.download.com`. For help with downloading and installing a spyware-checking program, see Chapter 12.

In addition, follow a few basic rules, which will make more sense after you read the later chapters of this book. (Don't worry: We mention them again in those later chapters, too.) Here they are:

- ✔ **Don't use Internet Explorer as your browser.** Most spyware is designed to use features of Internet Explorer to worm its way onto your computer. Instead, use Firefox, as described in Chapter 6.

- ✔ **Don't use Internet Explorer within other applications.** For example, some e-mail programs have an option to use Internet Explorer to display messages that contain HTML (Web formatting). Turn off these options.

Get rid of your Dell or Gateway software

Many computers come with Internet software created by the hardware manufacturers, designed to give you an easier Internet experience. Unfortunately, we find that these programs just give you a more *confusing* Internet experience because each program is renamed to add the name of the hardware manufacturer. (AOL used to do this, too.) If your Dell, Gateway, or other new computer comes with Dell, Gateway, or other Internet programs, we recommend that you ignore them and use the standard Windows stuff described in this chapter.

✓ **If you use Windows, turn on Automatic Updates, and download and install the updates it suggests.** Microsoft issues security fixes to Windows at least once a month. In Windows Vista, updates are already downloaded and installed unless you turned off Automatic Updates in the Security Center. To turn on Automatic Updates in Windows XP SP2, choose Start ⇨Control Panel⇨Security Center. In original Windows XP, choose Start⇨Control Panel⇨Performance and Maintenance⇨System. In the System Properties dialog box that appears, click the Automatic Updates tab. Choose the first or second option so that Windows lets you know when updates are available.

✗Our Favorite Internet Setup

You're probably wondering, "The authors of this book have used the Internet forever. What do they recommend as the very best way to connect to the Internet?" Okay, you're probably not wondering that, but we wish you were. And we've got the answer.

The best Internet setup (in our humble opinions) is this:

✓ A computer (Windows, Mac, or Linux — they're all good).

✓ A DSL or cable Internet account — broadband rocks!

✓ A *router*, to provide a firewall between your computer (or computers) and the Internet

You're Connected — Now What?

When you connect to your ISP (whether by dialup, DSL line, or cable Internet account), your computer becomes part of the Internet. You type stuff or click in programs running on your computer, and those programs communicate over the Net to do whatever it is they do for you.

Running lots of Internet programs

You can run several Internet applications at a time, which can be quite handy. You may be reading your electronic mail, for example, and receive a message describing a cool, new site on the World Wide Web. You can switch immediately to your Web browser program (usually Internet Explorer or — as we recommend — Firefox), look at the Web page, and then return to the mail program and pick up where you left off. Most e-mail programs highlight *URLs* (Web addresses) and enable you to go straight to your browser by clicking the URL in your e-mail message.

You're not limited to running programs that your Internet provider gives you. You can download a new Internet application from the Net and begin using it immediately — your ISP just acts as a data conduit between your computer and the rest of the Net.

To find out more about using the Web, see Chapter 6. If you want to start off with e-mail, read Chapter 13. Or, just flip through the rest of this book to see what looks interesting!

Getting off the Internet

If you dial in to the Internet (or AOL), you eventually want to disconnect (hang up). You don't have to log off, in most cases, but you do need to hang up the phone.

If you use a broadband account, you never need to disconnect. We love being able to saunter up to our computers at any time to check the weather, our e-mail, a good buttermilk waffle recipe, or which movies Joe E. Brown was in, without having to wait for our computer to reconnect.

You may have a bunch of programs running while you use the Internet, including your Web browser and your e-mail program. Only one of these programs, however, is the program that connects you to the Internet. That's the one you talk to when you're disconnecting from the Internet. In Windows, you disconnect from a dialup account by using the Dial-Up Networking or Dial-Up Connection program, which is usually a little icon on the Windows taskbar at the bottom of the screen, showing two flickering boxes. You can leave the rest of your programs (such as your Web browser and e-mail program) running even when you're not connected to the Net.

Chapter 5

Sharing Your Internet Connection

- -

In This Chapter

▶ Setting up a network at home

▶ Plugging together all your computers without wires

▶ Hooking up your laptop at home or on the road

- -

*T*hese days, lots of families have more than one computer — perhaps one in the office, one in the family room, and one in your teenager's bedroom. Hey, one of us has one in the kitchen for our family's calendar and address book. And that's not to mention the road warrior laptop.

Luckily, you don't need a separate Internet connection for each computer. Instead, you can connect the computers into a network — either with cables or through thin air with wireless connections — and then set them up to share one Internet connection. This chapter shows you how to set up both types of networks.

For those of you who already have a laptop or just got one, this chapter also talks about ways you can connect your laptop both at home and on the road.

Just One Computer for Internet Access? Naah

Many years ago, back when computers were large, hulking things found only in glass-walled computer rooms, a wild-eyed visionary friend of ours claimed (to great skepticism) that computers would be everywhere, and so small and cheap that they would show up as prizes in cereal boxes. We're not sure about the cereal boxes, but it's certainly true that the last time we went to put an old computer in the closet, there wasn't room because of all the other old computers in there. Rather than let them rust in the closet, you may as well get some use out of them by connecting them all to the Internet.

With a broadband connection, that turns out to be pretty easy. No more arguing about who's going to use the phone line next! No more pouting from the computer users who didn't get the cable or DSL hookup! Everyone can send e-mail, receive e-mail, chat, and browse the Web — all at the same time.

To share an Internet connection, you connect your computers to each other into a type of network called a *local-area network (LAN)*, and then you connect the LAN (rather than an individual computer) to the Internet. A local-area network is (drumroll, please!) a network that's entirely contained in one local area, like one building, and is connected via wires or wireless connections, with no phone lines within the LAN. Once the exclusive tool of businesses, LANs have become so cheap that they're showing up in homes — as long as your home is in one building, if you've got some computers connected to each other, it's a LAN.

Figure 5-1 shows a typical home network: A cable or DSL modem connects to a *hardware router,* a device that connects your LAN to your Internet connection. Normally, you would connect your PC to a network hub (for a wired network) or an access point (for wireless) — but a hardware router has a hub or access point built in. Then you connect the LAN to the rest of the computers around the house.

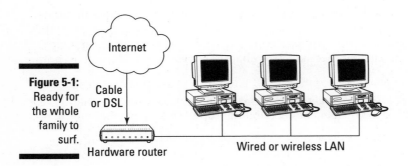

Figure 5-1:
Ready for
the whole
family to
surf.

The computers on your LAN don't all have to be running the same version of Windows — or running Windows at all. You can connect Windows computers, Macs, and Linux computers on the same LAN because they all speak the same networking protocol, the same protocol that the Internet itself uses.

First, Make a LAN

LANs come in two basic varieties: wired and wireless. In a wired network, a cable runs from each computer to a central box, whereas a wireless network uses radio signals rather than wires. (Either way, you need a central box, which we talk about in a minute.) If all your computers are in one room (or you're good at playing home electrician), a wired network is for you; otherwise, wireless is far easier to set up, although the pieces can be more expensive and the resulting network runs slower. Combos are also possible; most wireless equipment has a few jacks for wires to connect to the computers that are close enough to run cables.

The box in the middle — a hub or router

For any variety of current LAN, you need a special box that connects everything together. Here are the main kinds of boxes you have to choose from:

- A *hub* is a book-size box with a bunch of jacks for network cables. It serves as a wired connection point that links all your computers into a LAN.
- A *switch* is the same thing as a hub, but it's got a little extra circuitry to speed things up.
- An *access point* is the wireless equivalent of a hub, with a radio antenna or two, rather than jacks.
- A *router* is like a hub with the addition of Internet connection smarts, like a firewall (as described in Chapter 4).

Our advice is to go for a router; they're cheap ($40 to 80) and they'll save you days of hair-tearing grief because they keep most Windows worms out of your network. With a router, none of your computers needs to worry about connecting to the Internet — the router handles that.

Routers come in both wired and wireless versions. The wired versions have varying numbers of jacks, depending on how many computers you plan to connect to your wired LAN; the wireless ones have one jack for the cable to the modem, an antenna for the wireless network, and usually a few jacks for wires running to computers in the same room. For some perverse reason, wireless routers are usually cheaper than wired, even though the wireless ones include everything the wired ones do plus the wireless radio. So get a wireless router.

Setting up a router

Routers invariably come with a short Ethernet cable to connect the router to the cable or DSL modem, so connect your router to your modem, plug them in, and turn them on. An *Ethernet cable* (also known as *Category 5* or *Cat 5*) looks like a fat phone cable, with little plastic connectors that look just like phone plugs, but a little larger. (Even their technical names are a little larger; a phone connector is an *RJ-11 jack*, whereas an Ethernet connector is an *RJ-45 jack*.)

Configuring routers for DSL connections that require a username and password

For the most part, routers take care of themselves, but if you have the kind of DSL connection that requires a username and password, you need to put those into the router. If your DSL connection doesn't require a username and password, you can probably just skip this section, although you can come back later if a program you're installing requires you to change the router's configuration. Setup instructions for routers are all the same in concept, but they differ in detail from one router to another — so you may have to (gack!) glance at the instructions that came with the router.

Because the router doesn't have a screen or keyboard that would enable you to configure it, you use a computer connected to the router instead, via a Web browser. The router has its own Web address, accessible only from the computers on your LAN; it's usually a strange-looking all-numeric address. Even if you plan to have an entirely wireless LAN, the initial setup is a lot easier if you connect a PC (or Mac) to the router by using an Ethernet cable, at least for now, so that the router can figure out which computer it's supposed to be talking to. ("Hey, there it is at the other end of that wire!") Follow these steps:

1. **Turn off the router and the PC (or Mac).**

   Computers are usually happier if you plug and unplug stuff while the computer is turned off.

2. **Plug an Ethernet cable into the network adapter on your computer and plug the other end into one of the jacks on the router.**

3. **Turn on the router and then turn on the computer.**

4. **Fire up your Web browser, and type the address of the router's control page — its home page, with configuration settings.**

   Usually this page is at 192.168.0.1 (a special Web address reserved by the Internet powers that be for private networks like yours). If that Web address doesn't work, check the router's instructions.

5. **If your router's configuration page requires a password, check your router's manual to find out what it is, and type it in.**

   You see the configuration page for your router, something like the one shown in Figure 5-2.

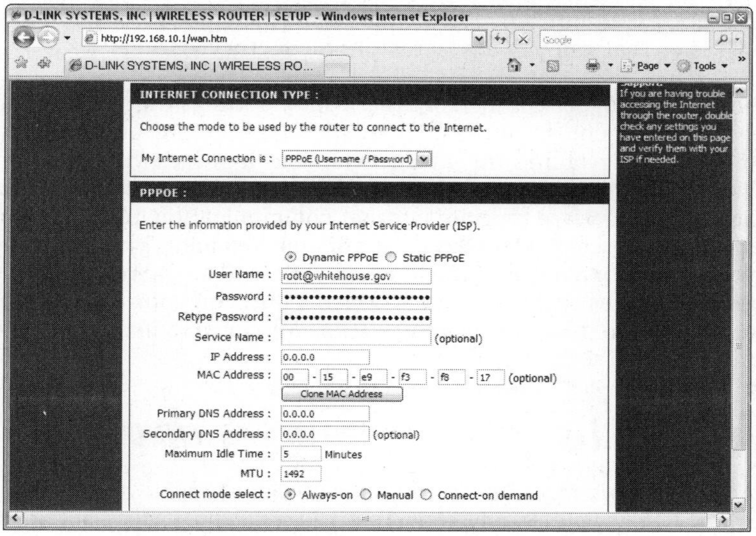

Figure 5-2:
Your router
doesn't
have a
screen, so
you talk with
it via your
Web
browser.

6. **If you have a broadband connection that uses a login and password, find the text box or field to enter your login name and password for your broadband connection.**

   Either follow the instructions in your router manual, or try clicking the tabs or links on the page until you find boxes with names like Username and Password. Connections that use passwords may be called *PPPoE* (Point-to-Point over Ethernet, if you must know). Type them in.

7. **If you see a Save, Done, or OK button or link, click it to make sure that the router saves your changes.**

   If there isn't any such button or link, don't worry.

Now your router knows how to log in to your DSL account.

Connecting your LAN to the modem

Plug the router into your DSL or cable modem, turn on the modem (if it's not on yet), restart the router (by unplugging and replugging the power cord), and verify that you can connect to the outside Internet. (Try a visit to our home page at `http://net.gurus.com`.) If that doesn't work, check the modem cable, and ensure that both the username and password setup are correct if your Internet connection needs them. Most routers have reset switches that you can use to restore the factory settings.

You can configure a bunch of other router settings that you shouldn't need to worry about unless you're planning to do something fancy. The firewall part of the router watches the Internet traffic as it passes through, and blocks traffic it doesn't like. Routers let through Web pages, e-mail, instant messages, and other standard types of Internet communication, but if you're going to do something special, like some types of online gaming, you may need to tell your router to allow additional types of data. If an online game or other program indicates that you need to "open a port" on your router, you need to come back to this router configuration Web page to make some changes.

Wiring up your computers into a LAN

After you have the router set up, if you want to create a wired LAN, you need wires. (Okay, you already knew that.) Specifically, LANs use Cat 5 Ethernet cable with RJ-45 connectors — it looks the same as the cable you use to connect your router to your modem. Cat 5 cable is available at any office supply store, electrical supply store, computer store, or even the occasional supermarket, and you can get it in varying lengths, from 10 feet to 50 feet or more. (If you need a longer cable, a computer store can make you one.) You need one cable for each computer.

For each computer — PCs, Macs, or whatever — plug one end of a Cat 5 cable into the computer's network adapter, the same jack into which the DSL and cable Internet modems plug. (See Chapter 4.) Plug the other end of the cable into the router.

After your computers are connected to each other, tell each computer about the LAN. Windows Vista makes it easy — as soon as you plug in your network cable, Vista contacts the router and sets up your connection. If it doesn't, choose Start➪Network, and on the menu bar, click Network and Sharing Center. You see which networks Vista thinks you're connected to, and you can click the Diagnose and Repair link to help fix the most common problems. (The most common problem: The cable isn't plugged in all the way at one end or the other.)

On each Windows XP computer on the network, follow this drill:

1. **Choose Start⇨All Programs⇨Accessories⇨Communications⇨Network Setup Wizard.**

   Another way to run the wizard is to choose Start⇨Control Panel⇨Network and Internet Connections and then click the Network Setup Wizard link.

2. **Follow the wizard's directions. When it asks what you want to do, choose the option labeled This Computer Connects through a Residential Gateway or through Another Computer on My Network.**

   The residential gateway is your router. On the next page, the wizard asks you to name your computer, as shown in Figure 5-3.

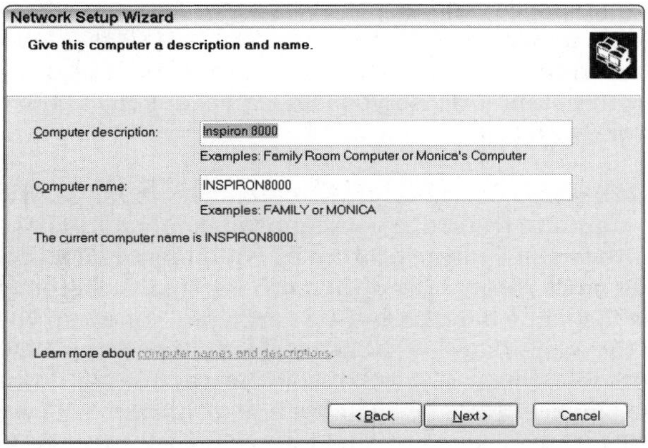

Figure 5-3:
Configuring
Windows
XP to
commu-
nicate on
your LAN.

Network Setup Wizard

Give this computer a description and name.

Computer description: Inspiron 8000

Examples: Family Room Computer or Monica's Computer

Computer name: INSPIRON8000

Examples: FAMILY or MONICA

The current computer name is INSPIRON8000.

Learn more about computer names and descriptions.

< Back   Next >   Cancel

3. **When the wizard asks, give the computer a network name (such as PLAYROOM, OFFICE, or JORDAN).**

   When the wizard asks for the workgroup name, use the *same* name for all the computers on your LAN. (We use WORKGROUP ourselves. Windows suggests MSHOME, which is fine too — just be consistent.)

If you connect a Mac to your LAN, it can probably see the LAN and work without your lifting a finger. If you do want (or need) to configure your network connection and you use Mac OS 9 or earlier, choose Apple⇨Control Panels⇨TCP/IP to access the TCP/IP control panel. Or, run the Internet Setup Assistant by choosing your hard disk, and then the Internet folder, and then Internet Setup

Assistant. In Mac OS X, your network software is named Open Transport. To configure it, open the System folder, and then the Control Panels folder, and then the TCP/IP control panel.

For more details on setting up your LAN, see *Home Networking For Dummies*, by Kathy Ivens (Wiley Publishing, Inc.).

Forget the Wires! Go WiFi

If you have computers in more than one room in the house, it's easier (though the hardware comes at a higher price) to use WiFi than to snake wires through the walls or basement.

Most laptop PCs have WiFi built in. For computers that don't, you can get WiFi PC cards, WiFi doozits with USB connectors, and (less often) WiFi add-in cards for desktop computers. WiFi makers do a remarkably good job of adhering to industry standards, so you can expect anyone's .11b or .11g WiFi equipment to work with anyone else's.

The main practical difference among WiFi equipment is range. WiFi components have one standard feature in common: laughably optimistic estimates of how far away they can be from other WiFi equipment and still work. Bigger antennas get you more range — as does more expensive equipment. WiFi radio waves use the same band as 2.4GHz cordless phones, so you can expect roughly the same range — like a cordless phone, your WiFi connection will probably work in most parts of your house, but not down to the end of your driveway. If you have a normal-size house, normal WiFi works fine. If you live in a $900,000 mansion, you might have to spring for the $100 WiFi card rather than the $50 one.

Set a password, for Pete's sake!

You would probably notice if a random stranger walked into your house and plugged into your wired network. (At least, we like to think you would notice.) However, if you have a WiFi network and a stranger is out on the street with a laptop scanning the area for unprotected wireless access points (a practice known as *wardriving*), he can connect to your WiFi network and you can't easily tell. Some people don't care — at least until they realize that wardrivers can see *all* the shared files and printers on your LAN, and can send spam (and worse) through your network connection. You may well be able to hop on to your neighbors' WiFi networks, and they on yours, which may or may not be okay, depending on how much you like your neighbors.

TECHNICAL STUFF

What can talk WiFi, and why A, B, and G aren't all that different

The engineers who design network equipment really enjoy making improvements. So, it's no wonder that there's more than one flavor of wireless network. Network standards are set by professional organization IEEE (the Institute of Electrical and Electronics Engineers, at http://ieee.org), in its standards group 802. (Yes, there really were 801 other groups ahead of it.) Group 802 has splintered into about two dozen subgroups, of which the most relevant are 802.3, which handles wired Ethernet, and 802.11, which is wireless Ethernet. The .11 group assigns letters to projects as they're set up, so 802.11b is the original 11-megabit (millions of bits per second) WiFi that became popular around 2000, and 802.11g is a faster 54-megabit version that is most common now.

Fortunately, .11b and .11g can talk to each other, at the slower .11b rate that's plenty fast for normal people. Some cards also handle .11a, which came out *after* .11b (it started first but took longer to finish) — it's faster than .11b but not compatible with it. All versions of .11 can be called WiFi, so when you get WiFi equipment, be sure that it says *802.11b* or *802.11g* on the box, to ensure that it works with all the other WiFi equipment you're likely to encounter.

Fortunately, all WiFi systems have optional passwords. Cryptographers laugh derisively at the poor security of WiFi passwords, but they're adequate to make wardrivers and nosy neighbors go bother someone else. (If you have serious secrets on your network, don't depend on WiFi passwords. A bad guy using a laptop and one of the widely available WiFi password-cracker programs can gather enough data from your network to break any password in less than a week. If you need better cryptographic protection, it's available, but it's not exactly a do-it-yourself project to set up.)

Those creative WiFi engineers created several flavors of passwords, too. The most widely used are called *WEP*, a term that allegedly means Wired Equivalent Privacy (which it's not). WEP passwords come in two sizes: 64 and 128 bits. Use 128 unless you have old equipment that can do only 64, in which case, 64 will do. (Your entire network has to use the same size.) The password can be represented as either a text string or a hexadecimal (base-16, also called *hex*) number — we leave it to you to choose which would be easier for you to type and remember. If you use 64-bit WEP, your password (in text format) must be exactly 7 characters long. For 128-bit WEP, you need a 13-character password. If you want to use a shorter password, pad it out with digits or punctuation.

Newer WiFi equipment uses a more secure password scheme: Wireless Privacy Access (WPA). If all your WiFi equipment can handle it, use WPA rather than WEP. WPA passwords can be almost any length — you aren't limited to exactly 7 or exactly 13.

The easiest way to set the password is to set it up at the same time you set up your network, as described in the next section.

Making the WiFi connection

To create a WiFi system, follow these steps:

1. **Get your router set up, and then set up your computers to connect to it.**

   See the section "Setting up a router," earlier in this chapter.

2. **Use your Web browser to display the router's control page (usually at** `192.168.0.1`**) so that you can configure the router.**

3. **Find the page where you can configure the router's WiFi settings.**

   What you click depends on your router. On our D-Link router, we clicked Setup and then Wireless Settings to get to the page shown in Figure 5-4. Look for a page with settings about wireless, a network name, and wireless security.

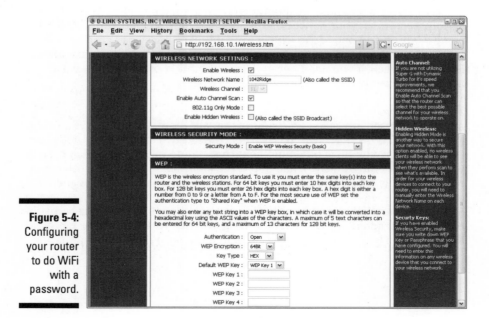

Figure 5-4:
Configuring your router to do WiFi with a password.

4. **Give your network a name. Every WiFi network has a name.**

   With typical machine imagination, your router suggests something like `linksys` (a router manufacturer) or `dlink` (another manufacturer) or `default`. We suggest something like `FredsHouse` so that any neighbors who happen on it know that it's you.

5. **Turn on WiFi passwords and set one, as described in the preceding section.**

   Your router probably has lots of other options — such as MAC cloning (less fruit-related than it sounds, and nothing to do with Macintosh computers), all of which you can ignore.

6. **When your router is up and running and your PC (or Mac) can see the Internet (that is, you can display Web pages), you're done configuring the router for your WiFi network.**

Now, at last, you can cut the cord and go wireless. On each PC, you need to tell it which WiFi network to use, and what the password is. On Windows Vista, the setup is quick:

1. **Choose Start⇨Connect To.**

   You see a window with a list of available networks, one of which is yours. If you have neighbors with WiFi networks, it may show them, too, but don't use your neighbors' networks unless they give you permission.

2. **Double-click your network.**

   In a moment, you see a dialog box that asks for the security key or pass phrase.

3. **Enter the network password, exactly as you did on the router, and click Connect.**

   Vista retrieves network settings from the router, and in a few seconds you're online. If you have trouble typing the password, click the box to display the characters of the password (unless, we suppose, someone you don't trust is looking over your shoulder.)

If you're using Windows XP SP2, the process is also fairly painless:

1. **Click Start⇨Connect To⇨Wireless Network Connection.**

2. **After your PC sniffs the airwaves for a moment, Windows shows you a list of available networks, including the one you just set up.**

3. **Click your network's name and then the Connect button at the bottom of the window.**

   4. **Windows asks you to type the password, twice. Type the password, whether it's text or hexadecimal, exactly as you did on the router.**

   5. **Click OK, and you should be online.**

Both Windows XP and Vista remember the wireless setup; in the future, it connects automatically.

Using Your Laptop at Home and Away

The whole point of having a laptop computer is to take it with you when you travel — and what fun is traveling with a computer if you can't use it to check your e-mail 17 times a day? After you set up your laptop on a home WiFi network by following the instructions earlier in this chapter, you already know most of what you need to know to use it on other networks when you travel.

Home and office setup

Lots of people have laptops they take back and forth between home and the office. A lot of variables are involved in doing this successfully, depending on not only your particular laptop but also the networks you use at home and at the office. In general, however, this is how the various setups should work:

- ✔ If both home and the office have wired networks, your computer should work when it's plugged into either network. If your computer doesn't connect at work, talk to your network administrator.

- ✔ If your office has local shared files and printers and your house doesn't, or vice versa, Windows complains and sulks if it can't find them. As long as you don't try to print to a printer that's at the other place, though, you can go online just fine.

- ✔ If both the home and office networks are wireless, or one is wireless and the other is wired, set up each one as described earlier in this chapter, and your PC should automatically recognize whichever is available — that is, the network where you are.

Getting WiFi with your latte

In olden days, people would go to a coffee shop, order cups of coffee, of which there was a maximum of two kinds, regular and decaf, and then chat with people sitting *right next to them*. Now, of course, that's hopelessly 20th century. We cruise into the coffee shop with our laptop, order a half-caf decaf mocha cappuccino grande with two percent milk, cocoa drizzle, hold the sprinkles, and we put on our headphones and talk or exchange messages with people thousands of miles away, utterly ignoring the losers at the next table. The magic of WiFi makes this possible, as coffee shops install WiFi *hotspots* (public areas with WiFi Internet access) to which customers can connect.

The amount of effort needed to get online at your coffee shop varies from none to way too much. At some places, the management has enough confidence in their product to figure that if they can get you to stick around, you'll keep buying coffee, so WiFi is free to the customers. (The coffee shop where John is sometimes found is in this category.) You turn on your computer; click the Start⇨Connect To menu — if your computer doesn't look for a WiFi network by itself; click the name of the shop's network when it appears; tell it that, yes, you really want to connect to that insecure network; and you're on. The next time you come back, your computer remembers the network and connects automatically.

Windows Internet Connection Sharing? Get a router!

Windows Vista and XP come with Internet Connection Sharing (ICS) — adequate built-in router software — but there's not much point in using it: You need a hub or router in order to connect your computers into a LAN anyway. With ICS, the computer running ICS must be awake and alert for any other computer to connect, and problems with that computer ("Rats! My game just crashed!") cause connection trouble for all the other computers. Who needs the hassle?

If you insist on using Internet Connection Sharing, be sure that the computer you plan to use is connected to both your cable or DSL modem and the wireless LAN, and that you leave the computer on all the time (it can't act like a router when it's turned off). What you do next depends on which version of Windows that computer is running:

✔ **Windows Vista:** Choose Start⇨Control Panel and open the Network and Sharing Center. Find the connection you want to share, and click View Status. In the small window that opens, click Properties and then Continue. In the properties window that opens, click the Sharing tab.

✔ **Windows XP:** Choose Start⇨All Programs⇨Accessories⇨Communications⇨New Connection Wizard (the same Wizard used to set up your Internet connection), and choose Set Up a Home or Small Office Network. The wizard steps you through the configuration of the *ICS server* (the computer that connects to the Internet) and the *ICS clients* (the rest of the computers).

Either way, if you have an Internet connection that requires you to log on, your ICS server (with luck) logs on automatically when someone on the LAN wants to connect to the Internet. Otherwise, you have to use the ICS client program to poke the router awake before you log on. If you have always-on broadband, the Internet will just be there when you need it.

Other places are less confident. A typical large chain — let's call it Ahab's — made the WiFi a profit center, so you have to pay by the hour. This adds an extra, annoying step to the connection process, the one where you pay. After your computer is turned on, fire up your Web browser. No matter what your home page is, the network is set up so that your browser shows *their* home page, which allows you to make payment arrangements.

There are about as many ways to pay for WiFi access as there are flavors of coffee. Maybe you buy or are given a ticket at the counter with a code number to enter. More likely, the coffee shop made a deal with one of the large, national mobile phone providers, T-Mobile or Cingular, that make a sideline of WiFi, as shown in Figure 5-5. In this case, you pay with a credit card, either by the hour (at about $6 an hour) or by buying a package of hours. You sign up via your Web browser — the WiFi network lets you connect to the signup page for free, but you have to sign up and pay to do anything else. If you plan to drink a great deal of coffee, you can sign up for a monthly flat-rate plan.

Figure 5-5:
Logging on from the road.

It's not hard to get into the WiFi cafe biz, so you can also find lots of tiny little providers. Many of the providers have reciprocal agreements and alliances, such that (for example) if you sign up with someone who belongs to the iPass group, you can use another iPass member's WiFi hotspot.

WARNING!

Snoops at the coffee shop

Although we think that a lot of concerns about Internet network security are overblown, one place where it's a real issue is on public WiFi networks, like the ones in hotels and coffee shops. Those networks frequently have no passwords, which means that *anyone on that network can snoop on your network connection.* Even if everyone in the coffee shop seems nice, a snoop might be sitting in a car out by the curb. And in a hotel, of course, you have no idea who's in all the nearby rooms.

Fortunately, a few simple precautions will keep you safe. When visiting Web sites, make sure that any site where you type in a password or other private info uses *SSL encryption:* The address starts with `https://` and the little lock in the corner is locked. If the site doesn't have SSL encryption, wait until you get home. For advice on securing your mail program, see the section "The mail problem," at the end of this chapter.

Airports, hotels, and beyond

Coffee shops are hardly the only places that offer WiFi. If you spend much time in airports (John does because he's on a lot of advisory boards), you find lots of WiFi — with about the same options as in the coffee shops. The same two providers dominate (Figure 5-5 shows T-Mobile in an airline club in Chicago), with a lot of little local ones as well. After a while, frequent travelers learn WiFi folklore — say that there's free WiFi in the airline club on the third level of the Pittsburgh airport, and even if you're not a member, you can use it if you sit in one of the chairs near the door.

Hotels, like cafes, either treat WiFi as a service — like the ice machine on each floor — or a profit center, like your room's minibar full of overpriced beer. Some hotels still offer wired Ethernet (in which case a cable on the desk in your room plugs into your computer), and others go WiFi. If you're at an ice-machine-style hotel, you may just be able to turn on your computer and go online with no fuss, or you may have to sign in through your browser, even though you don't have to pay. Some hotels with WiFi give you a slip of paper with a login code when you register, to deter visitors who would otherwise sit in the lobby and use it for free. In minibar-style hotels, you have to log in through your browser. Most hotels put the charge on the room bill; some want your credit card number so that they can bill you separately. The typical charge is $10 per day, noon to noon, but we've seen hourly rates, lower rates, and higher rates.

If you encounter a problem with a hotel's Internet service, rarely does anyone at the hotel know anything about it, but they should be able to give you an 800 number you can call to talk to someone at the company that actually provides the service.

The mail problem

WiFi connections in coffee shops, airports, and hotels sure are convenient, but remember: *They aren't private.* This is a particular problem when you send and receive e-mail, because you usually want your mail to be private *and* because your computer needs to send your network login and password over the Internet back to your mail server to pick up your mail. With a modest amount of advance planning, it shouldn't be hard to get your mail working securely on the road.

The simplest approach is Web mail — a secure Web site where you can log in to read and send mail. It's worth checking to see whether your mail system offers optional Web mail. If so, even if you don't use it at home, you might want to use it on the road, particularly if the Web mail offers a secure server. See Chapter 13 to find out how Web-based mail works and for instructions for using it. Normally, we don't worry about secure Web sites (`https://` versus `http://`), but public WiFi is one of the few cases where people might actually be snooping and the `https` security helps.

If you want to use your mail program, you have to slog through a fairly painful one-time process to set up secure mail. Because it involves adjusting the setup of your mail program, we cover it in Chapter 14, so flip ahead and check it out.

Part III
Web Mania

The 5th Wave   By Rich Tennant

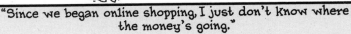

"Since we began online shopping, I just don't know where the money's going."

In this part . . .

No doubt about it, the Web is *the* happenin' place. For many people, the World Wide Web *is* the Internet. We explain what the Web is and how to get around, along with great tips about how to actually find stuff you're looking for among the millions of clamoring Web pages. We take a break to listen to lots of online music and watch online videos. Then, relaxed and refreshed, we tell you about Web shopping and Web banking so that you can confidently spend and save your money online, and then we wrap up with ways to get free (and almost free) software and other downloadable stuff from the Web.

Chapter 6

Welcome to the Wild, Wonderful, Wacky Web

*P*eople now talk about the *Web* more than they talk about the *Internet*. The World Wide Web and the Internet are not the same thing — the World Wide Web (which we call the Web because we're lazy typists) lives "on top of" the Internet. The Internet's network is at the core of the Web, and the Web is like an attractive parasite that requires the Net for survival.

This chapter explains what the Web is, where it came from, how to install and use the Firefox browser (which we prefer over Microsoft's Internet Explorer browser), and how to use both Web browsers to display Web pages. If you're already comfortable using the Web — and you've switched to Firefox — skip ahead to Chapter 7.

What Is the Web?

So what is the Web already? The Web is a bunch of "pages" of information connected to each other around the globe. Each page can be a combination of text, pictures, audio clips, video clips, animations, and other stuff. (People add new types of other stuff every day.) What makes Web pages interesting is that they contain *hyperlinks,* usually called just *links* because the Net already has plenty of hype. Each link points to another Web page, and, when you click a link, your browser fetches the page the link connects to. (Your *browser* is the program that shows you the Web — read more about it in a couple of pages.)

The other important characteristic of the Web is that you can search it — all ten billion or so pages. For example, in about ten seconds, you can get a list of Web pages that contain the phrase *domestic poultry* or your own name or the name of a book you want to find out about. You can follow links to see each page on the list to find the information you want. See Chapter 8 to find out how to use a search engine to search the Web.

Linking up Web pages

Each page your browser gets for you can have more links that take you to other places. Pages can be linked to other pages anywhere in the world so that when you're on the Web, you can end up looking at pages from Singapore to Calgary, or from Sydney to Buenos Aires, all faster than you can say "Bob's your uncle," usually. Most of the time, you're only seconds away from any site, anywhere in the world. This system of interlinked documents is known as *hypertext.*

Figure 6-1 shows a Web page (our Web page, in fact). Each underlined phrase is a link to another Web page.

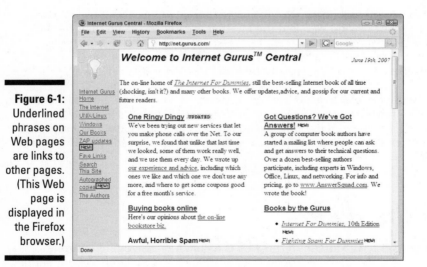

Figure 6-1:
Underlined phrases on Web pages are links to other pages. (This Web page is displayed in the Firefox browser.)

Links can create connections that let you go directly to related information. These invisible connections between pages are like the threads of a spider web — as you click from Web page to Web page, you can envision the Web created by the links. What's so remarkable about the Web is that it connects pieces of information from all around the *planet,* on different computers and in different databases (a feat you would be hard pressed to match with a card catalog in a brick-and-mortar library).

Where did the Web come from?

The World Wide Web was invented in 1989 at the European Particle Physics Lab in Geneva, Switzerland, an unlikely spot for a revolution in computing. The inventor is a British researcher named Sir Tim Berners-Lee, who is now the director of the World Wide Web Consortium (W3C) in Cambridge, Massachusetts, the organization that sets standards and loosely oversees the development of the Web. Tim is terrifically smart and hard working and is the nicest guy you would ever want to meet. (Margy met him through Sunday school — is that wholesome or what?)

Tim invented *HTTP* (HyperText Transport Protocol), the way Web browsers communicate with Web servers; *HTML* (HyperText Markup Language), the language in which Web pages are written; and *URLs* (Uniform Resource Locators), the codes used to identify Web pages and most other information on the Net. He envisioned the Web as a way for everyone to both publish and read information on the Net. Early Web browsers had editors that let you create Web pages almost as easily as you could read them.

For more information about the development of the Web and the work of the World Wide Web Consortium, visit its Web site, at www.w3.org. You can also read Tim's book, *Weaving the Web* (HarperOne, 1999). Tim was knighted in 2004, and because he's British, he accepted the title and became Sir Tim.

Name that page

Before you jump onto the Web (boing-g-g — that metaphor needs work), you need to know about one more basic concept. Every Web page has a name attached to it so that browsers, and you, can find it. Great figures in the world of software engineering (well, okay, it was Sir Tim Berners-Lee) named this name *URL,* or *Uniform Resource Locator.* Every Web page has a URL, a series of characters that begins with http://. (How do you say "URL"? Everyone we know pronounces each letter, "U-R-L" — no one says "earl.") Now you know enough to go browsing. For more entirely optional details about URLs, see the later sidebar "Duke of URL."

Browsing to Points Unknown

It's time to check out the Web for yourself. To do this, you need a *browser,* the program that gets Web pages and displays them on your screen. Fortunately, if you have any version of Windows written in the past 12 years, any recent Mac, or any computer with Internet access, you probably already have one.

Here are the two most popular browsers:

- ✔ **Internet Explorer (IE)** is the browser that Microsoft has built into every version of Windows since Windows 98. The latest version is 7.0, which comes with Windows Vista and is available as a free download for many earlier versions of Windows. IE 6.0, which came with Windows XP, looks a little different but works almost the same.

- ✔ **Firefox** is the latest browser from the open source Mozilla project at www.mozilla.org. You can download Firefox for free for Windows, Macs, and Linux computers; the latest version as of mid-2007 is version 2.0. Firefox runs faster than Internet Explorer and is much, much less susceptible to spyware. See the nearby sidebar "Recommendation: Switch from Internet Explorer to Firefox."

We describe both Internet Explorer and Firefox in detail in this book. If you don't have a browser, or you want to try a different one, see the section "Getting and Installing a Browser," later in this chapter.

Recommendation: Switch from Internet Explorer to Firefox

Both programs are free and downloadable from the Internet, but beyond that, they have some important differences.

The advantages of Firefox

- ✔ Firefox runs faster. It's smaller and quicker.

- ✔ Firefox doesn't use ActiveX controls, a feature of Internet Explorer that spyware uses to infect your computer.

The advantages of Internet Explorer

- ✔ Some Web sites (mainly sites run by Microsoft itself) require Internet Explorer because they use ActiveX controls.

- ✔ If you use Windows, you already have Internet Explorer because it comes bundled with Windows.

- ✔ A few add-ins work only with Internet Explorer.

Both IE and Firefox work fine for displaying and printing Web pages — don't get us wrong. However, we think that the security issue — avoiding spyware — trumps all other considerations hands down, and we recommend that you install Firefox and use it except for the few Web sites that require Internet Explorer. You can have both browsers installed at the same time — you can even have both running at the same time — so switching to Firefox doesn't mean that you can never use Internet Explorer again.

If you decide to try Firefox, you can choose Help⇨For Internet Explorer Users to see a pageful of helpful information. This chapter describes Firefox 2. Upgrade if you have an older version, and accept Firefox's offer to install upgrades automatically.

Mac users have a choice of Safari, which comes standard on all recent Macs, and Firefox. They're both fine browsers, but we slightly prefer Firefox because it works the same on all our different computers.

Web Surfing with Your Browser

When you start Firefox, you see a screen similar to the one shown earlier, in Figure 6-1. The Internet Explorer 7 window looks like the one shown in Figure 6-2 — most of the buttons are gone. Internet Explorer 6.0, which many Windows XP users still use, looks more like Firefox than like IE 7.

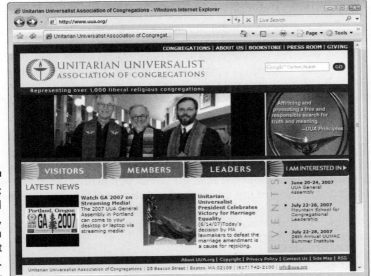

Figure 6-2: Your typical Web page, viewed in Internet Explorer 7.

Which page your browser displays at startup depends on how it's set up. Many ISPs arrange for your browser to display their home pages; otherwise, until you choose a home page of your own, Internet Explorer tends to display a Microsoft page, and Firefox usually shows a Mozilla-branded Google search page.

At the top of the window are a bunch of buttons, the Address box (which contains the URL of the current page), and a search box (for searching for Web pages by topic). Remember that URLs, or Web addresses, are an important part of Web lore because they're the secret codes that name all the pages on the Web. (For details, see the nearby sidebar "Duke of URL.")

The main section of the browser window is taken up by the Web page you're looking at. After all, that's what the browser is *for* — displaying a Web page! The buttons, bars, and menus around the edge help you find your way around the Web and do things like print and save pages.

Getting around

You need two simple skills (if we can describe something as basic as a single mouse click as a skill) to get going on the Web. One is to move from page to page on the Web, and the other is to jump directly to a page when you know its URL.

Moving from page to page is easy: Click any link that looks interesting. That's it. Underlined blue text and blue-bordered pictures are links, and sometimes other things are, too. Anything that looks like a button is probably a link. You can tell when you're pointing to a link because the mouse pointer changes to a little hand. If you're not sure whether something is a link, click it anyway because if it isn't, clicking doesn't hurt anything. Clicking outside a link selects the text you click, as in most other programs. Sometimes, clicking a link moves to you a different place on the same page rather than to a new page.

Backward, ho!

Web browsers remember the last few pages you visited, so if you click a link and decide that you're not so crazy about the new page, you can easily go back to the preceding one. To go back, click the Back or Previous button on the toolbar (its icon is an arrow pointing to the left, and it's the leftmost button on the toolbar) or press Alt+←.

Sometimes, clicking a link opens the new page in a new browser window — your browser (IE or Firefox) can display more than one Web page at the same time, each in its own window. If a link opens a new window, the Back button does nothing in that window.

Going places

These days, everyone and his dog has a home page. A *home page* is the main Web page for a person or organization. Part V of this book shows you various ways to make one for yourself and your dog, children, hobby, or business.

Duke of URL

The World Wide Web will eventually link together all the information in the known universe, starting with all the stuff on the Internet. (This statement may be a slight exaggeration, but not by much.) One key to global domination is to give everything a name so that no matter what a Web page link refers to, a Web browser can find it and know what to do with it.

Look at this typical URL, the one for the Web page shown earlier, in Figure 6-1:

```
http://net.gurus.com/index.
    phtml
```

The first item in a URL, the letters that appear before the colon, is the *scheme,* which describes the way a browser can get to the resource. Although ten schemes are defined, the most common by far is HTTP, which stands for HyperText Transfer Protocol, the Web's native transfer technique. (Don't confuse HTTP, which is the way pages are sent over the Internet, with HTML, which is the system of formatting codes in Web pages.) HTTP is the language that your browser uses to request a Web page from the Web server on which it's stored, and that the Web server uses to send you back the page you want to see.

Although the details of the rest of the URL depend on the scheme, most schemes look similar. Following the colon are two slashes (always forward slashes, never backslashes) and the name of the host computer on which the resource lives; in this case, net.gurus.com (one of the many names of John's Internet host computer). Then comes another slash and a *path,* which gives the name of the resource on that host; in this case, a file named index.phtml.

Web URLs allow a few other optional parts. They can include a *port number,* which specifies, roughly speaking, which of several programs running on that host should handle the request. The port number goes after a colon after the host name, like this:

```
http://net.gurus.com:80/index.
    phtml
```

The standard http port number is 80, so if that's the port you want (it usually is), you can leave it out. Finally, a Web URL can have a *query part* at the end, following a question mark, like this:

```
http://net.gurus.com:80/index.
    phtml?chickens
```

When a URL has a query part, it tells the host computer more specifically what you want the page to display. (You rarely type query parts yourself — they're often constructed for you from fill-in fields on Web pages.)

When you type a URL into your Web browser, you can leave out the http:// part because the browser adds it for you. Lazy typists, unite! When a Web address starts with www, you can usually leave that out, too.

Two other useful URL schemes are mailto and file. A mailto URL looks like this:

```
mailto:internet11@gurus.com
```

That is, a mailto link is an e-mail address. Clicking a mailto URL runs your e-mail program and creates a new message addressed to the address in the link.

The file URL specifies a file on your own computer. The URL looks like this:

```
file:///C|/www/index.htm
```

On a Windows computer, this line indicates a Web page stored in the file C:\www\index.htm on your own computer. The colon turns into a vertical bar (because colons in URLs mean something else), and the backslashes turn into forward slashes. File URLs are useful mostly for looking at a Web page you just created and saved on your hard drive.

Companies advertise their home pages, and people send e-mail talking about cool sites. When you see a URL you want to check out, here's what you do:

1. **Click in the Address box near the top of the browser window.**

   Pressing F6 also gets you to the Address box.

2. **Type the URL in the box.**

   The URL is something like `http://net.gurus.com` — you can just type **net.gurus.com**. Be sure to delete the URL that appeared before you started typing.

   You can leave the `http://` off the URLs when you type them in the Address box. Your browser can guess that part!

3. **Press Enter.**

If you receive URLs in e-mail, instant messages, or documents, try clicking them — many programs pass the addresses along to your browser. Or, use the standard cut-and-paste techniques and avoid retyping:

1. **Highlight the URL in whichever program it appears.**

   That is, use your mouse to select the URL so that the whole URL is highlighted.

2. **Press Ctrl+C (⌘+C on the Mac) to copy the info to the Clipboard.**

3. **Click in the Address box to highlight whatever is in it.**

4. **Press Ctrl+V (⌘+V on the Mac) to paste the URL into the box, and then press Enter.**

Bad guys can easily create e-mail messages where the URL you see in the text of a message isn't the URL you visit; the bad guys can hide the actual URL. Keep this in mind if you get mail that purports to be from your bank — if you click the link and enter your account number and password in the Web page that appears, you may be typing it into a Web site run by crooks rather than by your bank. See Chapter 2.

When you type a URL or click a link, the Web site you were looking for may have died long since. You may see an error message, or the Web address may have been taken over by an unrelated organization. Don't be too shocked if a site you heard about has been replaced by an unrelated advertisement or a porn site.

The best place to start browsing

You find out more about how to find things on the Web in Chapter 8, but for now, here's a good way to get started: Go to the Yahoo! News page. (Yes, the name of the Web page includes an exclamation point — it's very excitable. But we leave out the exclamation point throughout this book because we find it annoying.) To get to Yahoo News, type this URL in your browser's Address box and then press Enter:

```
http://news.yahoo.com
```

The Yahoo Web site includes lots of different features, but its news site should look familiar — it's like a newspaper on steroids. Just nose around, clicking links that look interesting and clicking the Back button on the toolbar when you make a wrong turn. We guarantee that you'll find something interesting.

For information related to the very book you're holding, go to this URL: `http://net.gurus.com`. Follow the links to the page about our books or about the Internet, and then select the pages for readers of *The Internet For Dummies,* 11th Edition. If we have any late-breaking news about the Internet or updates and corrections to this book, you can find them there. If you find mistakes in this book or have other comments, by the way, please send e-mail to us at `internet11@gurus.com`.

What not to click

The Web has some bad neighborhoods, and it's not always safe to click whatever you see. For example, clicking a link on a Web page can download and install a program on your computer, and that program might not be one you want to be running. So exercise judgment when clicking.

Here are some links *not* to click:

- Don't click ads claiming that you just won the lottery or a free laptop or anything else too good to be true.
- Don't click messages on Web pages claiming that your computer is at risk of some dire consequence if you don't click there. Yeah, right.
- Don't click OK in a dialog box that asks about downloading or installing a program, unless you're deliberately downloading and installing a program (as we describe in Chapter 12).
- Don't click any link that makes you suspicious. Your instincts are probably correct!

This page looks funny

Sometimes a Web page gets garbled on the way in or you interrupt it (by clicking the Stop button on the toolbar or by pressing the Esc key). You can tell your browser to get the information on the page again. Click the Reload or Refresh button, or press Ctrl+R.

Get me outta here

Sooner or later, even the most dedicated Web surfer has to stop to eat or attend to other bodily needs. You leave your browser in the same way you leave any other program: Choose File⇨Exit (File⇨Close for Internet Explorer) or click the Close (X) button in the upper-right corner of the window. Or, just leave the program running and walk away from your computer.

Getting and Installing a Browser

Chances are, a browser is already installed on your computer. If your browser is antiquated, or if you want to try Firefox, you can install a browser. If you use a version of Internet Explorer older than 6.0, you're missing lots of new features. Fortunately, browser programs aren't difficult to get and install, and both IE and Firefox are free.

Even if you already have a browser, new versions come out every 20 minutes or so, and it's worth knowing how to upgrade because occasionally the new versions fix some bugs so that the browsers are better than the old versions. Microsoft gives away Internet Explorer, and the Mozilla project gives away Firefox, so you might as well upgrade to the current version. (One can complain about many aspects of Internet Explorer, but not its price, unless you worry about software monopolies, as do we and many others.)

Getting the program

To get or upgrade Firefox (for Windows, Mac, or any of the other dozen computers it runs on), visit www.mozilla.com. To get or upgrade Internet Explorer for Windows XP or 2003, go to www.microsoft.com/ie. Use your browser to go to the page and then follow the instructions for finding and downloading the program. You might also want to consult Chapter 12 for details.

If you're upgrading from an older version of your browser to a newer one, you can replace the old version with the new one. The installation program should be smart enough to remember some of your old settings and bookmarks (favorites).

Running a new browser for the first time

To run your new browser, click the browser's attractive new icon. If you use Windows Vista or XP, the default browser also appears at the top of the lefthand column of the Start menu, too.

Firefox asks whether you want to import your settings — including your bookmarks and favorites — from another browser program. If you've already been using the Web for a while and have built up a list of your favorite Web sites, take advantage of this opportunity to copy your list into Firefox so that you don't have to search for your favorite sites all over again.

The first time you run Internet Explorer, it might run either the Internet Connection Wizard or the New Connection Wizard, which offer to help you get connected to the Internet. If it does, see Chapter 4 for details.

You've got your browser, you know what Web pages and links are, and you're ready to hit the Web running!

Chapter 7

Taking Your Browser for a Spin

*I*f you've read Chapter 6, you're all set to browse the Web. But to be an efficient, downright clever Internaut, you need to know about some other browser features, like printing Web pages, displaying more than one Web page at the same time, and storing the addresses of Web pages that you like to visit often. You also need to know how to handle spyware, an Internet menace that is described in Chapter 2. This chapter is your guide to these extra features and how you can make the most of them right away.

TIP

Some people hardly ever close their browsers, which probably isn't a good idea for their long-term mental stability. (Naturally, we're not talking about anyone *we* know! Definitely not.) If you're such a person, however, remember that your browser *caches* pages — it stores the pages temporarily on your hard disk for quick retrieval. If you want to make sure that you're seeing an up-to-date version of a page, reload it. Click the Reload or Refresh button on your browser's toolbar or press Ctrl+R.

Hey, how about us Mac users?

Macs have always been famous for their slick, easy to use software, and the Internet software is no exception. Recent Macs (OS 10 or later) come with a nice Web browser named Safari. Although it's unrelated to Firefox or Internet Explorer (it's based on a European browser named Konqueror), the way it works is remarkably similar to Firefox and Internet Explorer. It has bookmarks, tabbed browsing, printing, and everything else. You use the ⌘ key rather than

Ctrl for the keyboard shortcuts, and nearly all the rest of the keys work the way they do in the other two browsers.

Or, you can do what we do and use Firefox, which works very nicely on a Mac, just like it does on Windows with ⌘ instead of Ctrl. You can use Safari to visit www.mozilla.com to download and install Firefox, and then use it instead of or alongside Safari.

Saving Stuff from the Web

Frequently, you see something on a Web page that's worth saving for later. Sometimes it's interesting information, a picture or some other type of file, or even the entire Web page. Fortunately, saving stuff is easy.

There's not much point to saving an entire Web page. Web pages are usually made up of several files — one for the text, one for each picture, and sometimes other files, so your browser can't just save the page in a file. However, you can save images and text from a page.

If you want to remember a page and come back to it, *bookmark* it in your browser, as explained later in this chapter.

Saving text from a page

You can copy and paste text from a Web page into a word processing document or another type of file. Select the text with your mouse (click and drag the mouse over the text) and press Ctrl+C to save the text in your computer's clipboard. Then switch to the word processing or other program, position the cursor where you want the text to appear, and press Ctrl+V to paste it. Easy enough!

Saving an image

To save an image you see on a Web page, follow these steps:

1. **Right-click the image.**

2. **Choose Save Image As (in Firefox) or Save Picture As (in Internet Explorer) from the menu that appears.**

3. **In the Save Image or Save Picture dialog box, move to the folder or directory in which you want to save the graphics file, type a filename in the File Name text box, and click the Save button.**

A note about copyright: Almost all Web pages, along with almost everything else on the Internet, are copyrighted by their authors. (A notable exception is U.S. federal government Web sites, which are all free of copyright.) If you save a Web page or a picture from a Web page, you don't have permission to use it any way you want. Before you reuse the text or pictures, send an e-mail message to the owner of the site. If an address doesn't appear on the page, write for permission to `webmaster@domain.com`, replacing *domain.com* with the domain name part of the URL of the Web page.

Printing pages

To print a page, click the Print button on the toolbar, press Ctrl+P, or choose File⇨Print. The browser has to reformat the page to print, which can take a while, so remember that patience is a virtue. Fortunately, each browser displays a progress window to let you know how it's doing.

If the page you want to print uses frames (a technique that divides the browser window into sub areas that can scroll and update separately), click in the part of the window you want to print before printing. Otherwise, you might get only the outermost frame, which usually has just a title and some buttons.

Filling In Forms

In a Web page, a *form* is a page with boxes you can type in, check boxes you can select, and other clickable stuff that you can use to fill out the form. Then you click a Submit button (or a button with some other name) to send in the information you entered. Figure 7-1 shows a typical form.

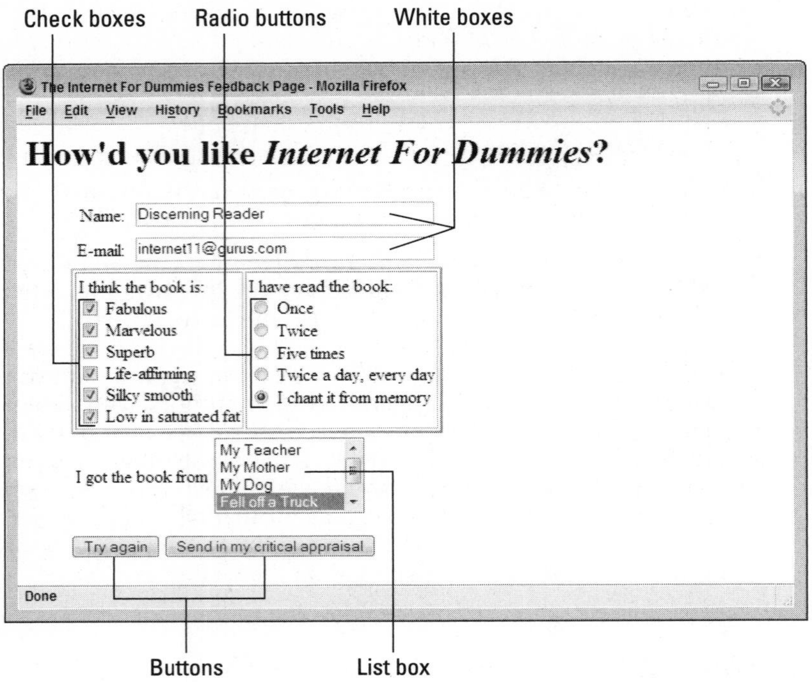

Check boxes   Radio buttons   White boxes

Figure 7-1:
Just fill out
a few forms.

Buttons   List box

Little boxes all the same

Text boxes in a form are white, fill-in boxes in which you type, in this case, your name and e-mail address. *Check boxes* are little square boxes in which you check whichever ones apply (all of them, we hope, on our sample form). *Radio buttons,* the little round buttons, are similar to check boxes except that you can choose only one of them from each set. In Figure 7-1, you also see a *list box,* in which you can choose one of the possibilities in the box. In most cases, you see more entries than can fit in the box, so you scroll them up and down. You can usually choose only one entry, but some list boxes let you choose more.

Forms also include buttons that determine what happens to the information you entered into the form. Most forms have two such buttons: one that clears the form fields to their initial state and sends nothing, and one, usually known as the *Submit* button, that sends the filled-out form back to the Web server for processing.

Some Web pages have *search boxes,* which are one-line forms that let you type some text for which to search. Depending on the browser, a Submit button may be displayed to the right of the text area, or you may just press Enter to send the search words to the server. For example, the Google search page at `www.google.com` has a box in which you type a word or phrase; when you press Enter or click the Google Search button, the search begins. (See Chapter 8 to find out what happens!)

Remember the address!

Your browser can remember the entries that you frequently type into Web page forms, like your name and address. As you type, your browser may try to spot entries you made before and suggest the rest of the entry so that you don't have to type it. If a suggestion pops up from your browser as you're filling in a form, you can click the suggestion to accept it. If you don't like the suggestion, just keep typing.

Using Secure Web Pages

When you fill out a form on a Web page, you may need to provide information that you prefer to keep private — your credit card number, for example. Not to worry! Browsers can *encrypt* the information you send to and receive from a *secure Web server.* You can tell when a page was received encrypted from the Web server by the little padlock icon in the middle or on the right end of the status bar, at the bottom of the browser window. If the padlock appears open or doesn't appear, the page wasn't encrypted. If the little lock is locked, encryption is on. To make it clearer, Internet Explorer displays the padlock icon at the right end of the Address box, too, and Firefox shows the whole Address box in yellow.

Typed-in data in forms on secure pages are almost always sent encrypted, making it impossible for anyone to snoop on your secrets as they pass through the Net. Encrypted pages are nice, but in practice, it's unlikely that anyone is snooping on your Web session anyway, encrypted or otherwise. The real security problems are elsewhere (refer to Chapter 2).

Firefox and Internet Explorer (IE) have the habit of popping up little boxes to warn you about the dangers of what you're about to do. They display a box when you're about to switch from encrypted to nonencrypted (or back again) transmissions. Most of these warning boxes include a check box you can select to tell the program not to bother you with this type of warning again. After you read the warning, select the check box so that your browser can stop nagging you.

Who Can Remember All Those Passwords?

Not us. Many Web sites ask you to enter a username and password. If you're buying something from an online store like Amazon.com, you create an account with a username and password that you enter each time you want to buy something. Amazon.com remembers your name, address, and credit card information as part of your account, so you don't need to enter it each time. If you want to read the *New York Times* online at `http://nytimes.com`, you create an account with a password, too. The account remembers what kinds of news you're interested in reading. After you use the Web for a while, you pile up a heap of usernames and passwords.

Firefox and Internet Explorer offer to remember your usernames and passwords for you. Using this feature can be dangerous if other people use your computer or if you use a computer in a public place, like a library or an Internet café. But if you're the only person who uses your computer, you may want to let your browser do the work of remembering some, if not all, of your usernames and passwords.

When you get to a Web page that asks for a username and password, your browser may pop up a little window offering to remember the username and password that you enter, similar to Figure 7-2. If you click Yes, the next time you arrive at the same page, your browser may fill in your username and password for you.

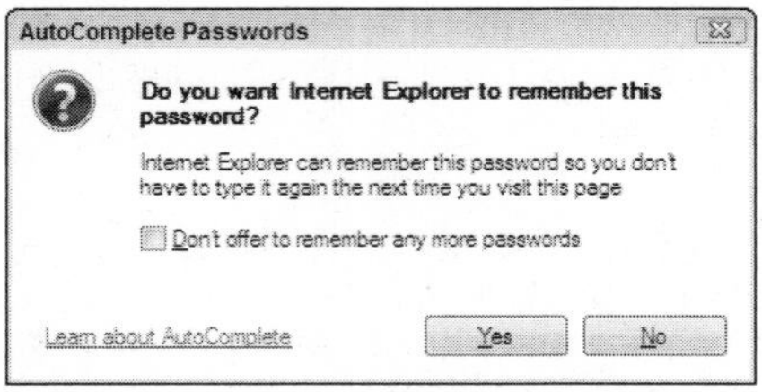

Figure 7-2:
Your
browser
can store
your
passwords
for you.

You can control whether and how your browser stores these passwords. In Firefox 2.0, follow these steps:

1. **Choose Tools⇨Options.**

   You see the Options dialog box, with a list of the categories of options across the top.

2. **Click the Security category.**

Here you find the following options:

- Select the Remember Passwords for Sites check box to clear the check mark if you want to turn off this feature (or click it again to turn it back on).

- Click the Show Passwords button to review or delete usernames and passwords that Firefox is remembering for you.

- Click the Use a Master Password check box to set a master password that you need to type only once, at the beginning of each Firefox session. (This option reduces the number of passwords you need to remember while maintaining some security.)

3. Click OK to close the Options dialog box.

In Internet Explorer, remembering usernames and passwords is the job of the AutoComplete feature, which you set up by following these simple steps:

1. Choose Tools⇨Internet Options.

You see the Internet Options dialog box.

2. Click the Content tab.

This tab contains sections for the Content Advisor (which can censor Internet pages for your kids), certificates (which are used for secure Web pages), AutoComplete, and RSS feeds (which are described in Chapter 17).

3. In the AutoComplete section, click the Settings button.

If you have Internet Explorer 6, click the AutoComplete button in the Personal Information section. Either way, you see the AutoComplete Settings dialog box.

4. Click the check boxes to control which kinds of entries IE stores: Web addresses, form entries, usernames, and passwords.

IE doesn't show you a list of the passwords you saved, but you can turn the feature on and off by selecting the Prompt Me to Save Passwords check box.

5. Click OK to close the AutoComplete Settings dialog box, and click OK again to close the Internet Options dialog box.

Depending on who else has access to your computer, you might let your browser remember only passwords to accounts that don't involve spending money or revealing personal information. For example, if we have an account at a Harry Potter fan site that enables us to participate in online discussions, the danger of having someone break into this account is a lot less daunting than the thought of someone hacking into an online bank account. Unless your computer is in a physically secure place, don't let your browser remember passwords that have any real power.

Viewing Lots of Web Pages at the Same Time

Internet Explorer and Firefox can display several pages at once — a feature we love. When we're pointing and clicking from one place to another, we like to open a bunch of windows so that we can see where we've been and go back to a previous page just by switching to another window. Better yet, both browsers can display lots of Web pages in one window, by using tabs (as explained in the section "Tab dancing," later in this chapter). You can also arrange windows side by side, which is a good way to, say, compare prices for *The Internet For Dummies,* 11th Edition, at various online bookstores. (The difference may be small, but when you're buying 100 copies for everyone on your Christmas list, those pennies can add up. Oh, you weren't planning to do that? Drat.)

Wild window mania

To display a page in a new Internet Explorer or Firefox window, click a link with the right mouse button and choose Open in New Window (or Open Link in New Window) from the menu that pops up. To close a window, click the Close (X) button in the upper right corner of the window frame, or press Alt+F4, the standard close-window shortcut. Macs don't have a right mouse button, so hold down the button you use to display contextual menus. (The default is the Control key.) You close all Mac windows the same way — by clicking the button in the upper left corner of the window. Users with three-button mice can open a link in a new window by clicking the middle button.

Short attention span tips

If you have a slow Internet connection, use at least two browser tabs or windows at the same time. While you're waiting for the next page to arrive in one tab or window, you can read the page that arrived a while ago in the other tab or window.

If you ask your browser to begin downloading a big file, it displays a small window in the corner of your screen. You can click back to the main browser window and continue surfing while the download continues.

Warning: Doing two or three things at a time in your browser when you have a slow Net connection is not unlike squeezing blood from a turnip — only so much blood can be squeezed. In this case, the blood is the amount of data your computer can pump through your modem. A single download task can keep your Internet connection close to 100 percent busy, and anything else you do shares the connection with the download process. When you do two things at a time, therefore, each one happens more slowly than it would by itself.

You can also create a new window without following a link: Press Ctrl+N in either IE or Firefox. (Mac users should think "Alt" and "Apple" for "Ctrl.")

Tab dancing

Firefox and IE 7 have *tabs,* which are multiple pages that you can switch among in a window. (IE 6 doesn't.) Figure 7-3 shows a Firefox window with three tabs. Just click any of the tabs near the top of the window to show the different pages — the tabs are just above the top edge of the Web page, and below the browser's menu and toolbars. Press Ctrl+T (or choose File⇨New Tab; IE users have to press Alt first to see the menu) to make a new, empty tab. Click the X at the right end to get rid of the current tab.

Figure 7-3:
A Firefox window with three tabs.

As with multiple windows, you can have one tab loading in the background while you're reading another tab, and little rotating arrows on the tab bar show you which ones are loading and which are ready. For most purposes, we find tabs more convenient than windows, but multiple windows are great if you want to compare two Web pages side by side. You can use both tabs and windows; each window can have multiple tabs.

A Few of Your Favorite Things

You'll find some Web pages that you want to visit over and over again. (We've each visited the Google Web site thousands of times by now.) The makers of fine browsers have, fortunately, provided a handy way for you to remember those URLs, so you don't have to write them on the wall and type them back in later.

The idea is simple: Your browser lets you add a Web address to a list on your computer. Later, when you want to go back, you just go to your list and pick the page you want. Firefox calls these saved Web addresses *bookmarks;* Internet Explorer calls them *favorites.*

Bookmarking with Firefox

Firefox has a Bookmarks choice on its menu that displays your current list of bookmarks. To bookmark a Web page — that is, to add the address of the page to your bookmarks — choose Bookmarks⇨Bookmark This Page, or press Ctrl+D, or drag the little icon at the left end of the Address box up to the Bookmarks menu item.

After you create a bookmark, it appears as an entry on the Bookmarks menu. To go to one of the pages on your bookmark list, just choose its entry from the menu.

If you're like most users, your bookmark menu gets bigger and bigger and crawls down your screen and eventually ends up flopping down on the floor, which is both unattractive and unsanitary. Fortunately, you can smoosh (technical term) your menu into a more tractable form. Choose Bookmarks⇨Organize Bookmarks to display your Bookmarks window (as shown in Figure 7-4). Or, press Ctrl+B to display your bookmarks list down the left side of the Firefox window.

Figure 7-4:
The Firefox Bookmarks window includes commands for moving, editing, and deleting bookmarks.

You can go to any bookmark by double-clicking it. (You can leave this window open while you move around the Web in other browser windows.) You can also add separator lines and submenus to organize your bookmarks and make the individual menus less unwieldy. Submenus look like folders in the Bookmarks window.

In the Bookmarks window, click the New Separator button to add a separator line and the New Folder button to add a new submenu. After you create a folder, you can drag bookmarks, separators, and folders up and down to where you want them in the Bookmarks window. Drag an item to a folder to put it in that folder's submenu, and double-click a folder to display or hide that submenu. Because any changes you make in the Bookmarks window are reflected immediately on the Bookmarks menu, it's easy to fiddle with the bookmarks until you get them arranged as you like. Firefox starts out your bookmarks with pages that the Firefox developers want you to look at, but feel free to delete them if your tastes are different from theirs.

When you're done fooling with your bookmarks, choose File⇨Close or press Ctrl+W to close the Bookmarks window.

Creating one-click bookmarks in Firefox

The Bookmarks toolbar is a row of buttons that usually appears just below the Address box. (If it isn't there, choose View⇨Toolbars⇨Bookmarks Toolbar to display it.) This row of buttons gives you one-button access to a bunch of Firefox developers' favorite Web sites. Wouldn't it be nice if your favorite Web sites appeared there instead? No problem! When you organize your bookmarks in the Bookmarks window, stick your top favorite sites in the Bookmarks Toolbar Folder — any sites in this folder automagically appear on the Bookmarks toolbar. You can even add folders with bookmarks in them. Feel free to delete the bookmarks that come with Firefox if they aren't useful to you.

Storing favorites with Internet Explorer

Internet Explorer uses a URL-saving system similar to Firefox's, although it calls the saved URLs *favorites* rather than bookmarks: You can add the current page to your Favorites folder and then look at and organize your Favorites folder. If you use Windows, this Favorites folder is shared with other programs on your computer. Other programs also can add things to your Favorites folder, so it's a jumble of Web pages, files, and other things. (To avoid insanity, most people use favorites only for Web pages.)

IE 7 has two little favorites icons just above the upper left corner of the Web page. To add the current page to your Favorites folder, click the Add to Favorites icon (a gold star with a green plus sign) and choose Add to Favorites from the menu that appears, or press Ctrl+D. In IE 6, choose Favorites⇨Add to Favorites. The Add a Favorite dialog box, shown in Figure 7-5, displays the page name (which you can edit) and the folder in which the favorite will be saved. Click the Create In box to choose a folder, or click the New Folder button to make a new folder to contain the page's address. Click Add when you're ready to save the favorite.

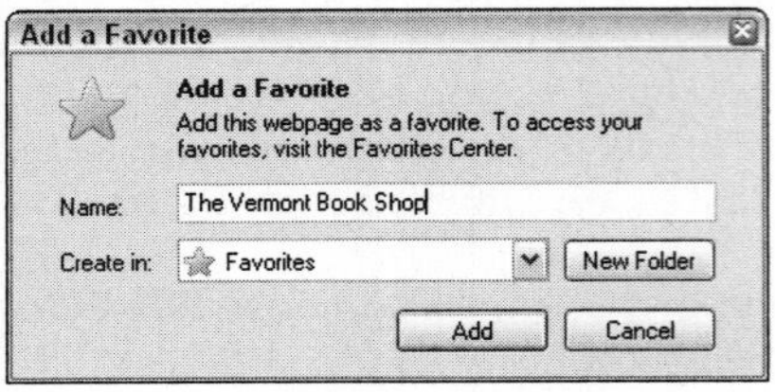

Figure 7-5:
Adding a
Web page
to your
Internet
Explorer
favorites.

Add a Favorite	⊠
☆ **Add a Favorite** Add this webpage as a favorite. To access your favorites, visit the Favorites Center.	
Name: The Vermont Book Shop	
Create in: ☆ Favorites ▼ New Folder	
Add Cancel	

In Internet Explorer 7, the Favorites Center icon (the gold star) displays your list of favorites in a separate little window — it's like the Bookmarks menu in Firefox. Click a page name to display that page, or click a folder to see (and click) the favorites that the folder contains.

In Internet Explorer 6, the Favorites button on the toolbar displays the list down the left side of the browser window; click the Favorites button (or press Ctrl+I) again to make the list go away. IE 6 also has a Favorites command on the menu that displays your favorites list — click an entry to display the page.

If you want to reorganize your Favorites folder, click the Add to Favorites icon and choose Organize Favorites from the menu that appears. (In Internet Explorer 6, choose Favorites⇨Organize Favorites from the menu.) The Organize Favorites window lets you create folders for your favorites, move favorites around, edit them, and delete them. To see what's in a folder, click it. When you're done organizing your favorite items, click Close.

Creating one-click bookmarks in Internet Explorer

Have you noticed the Links toolbar, which usually appears just below or to the right of the Address box? (If it isn't there, click the Tools icon above the right corner of the Web page and choose Toolbars⇨Links to display it. In Internet Explorer 6, choose View⇨Toolbars⇨Links.) You might never want to visit any of the sites that appear by default on this toolbar, but you can put your favorite Web sites there instead. When you organize your favorites, drag your top favorite sites and folders into the Links folder — any sites in the Links folder automagically appear on the Links toolbar. Delete any sites in the Links folder that aren't your favorites. This feature is seriously handy for Web sites you visit often.

Customizing Your Browser

As a serious Internet user, you'll probably spend way, way too much time in front of your Web browser. To make the Web as fun and efficient as possible, you can customize your browser to work the way you like.

Knowing where to start

When you run your browser, it displays your *start page*. Firefox usually starts on a Mozilla Web page, and Internet Explorer usually starts on a Microsoft page. Why not tell your browser to start where *you* want to start? You may want to start at the Yahoo page (www.yahoo.com), which we describe in Chapter 6; or Google (www.google.com); or Wikipedia (http://en.wikipedia.org for the English language encyclopedia).

In Firefox: You can tell Firefox not to load any Web page, or to load any page you like, when you start the program:

1. **Choose Tools⇨Options.**

   You see the Options dialog box, as shown in Figure 7-6.

2. **Click the Main category icon, if it isn't already selected.**

   This category may already be selected, and its settings appear in the rest of the Options dialog box. The setting we're concerned with is Home Page — the Web page that Firefox displays on startup. (We think it ought to be called Start Page, but no one asked us.)

3. **To choose a page to start with, type the URL of a page into the Home Page text box.**

   To make the current page your home page, click (you guessed it!) the Use Current Pages button.

4. **Click OK.**

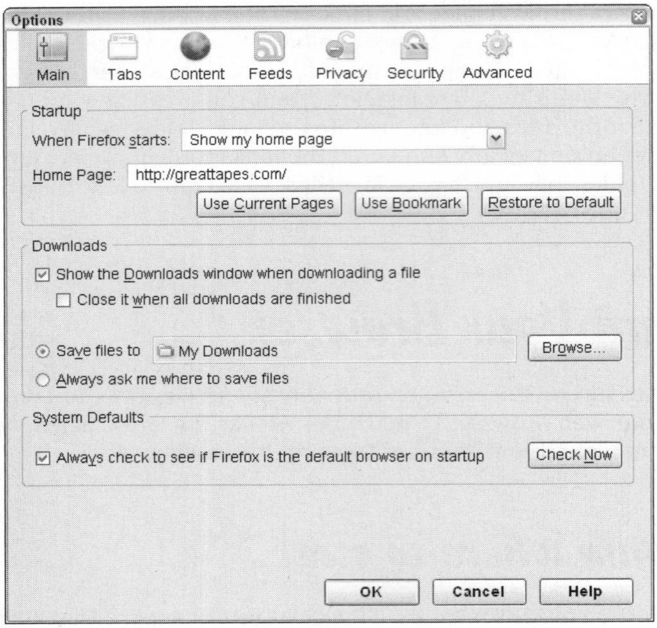

Options

Main | Tabs | Content | Feeds | Privacy | Security | Advanced

Startup

When Firefox starts: Show my home page

Home Page: http://greattapes.com/

Use Current Pages | Use Bookmark | Restore to Default

Downloads

☑ Show the Downloads window when downloading a file

☐ Close it when all downloads are finished

◉ Save files to ☐ My Downloads   Browse...

○ Always ask me where to save files

System Defaults

☑ Always check to see if Firefox is the default browser on startup   Check Now

OK | Cancel | Help

Figure 7-6:
In the
Options
dialog box,
configure
Firefox to
start with
your favorite
Web site.

You can set Firefox to display a bunch of pages when it starts up, each on its own, separate tab. For example, you might want to have Firefox open a weather-reporting page (like Weather Underground at `www.wunder ground.com`), the *New York Times* (`http.nytimes.com`), or even something silly (like `http://cuteoverload.com`), each time you start Firefox. First, display the Web pages you want to start with. Then choose Tools⇨Options, click Main, click Use Current Pages, and click OK.

In Internet Explorer: Follow these steps to change your start page:

1. **Display the Web page you want to use as your start page.**

2. **Click the Tools icon above the upper right corner of the Web page and choose Internet Options from the menu that appears.**

   In Internet Explorer 6, choose Tools⇨Internet Options from the menu. You see the Internet Options dialog box, as shown in Figure 7-7.

3. **Click the General tab, along the top of the dialog box.**

   It's probably already selected, but we say this in case you've been looking around at what's on the other tabs.

Internet Options

General | Security | Privacy | Content | Connections | Programs | Advanced

Home page

To create home page tabs, type each address on its own line.

http://salzburgseminar.org/

[Use current] [Use default] [Use blank]

Browsing history

Delete temporary files, history, cookies, saved passwords, and web form information.

[Delete...] [Settings]

Search

Change search defaults.

[Settings]

Tabs

Change how webpages are displayed in tabs.

[Settings]

Appearance

[Colors] [Languages] [Fonts] [Accessibility]

[OK] [Cancel] [Apply]

Figure 7-7:
The Internet Options dialog box has settings for Internet Explorer, including which Web page to display on startup.

4. **In the Home Page section, click the Use Current button.**

   The URL of the current page appears in the Address text box. To start with no page, click the Use Blank button.

5. **Click OK.**

IE 7 also has a nifty command to add a page to your home set of tabs. Just above the top of the Web page, in the middle, is a Home icon. Click the down arrow to the right of the Home icon and choose Add or Change Home Page from the menu that appears. You can choose to use this page as your start page, or to add this page to the set of pages that IE displays when you start the program.

Fixing your Firefox window

If someone else uses your browser and your browser window ends up looking like any of the following, you can easily put it back to normal:

✔ **If the whole top of the window is gone** — you have no window title bar or menu bar — you're in Full Screen mode. Press F11 to return to normal.

✔ **If some of your toolbars are missing,** choose View➪Toolbars. If a check mark doesn't appear to the left of one of the toolbars, choose it to put a check mark back in front of it and to redisplay that window component.

✔ **If the buttons on your toolbar aren't the buttons you're used to,** right-click the toolbar anywhere except on the Back and Forward icons and choose Customize from the menu that appears. Click Restore Default Set and then click Done.

Fixing your Internet Explorer window

IE 7 has no menu bar — no File-Edit-View set of commands that you're probably used to. Luckily, if you want the menu bar back, you can have it. Click the Tools icon and choose Menu Bar from the menu that appears. Phew! That's better! Or, if you want it for just a moment, press the Alt key.

If your browser, particularly IE, still looks strange, especially if it's showing a lot of ads that you didn't ask for, your computer is probably infected with spyware. See Chapter 2 for a definition of spyware, and the section "Detecting spyware" in Chapter 4 for advice on getting rid of it.

Erasing history

Both IE and Firefox keep a *history list* of the Web sites you've been to. No, your browser isn't spying on you; the history list remembers pages you went to earlier, even days ago, so that you can find them again. In Firefox, the History command on the menu displays where you've been. You can also press Ctrl+H to display the list down the left side of your browser window, arranged by day. Close the history list by clicking the X in its upper right corner.

In Internet Explorer 7, the history list is associated with the Back and Forward buttons. Click the down-pointing arrow between the Forward button (the white, right-pointing arrow icon) and the Address box, and IE displays the pages you've been to recently. You can choose History from the list to display your history list down the left side of your browser window. (In Internet Explorer 6, choose View⇨Explorer Bar⇨History to see your history list.)

Your browser also uses the history list to provide a drop-down list of URLs you've typed. At the right end of the Address box is a down-pointing arrow. When you click it, a list of recently visited URLs drops down. Some of our readers have asked us how to clear out that box, presumably because they meant to type www.disney.com, but their fingers slipped and it came out www.hot-xxx-babes.com instead. (It could happen to anyone.) Because some of the requests sounded fairly urgent, here are the gruesome details:

✔ **In Firefox,** choose Tools➪Clear Private Data to display the Clear Private Data dialog box. Choose which kinds of information you want Firefox to forget (probably your browsing history) and click Clear Private Data Now.

✔ **In Internet Explorer,** click the Tools icon and choose Delete Browsing History from the menu that appears. (Hmm, it's right up at the top. There must be a lot of sloppy typists out there.) In the Delete Browsing History dialog box, click the Delete History button, and click Yes. (In Internet Explorer 6, click Tools➪Internet Options and click the General tab. The History section of the Internet Options dialog box includes a box where you can type the number of days to keep the list of Web sites you've viewed. You can also find a Clear History button.)

If you're using someone else's computer, and especially if you're using a public computer in a library or Internet café, it's a good idea to delete your browsing history and any other information about your session that might be stored on the computer. In Internet Explorer 7, choose Tools➪Delete Browsing History and click the Delete All button. In Firefox, choose Tools➪Options, click the Privacy icon, and click the Clear Now button in the Private Data section.

Cookies Are (Usually) Your Friends

To enhance your online experience, browser makers invented a type of special message that lets a Web site recognize you when you revisit that site. They thoughtfully store this info, called a *cookie,* on your very own machine. See the section "Cookies aren't so bad" in Chapter 2 for a full description of cookies, and how they compare to more serious security threats. In both Firefox and Internet Explorer, you can control which sites can store cookies on your computer.

Controlling cookies in Firefox

Choose Tools➪Options, click the Privacy category, and look in the Cookie section. If the Accept Cookies from Sites check box isn't selected, select it. Set the Keep Until option to They Expire. (Who wants a dead cookie, anyway?) Or, if you want to decide which sites can store cookies on your computer, set Keep Until to Ask Me Every Time. Firefox doesn't give you the option of accepting first-party cookies and refusing third-party cookies, except by configuring it to ask you each time a site wants to set a cookie.

You can specify which sites can and cannot store cookies by clicking the Exceptions button. You can enter the Web addresses that you definitely trust with cookies (like the shopping sites that you frequent) or that you don't trust (like advertising sites).

You can take a look at the cookies on your computer at any time. Click the Show Cookies button and scroll down the list of sites. If you see some that you don't recognize or that sound suspicious, click the Remove Cookies button.

Controlling cookies in Internet Explorer

Use the Tools⇨Internet Options command to display the Internet Options dialog box. The cookie controls are on the Privacy tab (shown on the left side of Figure 7-8), so click it. By default, Internet Explorer sets your privacy level to Medium, allowing cookies from the server you contacted but not from *third-party* servers (ones other than the one that provided the page you're viewing).

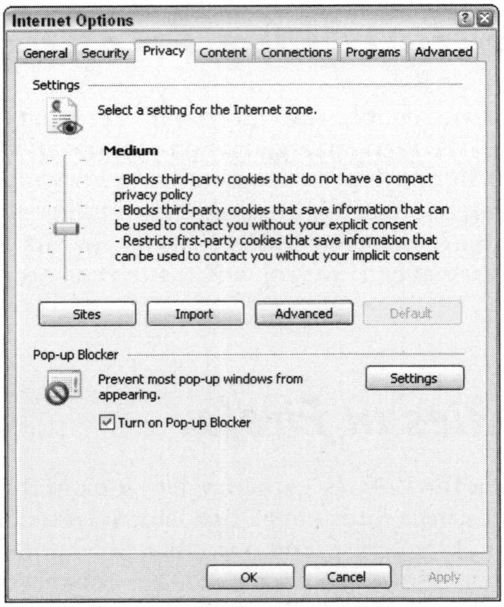

Figure 7-8:
Internet
Explorer,
cookies, and
you.

Third-party servers usually deliver advertisements and those annoying pop-up and pop-under ads. You can elect to manage them yourself by clicking the Advanced button to see the Advanced Privacy Settings dialog box and then selecting the Override Automatic Cookie Handling check box. The options are shown in this list:

✔ **First-party cookies:** You can choose to accept, block, or be prompted to choose, although this option gets tiresome very quickly if you encounter a lot of cookies. Some sites can store three or more cookies *per page*.

✔ **Third-party cookies:** Just say no to (that is, choose Block) third-party cookies.

✔ **Always allow session cookies:** This option lets all session cookies through, a type of cookie used to track a single instance of your visit to a Web site. These cookies are commonly used by shopping sites such as Amazon.com, and are harmless.

Blocking Pop-up Windows

Pop-up windows, as described in Chapter 2, are browser windows that open without you asking for them, usually at the command of the Web site you are viewing. Some Web sites display so many pop-ups that your computer becomes unusable until you can close them all. If you've encountered these sites, you'll be glad to year, both Firefox and Internet Explorer can block most (though not all) pop-up windows.

No pop-ups in Firefox

In Firefox, choose Tools➪Options to open the Options window and click the Content category. You see an option to block pop-up windows, as shown in Figure 7-9. (We leave it selected.)

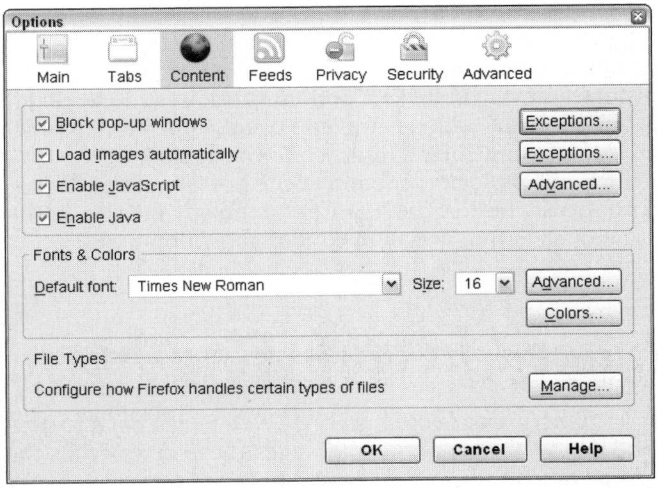

Figure 7-9:
Firefox,
pop-up
windows,
and you.

Blocking all pop-ups makes a few Web sites stop working. In particular, some shopping sites pop up small windows into which you have to type credit card verification information. Firefox thoughtfully includes an Exception button where you can specify Web sites whose pop-ups are okay with you.

When a Web site tries to display a pop-up, you see at the top of the Web page a message saying "Firefox prevented this site from opening a popup window." Click the Options button and choose from the menu that appears:

✔ **Allow popups from *sitename*** puts this site on your Allowed list.

✔ **Enable Popup Blocker Options** displays the Allowed Sites dialog box so that you can edit your list of sites.

✔ **Don't show this message when popups are blocked.**

Click the red X at the right end of the message to make the message go away.

Unfortunately, as quickly as browser makers add pop-up blockers, Web site creators come up with new ways to spawn pop-ups. If you still see too many pop-ups for your taste, consider installing the free Adblock Plus Firefox add-on. Go to `https://addons.mozilla.org/firefox` and look for Adblock Plus. When you find its page, click the Install Now link to download and install it into Firefox.

Blocking pop-ups in Internet Explorer

What about Internet Explorer? Microsoft finally added a pop-up blocker in response to Firefox's growing popularity. If you keep your Windows installation up-to-date with Windows Update, your IE includes the pop-up blocker. If not, go to `http://windowsupdate.microsoft.com` to get the latest version of IE.

IE's pop-up blocker also displays a "Pop-up blocked" message at the top of the Web page whenever it blocks a pop-up window, and clicking the message displays a similar set of options. You can tweak your pop-up blocking options at any time by choosing Tools⇨Internet Options, clicking the Privacy tab, and looking at the Pop-Up Blocker section at the bottom of the dialog box. The check box controls whether the feature is enabled, and the Settings button shows the list of sites that are allowed to display pop-ups.

Getting Plugged In with Plug-Ins

Web pages with pictures are old hat. Now, Web pages have to have pictures that sing and dance or ticker-style messages that move across the page, or they have to be able to play a good game of chess with you. Every month, new types of information appear on the Web, and browsers have to keep up. You can extend your browser's capabilities with *plug-ins* — add-on programs that glue themselves to the browser and add even more features. Internet Explorer can also extend itself by using *ActiveX* controls, which are another type of add-on program.

What are you to do when your browser encounters new kinds of information on a Web page? Get the plug-in program that handles that kind of information and glue it onto the browser program. *Star Trek* fans can think of plug-ins as parasitic life forms that attach themselves to your browser and enhance its intelligence.

A parade of plug-ins

Here are just a few of the useful plug-ins out there:

✔ **Flash Player:** Plays both audio and video files as well as other types of animations. Widely used on Web pages, it's available at www.adobe.com/products/flashplayer/.

✔ **RealPlayer:** Plays *streaming* sound and video files while you download them. A free player is available at www.real.com/realplayer.html, along with more powerful players that cost money. You may have to browse around to find the free player, but the other players are also a good value (most cost less than $30). Our favorite site with streaming audio is the National Public Radio Web site (www.npr.org), where you can hear recent NPR radio stories. Another favorite is the BBC at www.bbc.co.uk with news in 43 languages (really) and other BBC programs 24 hours a day.

✔ **QuickTime:** Plays video files as you download them. Available at www.apple.com/quicktime/download.

✔ **Adobe Acrobat:** Displays Acrobat files formatted exactly the way the author intended. Lots of useful Acrobat files are out there, including many U.S. tax forms (at www.irs.ustreas.gov). You can find Acrobat at www.adobe.com (or, more precisely, at www.adobe.com/products/acrobat/readstep.html if you don't mind some extra typing).

How to use plug-ins

After you download a plug-in from the Net, run it (double-click its icon, or its filename in My Computer (XP) or Computer (Vista) to install it. Depending on what the plug-in does, you follow different steps to try it out — usually, you find a file that the plug-in can play and watch (or listen) as the plug-in plays it.

After you install the plug-in, you don't have to do anything to run it. The plug-in fires up automatically whenever you view a Web page containing information that requires the plug-in.

To confuse matters, Firefox also allows you to install add-in programs written in its own, special extension language. Go to `https://addons.mozilla.org/firefox` to find out more about them. Popular add-ons include programs to display maps or weather forecasts, see the inner workings of Firefox, or see price comparisons from other Web sites.

Chapter 8

Needles and Haystacks: Finding Almost Anything on the Net

In This Chapter

▶ Starting with basic search strategies

▶ Finding what you're looking for on the Web

▶ Finding people on the Web

▶ Making use of built-in searches in your browser

"*O*kay, all this great stuff is out there on the Internet. How do I find it?" That's an excellent question and thanks for asking. Questions like that are what make this country strong and vibrant. We salute you and say, "Keep asking questions!" Next question, please.

Oh, you want an *answer* to your question. Fortunately, quite a bit of (technical term follows) stuff-finding stuff is on the Web. More particularly, free services called *search engines* and *directories* are available that cover most of the interesting material on the Web. There's even a free encyclopedia, written by Internet users like you.

You can search in dozens or hundreds of different ways, depending on what you're looking for and how you prefer to search. Search can take some practice because billions of Web pages are out there, most of which have nothing to do with the topic you're looking for. (John has remarked that his ideal restaurant has only one item on the menu, but it's exactly what he wants. The Internet is about as far from that ideal as you can possibly imagine.)

To provide a smidgen of structure to this discussion, we describe several different sorts of searches:

✔ **Topics:** Places, things, ideas, companies — anything you want to find out more about

✔ **Built-in searches:** Topic searches that a browser does automatically, and why we're not always thrilled about that

> ✔ **People:** Actual human beings whom you may want to contact, find out more about, or spy on

> ✔ **Goods and services:** Stuff to buy or find out about, from mortgages to mouthwash

To find topics, we use the various online search engines and directories, such as Google and Yahoo. To find people, however, we use directories of people — and those are (fortunately) different from directories of Web pages. Wondering what we're talking about? Read on!

Your Basic Search Strategy

When we look for topics on the Net, we always begin with a search engine, usually Google. (The word *google* has now been "verbed," much to the dismay of Google's trademark lawyers.)

You use all search engines in more or less the same way:

1. **Start your Web browser, such as Firefox or Internet Explorer.**

   Flip to Chapter 6 if you don't know what a browser is.

2. **Go to your favorite search engine's home page.**

   You can try one of these URLs (Web addresses): `www.google.com`, `www.yahoo.com`, or `http://dmoz.org`. We list the URLs of other search sites later in this section.

   Or, just click in the search box in the upper right corner of your browser window, to the right of the address box.

3. **Type some likely keywords in the Search box (either your browser's search box or the search box that appears on the search engine's home page) and press Enter.**

   After a delay (usually brief, but after all, the Web *is* pretty big), the search engine returns a page with some links to pages that it thinks match your keywords. The full list of links that match your keywords may be way too long to deal with — say, 300,000 of them — but the search engine tries to put them in some reasonable order and lets you look at them a screenful at a time.

4. **Adjust and repeat your search until you find something you like.**

   One trick is to pick keywords that get at your topic from two or three different directions, like `ethopian restaurants trumansburg` or `war women song`. After some clicking around to get the hang of it, you find all sorts of good stuff.

TIP

Search engine, directory — what's the difference?

When we talk about a *directory,* we mean a listing like an encyclopedia or a library's card catalog. (Well, like the computer system that *replaced* the card catalog.) A directory has named categories with entries assigned to them partly or entirely by human catalogers. You look things up by finding a category you want and seeing what it contains.

A *search engine,* on the other hand, periodically looks at every page it can find on the Internet, extracts keywords from them (by taking all the words except for *the, and,* and the like), and makes a big list. (Yes, that takes a lot of computers. Google has several hundred thousand of them.) They then try to figure out which pages are most important, using factors such as how many other sites link to that page, and give each page a score. You use the search engine by specifying some words that seem likely, and it

finds all the entries that contain that word, ranking them by their score.

We think of the index in the back of the book as a hard-copy equivalent of a search engine; it has its advantages and disadvantages, as do directories, which are more like this book's table of contents. Directories are organized better, but search engines are easier to use and more comprehensive. Directories use consistent terminology, and search engines use whichever terms the underlying Web pages use. Directories contain fewer useless pages, but search engines are updated more often.

Some overlap exists between search engines and directories — Yahoo includes a directory and a search engine; Google, which is mainly a search engine, includes a version of the Open Directory Project (ODP) directory.

5. **If the search engine is producing results too scattered to be useful and you can't think of any better keywords, try one of the directories: the Open Directory Project (ODP) at `http://dmoz.org` or Yahoo Directory at `http://dir.yahoo.com`.**

    When you see a list of links to topic areas, click a topic area of interest. In the directory approach, you begin at a general topic and get more and more specific. Each page has links to pages that become more and more specific until they link to actual pages that are likely to be of interest.

Search, Ho!

Once upon a time in an Internet far, far away, lots of search engines and directories all battled with each other to see which would be the favorite. There were AltaVista and Dogpile and lots of other sites you can find in earlier editions of this book. Well, it seems that the first pangalactic search war is pretty

---

The lazy searcher's search page

You may feel a wee bit overwhelmed with all the search directories and search engines we discuss in this chapter. If it makes you feel any better, so do we.

To make a little sense of all this stuff, we made ourselves a search page that connects to all the directories and search engines we use — call it one-stop searching. You can use it, too. Give it a try at http://net.gurus.com/search.

In the not unlikely event that new search systems are created or some of the existing ones have moved or died, this page gives you our latest greatest list and lets you sign up for e-mailed updates when we change it.

---

much over, with Google and Yahoo the victors — at least for now. However, Microsoft is trying to mount a new campaign, and a new challenge is coming from the open source world, particularly the Open Directory Project. Visit http://net.gurus.com/search for all the exciting developments.

Google, our favorite search engine

Our favorite Web search engine is Google. It has little robots that spend their time merrily visiting Web pages all over the Net and reporting what they see. It makes a humongous index of which words occurred in which pages; when you search for something, it picks pages from the index that contain the words you asked for. Google uses a sophisticated ranking system, based on how many *other* Web sites refer to each one in the index. Usually, Google's ranking puts the best pages first.

Refining your search

Using Google or any other search engine is an exercise in remote-control mind reading. You have to guess words that will appear on the pages you're looking for. Sometimes, that's easy — if you're looking for recipes for Key lime pie, key lime pie is a good set of search words because you know the name of what you're looking for. On the other hand, if you have forgotten that the capital of France is Paris, it's hard to tease a useful page out of a search engine because you don't know which words to look for. (If you try France capital, you find info about investment banking and Fort de France, which is the capital of the French overseas département of Martinique. Many people must ask this question, because Google takes pity on you and tells you at the top: "Capital: Paris.")

Now that we have you all discouraged, try some Google searches. Direct your browser to www.google.com. You see a screen like the one shown in Figure 8-1.

Type some search terms, and Google finds the pages that best match your terms. That's "*best* match," not "match" — if it can't match all the terms, it finds pages that match as well as possible. Google ignores words that occur too often to be usable as index terms, both the obvious (ones such as and, the, and of) and merely routine (terms such as internet and mail). These rules can sound somewhat discouraging, but in fact it's still not hard to get useful results from Google. You just have to think up good search terms. Try that recipe example by typing **key lime pie** and clicking the Search button. You get a response like the one shown in Figure 8-2.

Figure 8-1:
Google,
classic
style.

Figure 8-2:
Plenty
of pages
of pie.

The number-one reason a search doesn't find anything

Well, it may not be *your* number-one reason, but it's *our* number-one reason: One of the search words is spelled wrong or mistyped. John notes that his fingers insist on typing *Interent,* which doesn't find much — other than Web pages from other people who can't spell or type. Google often catches spelling mistakes and helpfully suggests alternatives. We sometimes use a Google search to check the preferred spelling of words that haven't made it into the dictionary yet. (Thanks to our friend Jean Armour Polly, for reminding us about this problem.)

Your results won't look exactly like Figure 8-2 because Google will have updated its database since this book went to press. Most of the pages that Google found do, in fact, have something to do with Key lime pie — some have pretty good recipes. Google says it found 371,000 matches (yow!) but in the interest of sanity it shows you about 100 of them, 10 at a time. Although that's still probably more than you wanted to look at, you should at least look at the next couple of screens of matches if the first screen doesn't have what you want. Because the list includes a lot of restaurants with Key lime pie on the menu and a hair salon named *Key Lime Pie,* you can just narrow the search by adding the keyword recipe. Search engines are pretty dumb; you have to add the intelligence. At the bottom of the Google screen are page numbers; click Next to go to the next page.

The links in the right column are "sponsored" links — that is, paid ads, ranked by how much the advertiser was willing to pay. Often they're worth clicking, but remember that they're ads.

The I'm Feeling Lucky button searches and takes you directly to the first link, which works, well, when you're lucky.

Even more Google options

Although Google looks very simple, it has plenty of other options that can be handy:

- ✔ **You can get there from here.** Type in a street address, and Google offers a link to a map. Type in a person's name and a full or partial address, at least the state abbreviation, and Google gives you addresses and phone numbers. Type in a phone number, and it often gives you the name and address. (Try typing **202-456-1414**). The information is all collected from public sources, but if you find this a bit too creepy, look yourself up and if it finds you, it includes a link to a page where you can have your info removed.

✔ **You can search Usenet for information.** *Usenet* is the giant collection of Internet *newsgroups* (online discussion groups) that has been around since before the Web. Simply click the More link above the Google search box, and choose Groups from the menu that appears. If a topic has been discussed in the past 26 years on Usenet (as it seems most topics have), this technique is the best way to find the messages about that topic. It's a great place to find out how to fix computer problems — most likely, whatever question you have has been asked and answered on Usenet, and Google has all of it. (John found things there that he wrote in 1981.) To browse around Usenet newsgroups, start at `http://groups.google.com`. For a description of Usenet, see `http://net.gurus.com/usenet`.

✔ **You can search for images as well as for text.** Simply click the Image link on any Google search page. Google has no idea what each image is but looks at the surrounding text and the filename of the image and does a remarkably good job of guessing. If you do an image search for **key lime pie**, you indeed see dozens of pictures of tasty pies. A safe-search feature omits pictures of naked people and the like. If you turn off safe search, you can find some impressively unsafe pictures.

✔ **You can get the news.** Google News (click the News link or start at `http://news.google.com`) shows a summary of current online news culled automatically from thousands of sources all over the world. *Warning:* If you're interested in current events, you can easily waste 12 hours a day following links from here.

✔ **You can limit your search to documents in a specific language.** No sense in finding pages in a language you can't read, although Google has a sub-system that can try, with mixed success, to translate pages from some other languages. Click the Preferences link to the right of the search box.

✔ **You can do painless arithmetic.** Google is even a calculator. Type **2+2** and Google says `2 + 2 = 4`. It knows units, so if you type **4 feet 8.5 inches**, Google says `4 feet 8.5 inches = 1.4351 meters`.

Searching from your cellphone

Google isn't limited to the Internet; you can use it from your cellphone. Google has a special five-digit phone number — 46645 (GOOGL) — that you can text from any phone that can do text messages. Here's how:

1. **Compose a text message to the phone number 46645 (GOOGL).**

2. **In the text of the message, type a Google search command.**

Handy search engine targeting tips

Google makes it easy to refine your search more exactly to target the pages you want to find. After each search, your search terms appear in a box at the top of the page so that you can change them and try again. Here are some tips on how you may want to change your terms:

✔ If two or more words should appear together, put quotes around them, as in `"Elvis Presley"`. You should do that with the pie search ("key lime pie")

because, after all, that's what the pie is called, although in this example, Google is clever enough to realize that it's a common phrase and pretends you typed the quotes anyway.

✔ Use + and − to indicate words that must either appear or not appear, such as `+Elvis +Costello -Presley` if you're looking for the modern Elvis, not the classic one.

Here are some search commands you can use:

- For driving directions, type the two addresses separated by *to*. For example, type **1600 Pennsylvania Avenue, Washington DC to 1 Fifth Avenue, New York, NY**.

- For nearby restaurants, type the name or type of restaurant followed by the city and state or the zip code. For example, type **pizza Middlebury VT**.

- For movie times, type the name of the movie followed by the city and state or zip code.

- For help with other commands you can use, type **help**.

3. Send the message.

Within a few minutes, you receive a text message back from Google with the results of your search.

See Google SMS, at `http://sms.google.com`, for more information. If your phone has a Web browser, you can use Google from that, too, the same way you visit any other Web page.

Browsing with Directories

Sometimes a Web search just doesn't find what you're looking for. Coming up with the right search terms can be tricky if no specific word or phrase sums up what you want to know. This is the moment to try a Web directory. If you know in general but not in detail what you're looking for, clicking up and down through directory pages is a good way to narrow your search and find pages of interest.

We recommend two Web directories: ODP and Yahoo.

ODP: It's open, it's big, and it's freeeee

Wouldn't it be nice if there were a really big directory with as much stuff as a search engine? Sure, but who'd ever be able to pay people to build a directory that big? Nobody — but volunteers do it for free. Netscape started the Open Directory Project (ODP), a volunteer effort to create the world's biggest and best Web directory. Propelled by the same community spirit that built Linux, Mozilla Firefox, and Wikipedia, ODP has indeed become a killer Web directory. Because ODP is available for anyone to use for free, dozens of search engines provide ODP along with their own index information. For example, Google's version is at `www.google.com/dirhp`.

Google does more than search

Here are a bunch of other Web-based services that Google offers. (As far as we can tell, all these services are part of Google's Grand Plan for Global Domination, but the services are free and good, so we use them.)

You can find files fast on your own computer. Google offers Google Desktop, a program you can download to your PC, that lets you do Google-like searches (while getting Google-like ads) of the contents of your PC's hard drive. We find it particularly useful for finding old files and e-mail messages that we're convinced are somewhere on our computers. Download it from `http://desktop.google.com`.

You can see a map of almost anywhere. Google Maps enables you to type in an address and see a map of the area, a satellite photo of the same area, or both superimposed. Try it at `http://maps.google.com`. Or, if you're tired of hearing about Google all the time, try MapQuest, at `www.mapquest.com`, another excellent map site. Even cooler is Google Earth (at `http://earth.google.com`), which displays 3-D maps and images.

You can create and store word processing documents and spreadsheets. Why get Microsoft Word or Excel or WordPerfect when Google Docs & Spreadsheets can do the job? Go to `http://docs.google.com`, create a free Google account, and go to it. All you need is your browser. Neither the word processor nor the spreadsheet program is as powerful as PC-based programs like Word and Excel, but for basic documents, they do the job. One of the nicest features is that you can share your documents and spreadsheets with your co-workers and friends so that they can see and edit the documents, too.

You can send and receive e-mail. We tell you about Google Mail (Gmail) in Chapter 13.

You can organize and display your digital photos. Google offers the Picasa program (at `http://picasa.google.com`), which helps you organize your photos, provides a photo editor, and enables you to upload them to your own photo Web site.

Google adds more features almost every week. To see what it's offering, start at `www.google.com`, click More, and choose a feature from the menu that appears.

You may already be an expert

The Open Directory Project depends on volunteers to manage a category. If you search for something, look at what's in the category, and think "Sheesh, I could do better than that," perhaps it's time to volunteer and do so. The time commitment for a single category is modest — just a few minutes a week to see what has been suggested, and edit, add, or reject it.

To volunteer, click the Become an Editor link on any dmoz.org window. A small questionnaire asks who you are, why you're interested, and which entries you want to add to your category.

If you're accepted (most people are if they have some new pages to suggest for the category), you can start editing in a day or two. There are tutorials and mailing lists for editors, so you don't have to do it all by yourself.

John edits the categories for *compilers,* a kind of software that's a professional interest from his grad-school days, as well as the one for Unitarian church camps because he was looking for one camp, saw the category, and thought "Sheesh, I could — oh, right."

ODP lives at www.dmoz.org, (*dmoz* stands, more or less, for *D*irectory *Moz*illa). The directory is a set of categories, subcategories, sub-subcategories, and so on down to an impressive level of detail. Each category can — and usually does — contain a bunch of Web pages. You can either start at the top directory level and click your way through the categories, or search within the directory to find pages and then look at the categories that include interesting pages. Because those pages have all been at least glanced at by a person, they're probably of higher quality than the mechanically collected ones in the general Google list. You see not only the relevant Web pages but also links to related categories. ODP has so many categories that you often have to click around to find the exact subcategory you want — but when you find it, you generally find some interesting links. (If you don't, see the nearby sidebar "You may already be an expert".)

Yahoo for directories!

Yahoo (yes, you normally see it with an exclamation point, but we don't like to yell) is one of the oldest directories — and still a pretty good one. You can search for entries or click from category to category until you find something you like. Start at http://dir.yahoo.com. (At least the page name doesn't use an exclamation point.) As with all Web pages, the exact design may have changed by the time you read this section. A whole bunch of categories and subcategories are listed; click any of them to see another page that has even more subcategories and links to actual Web pages. You can click a link to a page if you see one you like, or click a sub-subcategory, and so on. Figure 8-3 shows the Yahoo Directory page for Recreation & Sports.

Early on, it was easy to submit a Web page to Yahoo by simply entering it into the Submissions page and waiting a week or so for the editors to look at the new page. Now the site is so popular that normal submissions take a long, long time (months) before anyone on staff looks at them, unless you pay them $299 a year for the "express" service. You can draw your own conclusions about how that affects what gets into Yahoo (and what doesn't), and why we like dmoz.org.

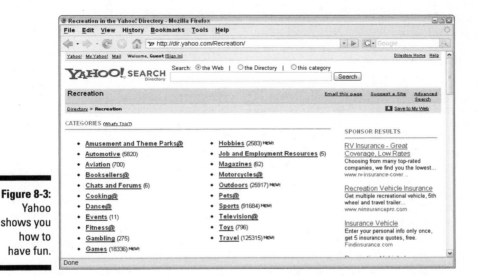

Figure 8-3:
Yahoo
shows you
how to
have fun.

For facts, try Wikipedia first

Wikipedia, www.wikipedia.org, is an encyclopedia you can use for free over the Internet, and it looks like the page shown in Figure 8-4. *Wiki* means fast in Hawaiian (actually, *wikiwiki* does), and Wikipedia has earned its name. The Wikipedia project, which started in 2001, has grown to almost 2 million articles in English, covering almost every conceivable topic, from the Battle of Dunkirk to Dummies books, and, yes, there's even a Key lime pie article, where we discover that "Proper Key lime pie is made with canned sweetened condensed milk, for fresh milk was not a common commodity in the Florida Keys before modern refrigerated distribution methods."

If you're looking for the scoop on most topics, Wikipedia is a great place to start. You can search on both article titles and article text. Words in the article body that are highlighted in blue link to other articles in Wikipedia. Many

The 404 blues

More often than we want to admit, when you click a link from a search results page, you see — rather than see the promised page — a message such as `404 Not Found`. What did you do wrong? Nothing. Web pages come and go and move around with great velocity, and the various Web search engines were designed as delivery vehicles (not garbage trucks), so they do a lousy job of cleaning out links to old, dead pages that have gone away.

At least the search engines are a bit better in this regard than the manual directories. That's because search engines have software robots that revisit all the indexed pages every once in a while and note whether they still exist. Even so, many lonely months can pass between robot visits, and a great deal can happen to a page in the meantime. Google *caches* (stores) a copy of most pages it visits, so even if the original has gone away, you can click the Cache link at the end of a Google index entry to see a copy of the page as it was when Google last looked at it.

Here are some other ways to chase down a tantalizing link that has wandered off into nowhere:

✔ The Internet Archive operates a nifty service, the Wayback Machine, that can retrieve older versions of Web sites. Enter your broken link in its search box at `www.archive.org`. (Yes, this site owns a lot of computers too.)

✔ Sometimes Web sites try to tidy up a bit and move their files around in the process. If the broken link is a long one, say, `www.frobliedoop.org/glompty-dompty/snrok/amazingtip.html`, try its shorter versions: `www.frobliedoop.org/glompty-dompty/snrok` or `www.frobliedoop.org/glompty-dompty` or even `www.frobliedoop.org` to find clues to where they put that tip. Also try a Google search on just the filename, `amazingtip.html`. You might find a copy at another Web site.

✔ Finally, we should mention that Web sites sometimes shut down, either because of equipment failure or for periodic maintenance. (Late nights, Sunday mornings, and major holidays are favorite times for the latter.) Your 404'd link just might magically work tomorrow.

Bad links are all just part of life on the online frontier — the high-tech equivalent of riding your horse along the trail in the Old West and noticing that there sure are a lot of bleached-white cattle skulls lying around.

articles also have links to external Web sites that have more information on the topic. Articles are created and edited by a volunteer team of more than 75,000 active contributors. There are Wikipedias in dozens of other languages as well. (Check out `http://is.wikipedia.org` if you ever wondered what Icelandic looks like.)

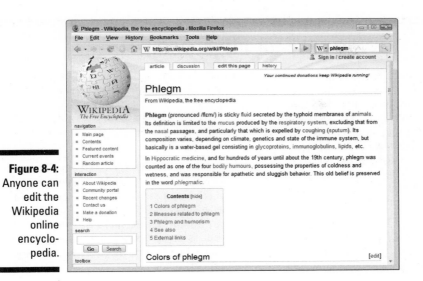

Figure 8-4:
Anyone can edit the Wikipedia online encyclopedia.

Anyone can edit a Wikipedia article any time they want. That might seem a prescription for chaos, but most articles are watched over by interested volunteers, and inappropriate edits are quickly reversed, so the overall quality remains remarkably high.

If the idea of editing encyclopedia articles on your favorite subjects sounds appealing, talk to your family first. Wikipedia can be very addictive.

Articles are supposed to reflect a neutral point of view (NPOV, in Wikispeak), but a few topics — like abortion, creationism, and Middle East politics — are continually debated. Wikipedia isn't as authoritative as conventional works like *Encyclopædia Britannica,* but its articles are usually up to date and to the point, with side issues dealt with by links to other articles. One particularly cool thing on Wikipedia is its collection of comprehensive lists, http://en. wikipedia.org/wiki/Category:Lists, on all sorts of arcane subjects. One of our favorites is the list of countries with mains power plugs, voltages, and frequencies; type **mains power systems** in the Search box to find it.

If you search Google for a topic, there's a good chance that a Wikipedia article will show up as one of the links Google returns. That link might be a good place to start reading.

Here ends our survey of Key lime pies. Wait just a minute while we run down to the kitchen and have another piece.

Who pays for all this stuff?

You may be wondering who pays for all these wonderful search systems. Advertising supports all except two of them. On every page of most search systems, you see lots and lots of ads. It used to be that ad revenue was pretty skimpy, hence the dotcom bust of 2000, but then the search sites discovered an important secret: When you enter keywords, you're telling the search site something about your interests at the moment. That information turns out to be *very* valuable to advertisers. An automobile company might pay a lot to have its ad near the top of the results page when you search on `automobile dealer Kansas`. Some sites (notably Google) auction off prime ad placement. Google marks all such ads as "sponsored links." Usually they're on the right side of the results page, but sometimes they're on top with a colored background. (Surprise — these cost more.) Other search sites may not be so scrupulous. Advertisers pay Google when you click their links.

The exceptions are the Open Directory Project and Wikipedia, which work on the open-source model. The vast majority of contributors are unpaid volunteers. ODP gets a small amount of support from AOL's Netscape subsidiary, and Wikipedia is supported by grants and donations. If you use Wikipedia much, you should kick in a few bucks.

The Usual Suspects: Other Useful Search Sites

After you surf around Yahoo, Google, and ODP for a while, you may want to check out the competition. Here are some search Web sites that provide specialized types of searches:

- **Microsoft Live.com search at www.live.com:** Microsoft sees Google as a threat and is not about to cede the lucrative search business without a fight. Right now Live looks a lot like a ho-hum clone of Google, but the folks at Redmond have money to burn. And, big surprise, Live is the default search engine in Internet Explorer.

- **Amazon's A9.com at www.a9.com:** Amazon.com, the giant online books-and-everything-else store, has its own search engine that shows results in several columns from sources including Microsoft Live search, books from Amazon, Wikipedia, and a few others. We think it's kind of cluttered, but sometimes its results can be interesting.

- **About.com at www.about.com:** About.com is a directory with several hundred semiprofessional "guides" who manage the topic areas. The guides vary from okay to very good (Margy knows a couple of very good ones), so if you're looking for in-depth information on a topic, it's worth checking About.com to see what the guide has to say. About.com was purchased by the *New York Times* in 2005.

- ✔ **Bytedog at www.bytedog.com:** Bytedog assembles the results of searches at other search engines and presents them in a ranked list with cute dog graphics (cuter than Microsoft's, if you ask us). It takes a few extra seconds to respond, but that's because it's filtering out bad links before you have to deal with them. It also includes a Web directory. Bytedog is a project of a couple of students at the University of Waterloo, Ontario.

- ✔ **Other Web guides:** ODP has a directory of several hundred other guides: See http://dmoz.org/Computers/Internet/Searching for links to them.

Finding People

Finding people on the Internet is surprisingly easy. It's so easy that, indeed, sometimes it's creepy. Two overlapping categories of people-finders are available: those that look for people on the Net with e-mail and Web addresses and those that look for people in real life with phone numbers and street addresses.

Looking for email addresses

The process of finding e-mail and Web addresses is somewhat hit-and-miss. Because no online equivalent to the telephone company's official phone book has ever existed, directories of e-mail addresses are collected from the addresses used in Web pages, Usenet messages, mailing lists, and other more-or-less public places on the Net. Because the different directories use different sources, if you don't find someone in one directory, you can try another.

Because the e-mail directories are incomplete, there's no substitute for calling someone up and asking, "What's your e-mail address?"

The ten-minute challenge

Our friend Doug Hacker (his real name) claims to be able to find the answer to any factual query on the Net in less than ten minutes. We challenged him to find a quote we vaguely knew from the liner notes of a Duke Ellington album whose title we couldn't remember. He had the complete quote in about an hour but spent less than five minutes himself actually searching. How? He found a mailing list about Duke Ellington, subscribed, and asked the question. Several members replied in short order. The more time you spend finding your way around the Net, the more you know where to go for the information you need.

Googling for people

Type in someone's name and address to Google (for the address, type at least the state abbreviation, but more is better), and it shows you matches from phone book listings.

If you're wondering whether someone has a Web page, use Google or Yahoo to search for just the person's name. If you're wondering whether you're famous, use Google or Yahoo to search for your own name to see how many people mention you or link to your Web pages. (If you do it more than once, it's called *egosurfing*.) If you get e-mail from someone you don't know, search Google for the e-mail address — unless the message was spam, the address is bound to appear on a Web page somewhere.

Using other people-search sites

Here are some other sites that search for people:

- **Yellow pages directories at www.superpages.com, www.smartpages. com, and www.infousa.com:** Quite a few "yellow pages" business directories, both national and local, are on the Net. The directories in this list are some of the national ones. InfoUSA even offers credit reports and other unpleasantly intrusive information.

- **Yahoo People Search at http://people.yahoo.com:** You can search for addresses and phone numbers and e-mail addresses. If you don't like your own listing, you can add, update, or delete it.

- **WhoWhere at http://whowhere.lycos.com:** WhoWhere is another e-mail address directory. Although Yahoo usually gives better results, some people are listed in WhoWhere who aren't listed in other places.

- **Canada 411 at http://canada411.com:** Canada 411 is a complete Canadian telephone book, sponsored by the major Canadian telephone companies. *Aussi disponible en français,* eh? For several years the listings for Alberta and Saskatchewan were missing, leading to concern that the two provinces were too boring to bother with, but they're all there now, proving that they're just as gnarly as everyone else.

Getting the goods on goods and services

All the commercial directories and search engines now put shopping information somewhere on their home pages to help get your credit card closer to the Web faster. You can find department stores and catalogs from all over, offering every conceivable item (and some inconceivable items). We tell you all the dos, don'ts, and how-tos in Chapter 10.

We're from Your Browser, and We're Here to Help You

Microsoft and Mozilla keep trying to crowbar their way into the search engine market. (Who? Us? Opinionated?) Both take you directly to their respective preferred search system if you give them half a chance. These search systems aren't awful, but unless you're the kind of person who turns on the TV and watches whatever is on the first channel you come to, you'll probably find that you prefer to choose your own search engine.

If you type a word or phrase, rather than a Web address, into the IE, Firefox, or Safari address box, your browser takes you to your preferred search engine and displays the results of a search on what you typed. How convenient is that! You can specify which search engine you want this feature to use:

✔ **In Firefox,** you can choose a search engine from its short list by clicking the search engine icon to the right of the address box (and to the left of the search box). Click the icon and choose a different site. Or, choose Manage Search Engines to display a list of the search engines that Firefox knows about and add your favorites.

✔ **In Internet Explorer,** choose Tools⇨Internet Options, click the General tab if it's not already selected, and click the Settings button in the Search section.

✔ **Safari** appears to be fixated on Google.

Making a Custom Start Page

Many sites want you to use them as your *start page* (the page that your browser loads when it starts up, as described in Chapter 7). To encourage you to do so, these sites enable you to customize them to show all kinds of useful information just for you.

For example, if you create a free Google account, you can have a fancy, custom Google page rather than the boring, plain one that most folks use. Click the Sign In link in the upper right corner of the Google page, and create an account if you don't already have one (by clicking the Create an Account Now link). After you're logged in, a Personalized Home link appears in the upper right part of the Google page. Your Google Home page can include a clock, calendar, weather report, news headlines, and other features.

Yahoo provides similar features. (Actually, they predate Google's by several years.) From www.yahoo.com, click My Yahoo (or start at http://my.yahoo.com), click Sign In, and click Sign Up to create a free Yahoo account. Your My Yahoo page can contain news headlines, stock prices, sports scores, and RSS feeds. (See Chapter 17 to see how RSS newsfeeds work.)

Chapter 9

Music and Video on the Web

A thousand years ago, when we wrote the first edition of *The Internet For Dummies*, Internet content consisted almost entirely of text. (It was 1993, but it sure *feels* like a thousand years ago.) You could download a few archives of pictures, and there was this weird thing, the World Wide Web, that could mix together pictures and text, but for the most part, it was text: People's connections were so slow, downloading pictures took so long, and computer screens were so fuzzy that we stuck to text. The pictures you could download were single images, like cartoons or snapshots. Audio was nearly unheard of (so to speak), and video files were so bulky that even if you could find a clip and wait a week for it to download, it wouldn't fit on your computer's disk. By the late 1990s, Internet connections had sped up enough and screens had improved enough that pictures were normal fare — and audio was entering the mainstream enough that we put a sample voice message on our Web site, in case any of our readers had sound cards. (It's still there, at http://net.gurus.com/ngc.wav.)

Things have advanced a little since then. Ordinary users now have Net connections that run at several million bits per second — faster than the main backbones of the early 1990s — and computer disks have gotten enormous beyond imagining. Passing around audio and video over the Net has become practical and widespread. In fact, the amounts of available audio and video are now so vast that you could spend your entire life looking at online commercials without ever getting to anything worth watching. This chapter tries to bring a little order to the vast wasteland of online media.

To avoid writing *audio and/or video* a hundred more times in this chapter, henceforth we use the concise (albeit imprecise) term *media* to refer to them.

Seven Ways to Get Media and One Way Not To

You can get your media fix in approximately ten zillion different programs and formats. Fortunately, they fall into a modest number of categories: free, streaming, rented, purchased, shared, and outright stolen.

Receive it as a gift

The simplest approach is to download media offered for free and then play it. Visit www.nasa.gov/multimedia, where NASA has lots of free little movies on topics ranging from dust storms on Mars to how a roller coaster ride feels like taking off in the space shuttle. You can also find independent movies and videos from producers more interested in letting people see their work than charging for it. Visit http://epitonic.com for an eclectic collection of music by artists, some well known and some obscure, released so that people can listen to it and make their own mixes.

Borrow it

Even on a broadband connection, downloading a whole media clip can take a while. Rather than download first and play later, *streaming* media downloads and plays at the same time, thereby re-creating (in a complex digital manner) the way that radio and TV have worked since the 1920s. As with TV and radio, after it's streamed, it's gone — and if you want to play it again, you have to stream it again. Streaming audio can work over a dialup connection, but streaming video needs a broadband connection.

Most streaming media is provided *on demand:* You click a link and they send you whatever it is, sort of like a jukebox. Alternatively, some streaming media is a single program to which you can listen in and hear what's playing at any moment. Not surprisingly, this is called *Internet radio,* and in many cases these audio streams are actual radio programs, such as our local public radio stations at http://wrvo.fm (click Listen Live) in upstate New York and www.vpr.net (click Listen Online) in Vermont. We say more about Internet radio later in this chapter.

Rent it

A great deal of music isn't available for free, but it's available for cheap. Services such as Real Networks' Rhapsody (www.real.com/rhapsody)

offer monthly subscriptions that let you listen to large libraries of recorded music. You pay them a fixed monthly fee, and they let you click songs from their catalog to play them and to make and share playlists of your favorites. You can only listen online; to download for keeps or to copy to CD or to an iPod, you have to buy it.

These rental services have enormous catalogs of music, with each one claiming to be the largest. They really *are* large; while checking out Rhapsody, we were finally able to do a side-by-side comparison of Desi Arnaz's muscular late-1940s version of *Babalu* and his mentor Xavier Cugat's more elegant 1941 recording. (You'll just have to decide for yourself which one you like better.)

You can find video-rental Web sites too — not just for renting a DVD but also for downloading the video over the Internet and watching it on your computer. For example, MovieLink, at `www.movielink.com`, lets you download a movie, store it for up to 30 days, and watch it as many times as you like in any single 24-hour period. (That is, after you start watching it, you need to finish it within 24 hours, but you can watch it over and over during that 24 hours.) Note that MovieLink works only with Internet Explorer, not with Firefox.

Buy it

Apple's iTunes makes buying music easy. Go to `www.apple.com/itunes` to listen to the first little bit of any song in its catalog. If you like it, you can buy your own, permanent copy (for 99 cents) that you can copy to your iPod, play on your computer, or burn on a CD. You don't have to be a Mac user to like iTunes; you can play the tunes by using a Windows version of the iTunes program. (See the section "Organizing your music with iTunes," later in this chapter). It's no surprise that people buy in droves, making iTunes the biggest online store. Likewise, many more Web sites sell music either through a Web store or as an add-on to a rental service, most for about the same price as iTunes.

Already own it

You probably own a whole lot of digital music in the form of music CDs. Copying your music CDs to your computer is called *ripping*, and it's easy to do. Windows Media Player, iTunes, and other music programs can copy all the tracks from a CD and put the songs into your music library so that you can play them from your computer (without the CD) or copy them to your MP3 player.

When you rip music from CDs, you can specify which format to store the files in. We use the MP3 format because the files are smaller than some other formats and because every music player can handle MP3s.

Share it

Napster was the first well-known music-exchange service, allowing members to download MP3 music files from each other for free. The system was the first large-scale *peer-to-peer* (*P2P*) information exchange, where people exchange files with each other rather than download them from a central library. Eventually, the big record labels sued and shut it down because most of what people exchanged was in flagrant violation of the music's copyright. Napster was later reincarnated as a music rental system.

Two current popular file-sharing systems are BitTorrent (www.bittorrent.com) and LimeWire (www.limewire.com), which have thus far been able to fly under the legal radar. They are much like what Napster was, a network from which you can download music for free, a certain amount of which is provided against the wishes of the owners of said music. While you are downloading music from other people's computers, they are in turn downloading music from you, so they can significantly slow down your computer and your Internet connection. The music industry insists that these folks are morally reprehensible, but particularly with BitTorrent, people use it to share large amounts of entirely legal and legitimate material along with the dodgy stuff.

Subscribe to it

You can subscribe to audio programs over the Internet. A *podcast* is an audio file distributed over the Net for listening to on an iPod or other type of MP3 player or any computer with speakers. Many radio shows are available as podcasts; go to www.npr.org to find many of them. Lots of organizations and people make podcasts, too. See the section "Subscribing to podcasts with iTunes," later in this chapter, for instructions.

Steal it — um, no

Plenty of pirated stuff is still on the Net, and probably always will be. We expect that our readers, because they're of good moral character, wouldn't want to look for it, but if you do, you have to do so without our help.

What Are You Listening With?

The three most popular programs used for playing Web-based online media are Windows Media Player, Real Player, and Apple iTunes. The first two include separate player programs and plug-ins for Web browsers so that Web pages can embed little windows that show movies or play music. You eventually have to install all three if you want to handle all the links you click. All three work pretty well.

Windows Media Player

```
www.microsoft.com/windows/windowsmedia
```

Microsoft decided to create its own streaming audio and video formats and to bundle a player for them with Windows. The Windows Media Player (shown in Figure 9-1) program can play files in Advanced Systems Format (with the extension .asf or .asx), as well as most other formats. More recent versions added useful new features, so if you don't have Media Player version 11 or later, it's worth visiting Windows Update or the Media Player site to download it. (Media Player itself may nag you to upgrade if you have an older version.)

Downloads for the post-literate

Not all downloadable audio files contain music. A thriving niche market exists for what used to be called "talking books." You can download books, magazines, and just about anything you might otherwise read, as well as radio programs you might have missed. Although listening to downloaded books on your computer works fine — and it can be an essential tool for the visually impaired — it's kind of pointless if you can read the paper book faster than you can listen to it (and kick back on the patio while you're at it). But if you drive to work or go jogging, a talking book on CD in the car player (or copied to the MP3 player or iPod on your belt) is just the ticket.

The largest source of talking books is Audible.com (www.audible.com). You can buy individual books for book-like prices, or you can subscribe and get one or two books a month cheaper than you can by paying individually. Either way, the books you buy are yours to keep. They provide a reasonably nice program that you can download and install to keep track of the files for the books you bought and burn them onto CDs (*lots* of CDs — about 15 for a full-length book). Audible has also made deals with many other media programs, so you can get an Audible plug-in for iTunes that lets you copy your books to an iPod, as well as a plug-in for Windows Media Player for all the MP3 devices it handles, and so forth.

Audible usually offers a trial subscription with a couple of free books, and its catalog includes public-interest stuff like presidential inaugural speeches available for free if you want to try it out. *Warning:* John tried it out and ended up inventing errands that involved driving to far-away stores so that he could listen to the last CD of *The DaVinci Code*. On the other hand, Margy's husband survived a long commute thanks to his Audible subscription.

Click the Media Library tab on the left side of the Media Player window to see which audio and video files you have. Click Media Guide to browse links to popular music. Or, click Copy from CD to rip (copy) tracks from a CD that you put in your computer's CD drive. You can also burn music CDs by clicking the Copy to CD or Device tab.

RealPlayer

www.real.com

One system for playing streaming media files, the kind you borrow or rent, is RealPlayer, shown in Figure 9-2. Files in the Real format have the extension .ra or .ram. To play RealAudio files, you need the RealPlayer program, which you can download from www.real.com. The RealAudio player also handles RealVideo, which shows smallish moving pictures to go with your sound.

You have to download and install the player before you can use it. The installation process is a pain because Real desperately wants you to choose a player you have to pay for, and to fill out registration info so that it can add you to its marketing lists. You see a variety of ominous warnings if you decline to register. Just say no; it works fine with no registration and no pop-ups.

If you start RealPlayer directly, it includes a Web browser (it's really Internet Explorer) that opens the media-guide page with lots of stuff you can listen to or watch — and, it hopes, buy.

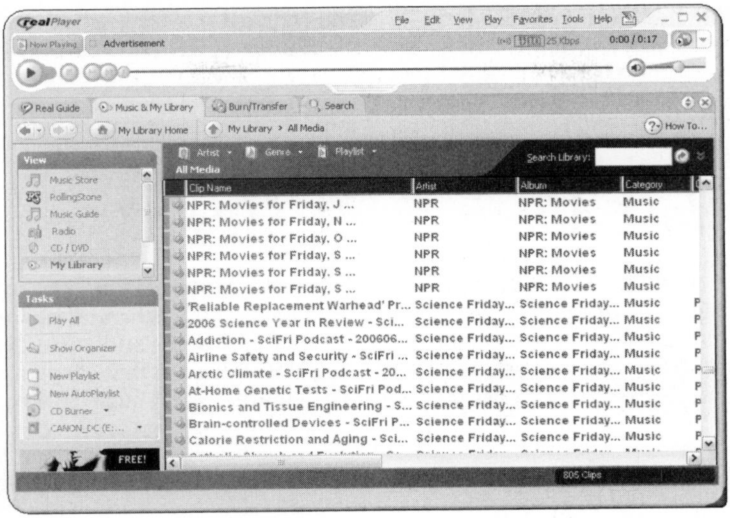

Figure 9-2:
Catching up
on the latest
media with
RealPlayer.

iTunes

`www.apple.com/itunes/download`

Another popular streaming player is Apple's iTunes, shown in Figure 9-3. You may have heard of it as a music store and a way to organize music, but iTunes can play all sorts of media, including videos. iTunes supports streaming video as well as audio in most popular formats.

Figure 9-3:
You can buy
music, rip
and burn
CDs,
organize
songs into
playlists,
subscribe to
podcasts,
and maybe
even wash
the dishes
with iTunes.

Apple has its own audio format, called MPEG-4 or M4P (with the file extension .m4p). If you buy music from the iTunes store, you can play it only with iTunes and transfer it only to an iPod. (Why should Apple make it easy to play music on MP3 players that it doesn't sell?)

Okay, How About Some Music?

One of the hottest activities on the Internet is downloading and exchanging music files with your friends in the MP3 file format. MP3 stands for *MP*EG level *3* (acronyms within acronyms — how technoid) and is simply the soundtrack format used with MPEG movies. Because that format is widely available and does a pretty good job of compressing music to a reasonable size for downloading, it has been adopted by music lovers on the Net.

You can play MP3 files with many different programs, including Windows Media Player, RealPlayer, and iTunes. This section explains how to use iTunes to organize music, subscribe to podcasts, make playlists, and listen to radio stations over the Internet, because all the programs are fairly similar. If you use Windows Media Player or RealPlayer, you get the general idea.

Naturally, Microsoft has the competing file format WMA, with the extension .wma. Real Player and iTunes can also handle WMA.

Organizing your music with iTunes

Apple's iTunes (www.apple.com/itunes) lets you buy legal, downloaded songs for the reasonable price of 99 cents each. Both Mac and Windows users can buy and play songs from iTunes by downloading the free iTunes program, which is excellent for keeping your songs organized even if you don't have an iPod or buy from the iTunes store.

Making playlists

In iTunes, you can organize your music into playlists, which are like your own, customized albums. One playlist can be music you like to listen to while washing the dishes, another playlist might be for your fabulous oldies collection. Or, each user of your computer can have his or her own playlist(s). You can have as many playlists as you like. (Margy has one playlist of the baritone parts she needs to learn for her women's barbershop group, and another playlist of instrumental jazz, 1960s rock, and Hindu chanting to listen to at work.)

You create a new playlist by choosing File⇨New Playlist or pressing Ctrl+N. You can name the playlist whatever you want, and then drag in music from your library. Dragging a song from the library to a playlist doesn't remove it from the library or copy the file — you can put the same song into multiple playlists, and all the while it continues to be stored in your general iTunes library just once.

Subscribing to podcasts with iTunes

Another nifty thing about iTunes and the iTunes music store is podcasts, which are sort of like audio magazines (see the section "Subscribe to it," earlier in this chapter). Radio programs, companies, musicians, comedians, and just plain people produce podcasts about a huge variety of different subjects, everything from *Grey's Anatomy* to the stock market.

To subscribe to a podcast, click the Music Store link in iTunes, and then click the Podcasts link. When you find a podcast that looks interesting, you can click an episode to listen to it on the spot or click the Subscribe button to receive all future episodes automatically. Podcasts are free, and iTunes downloads the latest episodes every time you start the program.

Real Player can also download music for 99 cents a track, or you can subscribe to the Rhapsody service for $10 a month (which offers unlimited online listening to its large catalog and downloads for 89 cents apiece). Several built-in links in Windows Media Player are for other music-rental and -download services, with similar prices.

If this blizzard of audio file types seems baffling, you're right — it is. Fortunately, most programs can read each other's formats, so you don't have to worry too much about which is which for typical downloads. We suggest that you experiment with a few programs and then use the one you like best. We like iTunes.

Playing Music after You Download It

If you want to listen to music while you're sitting in front of your computer, you're all set — fire up one of the media programs and listen. But we hear that some people actually have lives and want to listen to music in other places.

More threats and promises

Folks ripping their favorite tunes from CDs and e-mailing them to their 50 closest friends are a hideous threat to the recording industry, not to mention that they're violating copyright law. (The previous hideous threats, for those old enough to remember, were cassette tapes and home VCRs, which totally destroyed the music and movie industries. What — they didn't? Uh, well, *this* time it's different because, um, just because it is.) The industry's efforts to shut down Web sites that offer ripped songs for free downloading has been moderately successful, but private e-mail is hard to stop.

The recording industry came up with SDMI, a music file format of its own. The Secure Digital Music Initiative was intended to let you download but not share music. It flopped, partly because it had technical defects quickly analyzed and reported by enterprising college professors and students, and partly because nobody wanted crippleware music. The recording industry has been filing lawsuits against the most visible music sharers, on the peculiar theory that if it threatens and sues its customers, the customers' attitudes will improve and they will buy more stuff. Maybe someday the industry will figure out, as Apple did, that if it sells decent music at reasonable prices and lets customers listen to it the way they want to, people will pay for it.

You can buy a portable MP3 player that stores thousands of MP3 cuts so that you can listen while you jog, travel, or just hang out. It's like a Walkman, but you don't need tapes or CDs. You hook your MP3 player up to your computer whenever you want to download new tunes. These players can hold *weeks* of music. The most popular is the ubiquitous Apple iPod, but lots of other players are cheaper and work fine. Only iPods can play M4P (copy-protected) music and only files to which you own a license.

Ripper programs let you transfer music from your CDs to your computer disk in MP3 format. Real Player, iTunes, and Windows Media Player can all rip from CDs, and can burn new CDs of music you ripped and downloaded.

Windows Media Player, RealPlayer, and iTunes can all copy music from CDs to your computer, create CDs from your computer, and copy music to portable players. But if you want to use an Apple iPod, the program has to be iTunes.

Listening to Internet Radio

If you like to listen to music while you work, check out Internet radio stations. Like real radio stations, they offer a mix of music, talk, and sometimes commercials. Unlike real radio stations, they're extremely cheap to set up, so lots and lots of people do — providing lots of quirky little niche stations run by people all over the world. You listen to them with a streaming program, usually iTunes, Real Player, or Windows Media. Most are available for free, some require a subscription, and some have a subscription option to make the ads go away.

If you use iTunes, click the Radio link in iTunes to get started. You see a menu of different types of stations, and after choosing one of those, you can peruse stations from across the country at your leisure for free. Double-click a station to listen to it.

To get started, here are some directories of Internet radio stations:

✔ launch.yahoo.com — Yahoo's Launchcast.

✔ shoutcast.com — AOL's Shoutcast works best with its free Winamp media program.

✔ radio.msn.com — Microsoft's MSN Radio comes in a free version and a higher-quality paid version.

Another facet of Internet radio is listening on the Web to stations and programs that exist in real radio. The advantage is that you can listen to programs whenever and wherever you want, as long as you have a serviceable computer there. Most public radio programs are available for download at sites like www.npr.org, your local radio station's Web site, or the Web site of the program itself.

There's CDs, and then there's CDs

Although all CDs look the same, they don't all play the same. Normal audio CDs contain a maximum of about 74 minutes of music and work on every CD player ever made. When you burn a CD-R (the kind of CD you can write only once), you're making a normal audio CD. Because blank CD-Rs are so cheap (about 15 cents apiece if you buy them in quantity), the main disadvantage of this approach is that you end up with large stacks of CDs.

MP3 files are much smaller than audio CD files, so if you burn a CD full of MP3s, you can put about ten hours of music on each disc. DVD players and many recent CD players can play MP3 CDs. If you're not sure whether your player can handle MP3 CDs, just make one on your computer and try it in your player. It doesn't hurt your player, although you might see some odd error messages. Although rewritable CD-RWs don't work in normal CD players, players that can handle MP3 CDs can usually handle CD-RWs. Again, if you're not sure, try it; it doesn't hurt anything if it doesn't work.

Watching Movies on the Net

The original standard digital-movie format is *Moving Picture Experts Group (MPEG)*. MPEG was designed by a committee down the hall from the JPEG committee that defined file formats for scanned photos (practically unprecedented in the history of standards efforts) and was designed based on earlier work. MPEG files have the extension .mpeg or .mpg.

Microsoft, responding to the challenge of emerging standards that it didn't control, created its own formats. Audio/Visual Interleave (AVI) format is for nonstreaming video, with the extension .avi. Advanced Streaming Format (with the extension .asf or .asx) is for both streaming audio and video data.

Getting movies

Web browsers themselves can't play any of these video formats — you need to get a player program. You also need a reasonably fast computer to display movies in anything close to real time. RealPlayer and Windows Media Player handle movies (and are described earlier in this chapter). Adobe's Shockwave is also occasionally used for movies; if it's not already loaded on your computer, you can get a free player at www.adobe.com/shockwave/download/.

If you want to try watching movies online, visit www.ifilm.com, which has a large collection of short independent movies and trailers. All its movies are streamed, which means that they're shown in a little window on your screen. The Net just isn't fast enough to stream full-screen video, at least not yet.

The YouTube thing

Probably the largest Internet video phenomenon is YouTube (www.youtube.com). YouTube is a site like Google, but instead of being an Internet search engine for information at large, it's only for videos. On YouTube you can find everything from *Saturday Night Live* clips to previews for upcoming movies to strange homemade Lego flicks. According to the *New York Times*, people post more than 100 million videos on YouTube every *day*.

In the search box, you can type a word or phrase related to the video you're looking for, and YouTube displays a list of links of possible videos. Video-playing software is embedded in the Web site, so you don't need anything but an Internet connection to watch videos on YouTube. If you see a video you really like, and want to share with your 50 closest friends, you can click the

Share This Video link at the end of the video and e-mail it to them. The e-mail arrives with a link to the YouTube page that has the video on it.

Google has formed its own niche in the Internet movies world with Google Video (http://video.google.com), a site very similar to YouTube. Because Google now owns YouTube, the two sites are morphing into one. Another YouTube-like Web site is Metacafe (www.metacafe.com).

Watching real movies

If you can plan your movie viewing a little ahead of time, Movielink (www.movielink.com) may be for you. It rents full-length, full-screen movies you can watch on your Windows computer screen or, if your computer has a TV adapter (as many recent ones do), on your TV. To start, you have to sign up and install the player program. Then pick the movie you want and tell them to download it, at which point they charge your credit card about $4 and start the download, which takes about an hour. When the download is done (or even partly done, if you're in a hurry), you can watch it. It's sort of like making your computer into a VCR or TiVo. You can watch the movie any time during the month after you download it — but, after you start watching it, you have to finish within 24 hours. Alternatively, you can purchase movies and watch them as many times as you want.

Amazon.com offers the Unbox service, which is nearly identical to Movielink. After you install the player (again, Windows only), you can rent or purchase movies for download. Unlike with Movielink, you can also watch them on some models of TiVo and similar video players.

Two Web sites offer advertising-supported, professional-quality videos on your PC: Joost (pronounced "juiced," we imagine) at www.joost.com and BabelGum (from Italy) at www.babelgum.com. The sites are new, so check their selection of shows and how many ads they're throwing at you.

Another way of renting movies that involves a bit of planning is Netflix (www.netflix.com). The way it works is that you sign up for an account on their Web site (the starter account is 5 dollars per month), and, again on their Web site, you make a list of movies from the Netflix library, which is extremely extensive. Then Netflix sends you the DVD by mail, and as soon as you watch it, you send it back and Netflix sends you another one from your list. You can keep the DVDs as long as you want, but you don't get a new one until you send back the first one. You can use the Netflix Web site to add videos to your queue, reorganize your queue to control what will arrive next, rate movies you've seen, and see lists of recommended movies based on your ratings. Netflix has begun offering videos for download (for a fee), but the selection is limited — click the Watch Now tab.

Chapter 10

More Shopping, Less Dropping

The Internet is the world's biggest bazaar, with stores that carry everything from books to blouses, DVDs to prescription drugs, mutual funds to musical instruments, plane tickets to, uh, specialized personal products (don't read too much into that). Shopping online is convenient — no parking or standing in line — and allows you to compare prices easily. But is online shopping safe? Well, we've bought all kinds of products online, and we're still alive to tell the tale.

Shopping Online: Pros and Cons

Here are some reasons for shopping on the Net:

- ✔ Online stores are convenient and open all night, and they don't mind if you aren't wearing shoes or if you window-shop for a week before you buy something.

- ✔ Prices are often lower online, and you can compare prices at several online establishments in a matter of minutes. Even if you eventually make your purchase in a brick-and-mortar store, what you find out online can save you money. Shipping and handling is similar to what you pay for mail order, and you don't have to drive or park.

✔ Online stores can sometimes offer a better selection. They usually ship from a central warehouse rather than have to keep stock on the shelf at dozens of branches. If you're looking for something hard to find — for example, a part for that vintage toaster oven you're repairing — the Web can save you weeks of searching.

✔ Sometimes stuff just isn't available locally. (Two of the authors of this book live in small rural towns. Trumansburg, New York, is a wonderful place, but if you want to buy a book other than the three days a year the library has its book sale, you're out of luck. And Margy couldn't find a harmonium anywhere in the Champlain Valley.)

✔ Unlike malls, online stores don't have Muzak. (A few Web sites play background music, but we don't linger on those sites.)

On the other hand, here are some reasons why you shouldn't buy everything on the Net:

✔ You can't physically look at or try on stuff before you buy it, and in most cases, you have to wait for it to be shipped to you. (We haven't had much luck buying shoes online, f'rinstance.)

✔ Your local stores deserve support.

✔ You can't flirt with the staff at a Web store or find out about the latest town gossip.

The Credit Card Question

How do you pay for stuff you buy online? Most often you pay by credit card, the same way you pay for anything else. Isn't it incredibly, awfully dangerous to give out your credit card number online, though? Well, no.

When you use plastic at a restaurant, you give your physical card with your physical signature to the server, who takes it to the back room, does who-knows-what with it, and then brings it back. Compared with that, the risk of sending your number to an online store is pretty small. A friend of ours used to run a restaurant and later an online store and assures us that there's no comparison: The online store had none of the credit card problems that the restaurant did.

Many books (including earlier editions of this one) made a big deal about whether a Web site has a security certificate, which means that it shows a little lock in the corner of the Web browser window. The lock is nice to have, but the problem it solves, bad guys snooping on the connection somewhere between your PC and the seller's Web site, isn't a very likely one. We think you should worry more about whether a store selling something is well enough run that it actually ships you what you bought.

Take a credit card number, any number

One of the cleverer innovations in online banking is *virtual credit cards*. If you want to place an online credit card order with a merchant you don't entirely trust, first visit your bank's Web site and tell the bank how much the order will cost, and on the spot, it concocts a brand-new card number. Then you return to the merchant's site and order with that card number rather than with your regular number. As soon as the merchant places the charge, your bank links the new number to the merchant, so even if the merchant leaks the number, it's no good to anyone else. The number's credit limit is the amount you set when you created it, so if the merchant tries to overcharge you, the bank says no. You can also create virtual numbers good for a set number of charges, for subscriptions that require regular payments.

Different banks use different names for this service. Citibank and Discover call it *virtual numbers*. Bank of America calls it *ShopSafe*. Ask your bank whether it offers this service.

John found that virtual numbers also work for phone orders, mail orders, and any charge where you don't use the physical card. Because he's paranoid, he uses virtual numbers for everything from his electric bill to his college alumni association. But, don't use them for buying plane tickets or reserving hotel rooms; you may have to show a real card with the matching number when you show up.

Credit cards and debit cards look the same and spend the same, but credit cards bill you at the end of the month whereas debit cards take the money right out of your bank account. In the U.S., consumer protection laws are much stronger for credit cards. The important difference is that in case of a disputed transaction, *you* have the money if you used a credit card, but *they* have it if you used a debit card. Use a credit card to get the better protection and then pay the bill at the end of the month so that you don't owe interest.

If, after this harangue, you still don't want to send your credit card number over the Internet, most online stores are happy to have you call in your card number over the phone (although, likely as not, an operator halfway around the globe then enters your credit card number by using the Internet). If you're one of those fiscally responsible holdouts that doesn't do plastic, send a check or money order.

Paying at the Store

Buying stuff at an online store isn't much different from buying stuff at a regular store. In the simplest case, a store sells only one item per Web page, as shown in Figure 10-1. To buy it, you visit the page, you see the item, you enter the payment and shipping details, and they send it to you.

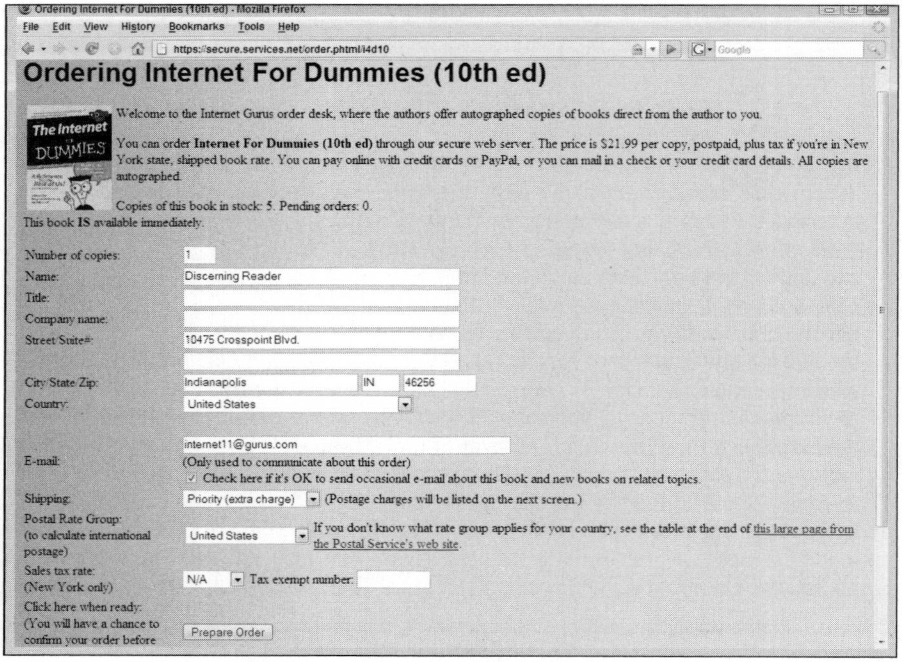

Figure 10-1:
You just
can't have
too much
quality
literature.

Most stores hope you will buy several items at once, so they use a *shopping cart* instead. Margy runs the little online kids' videotape store Great Tapes for Kids at www.greattapes.com. Originally, it had a single order page with an order form listing every tape in her rapidly expanding catalog. When the Great Tapes order form got hopelessly large, John reprogrammed it to provide a shopping cart to help track the items people order. (John will do practically anything to avoid writing.)

As you click your way around a site, you can toss items into your cart, adding and removing them as you want, by clicking a button labeled something like Add Item or Buy Now. When you have the items you want, you visit the virtual checkout line and buy the items in your cart. Until you visit the checkout, you can always take the items out of your cart if you decide that you don't want them, and at online stores they don't get shopworn, no matter how often you do that.

Figure 10-2 shows the Great Tapes for Kids shopping cart with two items in it. When you click the Proceed to Checkout button, the next page asks for the rest of your order details, much like the form shown earlier, in Figure 10-1.

Some stores even have the online equivalents of layaway plans and gift registries. For example, some Web shopping sites let you add items to a wish list that you can share with your friends so that you or someone else can buy the item for you later. Some sites offer gift certificates, too, for shopping online.

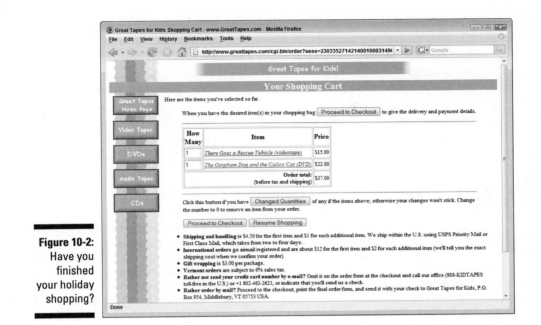

Figure 10-2:
Have you finished your holiday shopping?

How Little Do You Want to Pay?

As little as possible, of course. About 15 minutes after the second online store appeared, someone realized that you could look at the stores to find who charges how much for which item and then report back on your own Web site. Price comparison sites work really well *if* you can exactly identify what you want to buy. For books, consumer electronics, computers, and computer parts, it's always worth a look. But if you're looking for khaki pants, no two pairs are the same, and most of us would rather pay an extra ten bucks to avoid a pair that makes us look like a spandex-wrapped potato.

Comparison sites now work two ways. One is to visit store sites and "scrape" the prices. The other is to make a deal with interested stores and let them upload their prices directly, typically in return for a commission when users click through. Both methods work okay, but we have occasionally seen comparison sites showing different prices from the ones you get if you visit the store site directly. Here are a few of our favorites:

- ✔ **Froogle** (`http://froogle.google.com`) is Google's price comparison site. Stores upload prices, but Google doesn't charge them. (The search pages have ads on the right.) The searching is great, but the inventory is spotty.

- ✔ **PriceGrabber** (`www.pricegrabber.com`) has good coverage of everything from musical instruments to computer parts.

- ✔ **MySimon** (`www.mysimon.com`) compares prices from a wide variety of online stores, getting its information about high-tech products from CNET and about nontechnical products from Shopping.com.

- ✔ **Nextag** (`www.nextag.com`) also covers a wide range of products, but we would decline their offer to help you shop for online degrees.

- ✔ **ISBN.NU** (`http://isbn.nu`) checks prices for new books at a dozen online stores and tells you which has the best price. The site scrapes the prices and then uses the stores' affiliate programs to get paid.

Up, Up, and Away

We buy lots of airline tickets online. Although the online travel sites aren't as good as the very best human travel agents, the sites are now better than most agents and vastly better than bad travel agents. Even if you have a good agent, online sites let you look around to see what your options are before you get on the phone. Some airlines offer cheap fares on their own Web sites that aren't available any other way. They know that it costs them much less to let the Web do the work, and they pay you (in the form of a hefty discount) to use the Web.

The theory of airline tickets

Four giant airline computer systems in the United States — Sabre, Galileo, Worldspan, and Amadeus — handle nearly all the airline reservations in the country. (They're known as *CRSs,* or computer reservation systems, or *GDS,* for Global Distribution Systems.) Although each airline has a "home" GDS, the systems are all interlinked so that you can, with few exceptions, buy tickets for any airline from any GDS. Some of the low-price, startup airlines are available via GDS, but others, notably Southwest and Jet Blue, don't participate in any of these systems but have instead their own Web sites, where you can check flights and buy tickets.

In theory, all the systems show the same data; in practice, however, they get a little out of sync with each other. If you're looking for seats on a sold-out flight, an airline's home system is most likely to have that last, elusive seat. If you're looking for the lowest fare to somewhere, check all four systems (using different travel Web sites) because a fare that's marked as sold out on one system often mysteriously reappears on another system. Also check Orbitz (`www.orbitz.com`) which has direct-connect access to many airlines, bypassing GDS altogether.

Some categories of fares are visible only to travel agents and don't appear on any of the Web sites, particularly if you aren't staying over a weekend, so check with a good agent before buying. On the other hand, many airlines offer some special deals that are *only* on their Web sites and that agents often don't know about. Confused? You should be. We were.

The confusion is even worse if you want to fly internationally. Official fares to most countries are set via the IATA (International Air Transport Association) cartel, so computer systems usually list only the IATA fares for international flights. If you need to buy tickets less than a month ahead, you can often find entirely legal *consolidator tickets* sold for considerably less than the official price, so an online or offline agent is extremely useful for getting the best price. International airlines also have some impressive online offers, most notably from Cathay Pacific, which usually has a pass that includes a ticket from the United States to Hong Kong and then unlimited travel all over Asia.

Here's our distilled wisdom about buying tickets online:

- ✔ Check the online systems to see which flights are available and for an idea of the price ranges. Check sites that use different GDSs. (We list some sites at the end of this section.)

- ✔ After you find a likely airline, check that airline's site to see whether it has any special Web-only deals. If a low-fare airline flies the route, be sure to check that one, too.

- ✔ Check prices on flights serving all nearby airports. An extra 45 minutes of driving time can save you hundreds of dollars.

- ✔ Check with a travel agent (by phone, e-mail, or the agent's Web site) to see whether he can beat the online price, and buy your tickets from the agent unless the online deal is better.

- ✔ For international tickets, do everything in this list, and check both online and with your agent for consolidator tickets, particularly if you don't qualify for the lowest published fare. For complex international trips, such as around the world, agents can invariably find routes and prices that the automated systems can't.

- ✔ If you bid on airline tickets at a travel auction Web site, make sure that you already know the price at which you can buy the ticket so that you don't bid more.

Before looking at online agents, check out ITA Software (www.itasoftware.com). This company produces the fare search engine used by Orbitz and many airline sites. ITA's own site has a version of it that just searches and doesn't try to sell you any tickets, with more search options than most of their clients offer.

If you hate flying or would rather take the train, Amtrak and Via Rail Canada offer online reservations (www.amtrak.com and www.viarail.ca). If you're visiting Europe, you can buy your Eurail Pass online at www.raileurope.com and your London-to-continent Chunnel tickets at www.eurostar.com.

Major airline ticket sites, other than individual airlines, include

- ✔ **Expedia** (www.expedia.com): Microsoft's entry into the travel biz, now a part of the Interactive media empire.

- ✔ **Hotwire** (www.hotwire.com): Multi-airline site offering discounted left-over tickets.

- ✔ **Orbitz** (www.orbitz.com): The high-tech entry into the travel biz, with most airlines' weekly Web specials.

- ✔ **Travelocity** (www.travelocity.com): Sabre's entry into the travel biz. Yahoo Travel and the AOL travel section are both Travelocity underneath.

Fare comparison sites abound, including Kayak (www.kayak.com), Yahoo FareChase (http://farechase.yahoo.com), Mobissimo (www.mobissimo.com), and Sidestep (www.sidestep.com). We don't find any of them comprehensive enough to depend on, but they're worth a look if you want to try to find that elusive last cheap seat.

More about online airlines

Because the online airline situation changes weekly, anything more we print here would be out of date before you read it. One of the authors of this book is an air-travel nerd in his spare time; to get his current list of online airline Web sites, Web specials, and online travel agents, visit http://airinfo.aero.

Even More Places to Shop

Here are a few other places for you to shop on the Web. We have even bought stuff from most of them.

Books, music, and more

You can't flip through the books in an online bookstore as easily as you can in person (although Amazon.com comes pretty close by offering a selection of pages from many books). However, if you know what you want, you can get good deals.

Here are some of the top sites:

- ✔ **Advanced Book Exchange** (www.abebooks.com): ABE offers the combined catalogs of thousands of secondhand booksellers. You pay the same as you would in the used bookshop (plus shipping, of course), and you save hours of searching. Whether you're looking for a favorite book from your childhood or a rare, first-edition *For Dummies* book, this site is worth visiting.

- **AddALL** (www.addall.com): AddALL is another good used-book site offering titles from thousands of used-book stores as well as a price comparison service for new books.

- **Amazon.com** (www.amazon.com): Amazon.com is one of the great online-commerce success stories, springing up from nothing (if you call several million dollars of seed money nothing) to one of the Net's biggest online stores. Amazon has an enormous catalog of books and CDs and a growing variety of other junk, much of which can get to you in a few days. It also has an affiliates program in which other Web sites can refer you to their favorite books for sale at Amazon, creating sort of a virtual virtual-book-store. For an example, see our Web site, at http://net.gurus.com, where we have links to Amazon for every book we have written in case, because of an oversight, you don't already have them all. Amazon sells most books at less than list price. It also has used books, DVDs, and just about everything else from pogo sticks to underwear.

- **Powell's Books** (www.powellbooks.com), the country's largest independent (non-chain) bookstore, has a correspondingly large Web site offering new and used books. We like its e-mail newsletter with new and rediscovered books and author interviews.

- **Barnesandnoble.com** (www.bn.com): Barnes & Noble is the biggest bookstore chain in the United States, and its online bookstore is big, complete, and well done. You can even return online purchases at any of its stores. It also has a large selection of music.

- **J&R Music World** (www.jr.com): The online presence of one of New York's largest music stores has a huge selection of music CDs. You can also buy a stereo to listen to your new CDs and a refrigerator to keep appropriate beverages at hand.

Clothes

This section points out a few familiar clothing merchants with online stores. Directories such as Open Directory Project (ODP) and Yahoo have hundreds of other stores both familiar and obscure:

- **Lands' End** (www.landsend.com): Most of this catalog is online, and you can order anything you find in any of its individual printed catalogs along with online-only discounted overstocks. It also has plenty of the folksy blather that encourages you to think of the company in terms of a few folks in the cornfields of Wisconsin rather than a corporate mail-order colossus belonging to Sears Roebuck. (It's both.) Moderately cool 3-D virtual models attempt to show what your new clothes look like on a cyborg with chunky hips, just like yours.

- ✔ **REI** (www.rei.com): This large sports-equipment and outdoor-wear co-op is headquartered in Seattle. Members get a small rebate on purchases. The whole catalog is online, and you can find occasional online specials and discounts.

- ✔ **Eddie Bauer** (www.eddiebauer.com) has way more stuff than is available in its stores. (John gave up on the stores about the third time they said "Oh, you have to order that from the Web site.")

- ✔ **The Gap** (www.gap.com): This site has the same stuff you find in the stores, but for people of unusual vertical or horizontal dimension, it also has jeans in sizes the stores don't stock.

Computers

When you're shopping for computer hardware online, be sure that the vendor you're considering offers both a good return policy (in case the computer doesn't work when it arrives) and a long warranty.

Here are a few well-known vendors:

- ✔ **Dell Computers** (www.dell.com): This site has an extensive catalog with online ordering and custom computer system configurations.

- ✔ **Apple Computer** (http://store.apple.com): The Apple site has lots of information about Macintosh computers, and now it offers online purchasing of iPods and iPhones, too.

- ✔ **CDW** (www.cdw.com): This site has a good selection of hardware and software, and we've found it to be reliable.

- ✔ **PC Connection and Mac Connection** (www.pcconnection.com and www.macconnection.com): For computer hardware, software, and accessories, PC and Mac Connection is one of the oldest and most reliable online sources. And you can get overnight delivery within the continental U.S. even if you order as late as 2 a.m.!

Auctions and used stuff

You can participate in online auctions of everything from computers and computer parts to antiques to vacation packages. Online auctions are like any other kind of auction in at least one respect: If you know what you're looking for and know what it's worth, you can get some great values; if you don't, you can easily overpay for junk. When someone swiped our car phone handset, at eBay we found an exact replacement phone for $31, rather than the $150 the manufacturer charged for just the handset.

Many auctions, notably eBay (as shown in Figure 10-3), also allow you to list your own stuff for sale, which can be a way to get rid of some of your house-hold clutter a little more discreetly than in a yard sale. The *PayPal* service (www.paypal.com), now owned by eBay, lets you accept credit card pay-ment from the highest bidder by e-mail. (See Chapter 11 for more information about PayPal.)

Figure 10-3:
You can find just about anything for sale on eBay.

Online auction sites include

- ✔ **eBay** (www.ebay.com): This auction site is the most popular one on the Web, and people flock there to sell all sorts of stuff, from baby clothes and toys to computer parts to cars to the occasional tropical island. You can sell stuff, too, by registering as a seller. eBay charges a small commission for auctions, which the seller pays. Searching the completed auctions at eBay is also a terrific way to find out how much something is worth — you can see what people actually end up paying for items. If you're thinking of selling that rare Beanie Baby, search the completed auctions for the bad news that it's worth slightly less than it was when it was new.

- ✔ **Half.com** (www.half.com): This division of eBay is more like a consign-ment shop than an auction. Sellers list used items they want to sell, such as books (including textbooks), CDs, movies, video games, electronic equipment, and trading cards, at a fixed price. eBay keeps saying that it'll merge this site into its main eBay site, but it never does.

- ✔ **Yahoo Auctions** (`http://auctions.yahoo.com`): eBay was such a big hit that Yahoo decided to hold auctions, too. Although it's less popular than eBay, sometimes that means fewer people bidding against you.

- ✔ **Priceline.com** (`www.priceline.com`): This site sells airline tickets, hotel rooms, rental cars, and a grab bag of other items. It's not exactly an auction; you specify a price for what you want, and Priceline accepts or rejects it. Or, if that's too scary, you can just pay the posted price.

Food

To show the range of edibles available online, here are some of our favorite places to point, click, and chow down:

- ✔ **Cabot Creamery** (`www.cabotcheese.com`): This site sells the best cheese in Vermont. (Don't tell anyone that a lot of the milk comes from New York.)

- ✔ **Bobolink Dairy** (`www.cowsoutside.com`): A recovering software nerd and his family in rural New Jersey make and sell their own cheese — a rich, gooey, French-style cheese. The URL refers to cows out in the pasture rather than tied up in the barn.

- ✔ **Gimme Coffee** (`www.gimmecoffee.com`): Highly opinionated coffee from the wilds of upstate New York. Online orders and lots of advice on what to do with your coffee after it arrives; follow the Gimme Locations link to find pictures of the place John goes when in need of literary inspiration, also known as *caffeine*.

- ✔ **Gaspar's** (`www.linguica.com`): If you weren't aware that Portuguese garlic sausage is one of the four basic food groups, this site will fix that problem. Oddly, online orders incur steep shipping charges, but phone or fax orders are shipped free, so we print and fax the order form. Also check out the competition at `www.fragozo.com`.

- ✔ **The Kitchen Link** (`www.kitchenlink.com`): Search this site for the perfect recipe and then shop for the ingredients.

- ✔ **Peapod** (`www.peapod.com`): Peapod lets you shop for groceries online and then delivers them to your home. You have to live in an area that the parent grocery chains serve, the northeast and the Chicago area. If you live somewhere else, Netgrocer (`www.netgrocer.com`) delivers nonperishables by rather pricey overnight express.

Chapter 11

Banking, Bill Paying, and Investing Online

....

In This Chapter

▶ Managing your checking and savings accounts online

▶ Looking at your credit card statements online

▶ E-mailing payments with PayPal

▶ Managing your investments online

....

*O*nce upon a time, money was substantial stuff that glinted in the sun and clinked when you dropped it on the table. Investments were engraved certificates that you kept in your safe-deposit box if they worked out, and used as bathroom wallpaper if not. Well, that was then. Now money and investments are mere electronic blips scampering from computer to computer, and if you do any banking or investing, one of the computers they scamper through might as well be yours.

You can do just about any banking online that doesn't require physically handling pieces of paper, which means everything except depositing checks and withdrawing cash. For those, you have to use an ATM or, for the truly retro, physically visit a bank branch and talk to a human being. But we help you avoid that last option as much as possible.

Going to the Bank Without Ever Leaving Home

Nearly every bank in the country now offers online banking. They don't do it to be cool; they do it because online banking is vastly cheaper for them than ATMs or tellers. Because both you and your bank have a strong interest in making sure that the person messing around online with your accounts is *you*, the signup process is usually a bit complicated — with the bank calling you to verify that you signed up, or mailing you a paper letter with your password.

After you're signed up, you visit the bank's Web site and log in with your new user name or number and password. Each bank's Web site is different, but they all show you an account statement along the lines of the one from John's bank, shown in Figure 11-1.

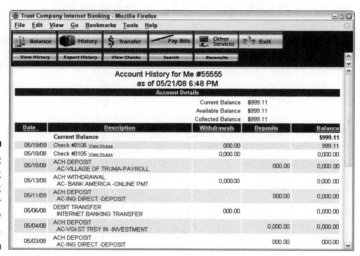

Figure 11-1:
A week
of bank
stuff, give or
take a few
details.

As you can see, deposits and withdrawals look like they do on a printed statement that you receive in the mail. If you click the View Image link next to a check number, it shows you a picture of the canceled check. The Automated Clearing House, or ACH, lines are described in a nearby sidebar.

If you use an accounting program like Quicken or Microsoft Money, banks invariably offer a way to download your account info into your program. Look for a link labeled Download or Export. In Figure 11-1, it's the small Export History button, near the upper left corner.

Details differ, but beyond the capability to check your statement, banks all offer roughly the same services, including transfers and bill paying.

Transferring money between bank accounts

If you have more than one account at a bank, a checking and savings account, some CDs, or a mortgage, you can usually move money from one account to another. In the account shown in Figure 11-1, the line that says "Internet

Banking Transfer" indicates that money has been transferred from the checking account to a mortgage account, to make the monthly mortgage payment. To get a better idea of how this works, here are the steps for transferring money from a checking account to a mortgage account (note again that the specific steps vary from bank to bank):

1. **Click the Transfer button (or whatever your bank's Web site calls it).**

2. **Enter the amount you want to transfer in the box labeled something like Amount.**

3. **Select the account that the transferred money is coming from, generally from a list of possible "From" accounts.**

4. **Select the account number that the transferred money is going to, generally from a list of possible "To" accounts.**

5. **Click the button labeled something like Transfer or Do It — it's done.**

ACH! It's better than a check!

For the past 150 years or so, the usual way to get money from one person's account at a bank to a second person's account at another bank has been for the first person to write a check and give it to the second person, who takes it to her bank and deposits it. (At least, that's the system in the U.S. — in Europe, the first person writes out a bank transfer and gives it to his bank to set up the payment.) Now that we're in the computer age, we have a high-tech replacement for this process: *Automated Clearing House (ACH)* transfers.

ACH transfers can do anything a check can do. Rather than print payroll checks, companies can use ACH to deposit the money directly into employees' bank accounts. The U.S. government uses ACH to make Social Security payments. You can use ACH to pay bills or to move money between accounts at different banks. For most purposes, ACH transactions are better than paper checks because they're faster and more reliable.

To identify the account to use for an ACH transfer, you need to provide the *routing number* that identifies the bank and the account number at that bank. The easiest way to find the routing number for your own checking account is to look at the line of funny-looking numbers printed along the bottom of one of your checks. The routing number consists of nine digits, usually printed at the left end of the line. The account number also appears on that line, and a check number (which ACH doesn't use) may appear, too. Savings accounts work for ACH transfers, too; to get the routing number, look at a check from the same bank or call the bank and ask.

You may be wondering "Can anyone who knows my account number suck money out of my account by using ACH?" Yes, but when you get your statement, you can challenge any bogus ACH transaction just as you can challenge a forged check and get your money back. In practice, ACH is safe and reliable, and we use it for our own accounts all the time.

It's that easy. Most banks handle transfers within the bank the same day; at John's bank you can enter a transfer as late as 7 p.m., which is handy when you remember at dinnertime that the mortgage is due today.

Many banks also let you make transfers to and from accounts at *other* banks, using ACH. To set up the transfers, you provide the other bank's routing code and account number. Depending on the bank, it may require a voided check from that account, verify that the account name is the same as your account name, or just believe the numbers you enter. After you set up a transfer, it's like a transfer within your own bank: You specify the accounts and the amount and then click. You can also transfer money between your bank and your mutual fund or brokerage account. In Figure 11-1, for example, the ACH deposits from ING DIRECT are from another bank, and the ACH deposit from VGI-ST TRSY is from a Vanguard mutual fund.

Transfers to other banks have two important differences: time and price. Even though the transfer is handled entirely electronically, it takes anywhere from two days to a week for the money to show up at the other end, depending on the other bank. The time it takes for any particular bank is pretty consistent, so if the transaction took three days last time, expect it to take three days next time. If you really need the money to be there so that you can write checks on it, allow a week, and keep an eye on your balances until you've done enough transfers to know how long they take.

The price for transfers varies from two bucks down to zero, with no consistency among banks. A transfer can be started from either the sending or receiving end; often, bank A charges you $1 if you tell it to *send* money to bank B, but if (instead) you tell bank B to *receive* the exact same money from bank A, it's free.

You can use PayPal to move money from just about any bank account to any other bank account for free. It's a handy, increasingly common way to do online transfers (and it's described later in this chapter).

Paying bills online

Writing checks is *so* twentieth century. Now you can pay most of your bills online. In many cases, you can arrange for automatic payments from your bank account for routine monthly bills. (In Figure 11-1, "Bank America" refers to the MasterCard bill.) We've arranged for payments for credit cards, the electric and gas companies, and mobile phones — a pretty typical mix. Each of these companies has its own procedure. We use a credit card example to show how this usually works. Figure 11-2 shows the online payment page at Capital One, a large credit card bank. When logged in to their Web site, you set up the payments by entering for your bank account the routing code and account number that ACH needs (see the preceding sidebar, "ACH! It's better than a check!"). After the payment info is set up, you visit the Web site, specify how much you want to pay, and the bill is paid from your bank account. Usually you get credit the same day, which is a big help to avoid paying credit card interest.

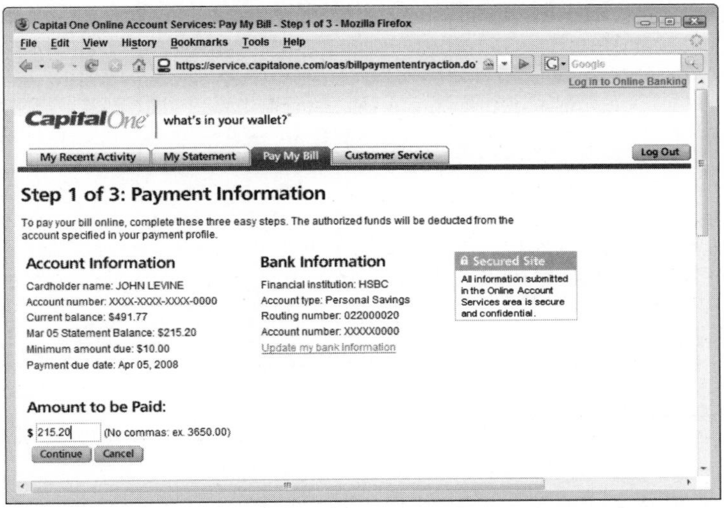

Figure 11-2:
Pay the credit card bill with one click.

If you want to automate all your bill paying, most banks can accommodate you with a *bill-pay* service. Most banks use one of a handful of specialized companies in this field. Usually you can choose from two levels of service: one only lets you pay bills from a list of about 300 large companies that want to send you your bill electronically; the other lets you pay anyone. Some banks provide bill pay for free, some charge, and some provide it for free as part of a package.

Figure 11-3 shows the bill payment service from John's bank. To set it up, you pick the companies to pay and then enter your account number and the name and address of the company if the bank doesn't already have it on file. Some bill-pay systems offer the option of *electronic presentment*, which means you get your bill on the Web rather than by paper mail. You also tell the system which bank account you want to pay the bills from. Then, to pay your bills each month, you just visit the bank's Web site and enter the amount to pay and the date. The bank automatically moves the money out of your account on that date.

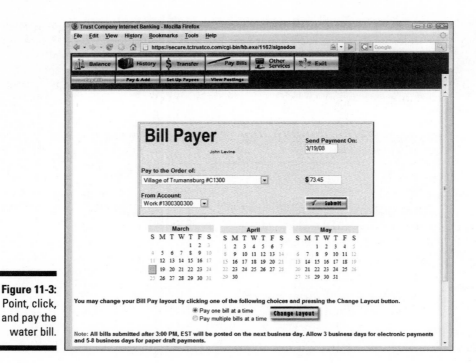

Figure 11-3:
Point, click,
and pay the
water bill.

If the payment service knows the payee's bank account info, it uses ACH to pay. Otherwise, the service prints an old-fashioned paper check and mails it.

Other online bank services

Because doing business over the Web is so much cheaper than doing it in person, banks are putting all sorts of other services online. Visit your bank's Web site to see what it offers. Among some of the services we've seen offered are

- ✔ Loan applications
- ✔ New accounts
- ✔ Retirement accounts
- ✔ Checkbook-balancing calculators

How safe are these banks, anyway?

When you open a bank account in person, you visit the bank and then look around to see that the bank looks like a bank, with tellers, people in suits, and a vault, which is good — or, you see a couple of people in a Winnebago with card tables and some money in cooler chests, which is bad. When you visit a bank's Web site, it's hard to tell a good one from a bad one. But it's not hard to do a little research.

Every real bank in the U.S. is a member of the Federal Deposit Insurance Corporation (FDIC). The FDIC has a nice-looking Web site at www.fdic.gov that has, among other things, detailed reports on each member bank. On the home page, click the Deposit Insurance link near the upper left corner, and then click Bank Find, at the top of the list. On that page, you can search by name or location. For example, to check out ING Bank, enter its full name (**ING bank, fsb**, as it says on its home page) and search. (For this particular bank, an alternative route to the same information is to click the FDIC icon on the bank's home page.) Either way, you see a reassuring page indicating that yes, it's insured. For more info, click Financial Information to see the bank's latest balance sheets. In this case, it says that the bank has $68 billion in assets and $5.7 billion in capital. Sounds like a bank to us.

Credit unions (joining one isn't a bad idea if you're eligible) are insured by the National Credit Union Association at www.ncua.gov. Click Credit Union Data in the pane down the left side of the screen, and then click the Find a Credit Union link near the middle of the page that appears.

A few recommended banks

These days, any bank you pass while driving down the street offers online banking, but some specialist banks do everything online. Although it is possible to do all your banking online, we prefer to have our main account at a local bank, where we can drop by and argue with the staff, and use an online bank for a high-interest savings account that you can't get at a local bank.

To give you a flavor of what's available, here are two banks we use and recommend:

- ✔ **HSBC Direct,** www.us.hsbc.com: A British bank that is, by some measures, the largest bank in the world.

- ✔ **ING Direct,** www.ingdirect.com: A large Dutch bank also with subsidiaries all over the world (not as large as HSBC, but still pretty big).

Both have U.S. subsidiaries that offer online accounts with better interest rates than most competitors and no minimum balances. HSBC has lots of physical offices, but for the high-interest online account, you have to sign up online. ING has an office in Wilmington, Delaware, that we walked past one time, but we didn't see any reason to go in.

To open an account at either bank, you fill out a form on its Web site, including the ACH info about your existing checking account to link to your new HSBC or ING account. After it's set up, you can move money back and forth between the accounts as needed. (Money you put into your ING account has to stay there for a week before you can get it back because the bank is chartered as a savings bank. HSBC's accounting limits you to six withdrawals each month.) Both also offer certificates of deposit, mortgages, home equity loans, and retirement accounts. HSBC is a full-service bank that offers free, no-minimum checking accounts and everything else a bank offers, all available online if you want it.

We've used both of these banks quite happily, but we give the nod to HSBC because it pays slightly more interest and gives you an ATM card you can use for withdrawals anywhere and deposits at HSBC branches. If you travel a lot, you pay no withdrawal fee at any HSBC machine anywhere in the world.

Combo banking

If you have an account with a stockbroker, such as the ones we list later in this chapter, it generally offers a check-writing option, which makes it act like a checking account, usually at very low cost. If you don't have a local bank you like, this option can be a good one.

Dealing with Credit Cards

Just about every credit card in the country offers online access for the same reason that bank accounts do — online transactions are a lot cheaper for them than if you call the 800 number.

Online credit card services start with applying for the card. Search Google for **credit cards**, and you find a phantasmagoria of offers. They change daily, but you can look for various goodies — no annual fee, bonuses and rebates, and low interest rates. Most of the sites that appear to compare cards are in fact selling one bank's cards, so treat their claims of unique and superior features with skepticism.

After you have your card, typical online conveniences include these:

- Check your balance and recent transactions.
- Pay your bill from your checking account.
- Apply for a credit line increase.
- Ask for copies of sales slips for charges you don't recognize, or challenge ones you think are bogus.
- Download account information into Quicken and other personal finance programs.
- Create single-use card numbers for online shopping. (Refer to Chapter 10.)

Different credit-card-issuing banks have somewhat different versions of these services, but it's difficult to compare them without getting the credit card first. For example, some banks let you set up automatic payments to pay each bill in full on the due date, getting the maximum use of your money without paying interest. At others, you have to visit their Web site each month to schedule the month's payment. Some have single-use card numbers, some don't. We would make a list of features, but it would be out of date before it was printed, so visit some bank Web sites to see what they're offering. (We compared two different banks in the tenth edition of this book, but then they merged, keeping the worst features of each. Sigh.)

Pay Your Pals with PayPal

Credit cards are easy to use — if you're *spending* money. Until recently, it has been all but impossible for individuals (rather than companies) to receive payments by credit card. Even small businesses found it expensive and time consuming to accept credit card payments. PayPal (www.paypal.com) has changed all that, and also provides an easy way to move money among accounts at different banks.

PayPal is a boon to individuals who sell at auction sites like eBay (which owns PayPal), but it has many other uses, too. PayPal makes it easy to start a small business on the Web: Small organizations can use PayPal to collect payments for events like dinners and amateur theater, nonprofits can accept donations, and it's just about the only way to make payments to individuals in other countries without paying a service charge larger than the amount you're paying.

If you plan to accept PayPal for your business, be sure to heed PayPal's warnings regarding shipping *only to verified buyer addresses.* Be sure to comply carefully with all the fine print to protect yourself against fraud. Most first-time sellers learn the hard way that it's they who pay the cost of fraud — and even the cost of their customers' innocent errors. PayPal's fraud rate is lower than that of most credit card fraud, but it's a case of *merchant beware* — know your customer and take appropriate steps to safeguard your transactions.

PayPal offers the following services, but you have to observe a few rules:

- ✔ To send money, you have to have a PayPal account. An account is easy (and free) to open.

- ✔ After you open an account, you can send money to anyone who can receive e-mail. If that person doesn't already have a PayPal account, she opens one when "cashing" your e-mail. The money you send can come from the balance in your PayPal account or from a bank account or credit card that you link to your PayPal account.

- ✔ After you have money in your account, you can use it to pay other people, move it to your linked bank account, or spend it with a debit card linked to your PayPal account.

- ✔ Individual accounts are free, but you can accept only small numbers of credit card payments. (There's a much higher limit on accepting payments sent from bank accounts, though.)

- ✔ Premier accounts have no such limit on accepting payments, but are charged a commission on each payment they receive.

The folks at PayPal encourage you to provide them with your bank account number so that when you pay somebody, PayPal can take the money directly. That way, they don't have to pay the credit card companies, and you can move any money you receive into your account with minimum hassle.

Be careful about giving your bank-account information to *anyone.* A variety of criminals send out huge numbers of notices, claiming to be from PayPal and claiming that you "must" provide them with your account number and password right away to clear up an account problem. Don't fall for it. PayPal will *never* ask you for your password or account information in an e-mail message — or anywhere other than on its Web site (at https://www.paypal.com). Help take a "byte" out of crime: Forward any such fraudulent e-mail to PayPal. Just go to the PayPal Web site and click the Security Center link.

When you first tell PayPal to link your account to a bank account, PayPal verifies your bank account number by making two random deposits of less than a dollar. You then have to tell PayPal the amount of the deposits to complete your registration. You can link several bank accounts to your PayPal account and then move money out of one account into PayPal, wait a few days for the transaction to be complete, and then move the money out of PayPal into a different account — all for free.

If you leave money in your PayPal account, it pays interest at a decent rate — but because PayPal is not a bank, your money is safer in your bank account. (Most U.S. bank accounts are insured, whereas PayPal accounts are not.) We recommend that you only leave money in PayPal that you're planning to use within a few days. If you're fortunate enough to need to keep a significant balance in an online account, ING Direct and HSBC (described earlier in the chapter) are real banks with deposit insurance and pay about the same as PayPal. Open an account at either, then link your PayPal account to your HSBC or ING Direct account, as well as to your main bank account.

Investing Your Money Online

If you invest in mutual funds or the stock market (something that's difficult to avoid these days unless you anticipate dying at an early age), you can find a remarkable range of resources online. An enormous amount of stock information is also available, providing Net users with research resources as good as professional analysts had before the advent of online investing.

The most important thing to remember about *all* online financial resources is that everyone has an ax to grind — and wants to get paid somehow. In most cases, the situation is straightforward; for example, a mutual fund manager wants you to invest with her funds, and a stockbroker wants you to buy and sell stocks with him. Some other sites are less obvious: Some are supported by advertising, and others push certain special kinds of investments. Just consider the source (and any vested interests they may have in mind) when you're considering that source's advice.

Mutual funds

Mutual funds are definitely the investment of the baby boomer generation. The world now has more mutual funds than it has stocks for the funds to buy. (Kind of makes you wonder, doesn't it?) Most fund managers have at least descriptions of the funds and prospectuses online, and many now provide online access so that you can check your account, move money from one fund to another within a fund group, and buy and sell funds — all with the money coming from and going to your bank account via ACH.

Well-known fund groups include

- ✔ **American Century:** A broad group of funds (www.american century.com)

- ✔ **Fidelity Investments:** The 500-pound gorilla of mutual funds; specializes in actively managed funds (www.fidelity.com)

- ✔ **Vanguard Group:** The other 500-pound gorilla; specializes in low-cost and index funds (www.vanguard.com)

Many online brokers listed in the following section also let you buy and sell mutual funds, although it almost always costs less if you deal directly with the fund manager. The Open Directory Project has a long list of funds and fund groups at http://dmoz.org/Business/Investing/Mutual_Funds.

Stockbrokers

Most well-known, full-service brokerage firms have jumped onto the Web, along with a new generation of low-cost online brokers that offer remarkably cheap stock trading. A trade that may cost $100 with a full-service firm can cost as little as $8 with a low-cost broker. The main difference is that the cheap firms don't offer investment advice and don't assign you to a specific broker. For people who do their own research and don't want advice from a broker, the low-cost firms work well. For people who need some advice, the partial- or full-service firms often offer lower-cost trades online, and they let you get a complete view of your account whenever you want. The number of extra services the brokerages offer (such as retirement accounts, dividend reinvestment, and automatic transfers to and from your checking account) varies widely.

Online brokers include

- ✔ **Charles Schwab,** www.schwab.com: The original discount broker offers somewhat more investment help than E-Trade and Smith Barney, but at a slightly higher price. Kathleen Sindell, the author of *Investing Online For Dummies* (Wiley) recommended them to us.

- ✔ **E-Trade,** www.etrade.com: This low-cost, no-advice broker also offers bank accounts, credit cards, boat loans, and just about every other financial service known to humankind.

- ✔ **Smith Barney,** www.smithbarney.com: This full-service broker offers online access to accounts and research info. It's a subsidiary of Citigroup, one of the largest banks in the world.

✔ **TD Ameritrade,** www.ameritrade.com: The low-cost, limited-advice broker, which is affiliated with Toronto-Dominion bank, is one of the largest Canadian banks. It has good online research tools and includes a checking account.

Most fund groups, including the ones in the preceding list, have brokerage departments — which can be a good choice if you want to hold both individual stocks and funds.

Portfolio tracking

Several services let you track your portfolio online. You enter the number of shares of each fund and stock you own, and the service can tell you — at any time — exactly how much they're worth and how much money you lost today. Some of them send by e-mail a daily portfolio report, if you want. These reports are handy if you have mutual funds from more than one group or both funds and stocks. All the tracking services are either supported by advertising or run by a brokerage that hopes to get your trading business:

✔ **My Yahoo:** (http://my.yahoo.com) You can enter multiple portfolios and customize your screens with related company and general news reports. You can also get lots of company and industry news, including some access to sites that otherwise require paid subscriptions. It's advertiser supported, comprehensive, and easy to use. We stock market junkies particularly like the streaming updates that continually update stock values in flickers of red (bad) and green (good).

✔ **Smart Money:** (www.smartmoney.com) The online face of *Smart Money* magazine lets you track portfolios and read news stories. Although the site really wants you to subscribe to the magazine, the free portfolio tracker isn't bad.

✔ **MSN MoneyCentral:** (http://moneycentral.msn.com) This service also has portfolios and lots of information, although we find it cumbersome to set up and more of a pain to use than My Yahoo. To use all its features, you have to use Internet Explorer.

Chapter 12

Swiping Files from the Net

. . . .

In This Chapter

▶ Using your Web browser to download files

▶ Sharing files with other Netizens

▶ Installing software you swiped from the Net

▶ Scanning downloaded files for purity and wholesomeness

▶ Text, graphics, audio, video, executable, and other types of files

. . . .

*T*he Internet is chock-full of computers, and those computers are chock-full of files. What's in those files? Programs, pictures, sounds, movies, documents, spreadsheets, recipes, *Anne of Green Gables* (the entire book and several of the sequels) — you name it. Some of the computers are set up so that you can copy some of the files they contain to your own computer, usually for free. In this chapter, we tell you how to find some of those files and how to copy and use them.

What Is Downloading?

Downloading means copying files from a computer Up There On The Internet "down" to the computer sitting on or under your desk. *Uploading* is the reverse — copying a file from your computer "up" to a computer on the Internet.

You probably won't be surprised to hear that you can download and upload files in three different ways:

✔ **Click a link on a Web page.** Web browsers can download files, too. In fact, they do it all time when they download Web pages so that you can see them.

✔ **Participate in a file sharing service.** Because these services are used to share material of dubious legality, which tends to install spyware on your computer, we don't recommend them. File-sharing services include LimeWire and BitTorrent.

✔ **Run a file transfer program.** *FTP* stands for File Transfer Protocol, an older (but still widely used) way that computers transfer files across the Internet.

You can also transfer files by attaching them to e-mail messages sent to other e-mail users, which we discuss in Chapter 13.

By far the easiest way to download files is by using your Web browser — clicking links is our favorite method of finding and downloading files.

How you download a file and what you do with it after you have it also depends on what's in the file. This chapter describes how to download pictures, programs, and other files. If you want to download music and video, refer to Chapter 9.

Downloading Pictures

To download a picture from the Web, follow these steps:

1. **Display the picture in your Web browser.**

2. **Right-click the picture.**

   A menu of commands appears. A small number of Web sites disable right-clicking pictures to prevent you from saving them. Oh, well!

3. **Choose Save Image As (in Firefox) or Save Picture As (in Internet Explorer).**

4. **In the Save Image or Save Picture dialog box that appears, tell your browser where to save the picture on your computer.**

   You can choose the folder where you want to put it and the filename to use.

5. **Click Save.**

That's all it takes!

Graphics files have special filename extensions that identify which graphics format the file is in. When you download a picture, you can change the name of the file, but *don't* change the extension. Common extensions are GIF, JPG, and TIF.

Art ain't free

As plentiful as art is on the Internet, consider this: Somebody had to work to create every one of those images. Some of the artists want to control what happens to their work, or even get paid for it. (What a concept.)

Just because a picture is on a Web page doesn't mean that no one owns it. Nearly all graphics on Web pages are copyrighted, and it's not legal to use the picture without getting permission from the copyright owner. No one will sue you for storing a picture on your computer (so far as we know — we're not lawyers) but don't plan on using downloaded graphics in your own Web site or publication without getting permission. Unless a picture comes from a site that specifically offers pictures as reusable *clip art* (art you can clip and use), you have to get permission to reuse the picture for most purposes — even to upload it to your own, noncommercial Web page.

To find clip art sources, search for **clip art** or **clipart** — and include a word or phrase describing what you need a picture of. Some of what you're shown is free, and some requires a subscription or payment per picture. We like www.clipart.com, which requires a subscription fee but offers a mountain of clip art and photos you can legally download and reuse.

Sharing pictures

We love sharing our family photos with other people, and the Web makes it easy. Also, sharing via the Web saves you the cost of making extra prints of your snapshots, and it's quick. Several Web sites enable you to upload your digital pictures to the site and share them with your friends and family. These photo-sharing sites make their money by selling prints — after your family sees that gorgeous shot of little Mary finger-painting with pudding, they'll *have* to have a copy for the fridge!

Here are a few good photo-sharing sites:

- **Kodak,** at www.kodakgallery.com: Formerly www.ofoto.com, it offers (not surprisingly) Kodak prints.

- **Picasa Web Albums,** at http://picasa.google.com: At this Google photo-sharing site, you can download and use (for free) its photo management program, Picasa.

- **Snapfish,** at www.snapfish.com: Hewlett-Packard now owns the site.

Downloading Programs

Lots of the programs that this book recommends can be downloaded from the Web, often for free. This section describes the process for downloading programs and getting them running.

The plan: Download, install, and run

When you download a program, you transfer a file from a computer on the Internet to your computer. But the program is still trapped inside the file — you usually need to take some additional steps to let it out. The file you download is usually an installation program, which you run to install the actual program. While you're at it, you'd be wise to scan the program for viruses before running it.

All these steps are described in the following pages — just keep reading!

Finding programs to download

The first step in downloading a program is to find it. In some cases, you already know the Web address where the file is available for download. For example, in Chapter 6 we recommend that you avoid Internet Explorer because it's a target for viruses and spyware. (Chapter 2 describes what we mean by viruses and spyware.) We suggest that you switch to Firefox, which is a free download from the Web site www.mozilla.com.

Free and not-quite-free-ware

Some software is free — it's freeware. *Freeware* is available for download for free with no strings attached. Firefox is freeware, as are many of the programs at www.tucows.com.

When the authors ask for a donation if you like the program — on the honor system — it's *shareware*. You can download and install the program for free (just like freeware), but if you keep using it, you should make a donation to the author. (If you don't, don't expect the program to be updated in the long run!) The site from which you download shareware should specify the

requested donation. You can usually also choose Help from the program's menu to find out how to make a donation.

Some downloaded programs are *trialware* or *crippleware*, which are time-limited or otherwise-limited versions of the program. You can use the downloaded program for free, but if you want the real, complete program, you need to pay for it. The program itself tells you its limitations, its price, and how to pay. Some programs don't limit their features, but they display ads unless you pay — a reasonable trade-off.

In other cases, you may hear about a program but not know where to find it. Google is your friend — search for the program's name and you will probably find its source.

Other good sources for downloadable programs are software libraries like these:

✔ Cnet's www.download.com and www.shareware.com are great sources for freeware and shareware. Includes recommendations and reviews.

✔ www.tucows.com (The Ultimate Collection Of Windows Software), now also includes Mac and Linux programs.

Downloading a file

Before you start downloading, make a folder to store all your downloaded files. In Windows, we make a folder in our My Documents folder, and we name it something like Downloaded Files or Downloads. (To create a folder in My Documents, launch Windows Explorer or My Computer, select the My Documents folder and choose File⇨New⇨Folder from the menu.)

Downloading a program file over the Web is easy: You click a link to it, frequently a link that says either Download or the name of the program. Your Web browser asks you what to do with the file. If it's a program (in Windows, a file with the extension .exe) or a ZIP file (with the extension .zip), the most reasonable thing for you to do is to save it to disk (in your Downloads folder) so that you can deal with it later.

If you're interested in downloading an Internet program, for example, you can go to TUCOWS, The Ultimate Collection of Windows (and Mac) Software, at www.tucows.com. After you're at the site, click links to choose the operating system you use, choose a site near you, and choose the type of programs you want to download. TUCOWS displays a list of programs available for downloading. Alternatively, type a program name into the Search box to find programs by that name. When you find the page about the program, you can download its program file; just click the name of the program or the Download Now button or another appropriate-sounding link.

Uncompressing and unzipping files

Most downloadable software on the Internet is in a compressed format to save both storage space on the server and transmission time when you download the file. Most software is *self-installing* — the file is (or contains) a program that does the necessary uncompressing and installing. Self-installing Windows files have the extension .exe or .msi, and non-self-installing compressed files have the extension .zip.

Our favorite downloaded program (aside from Firefox)

Google Desktop is a nifty freeware package that combines desktop search with desktop *gadgets*, little programs that sit on the side of your screen. The search automatically indexes all the files on your computer so that you can Google files on your own computer. The gadgets range from clocks and calendars to cricket scores and the current position of the International Space Station. Visit `http://desktop.google.com`, download it, and try it out. If you're running Vista, you have to confirm, as always, that you want to run the installation program as the administrator, and it asks whether to use Google's (rather than Microsoft's) gadget sidebar. Say yes — Google gadgets are better.

Viruses and spyware can be contained in `.exe` files, too, so don't run an executable file unless you're sure that you know what's in it! Stick with the software libraries we recommend in this chapter because they scan their files for viruses and spyware. Or, download programs directly from the software organization. (For example, get Firefox from `www.mozilla.com` and Google software from `http://google.com`.)

To install a self-installing file, just double-click the file to run it — and skip over to the later section "Installing the program." If a file is compressed, you need a program to open and uncompress it. Files with the file extension `.zip` identify compressed files (these files are called, amazingly, *ZIP files*). If you use Windows XP or Vista, the Compressed Folders feature pretends that ZIP files are folders, so you can open them directly in Windows Explorer windows. Just double-click the ZIP file to see what's inside it.

For older versions of Windows, programs such as WinZip (downloadable from `www.winzip.com`) can both unzip and zip things for you. (Mac users, see the nearby sidebar "Mac users say StuffIt.")

Mac users say StuffIt

Mac users can get programs named ZipIt, Unzip, or MindExpander from `www.macorchard.com`. The most popular is a shareware program, by Raymond Lau, known as StuffIt Expander. StuffIt comes in many flavors, including a shareware version and a commercial version from `www.stuffit.com`. StuffIt files of all varieties generally end with the extension `.sit`.

Scanning for Viruses

We warn you about viruses in Chapter 2 and encourage you to install a virus checker in Chapter 4. Chapter 14 describes how to configure your virus checker and how to tell your e-mail program not to run programs that you receive by e-mail. As you can tell, we take viruses seriously, and we think you should, too.

We all know that you practice safe software: You check every new program you get to make sure that it doesn't contain any hidden software viruses that may display obnoxious messages or trash your hard drive. If that's true of you (no fibbing, now), you can skip this section.

For the rest of you — make that all of us, these days — run a virus-scanning program at regular intervals and keep it updated. You never know what naughty piece of code you may otherwise unwittingly download to your defenseless computer!

Run your virus checker after you have obtained and run *any* new piece of software. Although the Web and FTP servers on the Internet make every effort to keep their software archives virus-free, nobody is perfect.

Installing the program

Okay, now you have the downloaded program file, and you know that it's safe to proceed. However, most downloaded programs are still trapped in an installation file — they aren't ready to use yet. For example, when you download Firefox, you get a file with a name like Firefox Setup 2.0.0.4.exe. (The .exe at the end tells you that it's a program; it's short for *exe*cutable.) That's not Firefox; it's the Firefox Setup program, which *contains* Firefox.

To install the program, double-click the name of the setup program in Windows Explorer or My Computer. The file should open itself and walk you through a wizard-style set of windows to collect any needed setup info — and then install itself. If you're using Vista, it pops up a box asking whether you want to become an administrator to do the installation. If you're sure that you trust the source of the program, click OK. The setup program probably creates an icon for the program on your desktop. In Windows, it may also add the program to your Start menu.

A small number of simple programs don't come with an installation program — you just get the program itself, and after it's unzipped, you need only run the program you extracted from the ZIP file. To make the program easy to run, you need an icon for it. You can create your own icon or menu item for the program. In Windows, follow these steps:

1. **Run either My Computer or Windows Explorer and select the program file (the file with the extension `.exe` or `.msi`).**

2. **Use your right mouse button to drag the filename out on the desktop or into an open folder on the desktop.**

   An icon for the program appears.

Another method is to choose Start⇨Programs or Start⇨All Programs, find the menu choice for the program, hold down the Shift key, drag the menu choice to the desktop, and release the Shift key. Windows copies the menu choice as an icon on the desktop.

To run your new program, you can just click or double-click the icon (depending on how you have Windows configured — try clicking first, and if nothing happens, double-click). Cool!

Configuring the program

Now you can run the program. Hooray! You may have to tell the program, however, about your Internet address or your computer or who-knows-what before it can do its job. Refer to the text files (if any) that came with the program — or choose Help from the program's menu bar — to get more information about how to configure and run your new program. The Web site from which you got the program may have some explanations, too.

Downloading Other Types of Files

If you want to download some other type of file — like a Word document, a spreadsheet, a database, or some other kind of file — you can use the same general steps:

1. **Find the file on the Web.**

   Search the Web for it, as described in Chapter 8.

Installing Mac programs

Like everything else on a Mac, installing software is pretty easy. Programs are packaged as .dmg files. Click the filename, and it opens like a little disk with a few files in it. One of those files is the program of interest, which you drag into the Finder's Application folder. That's it.

Then you can click the Eject button to close the .dmg file. Occasionally, the .dmg files are compressed as Zip or StuffIt files, which you first decompress (as described in the nearby sidebar "Mac users say StuffIt") and then open and drag, and then you're done.

2. **Follow the instructions on the Web page to download the file.**

   This step usually just means clicking a Download button.

3. **When your browser displays a Save or Save As dialog box, choose where to put the file.**

   If you have created a Downloads or Downloaded Files folder, put it there. Or, put it in the folder where you want the file to end up.

4. **Check the file for viruses.**

   See the section "Scanning for Viruses," earlier in this chapter, for details.

5. **Unzip the file if necessary.**

   If the file is large or you're downloading a group of files, the file or files may be compressed into a ZIP file. See the "Uncompressing and unzipping" section (earlier in this chapter) to find out how to uncompress the file.

6. **Open the file with its matching program.**

   If you downloaded a Word document, open it in Word. (Or, maybe Open Office, a nice freeware office suite you can download from www.open office.org.) If you aren't sure what kind of file you have or which program opens it, display the filename in My Computer or Windows Explorer and double-click the filename. If you have a program installed that can open the file, Windows should run the program and open the file automatically.

Your files are ready to use!

Downloading the old-fashioned way with FTP

Back before the Web was even invented, the Internet was up and running. (And yes, then-Senator Al Gore was a major player in getting the funding that made the Internet possible.) When you wanted to download a file, you used an FTP program — File Transfer Protocol. You needed to know the name of the server on which the file was stored and in which folder it was stored. If you want the retro FTP experience, see `http://net.gurus.com/ftp` for how FTP used to work — and still does.

Several Kinds of Files and What to Do with Them

The name of a file — in particular, its *extension* (the end of the name after the last period) — usually gives you a clue about the type of file it is. Although people usually try to be consistent and follow the conventions for filename extensions, file naming isn't a sure thing. Windows uses the extension to specify which program to use to open a file, so you may sometimes have to rename a file to an extension that will persuade Windows to use the right program. For example, if you double-click a file with the extension DOC, Windows runs Microsoft Word or WordPad (which are both associated with the DOC file extension) to open the file. If you rename a Word document to end with the extension GIF, Windows no longer knows that the file contains a document.

Hundreds of kinds of files exist, maybe thousands. Fortunately, they fall into some general categories:

- **Plain text:** Files that contain text, believe it or not, with no formatting codes. Text files contain readable text without any word-processor-style formatting codes. (What did you expect?) Sometimes, the text is human-readable text, such as the manuscript for the first edition of this book, which we typed into text files. Sometimes, the text is source code or data for computer programs. On PCs, text files usually have the file extension `.txt` (or no extension). You can look at these files by using Notepad, WordPad, or any word processor. Mac text files also often have the TXT file type. Read text files on a Macintosh with SimpleText, BBEdit Lite, or any word processor.

- **Executable:** Files you can execute, or run; in other words, programs. In Windows, these programs have the extension `.exe` or sometimes `.com`.

Executable programs are widely available for downloading for PCs and Macs. Executable files are specific to a kind of computer: A Mac executable file is useless on Windows and vice versa (unless you have special Mac software to run Windows programs, of course). Windows executable files have the file extension .exe. See the warnings about viruses earlier in this chapter before you run any of the files.

✔ **Compressed:** Archives, ZIP files, SIT files, and other compressed files, encoded in a special way that takes up less space but that can be decoded only by the corresponding *uncompressor.* Windows compressed files end with ZIP and appear as compressed folders. Mac compressed files are decoded with StuffIt.

✔ **Graphics:** High-quality digitized pictures; a large fraction of all the bits flying around the Internet is made up of them. About 99.44 percent of the pictures are purely for fun, games, and worse. We're sure that you're in the 0.56 percent of users who need the pictures for work. The most commonly used graphics formats on the Net are GIF, JPEG, and PNG. A nice feature of these file formats is that they do a pretty fair job of compression internally, as though they were prezipped. Dozens of commercial and shareware programs on PCs and Macs can read and write graphics files. Firefox and Internet Explorer can display them as well; just choose File⇨Open from the menu. The buttons and little pictures on Web pages are usually stored as GIF files, too.

✔ **Audio and video:** Files that contain pictures and sounds encoded in computer-readable form. Graphics files on Web pages are usually in GIF or JPEG format. Audio files can be in WAV (Windows audio), RAM (RealAudio), MP3 (music), WMA (Windows Media Player), or other formats. Video files contain digitized movies, in AVI, WMV, or MPEG format. Audio and video files — files that contain digitized sound and movies — can be found all over the Web, ranging from songs to radio shows to recorded books to full-length movies. For all kinds of music and video on the Web, refer to Chapter 9.

✔ **PDF:** Portable Document Format files (with the extension .pdf) are formatted documents, ready to view and print. The program that displays and prints PDF files is Acrobat Reader. If your computer doesn't already have it, you can download it from www.adobe.com/products/acrobat. Several free or cheap PDF creators are now available; we recommend Pdf995, at www.pdf995.com. You usually can't edit a PDF file, but when you print it, it looks great. The IRS offers tax forms as PDFs.

✔ **Formatted text documents:** Formatted text documents are frequently stored in Microsoft Word (DOC) or Rich Text Format (RTF) format. Unfortunately, different versions of Word store different types of DOC files; RTF is slightly more standard. OpenOffice Writer uses the extension .sxw.

Most word processing software can recognize a competitor's format and make a valiant effort to convert the format to something usable so that you aren't tempted to buy the other product. Windows comes with the WordPad program, which can open many Word documents.

✓ **Data:** Any other type of file. You can handle Excel (`.xls`) and PowerPoint (`.ppt`) files similarly, by opening them in the application.

Part IV
E-Mail, Chat, and Other Ways to Hang Out Online

The 5th Wave — By Rich Tennant

"You know, I liked you a whole lot more on the Internet."

In this part . . .

You've found out all about the Web, which is very, very slightly like TV because you're mostly looking at stuff that other people created. Now we turn to the part of the Internet that's very, very slightly like talking on the phone because you're talking (or typing) to other people. We start with e-mail, just about the oldest but still most useful Net service, for one-to-one conversations *and* discussions among larger e-mail communities. You'll find advice about how to use e-mail and how to keep safe from e-mail-borne spam and viruses. We finish with faster-paced modern alternatives, such as instant messages, online chat, and Internet phones.

Chapter 13

It's in the Mail: Sending and Receiving E-Mail

*E*lectronic mail, or *e-mail,* is without a doubt the most popular Internet service, even though it's one of the oldest and least glitzy. Although e-mail isn't as glitzy as the World Wide Web, more people use it. Every system on the Net supports some sort of mail service, which means that no matter what kind of computer you're using, if it's on the Internet, you can send and receive mail. Even some systems that aren't technically on the Internet — think cellphone or PDA (personal digital assistant, such as a Palm handheld or BlackBerry) — can do e-mail.

Regardless of which type of mail you're using, the basics of reading, sending, addressing, and filing mail work in pretty much the same way, so it's worth looking through this chapter even if you're not using any of the mail programs we describe here.

What's My Address?

Everyone with e-mail access to the Internet has at least one *e-mail address*, which is the cyberspace equivalent of a postal address or a phone number. When you send an e-mail message, you type the addresses of the recipients so that the computer knows where to send it.

Before you can do much mailing, you have to figure out your e-mail address so that you can give it to people who want to get in touch with you. You also have to figure out some of their addresses so that you can write to them. (If you have no friends or plan to send only anonymous hate mail, you can skip this section.)

E-mail addresses have two parts, separated by an @ (the *at* sign). The part before the @ is the *username* or *mailbox,* which is, roughly speaking, your personal name. The part after that is the *domain* where your mailbox is stored, usually the name of your Internet service provider (ISP), such as `aol.com` or `gurus.com`.

The username part

Your *username* is the name your ISP assigns to your account. If you're lucky, you get to choose your username; in other cases, ISPs standardize usernames, and you get what you get. You may choose (or be assigned) your first name as your username — or your last name, your initials, your first name and last initial, your first initial and last name, or a completely made-up name. Over the years, for example, John has had the usernames `john`, `john1`, `jrl`, `jlevine`, `jlevine3` (must have been at least three `jlevines` there), and even `q0246`; Margy tries to stick with `margy` but has ended up with `margyl` or `73727,2305` on occasion. A few ISPs assign names such as `usd31516`. (Ugh.)

For example, you can write to the president of the United States at `president@whitehouse.gov`. The president's username is `president`, and the domain that stores his mailbox is `whitehouse.gov` — reasonable enough.

Back when many fewer e-mail users were around and most users of any particular system knew each other directly, figuring out who had what username wasn't all that difficult. These days, many organizations assign usernames in a consistent format for all users, most often by using your first and last names with a dot (.) between them, or your first initial followed by the first seven letters of your last name. In these schemes, your username may be something like `elvis.presley@bluesuede.org` or `epresley@bluesuede.org`. (If your name isn't Elvis Presley, adjust this example suitably. On the other hand, if your name *is* Elvis Presley, please contact us immediately. We know some people who are looking for you.)

The domain part

A domain name for an ISP in the U.S. usually ends with a dot and a two- or three-letter code (which is the *top-level domain,* or TLD) that gives you a clue to what kind of outfit owns the domain name. The following list briefly explains which type of organization owns domains with which TLD codes:

- **Commercial organizations** typically own domain names ending in `.com`, which includes providers such as America Online (AOL) and MSN and also many companies that aren't public providers but that are commercial entities, such as `www.aa.com` (AMR Corporation, better known as American Airlines), `www.greattapes.com` (Margy's online video store), and `www.taugh.com` (John's hard-to-pronounce Taughannock Networks).

- **U.S. colleges and universities** typically own domain names ending in `.edu` (such as `www.yale.edu`).

- **Networking organizations** typically end with `.net`. These include both ISPs and companies that provide network services.

- **Government organizations** in the U.S. typically own domain names ending in `.gov`. For example, the National Do Not Call Registry, run by the Federal Trade Commission, is at `http://donotcall.gov`.

- **U.S. military organizations** typically own domain names ending in `.mil`.

- **Nonprofits** and **special interest groups** typically own domain names ending in `.org`. For example, the Unitarian Universalist Association (where Margy works) is at `uua.org`.

- **Organizations in specific countries** frequently own domain names ending in a two-letter country code, such as `.fr` for France or `.zm` for Zambia. See our Web site (at `http://net.gurus.com/countries`) for a listing of country TLD codes. Small businesses, local governments, and K-12 schools in the U.S. usually end with the two-letter state abbreviation followed by `.us` (such as John's community Web site at `www.trumansburg.ny.us`).

Where is your mailbox?

When you sign up with an ISP, the provider creates a mailbox for each of your usernames. Although some ISPs offer only one username with each Internet account, many ISPs offer up to five mailboxes with five different usernames for a single account so that each person in your family can have a mailbox. These mailboxes usually live on your ISP's mail server.

Who makes up these TLDs?

An international group (the Internet Corporation for Assigned Names and Numbers, or ICANN, at `http://icann.org`) is in charge of TLDs. In 1997, ICANN proposed adding some extra, generic domains, such as `.firm`, `.arts`, and `.web`. After a lengthy detour through a maze of international intellectual-property politics, the first new domains (`.biz` and `.info`) appeared in 2001. The result is confusion that practically guarantees that, more often than not, `whatever.biz` and `whatever.info` are owned by the same group that owns `whatever.com`, and when they're owned by someone else, they're usually sleazy knockoffs. ICANN has since added these domain extensions:

✔ `.name`: Personal vanity domains

✔ `.pro`: Licensed professional doctors, lawyers, and accountants

✔ `.coop`: Co-ops

✔ `.museum`: Museums

✔ `.aero`: Air travel

✔ `.jobs`: Job offers

✔ `.travel`: Travel in general

✔ `.mobi`: For people using cellphones and other mobile devices

✔ `.asia`: For people in Asia

✔ `.cat`: For people in Catalonia (that's where Barcelona is)

✔ `.tel`: An online directory for Internet telephone users

None is widely used, although `.mobi` has a reasonable chance of success because of enthusiastic support from mobile phone companies.

If you don't have an ISP (say, you connect from the public library), all is not lost. Many Web sites provide free mailboxes for you to use — try Hotmail at `www.hotmail.com` or Yahoo Mail at `http://mail.yahoo.com`. Google offers Gmail, its own free mail service, at `www.gmail.com`, which offers giant multigigabyte mailboxes with Google Search to find stuff in your old mail.

Putting it all together

Whenever you set up a mail program, you need to enter information about your e-mail mailbox. People switch mail programs from time to time (new versions often come out with swell new features), so write in Table 13-1 your e-mail address and other info that your ISP provided when you set up your account (and fold down the corner of this page so that you can find it again later). Capitalization never matters in domains and rarely matters in mailbox names. To make it easy on your eyes, therefore, most domain and mailbox names in this book are shown in lowercase. (Don't worry about the parts of the table you don't understand right away — we explain later in this chapter what *servers* are.)

TIP

Whaddaya mean you don't know your own address?

It happens frequently — you know the e-mail address you requested for your new account, but you're not absolutely positive that you got it. Before you give out your address to everyone you know, test it out by sending a message to a friend or two. Tell them to reply to your message when they receive it and to let you know which address your message came from. Or, send yourself a message and use your e-mail login name as the mailbox name. Then examine the return address on the message.

Better yet, send a message to *The Internet For Dummies* Mail Central, at `internet11 @gurus.com`, and a friendly robot will send back a message with your address. (While you're at it, tell us whether you like this book, because we authors read that mail and write back when time permits.) If you're planning on testing your e-mail repeatedly and don't care whether we read your message, send it to `test@gurus.com`.

Table 13-1	Information Your E-Mail Program Needs to Know	
	Description	*Example*
Your e-mail address	Your username followed by an @ and the domain name.	`internet11@ gurus.com`
Your e-mail password	The password for your e-mail mailbox (usually the same as the password for your account).	`dum3my`
Your incoming (POP3 or IMAP) mail server	The name of the computer that receives your e-mail messages. (Get this name from your ISP; skip it if you use Web-based mail or AOL.)	`email.gurus.com`
Is your incoming mail server POP3 or IMAP? __ POP __ IMAP __ Web mail __ AOL	Which protocol your server uses, and which your e-mail program needs to use to get your mail. Doesn't apply to Web mail or AOL.	
Your outgoing (SMTP) mail server	The name of the computer that distributes your outgoing mail to the rest of the Internet (often the same as the POP3 or IMAP server). Doesn't apply to Web mail or AOL.	`smtp.gurus.com`

My Mail Is Where?

If you use a regular mail program to read your e-mail, one of the things you have to set in your mail program is the *incoming mail server,* which holds your mail until your mail program picks it up. (AOL and Web mail users can skim this section.)

The usual way to pick up the mail is known as POP (Post Office Protocol). If you have broadband, you'll like the IMAP alternative, described in a nearby sidebar. To send mail, your e-mail program reverses the process and sends mail to your *outgoing mail server* (or *SMTP server,* for the badly misnamed Simple Mail Transfer Protocol).

Write the names of your incoming (POP3 or IMAP) and outgoing (SMTP) mail servers in Table 13-1. If you don't know what to write, ask your ISP or whatever organization hosts your e-mail mailbox. With luck, your mail program has the server names set automatically, but when the setup gets screwed up, you'll be glad that you know how to restore the settings.

If you use AOL as your ISP, you get a bunch of mailboxes as part of the service. AOL has its own mail system, so AOL users don't use POP, IMAP, or SMTP servers when they're using AOL's own software. However, AOL provides an IMAP server (`imap.aol.com`) in case you want to use some other e-mail program. MSN uses Hotmail for its mail system, so it doesn't do POP, IMAP, or SMTP either. Yahoo Mail provides Web-based accounts, but if you sign up for its premium service at $20 per year, it also provides a POP server in case you want to use an e-mail program rather than your browser to read your mail. Gmail provides POP access to all its Web mail users.

IMAP: Mail anywhere and everywhere

When you use POP to pick up your mail, the messages are downloaded to your PC and stored there, and are deleted from your mailbox on the mail server. If, like most people, you build up large files of saved messages, the saved messages are on your PC and accessible only from your mail program on that PC. Often that's good enough, but if you read your mail in more than one place (say, at home and at work), it can be a pain if you're one place and the saved message with a crucial work-related item (a recipe for Killer Tequila Nachos, for example) is in the other. IMAP solves this problem by storing all your mail on a mail server so that you can access it from any mail program, and you have the same set of mailboxes no matter which computer you use.

To use IMAP, you need a broadband connection at each of the places you read your mail, because IMAP is rather sluggish on dialup, and your mail provider has to offer IMAP service. Because all your mail folders are on your ISP's computer, see how much mail they let you store there because folders can get pretty big. One or two megabytes is pretty tight, whereas 100 megabytes should be plenty unless you mail around a lot of video files.

After your mail program sends a piece of e-mail to the outgoing mail server, you can't cancel it! (Note to AOL users: When you send a message to another AOL address, rather than over the Internet, you can cancel the message up until the moment that the other AOL user opens and reads it.)

Pick an E-Mail Program, Any Program

It's time for some hand-to-hand combat with your e-mail program — the program that reads and writes electronic-mail messages. The bad news is that countless slightly different and slightly incompatible e-mail programs exist. (So many of them exist that none of us felt up to the task of counting them.) You've got your freeware, you've got your shareware and your commercial stuff, and even more programs probably came with your computer. They all do more or less the same thing; they're all e-mail programs, after all.

E-mail programs of the world

Here's a quick rundown of types of e-mail accounts and the programs you can use with each:

- **Windows PC or Mac with a dialup or broadband Internet account:** You can use any of a long list of e-mail programs, including Thunderbird, Outlook, Outlook Express, Windows Mail, Eudora, Mail.app, and Entourage. See the later section "Setting Up Your E-Mail Program" for advice on choosing one and setting it up.

- **Corporate account:** If you use e-mail at work, your organization may use a different type of mail server: Microsoft Exchange. In addition to providing mail services, Exchange also provides shared calendars, to-do lists, and other nifty features. The most popular program that works with all Exchange features is Microsoft Outlook, so your organization probably insists that you use it, despite its security flaws. Outlook works somewhat like Outlook Express, which is described in the next section. To read about Outlook, get *Outlook 2007 For Dummies*, by Bill Dyszel (Wiley). IBM Lotus Notes is the main competitor to Exchange, with its own set of fancy features.

- **Web mail:** Many Web sites offer free e-mail accounts that you can access using your browser. The best known are Hotmail at www.hotmail.com, Yahoo Mail at http://mail.yahoo.com, Google's Gmail at http://gmail.google.com, and the newer AIM Mail (http://mail.aim.com). You use your browser to read and send mail. (Refer to Chapter 7 if you need help using a browser.)

✔ **America Online:** At long last, AOL now provides an IMAP server, so you can use standard mail programs to read your AOL mail! You now have three options for managing mail sent through AOL servers:

- *The AOL e-mail program:* Most AOL users read and send e-mail from the same AOL program that they use to connect to their account. Click the Read icon on the toolbar or any little mailbox icon you can find.

- *Another e-mail program:* You can use any Windows or Mac e-mail program that handles IMAP. These e-mail programs tend to have better features for reading and filing messages. We recommend that you use Thunderbird, which we describe later in this chapter.

- *Your Web browser:* Your third option is to do mail from the AOL Web site at www.aol.com, which has the advantage that you can use any Web browser from any computer.

Please don't call it a CrackBerry

One of the best innovations in e-mail, or the worst, depending on your point of view, is the *BlackBerry.* It's a combined mobile phone and e-mail device. Grown people in business suits nervously punch the Check Mail button every few seconds like trained lab rats, and when the entire BlackBerry system failed for a day in April 2007, you could hear the screams clear from the Arctic Circle to the Rio Grande.

On the other hand, if you really need to stay in touch every minute of every day, a BlackBerry is helpful. It can have its own e-mail address, or more often it gets copies of the same mail sent to your regular computer at work. You can read and send mail very much like you do on a regular computer, and with a little practice, you can get surprisingly efficient on the teensy keys and small screen.

None of us has a BlackBerry because the monthly charge is fairly high, we don't have an employer who pays the bill, and we don't really want to be *that* available. We do have mobile phones, and on mobiles that support SMS text messaging (all of them, these days), it's generally possible for people who know your phone number to send short e-mail messages that arrive as text messages on the phone. (Ask your mobile carrier what your phone's e-mail address is, and ask any teenager how to send and receive text messages.) SMS is too skimpy to do financial negotiations like they do on the BlackBerry, but for a quick note telling someone that a meeting has been moved or to ask a spouse to pick up a box of Cheez-It crackers on the way home, it's plenty and you pay only the regular text messaging price.

You can use your browser for e-mail

Even if you normally use an e-mail program like Thunderbird or Outlook Express to read your messages, check whether your ISP or other mailbox provider has a Web-based mail system. With a Web mail system, you can read your mail from any computer on the Internet, including computers at your friends' houses, public libraries, and Internet cafés. For example, if you have an account with EarthLink, you can use its Web site to read and send messages at any computer on the Net; go to `http://earthlink.net` and click the Web Mail link.

To find out whether your ISP provides Web mail, go to its Web site and look around or write to its support e-mail address. Most ISPs have a Web Mail or similar link on their home pages. You log in with the same mailbox name and password that you may have jotted down in Table 13-1.

Setting Up Your E-Mail Program

After you understand what an e-mail program is supposed to do, it's much easier to figure out how to make a specific e-mail program do what you want. We picked the two most popular e-mail programs to show you the ropes:

- **Thunderbird:** The people who created Firefox, the Web browser we describe in Chapter 7, have also written the excellent, free e-mail program Thunderbird. It works with regular Internet accounts as well as with AOL accounts. Refer to Chapter 12 to find out how to get hold of Thunderbird.

- **Outlook Express, and Windows Mail:** Windows 2000 and XP come with some version of *Outlook Express*, Microsoft's free e-mail program, which Vista renames to *Windows Mail*. We describe Outlook Express 6.0 for Windows XP and Windows Mail for Windows Vista. *Note:* Despite the similar name, Outlook Express is unrelated to Outlook 97, 98, 2000, XP, 2003, or 2007; those full-featured commercial programs are included in various versions of the Microsoft Office package.

To round out our discussion, we also describe a Web-based mail system, Yahoo Mail, which is on the Web at `http://mail.yahoo.com`. Microsoft Hotmail (`www.hotmail.com`), Google's Gmail (`www.gmail.com`), and AIM Mail (`http://mail.aim.com`) are similar. Our instructions for Yahoo Mail have to be a bit vague because (like all Web sites) they redesign it regularly.

Before you can use your e-mail program, you need to tell it two things:

- ✔ **Where your mailbox is stored** (usually on a mail server at your ISP)
- ✔ **Where to send outgoing mail** (usually to the same or another mail server at your ISP)

For Yahoo Mail and other Web-based e-mail servers, you create a mailbox for yourself, but you don't have to enter information about your mail server. Web-based e-mail already knows! Follow the instructions in the following sections to get up and running. Later sections describe how to send and receive mail by using each program.

Setting up Thunderbird

The Mozilla Foundation, which creates free, open-source software, has written Thunderbird to complement its excellent Firefox browser. Mozilla Foundation also offers the *Mozilla* browser, which combines a browser like Firefox, an e-mail program like Thunderbird, and a Web editor that's described in Chapter 18. AOL's version of Mozilla, Netscape 8, combines versions of these same programs. This section describes Thunderbird, but Mozilla Mail and Netscape 8 Mail work the same way.

Chapter 12 describes how to download and install programs; follow its procedures to download and install Thunderbird from www.mozilla.com.

 Start Thunderbird by clicking the desktop icon or choosing Start➪All Programs➪Mozilla Thunderbird➪Mozilla Thunderbird. If you use Mozilla or Netscape and have the mail module of the program installed, you can switch from the browser window to the mail window (which is very similar to the one in Thunderbird) by choosing Window➪Mail & Newsgroups. The first time you run Thunderbird, the Account Wizard runs, asking for your name, the type of e-mail account you have (POP or IMAP), your e-mail address, and your mail servers (incoming and outgoing), as described in the section "My Mail Is Where?" earlier in this chapter.

If you need to change your e-mail account information later or set up Thunderbird to work with a different e-mail account, choose Tools➪Account Settings. To run the Account Wizard again, click New Account. To change the settings for an existing account, choose the account, click the categories of settings below the account name, and change the settings that appear. Type your name, e-mail address, incoming mail server, and outgoing server, copying the information from Table 13-1. When you're done, you see your new account in the Account Settings window, which you can close.

The Thunderbird window looks like Figure 13-1. A list of your mailboxes (mail folders) appears in the upper left corner. To the right is a list of the messages in that mailbox and the text of the selected message.

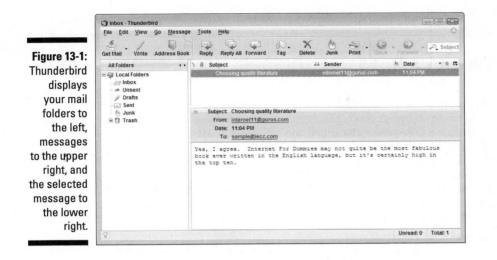

Figure 13-1:
Thunderbird
displays
your mail
folders to
the left,
messages
to the upper
right, and
the selected
message to
the lower
right.

If more than one person will use Thunderbird on the same account on one computer, each can have his or her own setup so that everyone can read his or her own mail rather than each other's. Choose Start➪All Programs➪ Mozilla Thunderbird➪Profile Manager to create a new profile for each person. If your computer runs Windows XP or Vista or you have a Mac and you give people separate accounts, each account has its own Thunderbird profile automatically.

Setting up Outlook Express

If you have Windows XP, you don't have to install Outlook Express — it's just there. In fact, we don't know of any way to truly get rid of it. (Microsoft claims that Internet Explorer is an integral part of Windows, and maybe Microsoft is getting ready to make the same claim about Outlook Express.)

To run Outlook Express in Windows XP: Choose Start➪E-mail Outlook Express, or Start➪All Programs➪Outlook Express. Or, double-click the Outlook Express icon on your desktop. (It's an envelope with blue arrows around it.) In earlier versions of Windows, the menu entry moved around a lot, on menus named Internet Programs and the like, so it's easier just to click the icon on your desktop.

The first time you run Outlook Express, the Internet Connection Wizard wakes up and asks some questions: Most of the answers you should already have written in Table 13-1. When prompted, type your name, your e-mail address, your incoming (POP or IMAP) mail server, your outgoing (SMTP) mail server, your username, and your password. Click Next after filling in the information that the wizard requests, and then click Finish when the wizard says that you can leave.

Outlook Express and Outlook: Point, click, uh-oh

Outlook Express and Windows Mail (because Microsoft includes them with Windows) and Outlook (because it comes with Microsoft Office) are slowly taking over the world of e-mail programs. Both for that reason and because a new security flaw is discovered about once a week, many viruses specifically target Outlook Express and Windows Mail. If you use them, you need to take a few precautions to protect yourself:

✔ **Never open an attachment or run a program that someone sends you, even if you know the sender.** Open an attachment only after you inquire whether the sender *meant* to send you the attachment. A virus often spreads when you open an infected message that contains a program that then launches itself and sends infected messages to everybody in your e-mail address book — all without your knowing it. If you get e-mail from someone you don't know, you should delete it without ever opening it.

✔ **Check the Microsoft Web site frequently (say, once a week) for security reports.** Go to windowsupdate.microsoft.com

for the latest security updates, including *patches* (corrections) for Outlook Express or Windows Mail and Internet Explorer. You have to use Internet Explorer to view this Web site because the site and the program are both from Microsoft. Be sure to download and install all security updates in the Critical Updates section. If you have Automatic Updates turned on in Windows XP or Vista, most updates are installed for you automatically.

✔ **Tell Outlook Express or Windows Mail to be careful.** If you don't expect to receive attached files, choose Tools⇨Options, click the Security tab, and select the Do Not Allow Attachments to Be Saved or Opened That Could Potentially Be a Virus check box. (Maybe Microsoft needs to run its check box names through the grammar checker!) Also select the Warn Me When Other Applications Try to Send Mail As Me check box — this setting may prevent a virus from surreptitiously spreading itself.

Better yet, switch to a safer e-mail program

At long last, you see the Outlook Express window, as shown in Figure 13-2. The layout is similar to Thunderbird's, displaying the Folders and Contacts lists, a message list, and the selected message.

If you need to add or change your e-mail accounts later, choose Tools⇨ Accounts from the Outlook Express menu. Click the Mail tab if it's not already selected. You can edit an account by clicking it and clicking the Properties button. Add an e-mail account (mailbox) by clicking the Add button.

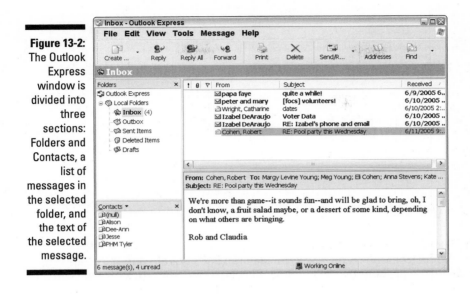

Figure 13-2:
The Outlook
Express
window is
divided into
three
sections:
Folders and
Contacts, a
list of
messages in
the selected
folder, and
the text of
the selected
message.

Setting up Windows Mail

The mail program that comes with Windows Vista is Windows Mail, but it looks a lot like Outlook Express.

To run Windows Mail, click Start@–>Windows Mail, or click the Windows Mail icon. The first time you run it, the Internet Connection Wizard wakes up and asks some questions: Most of the answers you should already have written in Table 13-1. When prompted, type your name, your e-mail address, your incoming (POP or IMAP) mail server, your outgoing (SMTP) mail server, your username, and your password. Click Next after filling in the information that the wizard requests, and then click Finish when the Wizard says that you may leave.

When you finish, you see the Windows Mail window, as shown in Figure 13-3. The layout is similar to Outlook Express's, displaying the Folders and Contacts lists, a message list, and the selected message.

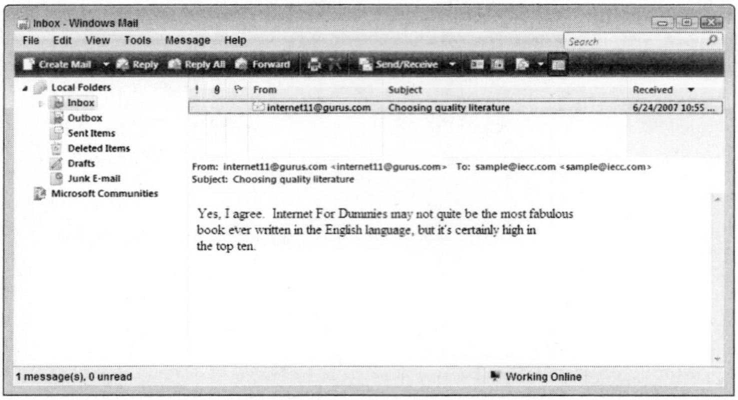

Figure 13-3:
The Windows Mail window has the three familiar sections.

If you need to add or change your e-mail accounts later, choose Tools⇨ Accounts from the menu. Click the Mail tab if it's not already selected. You can edit an account by clicking it and clicking the Properties button. Add an e-mail account (mailbox) by clicking the Add button.

Using Hotmail, Yahoo Mail, Gmail, AIM Mail, or other Web mail

Years ago, some genius had the idea of creating a Web site where you can sign up for an e-mail account and then log in to read and send messages. Your e-mail mailbox lives on the Web site's mail servers, and you use your browser, rather than a regular e-mail program, to read and send messages. The first such *Web mail* system was Hotmail (at www.hotmail.com, later bought by Microsoft). Other popular Web mail systems are Yahoo Mail (at http://mail.yahoo.com), AIM Mail (at http://mail.aim.com) and Google Mail, or Gmail (at www.gmail.com).

Yahoo Mail is our favorite Web-based mail service because of its wide range of features. (AIM Mail has good spam-blocking, though.) After you set up a free Yahoo ID, you get a mailbox, a Web site at http://geocities.com, an ID you can use when buying and selling in Yahoo's online stores and auctions, and access to a jillion other Yahoo services, from online games to a community advice area. Your Yahoo ID works when using Yahoo Messenger for instant messages, voice conferences, or videoconferences (see Chapter 16). The exact services (as well as the exact instructions for setting up and using a Yahoo Mail mailbox) vary from week to week because the Yahoo people change their Web site, but we can give you a general idea. Currently, the account is free as long as you check your mail at least every four months and as long as you don't mind using your browser to read your mail. If you sign up for a paid account, you get extra bells and whistles, including the ability to use an e-mail program to access your messages.

Hotmail, Gmail, and AIM Mail work similarly to Yahoo Mail: Just read their Web sites for instructions. If you have an account with an ISP that also provides Web mail, these instructions should give you a general idea of how the Web site works for sending and receiving messages.

To set up a Yahoo Mail mailbox, sign up for a Yahoo ID. (Don't worry: It's free). Two steps do the job:

1. **Go to** www.yahoo.com **and click the Mail icon.**

   Alternatively, you can go straight to http://mail.yahoo.com. You see links for signing in if you already have a Yahoo ID as well as a Sign Up Now link.

2. **Click the Sign Up Now link and fill in the forms with information about yourself.**

   They don't ask anything too nosy. Be sure to click the links to read the *terms of service* (rules of the game) and *privacy policy* (what they plan to do with the information you give them).

   In Table 13-1, you need to write only your e-mail address, which is your Yahoo ID followed by @yahoo.com. You don't need to fill in any other information. You're ready!

To access your Yahoo Mail mailbox, go to the Web site and log in:

1. **Go to** http://mail.yahoo.com.

   Or, click the Mail icon at www.yahoo.com.

2. **Sign in with your new Yahoo ID and password.**

   You see a Web page with links for sending (Compose) and reading (Check Mail) e-mail, as shown in Figure 13-4.

A cool thing about Web mail systems like Yahoo Mail, Gmail, AIM Mail, and Hotmail is that you can read and send messages from any computer on the Net. Your mailbox is stored on Yahoo's mail servers, and any computer with a Web browser can access it. Of course, no one can read your messages, or send messages as you, without typing your password. In this chapter and the next two, when we tell you how to send and receive mail with Yahoo Mail, keep in mind that you don't have to be at your own computer — you can check your mail from a friend's computer or from the computer at the public library. One downside is that reading and sending messages tends to be slower with Web mail than with an e-mail program because you have to wait for a new Web page to arrive every time you click a new message.

Figure 13-4:
Reading
mail in
Yahoo Mail.

Sending Mail Is Easy

Sending mail (whether through an e-mail program or through Web-based e-mail) is easy enough that we show you a few examples rather than waste time explaining the theory.

CC and BCC

The term *carbon copy* should be familiar to those of you who were born before 1960 and remember the ancient practice of putting sheets of carbon-coated paper between sheets of regular paper to make extra copies when using a typewriter. (Please don't ask us what a typewriter is.) In e-mail, a *carbon copy* is simply a copy of the message you send. All recipients, on both the To and CC lines, see who's getting the message — unless a recipient's e-mail address is typed in the BCC field instead. *Blind carbon copies* (BCCs) are copies sent to people without putting their names on the message so that the other recipients are none the wiser. You can figure out why you may want to send a copy to someone but not want everyone to know that you sent it

Sending e-mail with Thunderbird

Here's how to send an e-mail message by using Thunderbird:

1. **In Thunderbird, click the Write icon on the toolbar or press Ctrl+M.**

   Another window (the Compose window) opens with a blank message.

2. **Fill in the recipient's address (or recipients' addresses) in the To box.**

   If you want to send the same message to more than one person at a time, press Enter (rather than Tab). You can send this message to as many people as you want by pressing Enter after each address. When you're done including everybody in the To box, press Tab to move to the Subject box. If you want a recipient to be CC'ed or BCC'ed, click the To button next to the address and select Cc or Bcc from the list that drops down.

3. **Type the subject in the Subject box.**

   Make it specific. If you want help, don't type **Help!** as the subject. Type **Need help getting my cat not to spit out his pills**.

   Press Tab to move to the message box.

4. **Type the message in the big box.**

   The cursor should be blinking in the *message area,* the large, empty box where the actual message goes.

5. **Click the Send icon on the toolbar to send the message.**

   If you're connected to the Internet, the message wings its way to your ISP and on to the addressee. If you're not online, Thunderbird stores your message in the Unsent Messages folder.

6. **If you compose messages offline, when you next connect to the Internet, choose File⇨Send Unsent Messages.**

When you send a message in which you use formatting (such as boldface or italics, by using the toolbar buttons in the Compose window), Thunderbird may ask whether you really want to send the message using formatting. See the sidebar "To format or not to format," later in this chapter, to find out when to send formatted messages.

You can tell Thunderbird to check the spelling in your message before you send it. To use the spell checker, follow these steps:

1. **Choose Tools⇨Options.**

2. **Click Composition in the list on the left and select the Check Spelling Before Sending check box.**

   Each time you click Send to send a message, Thunderbird asks you about each word it doesn't recognize.

Sending e-mail with Outlook Express and Windows Mail

Here's how to send an e-mail message by using Outlook Express or Windows Mail:

1. **In Outlook Express or Windows Mail, click the Create Mail icon on the toolbar or press Ctrl+N.**

   You see a New Message window with boxes to fill in to address the message.

2. **In the To box, type the address to which to send the message and then press Tab to move to the CC box.**

   If you want to send a message to more than one address, type the addresses separated by commas or semicolons.

3. **If you want to send a copy of the message to someone, type that person's address in the CC box. Then press Tab.**

   If you want to send BCC copies, choose View⇨All Headers in the New Message window.

4. **In the Subject box, type a succinct summary of the message. Then press Tab again.**

5. **In the large, empty box, type the text of the message.**

   When you have typed your message, you can press F7 or choose Tools⇨Spelling to check its spelling.

6. **To send the message, click the Send icon on the toolbar or press Alt+S (not Ctrl+S, which means Save).**

   Outlook Express sticks the message in your Outbox folder, waiting to be sent. If you're connected to the Internet, Outlook Express may be configured to send the message immediately.

7. **Click the Send/Receive icon on the toolbar or press Ctrl+M.**

   Your message is on its way.

To tell Outlook Express or Windows Mail to check the spelling in your message, click the Spelling (ABC) button at the top of the New Message window.

If you use formatting commands to choose fonts and colors when you compose your message, some people may have trouble reading the message — specifically, people with older e-mail programs. If you get complaints, choose Format⇨Plain Text in the New Message window when you're composing the message. See the sidebar "To format or not to format," later in this chapter, for when to send formatted messages.

To format or not to format

A few years ago, someone got tired of e-mail's plain, unformatted appearance. After all, now that almost all computers can display boldface, italics, different fonts, and different font sizes, why not use them in e-mail? And formatted e-mail was born.

One problem is that not all e-mail programs can display formatted e-mail. Thunderbird, Outlook Express, Windows Mail, and Web-based mail systems can. The formatting usually takes one of two forms: *MIME,* in which the formatted text is sent like an attached file with the message, and *HTML,* in which Web page formatting codes are included in the text. If your mail program can't display formatted mail and you receive a formatted message, you see all kinds of gobbledygook mixed in with the text of the message, rendering it unreadable.

Another problem is that any HTML-formatted mail can potentially contain viruses, hostile Web pages that take over the screen, and other annoying or dangerous content. Some people turn off HTML mail, both the nice mail that you send and the nasty kind, to avoid having to deal with the nasty kind.

If you know that the person to whom you are writing uses an e-mail interface that can handle formatted e-mail, go ahead and use it. Boldface, italics, and color can add emphasis and interest to your messages although they're no substitute for clear, concise writing. If you receive formatted messages from someone, you can send him formatted messages, too. However, if you don't know whether your recipient's mail program can display formatted messages, don't use it. And, when sending messages to a mailing list (which we discuss in Chapter 16), don't use formatting — you never know who's on the list, who will receive your message, and which fonts their programs support.

Sending e-mail with Web mail, like Yahoo Mail, Gmail, Hotmail, and AIM Mail

After you have a Yahoo ID and Yahoo Mail mailbox, follow these steps (more or less — the Yahoo Mail Web site may have changed ten times since we wrote this). Other Web mail sites work similarly.

Here's how to send an e-mail message using Yahoo Web mail:

1. **Sign in.**

   Go to `http://mail.yahoo.com` (or click the Mail icon at `www.yahoo.com`) and sign in with your Yahoo ID and password.

2. **Click the Compose button (or any link about writing and sending a message).**

   Your browser displays a form with boxes for To (the address) and Subject and a large, unlabeled box for the text of the message.

3. **Type one or more addresses in the To box.**

   If you want to send your message to more than one address, separate each address with a comma.

4. **Type a subject line in the Subject box.**

5. **Type your message in the big box.**

6. **Scroll down and click the Send button.**

   If you want to check your spelling first, which is the polite thing to do, click the Spell Check button before clicking Send. That's all it takes!

Mail Coming Your Way

If you send e-mail, and in most cases even if you don't, you most likely receive it. The arrival of e-mail is always exciting, even when you get 200 messages a day. (It's exciting in a depressing kind of way, sometimes.)

You can do much of what you do with mail while you're not connected to your account. On the other hand, when you want to check your mailbox for your most current messages, you have to connect to the Internet.

Reading mail with your e-mail program

To check your e-mail with Thunderbird, Outlook Express, Windows Mail, or almost any other e-mail program, follow these steps:

1. **Make your Internet connection.**

   You can skip this step if your computer is always connected to the Internet or if it dials automatically whenever you need it to.

2. **Start your e-mail program if it's not already running.**

3. **If your program doesn't retrieve mail automatically, select the Check Mail or Send/Receive button on the toolbar to retrieve your mail.**

   If you have a full-time Internet connection, your e-mail program may retrieve your mail automatically, in which case you only have to start the program to get your mail. In addition, if you leave your e-mail program running, even hidden at the bottom of your screen as an icon, it may automatically check for new mail every once in a while. Most e-mail programs can even pick up mail while you're reading or sending other messages.

The program may play a tune, display a message, or show you a cute picture of a mailman delivering a letter when you receive messages. The mail appears in your inbox (usually in a window or folder named In or Inbox), showing one line per message. If you don't see it, double-click the In or Inbox mailbox in the list of mailboxes that usually appears on the left side of the window.

4. **To see a message, double-click the line or click the line and press Enter.**

   You see the text of the message, along with buttons for replying, forwarding, and deleting the message.

5. **To stop looking at a message, click the Close (X) button in the upper-right corner of the message window (the standard way to get rid of a window), or press Ctrl+W or Ctrl+F4.**

Here are some tips for displaying your inbox in specific e-mail programs:

- ✔ **Thunderbird:** To display your Inbox, click your e-mail address, account name, or Inbox in the Mail Folders list.

- ✔ **Outlook Express or Windows Mail:** If you don't see your Inbox, double-click the Local Folders item in the Folders list.

Reading mail with Web mail

To check your mail at Yahoo Mail, Hotmail, AIM Mail, Gmail, or any other Web mail system, try this:

1. **Make your Internet connection.**

   You can skip this step if your computer is always connected to the Internet or if it dials automatically whenever you need it to.

2. **Start your Web browser if it's not already running.**

3. **Go to the Web mail site and log in to your Web mail account with your username and password.**

   If the browser offers to remember your password for you and you're using a public computer, someone else's computer, or a computer you share with other people, decline its kind offer, to prevent others from getting into your mailbox.

4. **Click the Check Mail, Inbox, or other promising-looking button.**

   You see a list of the messages in your inbox.

5. **Click a message.**

   The Web mail system displays the text of the message, along with buttons for replying, forwarding, and deleting the message.

One-click surfing

Most e-mail programs display Web addresses as links. That is, if the text of a message includes a Web address (like `http://net.gurus.com`), the address appears underlined and perhaps in blue. Just click the link to display the page in your browser.

When you send messages, you don't have to do anything special to display a Web address as a link — the recipient's e-mail program should do this automatically.

Be sure to log out from the Web mail site when you're done reading and sending mail, especially if you're using a friend's computer or a computer in a public place. Otherwise, someone else can come along and read or send messages using your account.

When you use Web mail, rather than download mail to your own computer, you're managing your mail back on the server at headquarters. If you have more than one mail folder, you can use the same folders whether you move messages among folders in the mail program or on the Web.

Deleting messages from the message list

You don't have to read every single message before you delete it; sometimes you can guess from the sender's name or the Subject line that reading the message would be a waste of time. Buttons on the e-mail program's toolbar at the top of its window let you dispose of your mail. First, click once to highlight the message. Then (in most e-mail programs) click the Trash or Delete button on the toolbar to discard the message. You can do lots of other things with messages (such as reply, save, and forward), which we discuss in Chapter 15.

In Web mail, on the Web page that displays each message is some kind of Delete button. Some Web mail systems have a check box on the Web page that lists all the messages in your inbox folder, and a Delete button at the bottom of the list. To delete a bunch of messages, select their check boxes and then click Delete.

A Few Words from the Etiquette Ladies

Sadly, the Great Ladies of Etiquette, such as Emily Post and Amy Vanderbilt, died before the invention of e-mail. Here's what they may have suggested about what to say and, more important, what *not* to say in electronic mail.

E-mail is a funny hybrid, something between a phone call (or voice mail) and a letter. On one hand, it's quick and usually informal; on the other hand, because e-mail is written rather than spoken, you don't see a person's facial expressions or hear her tone of voice.

A few words of advice:

- ✔ When you send a message, watch the tone of your language.
- ✔ Don't use all capital letters — it looks like you're SHOUTING.
- ✔ If someone sends you an incredibly obnoxious and offensive message, as likely as not it's a mistake or a joke gone awry. In particular, be on the lookout for failed sarcasm.

Flame off!

Pointless and excessive outrage in electronic mail is so common that it has a name of its own: *flaming*. Don't flame. It makes you look like a jerk.

When you get a message so offensive that you just *have* to reply, stick it back in your electronic inbox for a while and wait until after lunch. Then . . . don't flame back. The sender probably didn't realize how the message would look. In about 20 years of using electronic mail, we can testify that we have never, ever, regretted *not* sending an angry message (although we *have* regretted sending a few — ouch).

When you're sending mail, keep in mind that the person reading it will have no idea what you *intended* to say — just what you *did* say. Subtle sarcasm and irony are almost impossible to use in e-mail and usually come across as annoying or dumb instead. (If you're an extremely superb writer, you can disregard this advice — but don't say that we didn't warn you.)

BTW, what does IMHO mean? RTFM!

E-mail users are often lazy typists, and abbreviations are common. Here are some of the most widely used:

Abbreviation	What It Means
AFAIK	As far as I know
BTW	By the way
IANAL	I am not a lawyer, (but. . . .)
IMHO	In my humble opinion
ROTFL	Rolling on the floor laughing
RSN	Real soon now (that is, any time in the next century)
RTFM	Read the manual — you could have and should have looked it up yourself
TIA	Thanks in advance
TLA	Three-letter acronym (for a three-letter acronym)
YMMV	Your mileage may vary

Another possibility to keep in the back of your mind is that it's technically easy to forge e-mail return addresses. If you get a totally off-the-wall message that seems out of character for the person that sent it, somebody else may have forged it as a prank. (No, we're not going to tell you how to forge e-mail. How dumb do you think we are?)

Smile!

Sometimes it helps to put in a :-) (*smiley* or *emoticon*), which means "This is a joke." (Try tilting your head to the left if you don't see why it's a smile.) In some communities, <g> or <grin> serves the same purpose. Here's a typical example:

```
People who don't believe that we are all part of a warm,
caring community who love and support each other are no
better than rabid dogs and should be hunted down and shot.
:-)
```

We feel that any joke that needs a smiley probably wasn't worth making, but tastes differ.

For more guidance about online etiquette, see our `http://net.gurus.com/netiquette` Web page.

How Private Is E-Mail?

Relatively, but not totally. Any recipient of your mail may forward it to other people. Some mail addresses are actually mailing lists that redistribute messages to many other people. We've gotten misrouted mail in our `internet11@gurus.com` mailbox with details of our correspondents' lives and anatomies that they probably would rather we forget. (So we did.)

If you send mail from work or to someone at work, your mail is not private because companies have the right to read all the employee e-mail that passes through their systems. You and your friend may work for companies of the highest integrity whose employees would never dream of reading private e-mail. When push comes to shove, however, and someone is accusing your company of leaking confidential information and the corporate lawyer says, "Examine the e-mail," someone reads all the e-mail. (This situation happened to a friend of ours who was none too pleased to find that all his intimate correspondence with his fiancée had been read.) E-mail you send and receive is stored on your disk, and most companies back up their disks regularly. If anybody really wants to read your mail, it's not hard to do. The usual rule is not to send anything you wouldn't want to see posted next to the water cooler or perhaps scribbled next to a pay phone.

If you really care about someone other than your intended recipient reading the content of your mail, you must *encrypt* it. The latest e-mail systems include encryption features that make the privacy situation somewhat better by scrambling a message so that anyone who doesn't know the keyword can't decode it.

Here are some of the most common tools for encrypted mail:

- ✔ **S/MIME:** Secure Multipurpose Internet Mail Extension is a standard encryption system that most popular mail programs support.

- ✔ **PGP:** Pretty Good Privacy is one of the most widely used encryption programs, both in the U.S. and abroad. Many experts think it's so strong that even the National Security Agency can't crack it. We don't know about that, but if the NSA wants to read your mail, you have more complicated problems than we can help you solve.

PGP is available for free on the Net. To find more information about privacy and security issues, including how to get started with PGP and S/MIME, point your browser to `http://net.gurus.com/pgp`.

To Whom Do I Write?

As you probably have figured out, one teensy detail is keeping you from sending e-mail to all your friends: You don't know their addresses. In this chapter, you find out lots of different ways to look for addresses. Start out with the easiest, most reliable way to find out people's e-mail addresses:

Call them on the phone and ask them.

Pretty low-tech, huh? For some reason, this technique seems to be absolutely the last thing people want to do. (See the sidebar, "Top ten reasons *not* to call someone to get an e-mail address.") Try it first. If you know or can find out the phone number, this method is much easier than any of the others.

Another way to find a person's e-mail address is by using an online directory. Wouldn't it be cool if some online directory listed everybody's e-mail addresses? Maybe, but the Internet doesn't have one. For one thing, nothing says that somebody's e-mail address has any connection to her name. For another, not everybody wants everybody else to know his e-mail address. Although lots of directories attempt to accumulate e-mail addresses, none of them is complete, most are somewhat out of date, and many work only if people voluntarily list themselves with the service.

This situation reiterates, of course, our point that the best way to find someone's e-mail address is to ask. When that method isn't an option, try Yahoo People Search at `http://people.yahoo.com`, which enables you to search by name and state. However, it's far from a complete database of addresses.

Top ten reasons *not* to call someone to get an e-mail address

10. You want to surprise a long-lost friend.

9. You want to surprise a long-lost *ex*-friend who owes you a large amount of money and thinks that she has given you the slip.

8. Your friend doesn't speak English. (That happens — a majority of Internauts are outside the U.S.)

7. You don't (or your friend doesn't) speak. (That happens, too — networks offer a uniquely friendly place for most people with handicaps; nobody has to know or care whether someone has a disability.)

6. It's 3 a.m. and you need to send a message right now or else you'll never get to sleep.

5. You don't know the phone number, and because of an unfortunate childhood experience, you have a deathly fear of calling directory assistance.

4. The phone takes only quarters; nobody around can break your $100 bill.

3. Your company has installed a new phone system, no one has figured out how to use it, and no matter what you dial, you always end up with Dial-a-Prayer.

2. You inadvertently spilled an entire can of soda into the phone and can't wait for it to dry out to make the call.

1. You called yesterday, didn't write down the answer, and forgot it. Oops.

Another approach is to go to a search engine like Google (www.google.com) or Yahoo Search (www.yahoo.com) and type the person's full name, enclosed in quotes. You see a list of pages that include the name — of course, many people may have the same name if your friend is named Allen Johnson or Bob Smith. Try searching for your own name and see what you find!

Chapter 14

Safe Mail: Protecting against Viruses, Spam, and WiFi Snoops

*O*kay, now you know how to send and receive e-mail. It's time to have a little chat about e-mail safety. If you've used e-mail, you probably have already seen spam and maybe even viruses. Take a look at Chapter 2 for definitions of these e-mail-borne menaces. This chapter describes how to protect yourself from them. Listen up.

I Think I've Got a Virus

A virus arrives on your computer as an attachment to an e-mail message. (Refer to Chapter 2 for a description of how viruses work.) In most e-mail programs (including Thunderbird), programs contained in attachments don't run until you click them — so *don't* open programs that come from people you don't know. Don't even open attachments from people you *do* know if you weren't expecting to receive them. Many successful viruses replicate themselves by sending copies of themselves to the first 50 people in an address book. Many viruses look like they come from someone who knows you.

In addition to taking care not to run viruses by opening attachments, you should set up your virus checker and e-mail program to catch as many viruses as possible and not to run them inadvertently. The following sections explain how.

Configuring your virus checker

In Chapter 4, we tell you to install a virus checker as soon as you get your computer connected to the Internet, but this topic is so important that we tell you again. You need to pay for a virus checker — we don't know of a good free one — and you need to pay annually to keep your subscription current for updates to the list of viruses that the checker checks for. Here are three of the many good virus checkers that are available:

- McAfee VirusScan, at www.mcafee.com
- Norton AntiVirus, at www.symantec.com
- F-Prot, at www.f-prot.com (a good deal if you have several computers, because you have to pay for only one license to run the program on all the computers in your house)

After your virus checker is installed, look at its configuration settings to make sure that the program downloads updates regularly. You can set up the program to connect to the Internet and download updates automatically. Most programs check for updates at least weekly. If you have an always-on Internet connection and you leave your computer on all the time, you can configure your program to check in the middle of the night so that it never disturbs you during the day. If you turn off your computer when you're not using it or if you have a dialup Internet account, you need to remember to run the program's update function regularly.

Most virus checkers look for viruses in two ways:

- Check e-mail messages as they arrive.
- Scan your whole computer (your hard disk) for viruses.

We recommend that you turn on both these options.

You can also configure what your virus checker does when it finds a virus in a file. You usually have options like these:

- **Disinfection:** Throws away the virus but keeps the rest of the file
- **Quarantine:** Moves the file to a safe place on your computer
- **Deletion:** Just kills it

We recommend that you set your virus checker to delete virus files. Infected files are unlikely to contain anything you want, and we can't see any reason to leave them lying around your hard disk.

Configuring Thunderbird against viruses

Thunderbird was designed to resist viruses: It doesn't use Internet Explorer to display formatted e-mail messages (as some other e-mail programs do), and it doesn't automatically open attachments. If you're running Thunderbird 2, you normally don't have to configure anything for virus protection.

If you're running a third-party virus filter, such as the ones listed in the previous section, choose Tools➪Options in the main window, click the Privacy button at the top of the options window and then the Anti-Virus tab, and be sure that the Allow Anti-Virus Clients to Quarantine Individual Messages check box is selected.

Configuring Windows Mail and Outlook Express not to run viruses

Some versions of Windows Mail, Outlook Express, and Outlook open attachments as soon as you view the message, which is a sure way to catch viruses. Outlook Express (which comes with Windows XP) provides a *preview pane* that displays a file and its attachments before you click it at all. Early versions of Outlook Express 5.0 and Outlook 97, 98, and 2000 allowed attached programs to do all kinds of horrible things to your PC. Luckily, Microsoft has changed the default settings on more recent versions of Outlook Express and Outlook.

Keeping Windows and Outlook Express updated

Outlook Express users should install Microsoft Windows XP Service Pack 2 (SP2), a free upgrade, and enable the automatic software update feature that comes with it. We say this with trepidation. We recommend that before you install SP2, you do a complete backup of your system so that you can go back if necessary. Also be sure to check the Microsoft site www.windowsupdate.com weekly for the latest bug fixes.

Checking security settings in Outlook Express or Windows Mail

Outlook Express and Windows Mail users should also check the program's configuration. Here's how:

1. **In Outlook Express or Windows Mail, choose Tools➪Options.**

   You see the Options dialog box, as shown in Figure 14-1.

2. **Click the Security tab.**

   The Virus Protection and Download Images sections both deserve your attention.

3. **Set the Internet Explorer security zone to Restricted Sites Zone.**

   If you work in a corporation and expect to receive programs from co-workers, you may need to change this setting; talk to your system administrator. For the rest of us, this is the safe setting.

4. **Make sure that the Warn Me When Other Applications Try to Send Mail As Me check box is selected. (Click it if it doesn't contain a check mark.)**

   If your computer is infected with a spyware or virus program that tries to use your computer as a spam-sending machine, this setting may prevent it.

5. **Select the Do Not Allow Attachments To Be Saved or Opened That Could Potentially Be a Virus so that it contains a check mark.**

   If you expect to receive programs, Excel spreadsheets, Word documents, or Access databases, you need to turn off this setting because all these types of files can contain viruses. Start out with it turned on, though.

6. **Select the Block Images and Other External Content in HTML E-Mail check box.**

   Images in e-mail may be Web beacons, which we describe in Chapter 2. Web beacons aren't viruses, but we don't like them anyway.

7. **Click OK.**

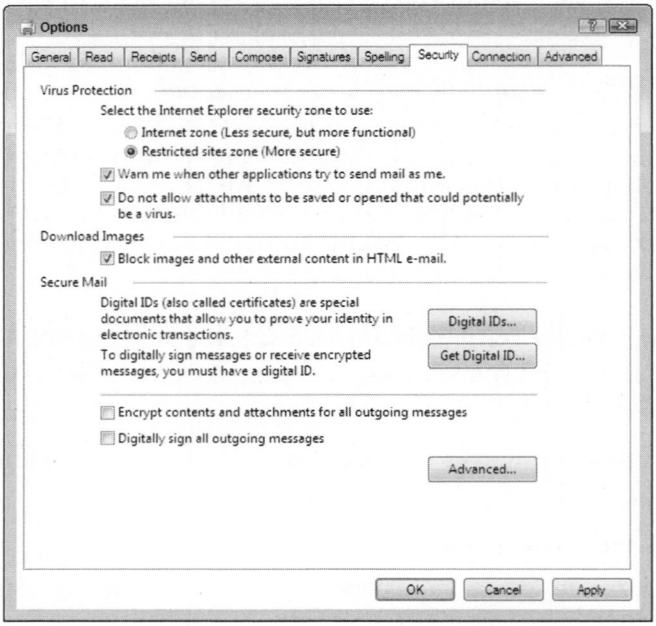

Figure 14-1:
Windows
Mail and
Outlook
Express
have virus
protection
settings.

Chain letters: Arrrrrgggghhh!

One of the most obnoxious things you can do with e-mail is pass around chain letters. Because all mail programs have forwarding commands, you can send a chain letter along to hundreds of other people with only a few keystrokes. Don't do it. Chain letters are cute for

A few chain letters just keep coming around and around, despite our best efforts to stamp them out:

✔ **Make big bucks with a chain letter:** These letters usually contain lots of testimonials from people who are now rolling in dough, and tell you to send $5 to the name at the top of the list, put your name at the bottom, and send the message to a zillion other suckers. Some even say, "This isn't a chain letter." (You're supposedly helping to compile a mailing list or sending reports or something — your 100 percent guaranteed tip-off that it's a chain letter). Don't even think about forwarding it. These chain letters are illegal in the U.S. even when they say that they aren't, and, besides, they don't even work. (Why send any money? Why not just add your name and send it on? Heck, why not just replace all the names on the list with yours?) Think of them as gullibility viruses. Send a polite note to the sender's postmaster to encourage her to tell users not to send any more chain letters. If you don't believe that they're illegal, see the Postal Service Web site at http://www.usps.com/cpim/ftp/pubs/pub300a_print.htm.

✔ **Big company will send you cash for reading e-mail:** This one has circulated with either Disney or Microsoft as the designated corporation. The message claims that the company is conducting a marketing test and that you can get big bucks or a trip to Disney World for sending along the message. Some claim that a sick child will receive 1 cent for each person you forward the message to. Yeah, right. A variation says that something interesting but unspecified will happen when you forward it; we suppose that's true if having all your friends find out you're a sucker is interesting. This chain letter isn't dangerous; it's just a waste of time — yours and everyone to whom you send it.

✔ **Hideous virus will wreck your computer:** Occasionally these are true; generally they're not, and when they are true, they tend to be about viruses that have been around since 1992. If you run software that's subject to viruses (Microsoft Outlook Express and Outlook are particularly vulnerable), look at the vendor's Web site and at the sites belonging to antivirus software makers for some more credible reports, downloadable updates, and antivirus advice. Some of the apparent virus warnings are themselves viruses. If a message shows up saying "Install this patch from Microsoft immediately to keep viruses out," it's not a patch; it's a virus.

Get This Spam Outta Here!

Spam is defined as unsolicited bulk e-mail, and we describe its history and sources in detail in Chapter 2. But you probably don't care about details — you just want it to go away.

One approach to spam is to ask your computer to figure out which messages are spam and then either trash them or put them in a separate folder so that you can trash them yourself. This seems like the perfect solution. The problem is how to get your computer to know what is spam and what is not. Many techniques are available, but none is perfect. Here are a few of the most common:

- **Blackhole lists:** A number of organizations circulate lists of Internet addresses that they consider to be sources of spam. Most ISPs subscribe to one or more of these blackhole lists and block all messages from listed sites. These ISPs block spam for you, at least the spam that comes from these Internet addresses. That's not all spam, but it's a start.

- **Content-based filters:** These filters look for words or phrases in the e-mail that are common in spam. They also note certain formatting errors that spammers seem to make often. Each text match earns a score. If a message scores above a certain threshold, it gets trashed. For example, messages with the word *Viagra* or the phrase *mortgage rate* are much more likely to be spam than other messages are.

- **Bayesian filters:** Tom Bayes was a mathematician who died 208 years before the Internet was born, but his groundbreaking work in statistics now helps computers figure out what is spam by being shown examples of messages that are spam along with others that are not. Many e-mail programs have built-in Bayesian filters. In your e-mail program, you might have noticed a button or menu option labeled something like This Is Junk. As you read your e-mail, you tell it which messages are spam. After a while, the program starts guessing based on the examples you give it, and redirects suspected spam into a Junk or Trash mailbox so that you don't have to read it. However, you do need to check the spam mailbox from time to time because the Bayesian filter may guess wrong and move good messages in with the bad.

All these methods make mistakes that let some spam through and block the occasional legit message. To reduce the latter problem, some e-mail systems *whitelist* senders listed in your e-mail address book, telling the filters that you always want to see messages from those senders — perhaps your boss or your significant other. Whitelists don't help you get messages from long-lost friends or people who just changed their e-mail addresses because their ISPs got bought out.

Filtering spam in Thunderbird

Thunderbird 2 contains a Bayesian filer that works pretty well after you give it some examples of what your spam looks like.

Telling Thunderbird to start filtering

First, set up your spam-filtering configuration settings, like this:

1. **Choose Tools⇨Account Settings. In the new window, click Junk Settings under your e-mail account.**

   You see the Junk Settings dialog box, as shown in Figure 14-2.

2. **Select the Enable Adaptive Junk Mail Controls check box if it's not already selected.**

3. **Select the check box labeled Do Not Mark Messages As Junk Mail If the Sender Is in Personal Address Book if it doesn't already contain a check mark in it.**

   Usually, people you know don't spam you.

4. **Click to select the Move New Junk Messages To check box if it doesn't already contain a check mark. Choose where to move your spam.**

   The default setting is a Junk folder, which sounds good to us.

5. **Clear any check mark from the Automatically Delete Junk Messages Older Than ___ Days check box.**

   Until your filter is well trained, don't let Thunderbird delete suspected spam before you have a chance to review it. It's terribly embarrassing to tell someone that you threw away their important message because your program thought it was spam.

6. **Click OK.**

   If you have set up more than one account, repeat this set of steps for each account in the Account Settings window.

Now Thunderbird is ready to distinguish the spam from the ham — the bad messages from the good. As you read the messages in your Inbox folder, each time you receive a spam message, click the Junk button on the toolbar. The message vanishes from your inbox, and Thunderbird analyzes the words in the message and makes a note that they're likely to appear in spam. The more spam messages you mark with the Junk button, the more Thunderbird knows about what spam looks like.

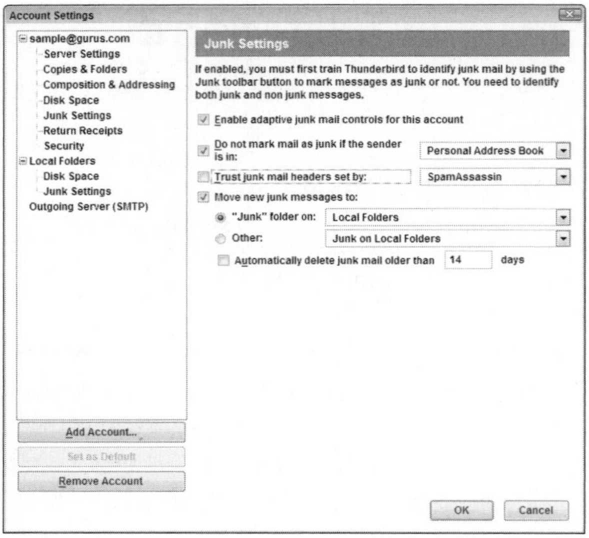

Figure 14-2:
Configuring
Thunderbird
to can your
spam.

Checking your Junk folder for real mail

From time to time (every week or so), open the Junk mail folder (or whatever folder you told Thunderbird to put suspected spam into in Step 4 in the previous section). The Junk mail folder appears on your list of folders, below your Inbox, Templates (form letters you send out), and Sent message folders. Click the Junk folder to see the list of messages. You don't need to open each message — reviewing the sender names and subjects is usually enough to find any good messages mixed in there.

If you see a good message in your Junk folder, select it and click the Not Junk button on the toolbar (it's where the Junk button usually is — the button turns into Not Junk when you open the Junk folder). This button tells Thunderbird to look at this message and to adjust the filters accordingly. Then drag the message back into your Inbox. When you're sure that all the messages in your Junk folder are indeed junk, delete them. The easiest way to do this is to click the first message and then scroll down and Shiftclick the last message — now all the messages in the Junk folder are selected. Press the Del key or click the Delete button on the toolbar to trash them.

Filtering spam in Outlook Express and Windows Mail

Outlook Express and Windows Mail don't have Bayesian filters, but they have a number of other spam-fighting features:

- ✔ **Junk E-mail Options:** (Windows Mail only) You can adjust the built-in spam filters.

- ✔ **Blocked Senders list:** If you get a message from anyone on this list, the message goes right into the trash.

- ✔ **Safe Senders list:** Messages from people on this list *don't* get marked as spam, even if the message looks like spam.

Here's how to use the features that Windows Mail and Outlook Express have.

Configuring your junk e-mail options

Windows Mail (but not Outlook Express) has a built-in junk mail filter. To configure it, follow these steps:

1. **Choose Tools⇨Junk E-mail Options. Click the Options tab if it isn't already selected.**

   You should see a window like the one shown in Figure 14-3.

2. **Select Low to pick the normal junk filter setting.**

   You can try High, but we find that it catches too much nonspam.

3. **Click the Phishing tab.**

4. **Select Protect My Inbox from Messages with Potential Phishing Links if it's not already set.**

   This feature is useful, but it raises some privacy concerns. Because it checks any Web URLs in the message against a list of known phishing sites maintained by Microsoft, the link information in your mail gets sent to Microsoft for checking.

5. **Click OK.**

You can use the Safe Senders and Blocked Senders tabs to list addresses of people whose mail you always and never want, respectively. On the Options tab, you can click Safe List Only, to accept mail only from people listed on the Safe Senders tab. This setting is way too restrictive for adults, but is appropriate for children, so you can set up a list of the friends and relatives from whom you expect them to be getting mail.

The International tab lets you block mail from addresses from certain top-level domains (the part of the e-mail address after the last dot) and in certain language encodings. We don't recommend the domain blocking, which tends to block more mail than you want, but if you don't speak Korean (or Arabic, Greek, Vietnamese, Chinese, or another language in the list) and don't know anyone in Korea, it's pretty safe to tell it to block mail encoded as Korean. Don't tell it to block US_ASCII or Western European or else you'll block most of your real mail.

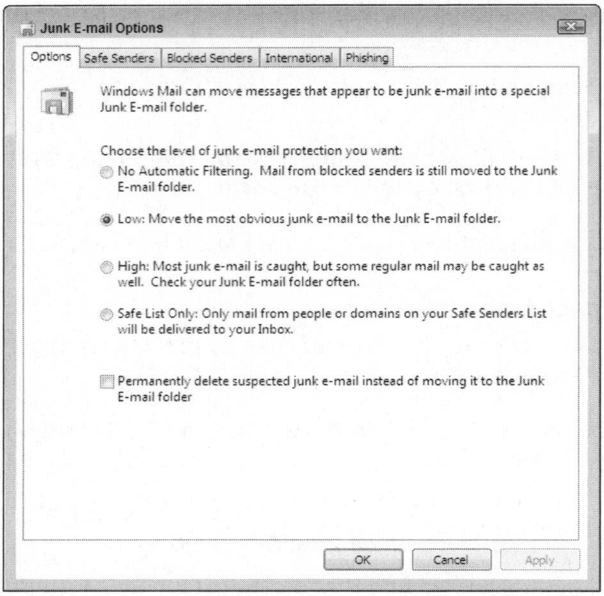

Figure 14-3:
Lots of ways
to block and
not block
junk in
Windows
Mail.

Blocking messages by sender

To block messages from a specific address, follow these steps:

1. **Open a message from the address.**

2. **In the window that displays the message, choose Message⇨Block Sender (Outlook Express) or Message⇨Junk Email⇨Add Sender to Blocked Senders List (Windows Mail).**

   You may see a message confirming that the address has been added to your Blocked Senders list.

3. **If you see a confirmation message, click OK.**

   The message you opened is still in your inbox; the program will block *future* messages, but doesn't do anything about this one. Just delete it!

Viewing your Blocked Senders list

You can look at or edit the Blocked Senders list later, in case you add a friend accidentally or you want to type a bunch of spammer addresses. Choose Tools⇨Message Rules⇨Blocked Senders List (in Outlook Express) or Tools⇨Junk Email Options and then click the Blocked Senders tab (Windows Mail) from the menu bar in the main window. You see the Message Rules dialog box with the Blocked Senders tab selected.

Messages from any addresses on your Blocked Senders list are shunted straight to your Deleted Items folder.

You can add more addresses to your Blocked Senders list by clicking the Add button and typing or pasting the address in the dialog box that appears. If you decide to accept messages from an address after all, you can delete it from the list by choosing the address and clicking Remove.

Blocking messages from entire domains

The Blocked Senders list can include entire domains. (A *domain* is the part of an e-mail address after the @.) For example, if you don't want to receive *any* mail from the White House, you can block all messages that come from *anything*@whitehouse.gov. Follow these steps to block all messages from an entire domain:

1. **Display the Blocked Senders list, as described in the preceding section.**

2. **Click the Add button.**

   You see the Add Sender dialog box.

3. **Type the domain name and click OK.**

   Leave the Mail Messages radio button selected. When you click OK, the new entry appears on your Blocked Senders list.

Reviewing your spam

From time to time, be sure to look through the messages that have been identified and filed as spam. Perfectly innocent messages may have been mislabeled as spam.

To look in your Junk E-mail folder in Windows Mail, double-click it on the folder list. The list of messages in that folder appears. Scroll through the messages; the unread messages appear in bold. (Spam you never saw should all appear in bold.)

If you see any good messages, select each one and click Not Junk to put them back in your Inbox.

Sneaky ways that spammers evade filters

Spammers are smart — if they weren't, outraged Internet users would have shut them down long ago. Every time spam filterers come up with another way to spot spam, spammers change what they send out. It's like a sped-up version of e-mail evolution.

Here are some tricks that spammers use to prevent your filters from catching their junk messages:

✔ **Funky capitalization:** Most mail filter programs look for the exact capitalization you specify. If your filter looks for `spammers rus.com` on the From line, you don't catch messages from `SpammersRus.com` or `spaMmersruS.com`.

✔ **No text:** Many spam messages contain almost no text — just a graphical image of text. When text is sent as a graphical image, filters can't read the text to spot the phrases you're looking for.

✔ **Wrods Speled w.r.0.n.g:** People are remarkably good at making sense of garbled text, so it's not hard to garble text enough to defeat filters and remain legible to people.

✔ **Hidden bogus codes:** E-mail messages can contain HTML formatting codes, which are enclosed in <angle brackets>. These formatting codes can create bold (with the <b> code) and italic (with <i>) text in your messages. However, lots of codes have no meaning in HTML, like <m> and <n>, so your e-mail program ignores them when displaying messages. However, if these meaningless codes are sprinkled in your messages, your filters are prevented from finding the words you have flagged. For example, a filter that's looking for `make money` doesn't match a message that contains `ma<m>ke mon<n>ey`.

What else can I do?

The Internet grew from a need for the easy and free flow of information, and everyone using it should strive to keep it that way. Check out these Web sites for information about spam and how to fight it technically, socially, and legally:

> ✔ **Fight Spam on the Internet!** (`http://spam.abuse.net`): A spam overview
>
> ✔ **Coalition Against Unsolicited Commercial Email** (`http://www.cauce.org`): Advocates for better antispam laws
>
> ✔ **Network Abuse Clearinghouse** (`www.abuse.net`): A complaint-forwarding service for e-mail abuse

We believe that spam is not just a technical problem and that only a combination of technical, social, and legal solutions will work in the long run. In the meantime, every ISP now does at least some spam filtering on incoming mail, and many let you "tune" their filters. Check with your ISP for the specific services it provides.

One-click surfing, but no phishing

Most e-mail programs convert URLs (Web site addresses) in your e-mail messages into links to the actual Web sites. You don't have to type these addresses into your browser. All you have to do is click the highlighted link in the e-mail message and — poof — your browser opens and you're at the Web site. If your e-mail program has this feature (all the programs mentioned in this chapter do), URLs in e-mail messages appear underlined and blue — a nice feature.

Unfortunately, this feature is abused by phishers. *Phishing* is sending faked e-mail that claims to be from your bank or other official organization to trick you into revealing personal information, and we describe it in Chapter 2. If you click one of these links and it takes you to a Web site that asks for a password, credit card number, or the like, don't give it any information!

Thunderbird and Windows Mail both have phish detection features. They're not perfect, but if either says that a link looks phishy, you probably don't want to click it.

Secure That Mail

If you have a laptop and you use it to read your e-mail in public WiFi hotspots, you may have a security problem. (Refer to Chapter 5 to find out what we mean by *WiFi* and *hotspot*.) Public WiFi setups allow anyone connected to the same hotspot (that is, anyone in the same café or area of the airport) to eavesdrop on what you type, including potentially seeing your e-mail username and password.

Fortunately, most mail programs and mail servers let you use a secure connection, the same kind that secure Web pages use, for incoming and outgoing mail. Setting up the secure connection can be a little tricky, but you have to do it only once.

Secure mail with Thunderbird

To set up secure mail in Thunderbird, follow these steps:

1. **Choose Tools⇨Account Settings.**

   You see the Account Settings window, with a list of your mail accounts on the left.

2. **Click Server Settings under your incoming mail account.**

   You may have to click the little + sign next to your account's name to see the Server Settings option.

   3. **Select the Use Secure Connection (SSL) check box.**

   4. **Click Outgoing Server (SMTP) at the bottom of the left column.**

      If you have several accounts set up, you may have to scroll down to find it.

   5. **Click Edit.**

   6. **Under Use Secure Connection, select TLS.**

   7. **Click OK.**

Now check your mail, and try sending yourself a message. If it doesn't work, your mail provider may not offer secure mail, or may offer it in a nonstandard way, and you have to call for help.

Secure mail with Outlook Express or Windows Mail

To set up secure mail in Outlook Express or Windows Mail, follow these steps:

   1. **Choose Tools⇨Accounts.**

   2. **Click the name of your mail account in the window that opens, and then click Properties.**

   3. **In the window that opens, click the Advanced tab.**

      There's a Security tab, but that's not what you want here.

   4. **Select the check boxes labeled This Server Requires a Secure Connection (SSL) for both incoming and outgoing mail.**

   5. **Click OK.**

Now check your mail, and try sending yourself a message, clicking the Send/Recv button to make Outlook Express or Windows Mail connect to the server. If it doesn't work, your mail provider may not offer secure mail, or may offer it in a nonstandard way, and you have to call for hel

Chapter 15

Putting Your Mail in Its Place

*A*fter you get used to using e-mail, you start sending and receiving enough messages that you had better keep it organized. This chapter describes how to delete, reply to, forward, and file messages in Thunderbird, Windows Mail, Outlook Express, and Web mail systems such as Yahoo Mail, Gmail, and Hotmail. (Refer to Chapter 13 to find out how to get started using these programs.)

After you read (or decide not to read) an e-mail message, you can deal with it in a number of ways, much the same as with paper mail. Here are your usual choices:

✔ Throw it away.

✔ Reply to it.

✔ Forward it to other people.

✔ File it.

You can do any or all these things with each message. If you don't tell your mail program what to do with a message, the message usually stays in your mailbox for later perusal.

Deleting Mail

When you first begin to get e-mail, the feeling is so exciting that it's difficult to imagine just throwing away the message. Eventually, however, you *have* to know how to get rid of messages, or else your computer will eventually run out of room. Start early. Delete often.

Throwing away mail is easy enough that you probably have figured out how to do it already. In Thunderbird, Windows Mail, and Outlook Express (and in most other e-mail programs, for that matter), the process goes like this:

Display the message or select it from the list of messages in a folder. Then click the trashcan, big X, or other trashy-looking icon on the toolbar, or press Ctrl+D or Del. (On the Mac, press ⌘+D or Delete.) In Yahoo Mail or other Web mail systems, click either the Inbox or Check Mail link to see a list of your messages. Then select the check box by the message and click the Delete button at the bottom of the list. When you're looking at a message in Web mail, you can click an X or Delete button, too.

You can delete mail without even reading it. If you subscribe to mailing lists (which we describe in Chapter 16), certain topics may not interest you. When you see the subject line in your list of messages, you can delete the message without reading it.

When you delete a message, most e-mail programs don't throw it away immediately. Instead, they file the message in your Trash or Deleted Messages mailbox or mail folder, or just mark it as deleted. From time to time (usually whenever you exit the e-mail program), the program empties your trash, truly deleting the messages. Until then, you can undelete it if you deleted it by mistake.

Back to You, Sam: Replying to Mail

Replying to mail is easy: Choose Message⇨Reply in Thunderbird, or Message⇨Reply to Sender in Outlook Express or Windows Mail. Or, click the Reply button on the toolbar or press Ctrl+R (⌘+R on the Mac). In Web mail, you usually see a Reply button.

When you have the reply message open, ask yourself two important questions:

✔ **To whom does the reply go?** Look carefully at the To line, which your e-mail program has filled out for you. Is that who you thought you were addressing? If the reply is addressed to a mailing list, did you really intend to send a message to the entire list, or is your reply of a more personal nature, intended only for the individual who sent the message? Did you mean to reply to a group? Are all the addresses that you think you're replying to included on the To list? If the To list isn't correct, move the cursor to it and edit it as necessary.

Occasionally you may receive a message that has been sent to a zillion people, and their addresses appear in dozens of lines in the To section of the message. If you reply to a message like this, make sure that your reply isn't addressed to the entire huge list of recipients.

Some e-mail programs have a separate Reply to All command or button that addresses your reply to both the people that the message was from and the people who received copies of the message (that is, to "To" people and the "Cc" people). Thunderbird, Windows Mail, and Outlook Express all have a Reply All button on the toolbar,

✔ **Do you want to include the content of the message to which you're replying?** Most e-mail programs include the content of the message to which you're replying, usually formatted to show that it's a *quotation* or *quoted text.* Edit the quoted text to include just the relevant material, so as not to bore or confuse the recipient with unrelated stuff. If you don't provide some context to people who get a great deal of e-mail, your reply makes no sense, so including part of the original message can be helpful. If you're answering a question, include the question in the response. You don't have to include the entire text, but give your reader a break. She may have read 50 messages since she sent you mail and may not have a clue what you're talking about unless you remind her.

When you reply to a message, most mail programs fill in the Subject field with the letters *Re:* (short for *re*garding) and the Subject field contents of the message to which you're replying.

Keeping Track of Your Friends

After you begin using e-mail, you quickly find that you have enough regular correspondents that keeping track of their e-mail addresses is a pain. Fortunately, every popular e-mail program provides an *address book* in which you can save your friends' addresses so that you can send mail to Mom, for example, and have it automatically addressed to chairman@exec.hq. giantcorp.com. You can also create address lists so that you can send mail to family, for example, and it goes to Mom, Dad, your brother, both sisters, and your dog, all of whom have e-mail addresses.

All address books let you do the same things:

✔ Save in your address book the address from a message you have just read.

✔ Use addresses you have saved for outgoing messages.

✔ Edit your address book.

The Thunderbird address book

Thunderbird has a good address book, and adding people to it is easy. Display the Address Book window by clicking the Address Book button on the toolbar, pressing Ctrl+2 (⌘+2 on the Mac), or choosing Tools⇨Address Book — you see a window that looks like Figure 15-1. You can add a new person to your address book by clicking New Card and filling out the form. To edit an entry, select it and click the Properties button on the toolbar. You can also create a *list* — that is, an address book entry that sends a message to a bunch of people (for example, the members of a committee or of your family). Click New List to create one.

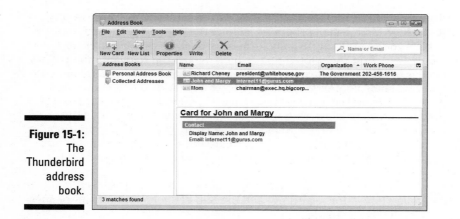

Figure 15-1:
The
Thunderbird
address
book.

To use the address book while you're composing a message, just start typing the person's name in your new message. As soon as Thunderbird sees a name that begins with the same letters as an address book entry, it displays the person's name. If more than one entry matches, you see a list you can choose from.

To create a mailing list for your use, click the New List button, which creates an empty list, and then type the addresses you want.

When you're reading a message in Thunderbird, you can add the sender's address to your address book by clicking the sender's name or address on the From line and choosing Add to Address Book from the menu that pops up. This opens a New Card window in which you can enter additional information about the person. Then click OK to add it to the address book.

The Outlook Express address book and Windows Mail contacts

In Outlook Express, to display and edit the address book, click the Addresses button on the toolbar. (You may need to widen the Outlook Express window to see it — it's near the right end of the toolbar in some versions.)

Add a new person by clicking the New button on the Address Book window's toolbar and choosing New Contact from the menu that appears. To change someone's entry, select the entry and click Properties on the toolbar.

The process of copying a correspondent's address into the address book is easy: Right-click the person's name in the list of messages, and choose Add Sender to Address Book from the menu that appears.

After you add some entries to your address book, you use them while you're creating a new message by clicking the little book icon to the left of the To or Cc line in the New Message window. In the Select Recipients window that appears, double-click the address book entry or entries you want to use — they appear in the Message Recipients list. Then click OK.

The Windows Mail address book

Windows Mail renamed and somewhat expanded the address book and calls it Contacts. To open the Contacts window, click the icon on the Windows Mail address bar that looks like a little flag. (Move your mouse over the icons, and it says Contacts when you're on the right one.)

To add a new contact, click the New Contact button and fill in as much info as you want in the Properties window that opens. To add an e-mail address, type it in the E-mail box, and then click the Add button to the right of that box. After you enter the contact info (name and one e-mail address is plenty), click OK. To change an entry, just click it in the Contacts window, and a Properties window opens, where you can change it.

To add an address from a message in a mailbox, right-click the person's name or address in the list of messages, and then select Add Sender to Contacts from the pop-up menu that appears.

When you're composing a mail message, click the little flag to the left of the To, Cc, or Bcc line, and a Select Recipients window opens. Double-click the one or ones you want, and then click OK to return to the message.

Web mail address books

Web mail systems (which we describe in detail in Chapter 13) include an address book — it's just too useful a feature to leave out. After you log in to your mail account by using your browser, click the Contacts, Addresses, or Address Book link to display your address book. Click the Add Contact, Create Contact, or similar button or link to add someone. Fill out the form that appears, and be sure to enter a *nickname* for the person: You can type the nickname when addressing an e-mail message rather than type the person's whole e-mail address. The form may include fields for the person's postal address and phone numbers, but you can leave them blank. Then click the Save or Save Contact button. (These instructions are approximate because Web mail sites change their button names all the time.) In the new version of Yahoo Mail, you can right-click an address in the message list and then choose Add Sender to Contacts from the pop-up menu.

Web mail systems provide several ways to address a message to someone in your address book. In Yahoo Mail, you can display a list of your contacts, as shown in Figure 15-2. When composing a message, try typing the person's nickname to see whether a matching entry appears in the window of address book entries, or click the To or Cc button to see a list of contacts from which to choose.

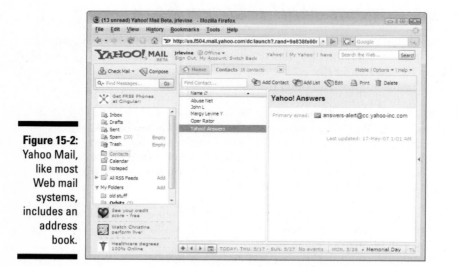

Figure 15-2:
Yahoo Mail,
like most
Web mail
systems,
includes an
address
book.

Fast forward

Whenever you're forwarding mail, be sure to delete uninteresting parts. All the glop in the message header is frequently included automatically in the forwarded message, and almost none of it is comprehensible, much less interesting, so get rid of it.

The tricky part is editing the text. If the message is short (a screenful or so), you probably should leave it alone:

```
>Is there a lot of demand for
    fruit pizza?
>
I checked with our research
    department and found that
    the favorite pizza
    toppings in the 18-34 age
    group are pepperoni,
    sausage, ham, pineapple,
    olives, peppers,
    sauerkraut, hamburger, and
    broccoli. I specifically
    asked about prunes, and
    they found no
    statistically significant
    response.
```

If the message is really long and only part of it is relevant, you should, as a courtesy to the reader, cut it down to the interesting part. We can tell you from experience that people pay much more attention to a concise, one-line e-mail message than they do to 12 pages of quoted stuff followed by a two-line question.

Sometimes it makes sense to edit material even more, particularly to emphasize one specific part. When you do so, of course, be sure not to edit to the point where you put words in the original author's mouth or garble the sense of the message, as in the following reply:

```
>I checked with
>our research department and
    found that the
>favorite pizza toppings ...
    and they
>found no statistically
    significant
>response.
```

This version of the original message is totally misleading — it twists the original text. Sometimes, it makes sense to paraphrase a little — in that case, put the paraphrased part in square brackets, like this:

```
>[When asked about prunes on
    pizza, research]
>found no statistically
    significant response.
```

People disagree about whether paraphrasing to shorten quotes is a good idea. On one hand, if you do it well, it saves everyone time. On the other hand, if you do it badly and someone takes offense, you're in for a week of accusations and apologies that will wipe out whatever time you may have saved. The decision is up to you.

Hot Potatoes: Forwarding Mail

You can forward e-mail to someone else. It's easy. It's cheap. Forwarding is one of the best things about e-mail and at the same time one of the worst. It's good because you can easily pass along messages to people who need to know about them. It's bad because you (not *you* personally, but, um, people around you — that's it) can just as easily send out floods of messages to recipients who would just as soon not hear *another* press release from the local Ministry of Truth (or another joke that's making the rounds). Think about whether you will enhance someone's quality of life by forwarding a message to him. If a message says "forward this to everyone you know," do everyone you know a favor and delete it instead.

Forwarding a message involves wrapping the message in a new message of your own, sort of like putting sticky notes all over a copy of it and mailing the copy and notes to someone else.

Forwarding mail is almost as easy as replying to it: Select the message and click the Forward button on the toolbar, or choose Message⇨Forward. Pressing Ctrl+L (⌘+L on the Mac) also works in Thunderbird, and Ctrl+F forwards in Windows Mail and Outlook Express. In Web mail systems, a Forward button usually appears when you view a message. The mail program composes a message that contains the text of the message you want to forward; all you have to do is address the message, add a few snappy comments, and send it.

The text of the original message appears at the top or bottom of the message, usually formatted as quoted text and preceded by a line that specifies whom the original message was from, and when. You then get to edit the message and add your own comments. (See the nearby sidebar "Fast forward" for tips about pruning forwarded mail.)

Cold Potatoes: Saving Mail

Saving e-mail for later reference is similar to putting potatoes in the fridge for later. (Don't knock it if you haven't tried it — day-old boiled potatoes are yummy with enough butter or sour cream.) Lots of your e-mail is worth saving, just as lots of your paper mail is worth saving. Lots of it *isn't,* of course, but we cover that subject earlier in this chapter.

You can save e-mail in a few different ways:

- ✔ Save it in a folder full of messages.
- ✔ Print it and put it in a file cabinet with paper mail. (Spare a tree; don't use this method.)

The easiest method usually is to stick messages in a folder. E-mail programs usually come with folders named In (or Inbox), Outbox, Sent, and Trash, and perhaps some others. But you can also make your own folders.

People use two general approaches in filing mail: by sender and by topic. Whether you use one or the other or both is mostly a matter of taste. For filing by topic, it's entirely up to you to come up with folder names. The most difficult part is coming up with memorable names. If you aren't careful, you end up with four folders with slightly different names, each with a quarter of the messages about a particular topic. Try to come up with names that are obvious, and don't abbreviate. If the topic is accounting, name the folder Accounting because if you abbreviate, you'll never remember whether it's Acctng, acct, or Acntng.

You can save all or part of a message by copying it into a text file or word-processing document. Select the text of the message by using your mouse. Press Ctrl+C (⌘+C on a Mac) or choose Edit➪Copy to copy the text to the Clipboard. Switch to your word processor (or whatever program into which you want to copy the text) and press Ctrl+V (⌘+V on the Mac) or choose Edit➪Paste to make the message appear where the cursor is.

Filing with Thunderbird

Thunderbird lists your mail folders down the left side of the window, starting with Inbox. Thunderbird provides folders named Inbox, Unsent Messages, Drafts, Sent, and Trash, but you can create your own folders. If you have a *lot* of messages to file, you can even create folders within folders to keep things organized. To make a new folder, follow these steps:

1. **Choose File➪New➪New Folder.**

   You see the New Folder dialog box.

2. **Type a name for the folder in the Name text box.**

   Make one named Personal, just to give it a try.

3. **Set the Create As A Subfolder Of drop-down box to the folder name in which you want the new folder to live.**

   Usually, you want your folder to be a subfolder of Local Folders, so set it to Local Folders and click Choose This for the Parent. Or, choose another folder; for example, you can have a folder named Personal, and inside that can be a folder for each friend you get messages from.

4. **Click OK.**

The new folder appears on the list of folders on the left side of the Thunderbird window. You can see the list of message headers for any folder by clicking the folder name.

You can save a message in a folder by dragging the message to the folder name — easy enough. Or, right-click the message, choose Move To from the menu that appears, and choose the folder from the list that appears.

When you compose a message, you can tell Thunderbird to save a copy of your message in a folder. While writing the message, choose Options⇨Send A Copy To and then choose a folder.

Filing with Windows Mail and Outlook Express

You start out with folders named Inbox, Outbox, Sent Items, Drafts, Deleted Items, and maybe Junk E-mail. To make a new folder, choose File⇨Folder⇨ New or File⇨New⇨Folder, give the folder a name, and choose which folder to put this new folder in. (Like Thunderbird, Outlook Express can have folders within folders — very convenient.)

Move messages into a folder by clicking a message header and dragging it over to the folder name, right-clicking the message on the message list and choosing Move To Folder, or choosing Edit⇨Move To Folder.

Filing with Web mail systems

To save a message in a folder in Yahoo Mail, just drag it from the list of messages into the new folder, like in a real mail program. Or, click the Move button and choose the folder where you want the message. To create a new folder, choose New Folder from the list of folders and click Move. Yahoo Mail shows you a menu of your folders.

Your folders appear in the list of folders down the left side of your browser window, under the My Folders heading. Your folders include Inbox, Sent, Draft, Spam, and Trash. Click a folder name to see the messages in that folder.

In Gmail, rather than put mail in folders, you label it. Click the More Actions drop-down menu and choose Apply Label from the menu that appears. If you want to create a label that you haven't yet used, choose New Label.

Handling Exotic Mail and Mail Attachments

Sooner or later, just plain, old, everyday e-mail isn't good enough for you. Someone's going to send you a picture you just have to see, or you're going to want to send a video clip of Fluffy to your new best friend in Paris. To send stuff other than text through the mail, a message uses special file formats. Sometimes, the entire message is in a special format, and sometimes people *attach* things to their plain text mail. The most widely used format for attaching files to messages is *MIME (Multipurpose Internet Mail Extensions)*. The programs we describe in this chapter can send and receive files attached with MIME, as do most e-mail programs on the planet — only a few, very old e-mail programs still can't.

When you receive a file that's attached to an e-mail message, your mail program is responsible for noticing the attached file and doing something intelligent with it. Most of the time, your program saves the attached file as a separate file in the folder you specify. After the file has been saved, you can use it just like you use any other file. If you see a picture in a message and you're not sure where it's saved, most programs let you right-click the picture and choose Save Image As to put the picture in the folder of your choice.

You can send the following types of files as attachments:

✔ Pictures, in image files

✔ Word processing documents

✔ Sounds, in audio files

✔ Movies, in video files

✔ Programs, in executable files

✔ Compressed files, such as ZIP files

E-mail viruses usually show up as attachments. If you get a message with an unexpected attachment, even from someone you know, **DON'T OPEN IT** until you check with the sender to make sure he or she sent it deliberately. Viruses often suck all the addresses from a victim's address book so that the virus can mail itself to the victim's friends. Some kinds of attachments can't carry viruses, notably GIF and JPG images. Refer to Chapter 14 for details.

Your ISP or Web-based mail service may place a limit on the size of your mailbox (the place on its server where your messages are stored until you pick them up). Google's Gmail and Yahoo Mail have high limits (at least 1GB), so other mail systems have been increasing their limits to match, but you may still run into a size limit if someone sends you a truly gigantic file (for example, a video file). One way to shrink the size of attached files is to ZIP them first, using the Windows XP Compressed Folders feature or a separate program like WinZip. Refer to Chapter 12 if you receive a ZIPped file (with the file extension .zip).

Thunderbird attachments

To attach a file to the message you're composing, click the Attach button or choose File⇨Attach. Then select the file you want to send. You can also insert a picture right into the text of the message by positioning your cursor where you want the picture to appear, choosing Insert⇨Image, and specifying the filename.

For incoming mail, Thunderbird displays any attachments that it can display itself (Web pages and GIF and JPEG image files). For other types of attachments, it displays a little description of the file, which you can click. Thunderbird then runs an appropriate display program — if it knows of one — or asks you whether to save the attachment to a file or to configure a display program, which Thunderbird then runs in order to display the attachment.

Windows Mail and Outlook Express attachments

In Windows Mail and Outlook Express, create a new message and then attach a file to a message by choosing Insert⇨File Attachment or by clicking the Attach button. (The Attach button, which looks like a paper clip, might be off the right side of the toolbar — make the Composition window wider to display it.) Then select the file to attach. Or, just drag the file into the message composition window. Then send the message as usual.

When an incoming message contains an attachment, a paper-clip icon appears in the message on your list of incoming messages and in the message header when you view the message. Click the paper clip to see the filename — double-click, and you may be able to see the attachment.

Microsoft has "solved" some of the chronic Outlook Express security problems by making Outlook Express and Windows Mail refuse to show you many attachments, including a lot of benign ones, such as attached text messages and PDF files. You can sort of fix this problem by choosing Tools⇨Options in the main window, clicking the Security tab, and then deselecting the Do Not Allow Attachments to Be Saved or Opened That Could Potentially Be a Virus check box. Then the program lets you open your attachments, although of course when someone *does* send you a virus, it cheerfully opens that one, too.

Web mail attachments

To attach stuff with Yahoo Mail, compose a message as usual. Then click the Attach File button and select the file on your computer to attach. Your Web browser, amazing beast that it is, copies the file right off your hard drive and sends it to the Yahoo Mail system to include in your message. When you return to the Yahoo Mail page where you're composing your message — the filename appears just below the subject line. Send the message as usual. Other Web mail systems work similarly.

When you get a message with attachments, a box appears at the bottom of the message, displaying the filename and size of the attachment. Click the Download File button to get the file onto your computer.

Teaching Your E-Mail Program to Sort Your Mail

After you begin sending e-mail, you probably will find that you receive quite a bit of it, particularly if you put yourself on some mailing lists (see Chapter 16). Your incoming mail becomes a trickle, and then a stream, and then a torrent, and pretty soon you can't walk past your keyboard without getting soaking wet, metaphorically speaking.

Fortunately, most mail systems provide ways for you to manage the flow and avoid ruining your clothes (enough of this metaphor already). Thunderbird can create *filters* that can automatically check incoming messages against a list of senders and subjects and file them in appropriate folders. Outlook Express has the Inbox Assistant, and Windows Mail has Message Rules, which can sort your mail automatically. Most other mail programs (and a few Web mail systems) have similar filtering features. If you sort mail into separate mailboxes for each mailing list or other category, you can deal with it a lot more efficiently.

For example, you can create filters that tell your mail program, "Any message that comes from the CHICKENS-L mailing list should be automatically filed in the Cluck mail folder." Figure 15-3 shows this type of filter in Thunderbird.

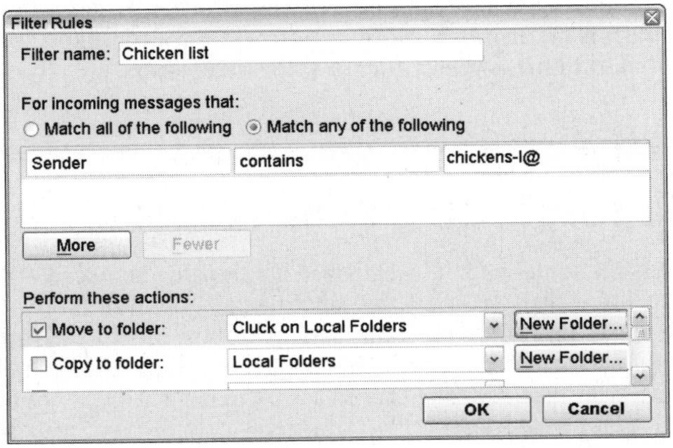

Figure 15-3:
Moving
poultry-
related
messages
to a
separate
folder for
immediate
attention.

You can create filters to highlight messages from particularly interesting friends, or delete certain messages (you know the ones we mean) so that you never have to see them. Here's how to do it for the main e-mail programs we discuss in this book:

- **Thunderbird:** Choose Tools⇨Message Filters to display the Message Filters window, where you can see, create, edit, and delete filters. Click New to create a new filter, and then specify a filter name (for your own reference), how Thunderbird can match incoming messages to this filter, and what to do with messages that match. Or, click the To or From address in a message and choose Create Filter from Message to make a filter for mail sent to or from that address.

- **Outlook Express and Windows Mail:** Tell the Inbox Assistant or Message Filters how to sort your mail into folders by choosing Tools⇨Message Rules⇨Mail. In the window that opens, you first choose a condition, which enables the program to identify messages based on the From line, Subject line, or message body. Then you select an action, which is usually to move the message to a folder. (Remember, Trash is a folder.) Then in the bottom part of the window, it will have written a little description of what it's going to do. Because you haven't yet told it what to look for or where to move the message, there are placeholders in the description you click to enter the words to match and the folder to use. Then click OK. This method is a lot simpler in practice than it is to describe; try making a rule to move messages with *pickle* in the subject line into a folder named Pickles and you'll get the hang of it.

- **Yahoo Mail:** Click the Options button on the Yahoo Mail Web page, and then the Mail Options entry on the menu that drops down, and then click the Filters heading. You can create, edit, or delete your filters.

All this automatic-sorting nonsense may seem like overkill, and if you get only five or ten messages a day, it is. After the mail really gets flowing, however, dealing with it takes much more of your time than it used to. Keep those automated tools in mind — if not for now, then for later.

Corresponding with a robot

Not every mail address has an actual person behind it. Some are mailing lists (which we talk about in Chapter 16), and some are *robots,* or programs that automatically reply to messages. Mail robots have become popular as a way to query databases and retrieve files because setting up a connection for electronic mail is much easier than setting up one that handles the more standard file transfer. You send a message to the robot (usually referred to as a *mailbot* or *mail server*), it takes some action based on the contents of your message, and then the robot sends back a response. If you send a message to `internet11@gurus.com`, for example, you receive a response telling you your e-mail address.

Chapter 16

Typing and Talking on the Net

*I*nternet e-mail is pretty fast, usually arriving in less than a minute. But sometimes that's just not fast enough. Instant-message (IM) systems let you pop up a message on a friend's screen in a matter of seconds. You can also tell your instant-message program the usernames of your friends and colleagues so that the program can alert you the instant that one of your buddies comes online and you can instantiate an instant message to them. (Excuse us, this gives us a headache. Just a moment while we get some instant coffee. Ahh, that's better.)

The good thing about instant messages is that you can stay in touch with people as fast as by talking to them on the phone. The bad thing about instant messages is that they also offer an unparalleled range of ways to annoy people. AOL Instant Messenger, discussed later in this chapter, has about two features to send and receive messages, and about 12 features to reject, denounce, erase, and otherwise deal with unwanted messages. (This may say more about AOL users than about the technology, of course.)

Gregarious people can chat with a whole bunch of people at once, either typing at the same time like a party line or sending messages to each other by e-mail or Web forums.

Of course, even better than typing messages to another person is talking right out loud. If your computer has a microphone and speakers, you can use IM or other systems to talk to people over the Net — even groups of people — with no toll charges. If you connect a digital video camera (or *webcam*) to your computer, your friends can even see you as you talk or type. It's not hard to do!

AIMing to Chat via Text

Instant messaging (IM'ing) lets you type short messages that appear in a window on someone else's computer. It's faster than e-mail but slightly less intrusive than a phone call, so far few people have their secretaries screen their IMs.

This chapter describes how to use the most popular IM system: AOL Instant Messenger. Windows Messenger and Yahoo Messenger work similarly, and have similar features. Skype, a voice-over-Internet program described in "Internet Phones and Voice Chat," later in this chapter, also includes IM chat.

AOL Instant Messenger (*AIM,* for short) is one of the simplest chat systems around. All it does is let you type messages back and forth. This chapter describes AIM version 6. If you use AOL, you can use either the separate AIM program we describe here or the AIM part of the regular AOL program (which does the same things although the windows are a little different).

Instant-message programs open a new window when one of your buddies sends you a message. If you have a program that blocks pop-up windows in your browser, IM windows aren't affected because pop-up blockers block only Web browser pop-ups.

Taking AIM

If you're an AOL user, you're already set up for instant messages. If not, you have to install the AIM program. AOL subscribers can also run the AIM program and use their AOL screen names when they're logged in to another kind of Internet account.

AOL, hyper-aggressive marketing organization that it is, has arranged for AIM to be bundled in with a lot of other packages. If you don't have it, visit www.aim.com and follow the directions on the Web page to download it. (See Chapter 12 for how to download and install programs from the Internet.)

When you install the program, you have to choose a screen name — which can be up to 16 letters long (be creative so that yours doesn't collide with one of the 40 million names already in use) — and a password. You also have to enter your e-mail address. AOL, refreshingly, doesn't want any more personal information. The e-mail address you give has to be real; AOL sends a confirmation message to that address, and you must reply or else your screen name is deleted. Normally, AIM runs in the background whenever you're online. If it's not running, click the AIM icon on your desktop.

The first time you use AIM, you enter your AIM or AOL screen name, as shown in the left part of Figure 16-1. Type your screen name and password and click Sign On. If you want to use AIM every time you're online, check the Save Password and Auto-Login boxes before signing on, and AIM signs you on automatically in the future. After you sign in, you see the AIM window, shown on the right of Figure 16-1.

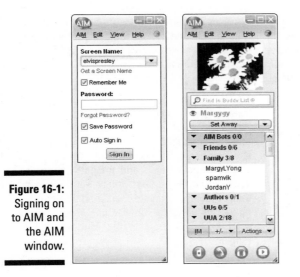

Figure 16-1: Signing on to AIM and the AIM window.

Getting your buddies organized

First you create your Buddy List, and then you can send messages.

When AIM opens, you see your *Buddy List*; that is, other AIM users you like to chat with. The window shows which of your many buddies are online now (everyone who's not currently listed in the Offline category). What? None of your pals appears? You need to add your friends' AOL or AIM screen names to your Buddy List.

In the AIM window, press Ctrl+D or choose Edit⇨Add Buddy from the menu to display the New Buddy window. Enter a nickname to use for your friend or coworker, an AIM username, and (optionally) a cellphone number (preceded by +1 for U.S. numbers). AIM can send IMs as text messages to cellphones. Click the Buddy Group button to choose which group to put your new buddy in. AOL provides a few groups, but you can also make your own, by choosing Edit⇨Add Group. Click Save to add your friend as a buddy.

Which instant-message system should I use?

Unfortunately, the instant-message systems don't talk to one another. Because the goal of all these systems is to help you stay in touch with your friends, use whichever one they use. If you're not sure who your friends are, AOL Instant Messenger is a good bet because it's easy to set up and works automatically with any AOL user; it's the same system that AOL uses internally. AIM, Yahoo Messenger, and Windows Messenger have similar features because when one adds something, the others tend to follow suit. All three are free; support text, voice, and video; and allow more than two people to chat. (We've held meetings on Yahoo Messenger with six people on voice and two on video and everyone typing snide comments at the same time.) If you have Windows XP or Vista, you already have Windows Messenger, which comes preinstalled.

The bottom line: Use whichever system your friends use. If you're really message-mad or you have friends on more than one system, you can run more than one messaging program at the same time. While we were writing this chapter, we had Windows Messenger, AOL Instant Messenger, and Yahoo! Messenger all running at once. It was an awful lot of blinking and flashing, but it worked.

Better yet, use a program that speaks all three IM languages. We know of and like two, both free. They are Pidgin, at www.pidgin.im, and Trillian, at www.ceruleanstudios.com, and they simultaneously handle every IM system you ever heard of. Trillian tries to install a bunch of extra applications and toolbars when you install it; say No unless you're sure you want them. Pidgin is plain old-fashioned freeware — no ads, no begging. For Mac users, Adium from www.adiumx.com is the Mac version of Pidgin.

You can drag a buddy from one group to another in the Buddy List or get rid of a buddy (by clicking the buddy and then pressing Del).

Getting buddy-buddy online

To send a message to someone, double-click the buddy's name to open a message window, type the message, and click the Send button or press Enter. AIM pops up a window (shown on Figure 16-2) on the recipient's machine and plays a little song, and you and your buddy can type back and forth. When you're done, close the message window.

Making noise with AIM

After you establish a conversation using AIM, you can switch to voice (assuming that both parties have computers equipped with microphones and speakers). Click the Talk button and click Connect. Your friend sees a window asking whether he wants to make a direct connection with you. If your friend accepts the invitation, you can chat using the microphone and speakers on your PC. Click Disconnect when you're done talking. See the section "Adding Voices and Faces," later in this chapter, for more about both voice and video on AIM.

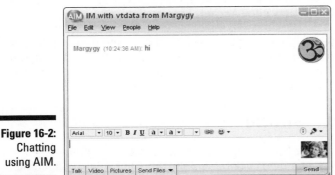

Figure 16-2:
Chatting
using AIM.

Buzz off

AOL evidently has a lot of ill-mannered users, because AIM has a system for warning and blocking users you don't like. If someone sends you an annoying message, you can choose People⇨Ignore in the chat window.

What if someone IMs you when you aren't online? You can tell AIM to show you missed messages by choosing Edit⇨Settings in the AIM window, which displays the Setting – Buddy List window. Click the Offline IM tab, choose the settings you want, and click Save. AIM can save up to 40 offline messages for as long as two weeks.

You can fine-tune whom you let send messages to you: Choose Edit⇨Settings, and then click the Privacy tab. You can limit messages to people on your Buddy List, permit access to specific people, or block specific people. You can also add or delete people from your Block list. We recommend choosing Allow Only Users on My Buddy List unless you like being contacted by total strangers at inconvenient moments.

The more the merrier — chatting with a group

AIM doesn't limit you to chatting with one person at a time. You can have several chat windows open at the same time, and have separate chats in each window. It can make you crazy, though, keeping track of a bunch of conversations, but teenagers do it every day.

An alternative is to have one chat window for more than just one other person. In a chat window, you can choose People➪Start a Buddy Chat and type the screen names of people you want to invite into a group chat window. AIM opens a new tab in your chat window and sends invitations to your buddies, and, assuming that they click Accept, you're all in!

You can control whether your multiple chats appear in separate windows or as separate tabs in one window. Choose View➪Ungroup All Tabs to make separate windows, or View➪Regroup All Tabs to display all chats in one window.

AIM on your phone

You can tell AIM to forward messages to your cellphone via text message. Choose Edit➪Settings, and then click the Mobile tab. Click Register a Mobile Device to display the signup page in your Web browser. AIM sends a text message to your phone with a code that you must type on the registration page, to prove that the phone is really yours. If you pay to receive text messages or you don't want to get them from all your AIM buddies, choose Edit➪Settings again, click the Mobile tab again, and choose whether to receive text messages from everyone on your Buddy List, only people on a Mobile Buddy List that you can set up, or everyone in the known universe (not recommended for your sanity).

Some obvious rules of messaging conduct

Sending someone an instant message is the online equivalent of walking up to someone on the street and starting a conversation. If it's someone you know, it's one thing; if not, it's usually an intrusion.

Unless you have a compelling reason, don't send instant messages to people you don't know who haven't invited you to do so. Don't say anything that you wouldn't say in an analogous situation on the street.

Most instant-message programs allow you to send and receive files. Unsolicited files from people you don't know are always spam, viruses, or both. Most virus checkers don't monitor file transfers via an IM program.

The messages you send with AIM and other chat programs may appear to be ephemeral, but anyone in the conversation can easily store the messages. Most IM programs have a log feature that saves the series of messages in a text file, which may be embarrassing later. In AIM, you control logging by choosing Edit➪Settings and clicking the IM Logging tab.

Finally, if someone tells you to give a series of commands or to download and install a program, don't do it. And never tell anyone any of your passwords.

Or, use Windows (Live) Messenger

Someone at Microsoft noticed that instant messaging was a niche in which the company didn't have the dominant program, and so they decided to issue everyone a copy of theirs. Windows XP comes with the latest instant-messaging program, Windows Messenger (which used to be named MSN Messenger), whereas Windows Vista has a Windows Live Messenger Download command on the Start menu.

We don't see the advantage of Windows Messenger over the other instant-message programs, but one nice thing is that it interconnects with Yahoo Messenger, so you can chat with people who use either system. (Or, you can use Pidgin, Adium, or Trillian to talk with people on all three major systems. See the earlier sidebar "Which instant-message system should I use?"). It supports voice and video, along with sending text messages to cellphones. Windows Live Messenger also has a nice Sharing Folder feature that allows you and a friend to share photos and other files.

Versions are available for Windows and Macs. Unless all your friends use Windows or Yahoo Messenger there's little reason to use it — but if they do (and you want to), you can download it from `http://get.live.com/ messenger`. See Chapter 12 for how to download and install programs. We recommend that you decline all the other programs that come along with Windows Live Messenger, by deselecting their check boxes during installation.

After Windows Live Messenger is installed, you can run it by choosing Start➪Windows Live Messenger. You sign in with your free Windows Live ID (previously known as a .NET Passport), if you created one; this account is the same one you use to read Hotmail, a type of Web mail account described in Chapter 13. The program, shown on the left side of Figure 16-3, works similarly to AIM, with a buddy list (contact list) and chat windows. You add people to your contact list by specifying their Windows Live e-mail address at Live.com or Hotmail.com or their Yahoo e-mail address at Yahoo.com. Then right-click a contact name and choose how to contact them — IM, e-mail, voice call, or video call (if you have a webcam). You can also make phone calls from your computer, but the calls aren't free.

Or, use Yahoo Messenger

Yahoo, the popular Web site, has its own instant-message program, named Yahoo Messenger. It pioneered multiperson voice and video chats back in 2001. We've held six-person voice-and-video conference calls using Yahoo Messenger for a total cost of $0. Yahoo Messenger can communicate with Windows Live Messenger, so there's no reason to install both programs, and it also has a photo-sharing feature. Yahoo Messenger can make and receive voice calls to real telephones, although it costs money. You can also use Yahoo Messenger to join Yahoo chat rooms, described in the section "Look Who's Chatting," later in this chapter.

Figure 16-3: Windows Live Messenger and Yahoo Messenger look a lot like AIM.

To get the program, go to `http://messenger.yahoo.com` and follow the directions to download and install the program. Yahoo Messenger is available in many versions, including versions for Windows, Macs, UNIX, and Palm, and a version that runs as a Flash applet in your Web browser — on *any* system that has a Flash-enabled browser.

When you download the program, it installs automatically. To log in, you create a free Yahoo ID for yourself. Go to the `http://messenger.yahoo.com` Web site and click the Sign In link if you already have a Yahoo ID, or click the Sign Up link if you don't. You can use your Yahoo ID for free Web mail, too, as described in Chapter 13. See Chapter 12 for how to download and install programs. We recommend clicking Custom Install during the installation and choosing to install only Yahoo Messenger, without the other miscellaneous programs. (Why glop up your computer?)

Yahoo Messenger, shown on the right side of Figure 16-3, looks and acts very much like AIM. Choose Contact⇔Add a Contact to add your friends who use Yahoo or Windows Messenger. Then you can right-click a contact and choose how you want to communicate with them — chat, text message to their cell-phone, voice message, phone call to their telephone number — you name it. After you're chatting, you can click the Conference button to add other people or choose Actions⇔View Webcam to view each other's webcams.

If you don't want to install a chat program, you can use Yahoo Messenger from your browser — go to the `http://webmessenger.yahoo.com` site to try it out. As of mid-2007, it provided only text chat.

Abbreviations and smileys

Typing is way slower than talking, so when people IM (or participate in online chat, described later in this chapter), they tend to abbreviate wildly. Many chat abbreviations are the same as those used in e-mail. Because IM is live, however, some are unique. We also list some common emoticons (sometimes called *smileys*) — funky combinations of punctuation used to depict the emotional inflection of the sender. If at first you don't see what they are, try tilting your head to the left. Table 16-1 shows you a short list of chat abbreviations and emoticons.

Table 16-1	IM and Chat Shorthand		
Abbreviation	**What It Means**	**Abbreviation**	**What It Means**
AFK	Away from keyboard	LTNS	Long time no see
A/S/L	Age/sex/location 35/f/LA)	LOL	Laughing out loud
BAK	Back at keyboard	NP	No problem
BBL	Be back later	OOC	Out of character (an RL aside during RP)
BRB	Be right back	PM	Private message (same as IM)
CYBER	A chat conversation of a prurient nature (short for *cybersex*)	RL	Real life (opposite of RP)
FTF or F2F	Face to face	ROTFL	Rolling on the floor laughing
IC	In character (playing a role)	RP	Role playing (acting out a character)
IGGIE	To set the Ignore feature, as in "I've iggied SmartMouthSam"	TTFN	Ta-ta for now!
IM	Instant message	WB	Welcome back
J/K	Just kidding	WTF?	What the heck?

(continued)

Table 16-1 *(continued)*

Abbreviation	What It Means	Abbreviation	What It Means
WTG	Way to go!	0:)	Angel
:) or :-)	A smile	}:>	Devil
;)	A wink	:P	Sticking out tongue
{{{{bob}}}}	A hug for Bob	*** or xox	Kisses
:(or :-(	Frown	<----	Action marker that appears before a phrase indicating what you're doing (<----eating pizza, for example)
:'(	Crying		

In addition to using the abbreviations in the table, chatters sometimes use simple shorthand abbreviations, as in If u cn rd ths ur rdy 2 chat.

Adding Voices and Faces

If you don't want to talk with or see people while you chat — that is, if you don't mind being limited to typing back and forth with your friends — skip this section. If you do want the audiovisual goodies, read on. You can use a webcam with AIM, Yahoo Messenger, and Windows Live Messenger.

Say what? Hooking up the sound

Almost every computer comes with speakers, which are connected to a *sound board* inside the computer. These speakers are what make the various noises that your programs make (like the AOL "You've got mail!" announcement). Most laptops have a built-in microphone, and most desktop computers also have a jack for a microphone. (Check your computer manual or ask almost any teenager for help with this.) If you don't have a microphone, you can get one that works with almost any computer. A mike should cost less than $20 at your local computer or office supply store.

To test your mike and speakers on a Windows machine, run the Sound Recorder program; try recording yourself and playing it back.

1. **Choose Start⇨All Programs⇨Accessories⇨Entertainment⇨Sound Recorder.**

2. **Click the red Record button to start recording, and the square Stop button to stop.**

   Talk, sing, or make other noises between your Start and Stop clicks.

3. **Click the triangular Play button to hear what you just recorded.**

   Click Record again to add to the end of your recording. Choose File⇨New to start over and throw away what you recorded.

4. **Choose File⇨Save to save it as a .WAV (audio) file.**

   We like to make .WAV recordings of our kids saying silly things and e-mail them — the recordings, not the kids — to their grandparents.

You can adjust the volume of your microphone (for the sound coming into the computer) and your speakers or headphones (for the sound coming out) by choosing Start⇨All Programs⇨Accessories⇨Entertainment⇨Volume Control. If a volume control for your microphone doesn't appear, choose Options⇨Properties, select the Microsoft check box so that a check mark appears, and click OK.

If you want to test how voices from the Net sound on your computer, type the URL http://net.gurus.com/ngc.wav into your browser and see what happens. You may need to click an Open or Open with Default Application button after it downloads. (Yes, that's John's mellifluous voice.)

If you can record yourself and hear the recording when you play it back, you're ready for Internet-based phone calls or chats!

I see you!

If you want other people to be able to see you during online conversations, consider getting a *webcam*. This small digital-video camera can connect to a computer. Webcams come in many sizes and shapes, and prices run from $30 to $300. More expensive webcams send higher-quality images at higher speeds, and come with better software. On the other hand, we've had great luck with a $36 webcam for chatting with friends and participating in videoconferences.

Most webcams connect to your computer's USB port, a little rectangular plug on the back of the computer. Older computers don't have USB ports. The better cameras connect to special video-capture cards, which you have to open your computer to install. For news and reviews about webcams, see the WebCam.com site at www.webcam.com.

If you own a digital video camera for taking video of your family and friends, you may be able to connect it to your computer for use as a webcam. Check the manual that came with the camera.

Viewing your chat buddies

When chatting in AIM with one other person, if both you and your friend have webcams set up, you can switch them on for use in your chat. Make sure that AIM knows about your webcam; choose Edit⇨Settings, click the Enhanced IM tab, and see whether the camera appears in the Video setting (it may just say Default Device).

To switch on your webcams, click the Video button at the bottom of the chat window. You see a message while AIM sets up the connection, and then your buddy's image appears! You can choose Actions in the video window to control the size of the video image.

Getting a webcam working with Yahoo Messenger, Windows Live Messenger, or Skype (described in the next section) works pretty much the same way as with AIM.

Internet Phones and Voice Chat

For about a decade, Internet phones were just around the corner. If you have a broadband Net connection, you're now near that corner. No Internet phenomenon would be complete without an arcane abbreviation, so this one is *VoIP,* for *Voice over Internet Protocol,* pronounced either V-O-I-P or to sound like a dripping faucet.

Some kinds of VoIP use a microphone and headphones plugged into the computer, but most people prefer the variety that use regular phones plugged into a *terminal adapter,* or TA. (See the nearby sidebar "The Hype about Skype" for the main exception.)

Signing up

Setting up VoIP phone service is moderately complicated, not unlike setting up regular phone service. You visit a VoIP provider's Web site and go through the signup process, which includes giving your payment info and picking your phone number, which can be either where you live or anywhere you want people to be able to call you as a local call. Most VoIP companies can also *port* your existing phone number away from your old phone company so that you don't have to change your number. (If you later hate your VoIP company, you can port it back, or to a different VoIP company.) The company then ships you the TA, which you plug into your Internet connection. Then you plug a regular phone into the TA, and you're ready to go.

Several VoIP companies sell combined routers (see Chapter 4) and VoIP terminal adapters through electronics stores. In that case, you set up your Internet connection with the router. Then you use your computer's Web browser to go to the VoIP company's Web site to activate the terminal-adapter part of the router, plug a phone into the phone jack on the router, and you're ready to go.

VoIP companies vary a lot, with local calling areas ranging from a single U.S. state to all of North America, Europe, and large parts of Asia. Calls to other customers of the same VoIP company are always free, so you might want to get the same one your friends have. See our Web site at `net.gurus.com/phone` for some suggestions about VoIP companies.

If you have a cable modem, your cable company may also offer VoIP. If it does. the quality of service is better than what you get with independent VoIP providers, so it's worth a close look.

The hype about Skype

Skype is a freeware VoIP service owned by eBay. It's located in Luxembourg, a tiny country in Europe whose main attraction is that it's not anywhere else. You download and install Skype on your computer from `www.skype.com`, set up a free account, and start using it to talk to other Skype users. You need a headset with headphones and a microphone, or a handset (which is like a phone handset) plugged into your computer. Skype's voice quality over most broadband is very good, much better than that of a normal phone.

Skype isn't limited to talking to other Skype users. You can set up a SkypeOut account to which you add money — from a credit card or as a bonus included with some computer headsets — and you can then call any normal phone in the world and pay by the minute. Rates are quite low, about 2¢/minute for the U.S., Canada, or Europe, and do not depend on where you're using Skype, only where you're calling. John once called home using his laptop via a WiFi connection in a hotel lobby in Argentina for 2 cents rather than the dollar a minute it would have cost from a payphone. You can also use SkypeIn — a real phone number for your Skype phone so that people can call you — for a monthly fee.

Skype lets you have conference calls of up to five people, any combination of Skype users and SkypeOut calls to regular phones. It includes an IM feature for typing with your friends while talking to them (or even when you're not talking to them). And it has a chat feature with SkypeMe, in which you set up a profile, set your online status to SkypeMe, and invite people to call. Skype users live all over the world, so with luck, you may make some new faraway friends.

Using your VoIP phone

It's a phone. When it rings, answer it. If you want to call someone, pick up the phone and dial. Most VoIP companies offer a full suite of phone features, like voice mail, call forwarding, and caller ID, usually controlled via a Web page rather than through the phone itself.

Around the Virtual Town Pump

Typing or talking to a few people is fun and interesting, but for really good gossip, you need a group. Fortunately, the Internet offers limitless opportunities to find like-minded people and discuss anything you can imagine. Clubs, churches, and other groups use the Internet to hold meetings. Hobbyists and fans talk about an amazing variety of topics, from knitting to *American Idol* and everything in between. People with medical problems support each other and exchange tips. You get the idea — anything that people might want to talk about is now under intense discussion somewhere on the Net.

You can talk with groups of people on the Internet in lots of ways, including these:

- ✔ **E-mail mailing lists,** in which you exchange messages by e-mail.
- ✔ **Web-based message boards,** where messages appear on a Web page.
- ✔ **Social networking sites,** like MySpace and Facebook, which are described in Chapter 17.
- ✔ **Usenet newsgroups** (the original Internet discussion groups), which you read with a *newsreading program.* For a description of Usenet newsgroups and how to read them, see our Web site at net.gurus.com/usenet. Or, go to http://groups.google.com on the Web and search for topics that interest you.

This section tells you how to participate in Internet-based discussions using e-mail mailing lists and Web message boards.

Mailing lists: Are you sure that this isn't junk mail?

An e-mail mailing list is quite different from a snail-mail mailing list. Yes, both distribute messages to the people on the list, but the messages on most e-mail mailing lists contain a discussion among the subscribers rather than junk mail and catalogs.

Here's how an e-mail mailing list works. The list has its own, special e-mail address, and anything someone sends to that address is sent to all the people on the list. Because these people in turn often respond to the messages, the result is a running conversation. For example, if the authors of this book hosted a discussion called *chocolate-lovers,* about the use and abuse of chocolate, and if the list-server program ran at `lists.gurus.com`, the list of the address would be `chocolate-lovers@lists.gurus.com`. (We do run a bunch of lists, but not one about chocolate. Yet.)

Different lists have different styles. Some are relatively formal, hewing closely to the official topic of the list. Others tend to go flying off into outer space, topic-wise. You have to read them for a while to be able to tell which list works which way.

Mailing lists fall into three categories:

- **Discussion:** Every subscriber can post a message. These lists lead to freewheeling discussions and can include a certain number of off-topic messages.

- **Moderated:** A moderator reviews each message before it gets distributed. The moderator can stop unrelated, redundant, or clueless postings from wasting everyone's time.

- **Announcement-only:** Only the moderator posts messages. Announcement mailing lists are essentially online newsletters.

Who handles all this mail?

Something or somebody has to take on the job of keeping track of who's on the mailing list and distributing messages to all the subscribers. This job is *way* too boring for a human being to handle, so programs usually do the job. (A few lists are still run by human beings, and we pity them!) Most lists are run by *list servers* or *mailing-list managers.* Popular list-server programs include LISTSERV, Lyris, Majordomo, MailMan, and many others, as well as Web-based systems, such as Yahoo Groups and Google Groups.

Talking to the human being in charge

Someone is in charge of every mailing list: the *list manager.* The list manager is in charge of helping people on and off the list, answering questions about the list, and hosting the discussion. If you have a problem with a list, write a *nice* message to the list manager. Remember that most list managers are volunteers who sometimes eat, sleep, and work regular jobs as well as maintain mailing lists. If it takes longer than you want, be patient. *Don't* send cranky follow-ups — they just cheese off the list manager.

The list manager's address is usually the same as the list address with the addition of *owner-* at the beginning or *-request* just before the @. For example, the manager of the `chocoloate-lovers@lists.gurus.com` list would be `chocoloate-lovers-request@lists.gurus.com`.

Getting on and off lists

To find out how to subscribe to a list, or how to unsubscribe to the list, take a look at the instructions that (with luck) came with whatever information you received about the mailing list. With most lists, you can subscribe, unsubscribe, and change your subscription settings from the Web — you go to a Web page and fill out a form. Generally you enter your e-mail address in a box on a Web page, click a Send or Subscribe button, and you're on the list. This is often more convenient than sending a command by e-mail.

Before you subscribe, be sure that you see a way to get *off* the list (an option that some marketing-oriented outfits neglect to provide).

You should receive a chatty, machine-generated welcoming message telling you that you have joined the list, along with a description of some commands you can use to fiddle with your mailing-list membership. Usually, this message includes a request to confirm that you received this message and that it was really you who wanted to subscribe. Follow the instructions by clicking a link or replying to this message, or doing whatever else the instructions say to do. Confirmation helps lists ensure that they aren't mailing into the void, and keeps people from sticking you on lists without your knowledge. If you don't provide this confirmation, you don't get on the list.

Don't delete the chatty, informative welcome message that tells you about all the commands you can use when you're dealing with the list. For one thing, it tells you how to get *off* the mailing list if it's not to your liking. We have in our mail program a folder named Mailing Lists, in which we store the welcome messages from all the mailing lists we join, so that we don't have to embarrass ourselves by asking for help with unsubscribing later.

To get off a list, you again visit the Web page for the list and follow the unsubscription instructions. *Don't* send a message to the list saying "Please unsubscribe me" because it just wastes the other subscribers' time.

Stupid mailing-list tricks

Most list servers know some other commands, including commands to hold your mail for a while, send you a daily message that includes all the postings for the day, and see a subscriber list. Refer to the instructions you received when you subscribed to the list for the exact commands, which vary depending on the list server software. (You did save the welcome message, didn't you?)

Sending messages to mailing lists

Okay, you're signed up on a mailing list. Now what? First, wait a week or so to see what sort of messages arrive from the list — that way, you can get an idea of what you should or should not send to it. When you think that you have seen enough to avoid embarrassing yourself, try sending something in. That's easy: You mail a message to the list address, which is the same as the name of the list — `chocolate-lovers@lists.gurus.com` or `dandruff-l@bluesuede.org` or whatever. Keep in mind that because hundreds or thousands of people may be reading your pearls of wisdom, you should at least try to spell things correctly. (You may have thought that this advice is obvious, but you would be sadly mistaken.) On popular lists, you may begin to get back responses within a few minutes of sending a message.

Some lists encourage new subscribers to send in messages introducing themselves and saying briefly what their interests are. Others don't. Don't send anything until you have something to say. After you watch the flow of messages on a list for a while, all this stuff becomes obvious.

Some mailing lists have rules about who is allowed to send messages, so just because you're on the list doesn't automatically mean that any messages you send appear on the list. Some lists are *moderated:* Any message you send in gets sent to a human *moderator* who decides what goes to the list and what doesn't. Although this process may sound sort of fascist, moderation can make a list about 50 times more interesting than it would be otherwise because a good moderator can filter out the boring and irrelevant messages and keep the list on track. Indeed, the people who complain the loudest about moderator censorship are usually the ones whose messages most urgently need to be filtered out.

Another rule that sometimes causes trouble is that many lists allow messages to be sent only from people whose addresses appear on the list, to prevent the list from getting overrun with spam. If your mailing address changes, you have to resubscribe or you can't post anything.

Boing!

Computer accounts are created and deleted often enough and mail addresses change often enough that a large list always contains, at any given moment, some addresses that are no longer valid. If you send a message to the list, your message is forwarded to these invalid addresses — and a return message (reporting a bad address) is generated for each of them. Mailing-list managers (both human and computer) normally try to deflect the error messages over to the list owner, who can do something about them, rather than to you. As often as not, however, a persistently dumb mail system sends one of these failure messages directly to you. Just ignore it because you can't do anything about it.

Sometimes you may get an "I'm away on vacation" message or a "Click here if you're not a spammer" message in response to list messages you send. *Don't respond to those, either* — vacation and anti-spam programs shouldn't even be responding to list mail. Forward them to the list manager, though, so that she can suspend those recipients' subscriptions until they get their software under control.

The fine points of replying to list messages

Often, you receive an interesting message from a list and want to respond to it. When you send your answer, does it go *just* to the person who sent the original message or to the *entire list?* It depends on how the list manager set up the list. About half the list managers set up their lists so that replies go automatically to just the person who sent the original message, on the theory that your response is likely to be of interest to only the original author. The other half set up the lists so that replies go to the entire list, on the theory that the list is a running public discussion. In messages coming from the list, the mailing-list software automatically sets the Reply-To header line to the address to which replies should be sent.

Fortunately, you're in charge of that feature. When you start to create a reply, your mail program should show you the address to which it's replying. If you don't like the address it's using, change the address. Check the To and Cc fields to make sure that you're sending your message where you want. Don't run the risk of sending a message such as, "I agree with you — aren't the rest of these people idiots?" to the whole list if you intend it for only one person.

While you're fixing the recipient's address, you may also want to fix the Subject line. After a few rounds of replies to replies to replies, the topic of discussion often wanders away from the original topic. Change the subject to better describe what is really under discussion, as a favor to the other folks trying to follow the discussion.

How to avoid looking like an idiot

After you subscribe to a list, don't send anything to it until you read it for a week. Trust us — the list has been getting along without your insights since it began, and it can get along without them for one more week.

You can determine which topics people really discuss and the tone of the list, for example. It also gives you a fair idea about which topics people are tired of. The classic newcomer gaffe is to subscribe to a list and immediately send a message asking a dumb question that isn't really germane to the topic and that was beaten to death three days earlier.

The number-two newcomer gaffe is to send a message directly to the list asking to subscribe or unsubscribe. This type of message should go to the list manager or list server program, *not* to the list itself, where all the other subscribers can see that you screwed up.

One last thing not to do: If you don't like what another person is posting (for example, some newbie is posting blank messages or "unsubscribe me" messages or is ranting interminably about a topic), don't waste everyone's time by posting a response on the list. The only thing stupider than a stupid posting is a response complaining about it. Instead, e-mail the person *privately* and ask him to stop, or e-mail the list manager and ask that person to intervene.

Posting to message boards

Mailing lists are great if you want to receive messages by e-mail, but some people prefer to read messages on the Web. These folks are in luck: *Message boards* are Web-based discussion groups that post messages on a Web site. They're also called *discussion boards*, *forums*, or *communities*. Like mailing lists, some message boards are readable only by subscribers, some allow only subscribers to post, and some are *moderated* (that is, a moderator must approve messages before they appear on the message board). Other message boards are more like bulletin boards: Anyone can post anytime, and there's no continuity to the messages or feeling of community among the people who post.

Many Web sites include message boards. Some Web sites are dedicated to hosting message boards on lots of different topics. Some sites host message boards that can also send the messages to you by e-mail, so they work as message boards and mailing lists rolled into one.

Excellent Web-based discussion sites

Here are some of our favorites:

✔ **About.com, at** www.about.com: About.com hires semipro experts in a wide variety of fields to host sites about each field. For example, the knitting site at http://knitting.about.com is run by a world-class knitter who posts articles and patterns and hosts one or more message boards about knitting. Find the Forums link in the list of topics down the left side of the screen. Figure 16-4 shows a discussion of knitting techniques.

✔ **Google Groups, at** http://groups.google.com: Google Groups started as a way for people to participate in Usenet newsgroups via the Web. Then Google provided a way to set up new groups, too. You can search by topic for groups or messages of interest.

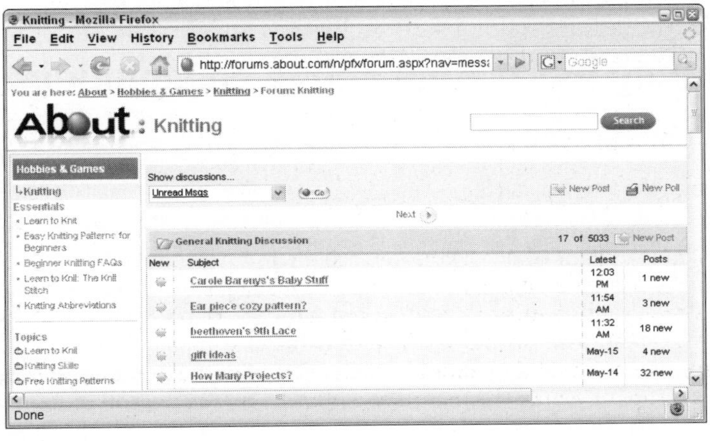

Figure 16-4: About.com hosts sites about hundreds (thousands?) of topics, each with a message board

✔ **MSN Groups, at** `http://groups.msn.com`: MSN Groups include message boards, live chat rooms, and other information. You can browse lists of groups by topic or search for groups with a particular word or phrase in its name. To join a group, you need to sign up for a free .NET Passport.

✔ **Yahoo Groups, at** `http://groups.yahoo.com`: Yahoo Groups include message boards and file libraries, and you can read the messages either on the Web site or by e-mail — it's your choice when you join a group. Yahoo Groups also feature calendars for group events and real-time chats right on the Web site. To join, you must first sign up for a free Yahoo ID, which also gets you a mailbox and free Web space — what a deal! You can also create your own Yahoo Group by clicking links — either a public group for all to join or a private group for your club or family.

Subscribing and participating

Most good message boards require you to register before you can subscribe, which means that you choose a username and password, and possibly provide your e-mail address, and respond to a message sent to that address. Registration makes it harder for spam-posting robots to take over the message board.

To subscribe to a community on one of these Web sites, just follow the instructions on the site. Some community Web sites let you read the messages posted to their lists without subscribing — you can click links to display the messages in your Web browser.

You can set up your own mailing lists or message boards, too. It's free because the sites display ads on their Web pages, and may even tack on ads to the postings on the list. If you have an unusual hobby, job, interest, or ailment, you may want to create a list to discuss it. Or, set up a list for a committee or family group to use for online discussions.

Finding interesting online communities

Tens of thousands of communities — in the form of mailing lists, message boards, and hybrids of the two — reside on the Internet, but there's no central directory of them. This is partly because so many lists are intended only for specific groups of people, like members of the board of directors of the First Parish Church of Podunk or students in Economics 101 at Tech State.

You can find some communities by searching the Web (as described in Chapter 8) and including the word or phrase, mailing list, community, forum, or message board. Or, start at `http://about.com`, `http://groups.google.com`, `http://groups.yahoo.com`, or `http://groups.msn.com` and search for your topic.

Look Who's Chatting

Online chat is similar to talking on an old-fashioned party line (or CB radio). In the infancy of the telephone system, people usually shared their phone lines with other families because stringing telephone lines was expensive. Everyone on the party line could join in any conversation, offering hours of nosy fun for people with nothing better to do. Online chat differs from IM chat because it's public and you usually don't know the other people in the discussion.

You begin chatting by entering an area of the Internet called an electronic *chat room* or *channel.* After you join a room, you can read on-screen what people are saying and then add your own comments just by typing them and clicking Send. Although several people participating in the chat can type at the same time, each person's contribution is presented on-screen in the order received. Whatever people type appears in the general conversation window and is identified by their screen names. On some chat systems, such as AOL, each participant can select a personal type font and color for his comments.

If one of the people in a chat room seems like someone you want to know better, you can ask to establish a *private room* or *direct connection,* which is a private conversation between you and the other person and not much different from instant messaging. And, of course, you might get such an invitation from someone else. It's not uncommon for someone to be in a chat room and be holding several direct conversations at the same time, although it's considered rude (not to mention confusing!) to overdo this.

You might also get asked to join a private chat room with several other people. We're not really sure just what goes on in those rooms because we've never been invited.

Where is everyone chatting?

Which groups of people you can chat with depends on which chat system you connect to. Here are a few places you can find groups of people chatting online:

- ✔ **America Online:** If you have an America Online account, you can chat with other AOL users. Get *AOL For Dummies*, by John Kaufeld and Ted Leonsis (Wiley) for a full description of AOL chat rooms.

- ✔ **Skype and other VoIP systems:** If you use Skype (described in the section "Internet Phones and Voice Chat," earlier in this chapter), you can choose the Live tab to join a public voice chat, or choose Chats⇨Start Public Chat to start your own.

✔ **Web sites:** Some Web sites include chat rooms, using a plug-in program that allows people to type at each other.

✔ **Yahoo Messenger:** In Yahoo Messenger, you can choose Messenger⇨ Yahoo Chat.

Chatting is pretty much the same from system to system, although the participants vary. This section gives a sense of the essence of chat no matter where you go to do it. We describe how to use Web-based chat rooms later in this chapter.

Each chat room has a name; with luck, the name is an indication of what the chatters there are talking about or what they have in common. Some channels have names such as *lobby,* and the people there are probably just being sociable.

Who am 1?

No matter which chat facility you use, each participant has a *screen name,* or *nickname,* often chosen to be unique, colorful, or clever and used as a mask. Chatters sometimes change their screen names. This anonymity makes a chat room a place where you need to be careful. On the other hand, one attraction of chatting is meeting new and interesting people. Many warm and wonderful friendships have evolved from a chance meeting in a chat room.

When you join a group and begin chatting, you see the screen names of the people who are already there and a window in which the current conversation goes flying by. If the group is friendly, somebody may even send you a welcome message.

As in real life, in a room full of strangers you're likely to encounter people you don't like much. Because it's possible to be fairly anonymous on the Internet, some people act boorish, vulgar, or crude. If you're new to chat, sooner or later you'll visit some disgusting places, although you'll find out how to avoid them and find rooms that have useful, friendly, and supportive conversations. Be very careful about letting children chat unsupervised (see Chapter 3). Even in chat rooms that are designed for young people and provide some supervision, unwholesome goings-on can take place.

Type or talk?

The original chat rooms consisted entirely of people typing messages to each other. Newer chat systems include *voice chat* (which requires you to have a microphone and speakers on your computer) and even video (which requires a webcam if you want other people to be able to see you).

Getting Used to Chat Culture

Your first time in a chat room can seem stupid or daunting or both. Here are some things you can do to get through your first encounters:

- ✔ Remember that when you enter a chat room, a conversation is probably already in progress. You don't know what went on before you arrived.

- ✔ Wait a minute or two to see a page full of exchanges so that you can understand some of the context before you start writing.

- ✔ Read messages for a while to figure out what's happening before sending a message to a chat group. (Reading without saying anything is known as *lurking*. When you finally venture to say something, you're *de-lurking*.) Lurking isn't necessarily a bad thing, but be aware that you might not always have the privacy you think you have.

- ✔ Some chat systems enable you to indicate people to ignore. Messages from these chatters no longer appear on your screen, although other members' replies to them do appear. This is usually the best way to deal with obnoxious chatters. You may also be able to get your chat program not to display the many system messages, which announce when people arrive, leave, or are ejected forcefully from the chat room.

- ✔ Scroll up to see older messages if you have to, but remember that on most systems, after you have scrolled up, no new messages appear until you scroll back down.

Online chat etiquette

Chatting etiquette isn't that much different from e-mail etiquette, and common sense is your best guide. Here are some additional chatting tips:

- ✔ The first rule of chatting is not to hurt anyone. A real person with real feelings is at the other end of the computer-chat connection. Don't insult people, don't use foul language, and don't respond to people who do.

- ✔ The second rule is to be cautious. You really have no idea who the other people are. Remember, too, that people might be hanging out in a chat room and quietly collecting information, and you might not notice them because they never say anything.

- ✔ Keep your messages short and to the point.

✔ Create a profile with selected information about yourself. Most chat systems have provisions for creating profiles (personal information) that other members can access.

Don't give out your last name, phone number, or address. Extra caution is necessary for kids: A kid should never enter her age, hometown, school, last name, phone number, or address. Although you don't have to tell everything about yourself in your profile, what you do say should be truthful. The one exception is role-playing chat, where everyone is acting out a fantasy character.

✔ If you want to talk to someone in private, send a message saying hi, who you are, and what you want.

✔ If the tone of conversation in one chat room offends or bores you, try another. As in real life, you run into lots of people in chat rooms that you *don't* want to meet — and you don't have to stay there.

As in society at large, online chat involves some contact with strangers. Most encounters are with more-or-less reasonable folks. For the rest, common sense dictates that you keep your wits about you — and your private information private. See Chapter 2 for some guidelines for staying safe while chatting with strangers.

Let's Chat

Whatever chat service you use, the idea is the same — you read other people's messages and chime in with your own. In this section, we describe Web-based chat because it's available to all Internet users without installing any extra programs.

Web-based chat sites have Java-based chat programs that your browser can download and run automatically. Some other Web chat sites require that you download a plug-in or ActiveX control to add chat capability to your browser. (see Chapter 7 for information on how to use plug-ins).

Finding some action

Some Web chat sites include

✔ ICG Chat, at `www.icq.com/icqchat`

✔ MSN Groups at `http://groups.msn.com`

✔ Userplane at `www.userplane.com`, which supports text, voice, and video chat

Many other Web sites have chats on the specific topic of the site. Search for **chat** at `http://.dmoz.org` or `www.google.com` for a variety of chat venues.

Starting to chat

Most chat sites have directories or search boxes so that you can find a group talking about a topic of interest. Actually, we find that after you get into the chat room, 93 percent of chats are about nothing at all, or general flirting, so you may need to shop around. Also, it may take a number of tries until you find a chat room where people are actually chatting — sometimes, everyone appears to have wandered off.

Most Web-based chat pages have a large window that displays the ongoing conversation, a smaller window that displays the screen names of the participants, and a text area where you type your messages. Figure 16-5 shows a chat room at Userplane.com. After you type your message, press Enter or click Send, and the message appears in the message window for you and everyone else in the chat room.

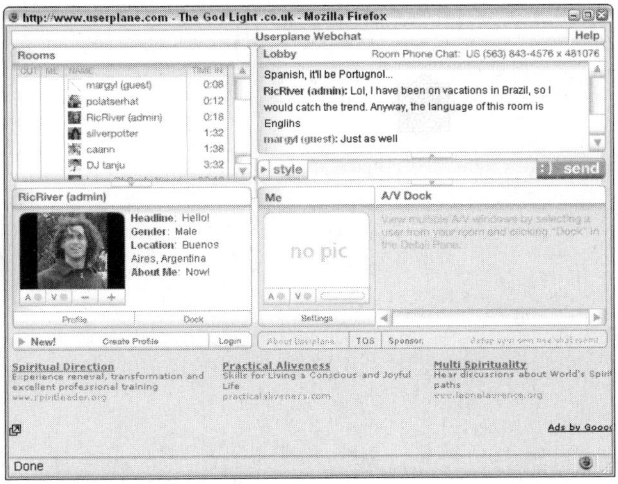

Figure 16-5: The Userplane site hosts lots of chat rooms.

In some chat rooms, you can click a name in the list of participants to see more information about that person, perhaps a name, location, or picture. Some chat rooms have links or buttons that enable you to turn on voice so that you can talk into your computer's microphone and hear other people from the speakers. And some have video buttons or links that can enable your webcam.

Part V
Putting Your Own Stuff on the Net

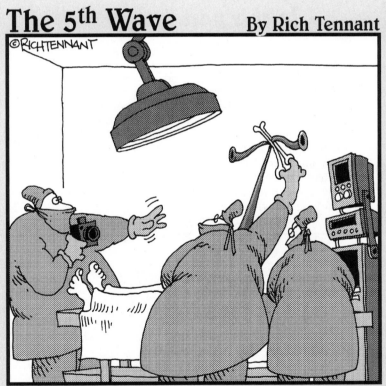

The 5th Wave   By Rich Tennant

"Ooo-wait! That's perfect for the clinic's home page. Just stretch it out a little further... little more..."

In this part . . .

The Internet is different from other computer networks because it's *flat* — every computer is, in principle, equal to every other. So there's no excuse for being a virtual couch potato and just looking at other people's stuff — you can publish your own stuff. We start with a look at all the ways to make or contribute to Web sites, like photo gallery sites, video-sharing sites, Weblogs, and social networking sites like MySpace and Facebook, including making your own Web site from scratch. Then we dive into virtual worlds, the parts of cyberspace inhabited by real people (sometimes remarkably large numbers of real people), one of whom can be you.

Chapter 17

Look Who Has a Web Site — You!

*B*ack at the dawn of the World Wide Web (18 years ago), the plan was that people all over the world would use it to communicate among themselves — a virtual rustic global village. That's not exactly how it turned out, with giant megamalls like Amazon.com making the Net a distinctly non-rustic experience. However, after you've used the Internet and browsed the Web for a while, you'll probably think of putting your own material on the Web. Hey, you've got interesting things to say, probably more interesting than a lot of Web sites that are out there!

You can create a Web site for yourself, consisting of one or many pages, with your own domain name. These days, you have a lot of options for posting information on the Web: writings, photos, songs, videos — you name it — without having to become a Web page guru. This chapter explains how to post pictures, audio files, and videos and sell stuff on the Web on many different types of sites. Chapter 18 describes how to make a roll-your-own Web site using a Web page editor. Chapter 19 covers how to participate in online games, including creating a persona, buying land, and making a new life on Second Life.

Lots of Ways to Post Your Own Stuff

You can post information on the Internet in dozens of different ways. Some require more startup effort than others. Here's an overview of the best methods for getting started with an online site:

✓ **Create photo galleries:** Many sites enable you to create an online gallery of photos or other pictures. You can make your gallery public or share it with only friends and family. See the section "Say 'Cheese!'" later in this chapter.

✓ **Share videos:** If you have home videos, animated movies, or other digital video you created or edited using software on your PC or Mac, you can post it on a number of video sites. See the section "The Internet's Funniest Home Videos," later in this chapter.

✓ **Sell stuff:** You can sell goods or services in an online storefront or auction. See the section "Setting Up an Online Shop," later in this chapter.

✓ **Participate in social networking:** Web sites such as MySpace and Facebook started as glorified personal ads, and have expanded to include photos, video, e-mail, blogs, polls — you name it. See the section "Presenting Your Online Self," later in this chapter.

✓ **Write a Web log (blog):** You can create an online diary or journal with chronological entries. The later section "What's in a Blog?" describes how to read blogs, and the section "Writing Your Own Blog" tells you how to do just that.

✓ **Produce podcasts:** If you're a musician, storyteller, minister, or teacher or you just think you have something to say, you can post digital recordings on the Web. See the section "Songs on the Net," later in this chapter.

✓ **Create a collaborative Web site:** A *wiki* enables you and your friends or co-workers to edit a set of Web pages together. See the section "Working Together on a Wiki," at the end of this chapter. Or, you can post word processing documents or spreadsheets that selected others can view or edit.

✓ **Engage in multiuser online gaming:** You can participate in online games, anything from contract bridge to complete alternative universes, as described in Chapter 19.

✓ **Build a handcrafted Web site:** You can use a Web page editor to create Web pages in almost any format, with almost any information. See Chapter 18 for an overview.

Safety concerns

Regardless of how you create your site, consider carefully what information you want to make public. Remember that everyone in the entire world will be able to read what you write, and it will be available online forever. (Sites such as the Wayback Machine at `www.archive.org` save copies of old Web sites.) Whatever you post now will be readable by future bosses, your children's teachers, potential dates — everyone.

We suggest that you not post your address (mailing or physical address, unless you have a post office box), phone number, or exact age (lie a little). Kids and youth should omit or fudge the names of their schools. You can even create an online persona for yourself, complete with a new name and personal details, as long as you don't use it to deliberately mislead people about yourself.

For more about safety concerns about social networking sites, read *MySpace Safety: 51 Tips for Teens and Parents*, by Kevin and Dale Farnham (from `howtoprimers.com`). Or, visit OnGuard Online, at `http://onguardonline.gov`, for safety tips from the U.S. government.

How do you choose what kind of site to create or where to post your material? Here are questions to get you started:

- ✔ **Do you want to share files with friends and family, or do you want to make a public site?** Some types of sites enable you to control who can see your material, whereas other types are designed to be completely public and open to the world. For private sites, consider photo-sharing sites, blogs, social networking sites, wikis, or Google Docs.

- ✔ **What kind of material do you want to post?** Do you have pictures, sound files, video, or writing? Maybe you have a word-processing document or spreadsheet that you want others to see or edit. Photo-sharing sites are for photos only, perhaps with captions and a little text. Blogs can combine text and photos. For videos, try YouTube or other video-sharing sites. For documents and spreadsheets, use Google Docs.

- ✔ **How much control do you want to have over the format of the site?** Each type of site listed in this chapter has its own, built-in format and limitations. If you want complete control over the format and position of material on your site, you need to create it from scratch (what we're calling a handcrafted Web site, described in Chapter 18).

We suggest that you read (or at least flip) through this chapter and the next before deciding. Also, check with your friends to see what they use and like.

Say "Cheese!"

If you want to put pictures on the Web for your far-flung family and friends to see, you can create a free account on one of a number of photo-sharing sites, like the one in Figure 17-1. (Family-friendly only, please.) Try one of these photo-sharing sites:

- ✔ **Flickr** (part of Yahoo), at www.flickr.com, lets you send photos from your Web browser, your e-mail program, or even your phone. Flickr gives you the choice of making photos public to all Flickr users, accessible only to specific groups of people, or completely private.

- ✔ **Kodak Gallery**, at www.kodakgallery.com, makes it easy to share photos with family and friends and get Kodak high-quality prints.

- ✔ **Picasa** (part of Google), at www.picasa.com or picasa.google.com, works with the free, downloadable Picasa program, which helps you organize, caption, and edit photos on your PC.

- ✔ HP's **Snapfish**, at www.snapfish.com, lets you set up online photo albums using either photos you upload or rolls of film you mail in to the site. You can share the albums and order prints.

After you create an account at one of these sites, you can upload photos into online photo albums by filling out forms on the Web site. Then you can share your albums with your friends. If you want, you can make your photos on these sites invisible to the general public — visible to only the people with whom you share the album.

Picture formats

Pictures come in dozens of formats. Fortunately, only three picture formats are in common use on the Web: GIF, PNG, and JPEG. Many lengthy ... er, *free* and *frank* discussions have occurred on the Internet concerning the relative merits of these formats. John, who is an Official Graphics Format Expert, by virtue of having persuaded two otherwise reputable publishers to publish his books on the topic, suggests that photographs work better in JPEG format, whereas clip art, icons, and cartoons are better in PNG or GIF. If you're in doubt, JPEG files are smaller, and download faster. PNG is a superior, new replacement for GIF, and its only disadvantage is that people with very old browsers (Netscape 3.0 and older, for example) can't easily view PNG files.

If you have a picture in any other format, such as BMP or PCX, you must convert it to GIF, PNG, or JPEG before you can use it on the Web. Windows comes with Paint, which you can run by choosing Start➪All Programs➪Accessories➪Paint. Or, check out Tucows, at http://tucows.com/Windows or Download.com at www.download.com for graphics programs that can do conversions. For the Mac, consider GraphicConverter at www.lemkesoft.de and click the American flag for the English version of the site.

You (and your friends) can also order prints of your uploaded photos — that's how these sites make their money. The prices for prints are reasonable, and we find these systems very convenient. You can print your photos as calendars, cards, books, and even postage stamps!

Figure 17-1: You can share your photos on the Web without having to create your own Web site.

Another way to share photos is to include them on a blog, as described in Chapter 18. Blogs are great if you want to use your photos to illustrate a narrative, like the story of your trip to Spain. You can also post photos on social networking sites like MySpace and Facebook.

The Internet's Funniest Home Videos

It would be hard to live in the 21st century and not have heard of YouTube, the popular video-sharing Web site that is owned by Google. YouTube and similar sites, like Google Video, store huge libraries of videos that you can search and watch. To watch videos on YouTube and other video-sharing sites, see the section "Watching movies on the Net" in Chapter 9.

You can post videos on these sites, too, as long as your video isn't longer than 10 minutes. Use your video camera to shoot a short movie and transfer it to your PC. This topic is too vast to cover here; see *Digital Video For Dummies,* 4th Edition, by Keith Underdahl (Wiley Publishing, Inc.), for more information about storing and editing videos on your computer. Then you can upload your video. On YouTube, you need to sign up for a free account first and then click the Upload Videos link on any YouTube page.

Kyte, at `www.kyte.tv`, enables you to upload videos from your cellphone, digital camera, or computer and distribute them to friends or the entire world via your MySpace pages, your own Web site, your blog, or people's cellphones. The Kyte Web site includes tools for editing your video, turning still photos into a slide show, and adding a soundtrack. People who are watching a Kyte video at the same time can even chat with each other. ("Wow — how did he do that?" or "Who is this loser?")

Setting Up an Online Shop

Selling stuff on the Internet used to take hundreds of thousands of dollars worth of software and programming talent. A number of sites now let you create a Web store for very modest fees. Here are a few:

- ✔ **Amazon.com Marketplace**, at `http://amazon.com`, is particularly easy to set up — click Sell Your Stuff to find out how to set up a seller account. The site even processes credit card sales for you, eliminating what was once a horrible pain in the neck.

- ✔ **eBay.com Stores**, at `http://pages.ebay.com/sellercentral`, enable you to sell items in auctions (for which eBay is famous) or at fixed prices (the Buy It Now option). Your store can have its own name and logo, and items in your store show up when people search eBay for merchandise.

- ✔ **Yahoo**, at `http://smallbusiness.yahoo.com`, enables you to create a storefront for a monthly fee.

To set up a store, you sign up for a free account at the Web site and then click the link to create the store. You provide information about the items you sell, including descriptions, prices, and shipping costs.

If you don't want to set up a whole store, you can still sell individual items either on consignment at sites like `www.half.com` or at auction at sites like `www.ebay.com`. eBay now owns Half.com, so when you set up an account to buy or sell items on one, you're ready to buy or sell on the other, too.

To sell an item on Half.com (or any other consignment site), first find the item you want to sell (as shown in Figure 17-2). Half specializes in books, movies, and music, and it has almost everything in print in its database. When you find your item, click the Sell Yours Now link, specify the condition of the item, add a description, and state your asking price. When you click the List Item link, your listing goes into the Half.com database and appears on the site within an hour. When you sell your item — which could be minutes, hours, or months later — Half.com keeps a commission.

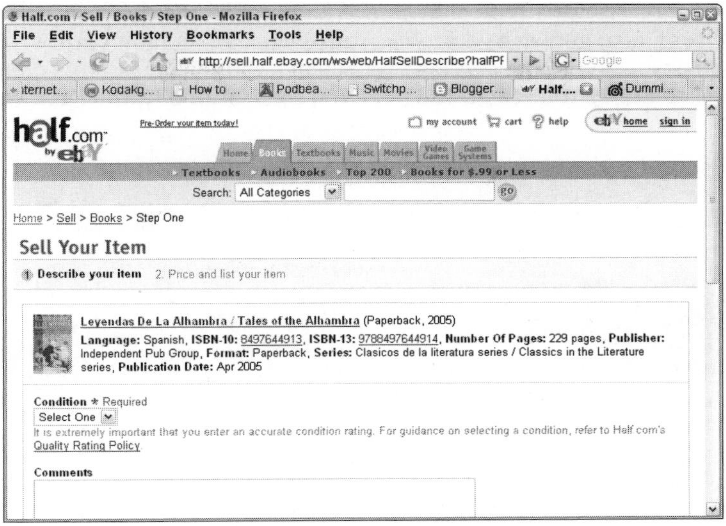

Figure 17-2:
You have a book to sell on Half.com.

Selling an item on eBay is a little more complicated. You need to write a description for the item and take or scan a digital picture of it. (For some items, like books and CDs, eBay may have your item in its Half.com database, and you can use its description and picture.) Start at `www.ebay.com`, click the Sell tab or link, and follow the directions. Auctions can last as long as seven days. eBay charges you a listing fee, although if your item doesn't sell, you can usually relist it (try again, perhaps with a lower starting price) for free.

Presenting Your Online Self

MySpace and Facebook are *social networking sites* that make it easy to make a Web page about yourself without having to know how to use HTML. Then you can use your Web page to communicate with friends, organize events, create committees, and meet new people.

Social networking sites have become hugely popular with teenagers and young business owners trying to branch out in their social and financial assets. Many musical groups (especially rock bands) have also found MySpace to be a good place to communicate with fans. And every political candidate who's serious needs a MySpace or Facebook presence. Since their creation, MySpace and Facebook have been a way for people to publish their thoughts and ideas on the Internet, free of charge. They have also opened up a huge window for up-and-coming musicians, poets, and other performers, helping many people rise in their careers.

Figure 17-3 shows a typical MySpace page (okay, it's the page of one of the authors), also known as a *profile*. Your page can include photos, videos, a blog (described in the section "What's in a Blog?" later in this chapter), and other elements to present the Real You (or, optionally, the Fake You).

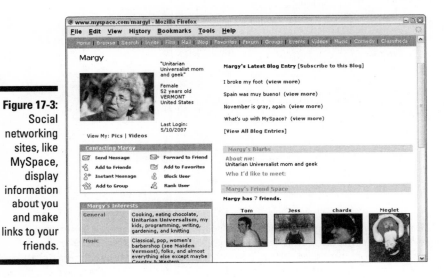

Figure 17-3:
Social networking sites, like MySpace, display information about you and make links to your friends.

You can find a bunch of social networking sites, including these:

- ✔ **Bebo** (www.bebo.com) lets you draw pictures on other people's whiteboards or add quizzes and polls to your profile.
- ✔ **Facebook** (www.facebook.com) was started for college students but now welcomes everybody.
- ✔ **MySpace** (www.myspace.com) is directed primarily at high school students, artists, and bands.
- ✔ **Xanga** (www.xanga.com) was original a blogging site, but added photos and videos.

MySpace and Facebook are the most popular, so those are the sites we describe in this section.

Different sites have different age restrictions for users, along with rules that apply to all users regardless of age. The MySpace terms of service (*ToS*, in the lingo) prohibit posting your phone number, street address, nude photos, sexually explicit subject matter, and commercial advertisements (except for theirs, of course), and requires users to be at least 14 years old. Facebook requires users to be 13 and in high school or college, or 18 or older.

Setting up your social site

To create your own page on a social networking site, the steps go like this:

1. **Go to the Web site where you want to create a site,** like www.myspace.com or www.facebook.com.

2. **Find the Sign Up Now or Register button.** Follow the instructions to create an account, which is free. Some sites send a confirmation message to your e-mail, containing a list that you must click to prove that your address is what you say it is. On MySpace, you specify a username that becomes part of the Web address of your site (if your username is elvis-presley on MySpace, your site is www.myspace.com/elvispresley).

3. **Set up your account.** Depending on the site, you're asked for different kinds of information. Facebook prompts you to join one or more networks based on geography (people in your town), people who went to your college, or people at your company.

4. **Edit your profile.** Click the Profile or Edit Profile button or link to enter the information you want to display on your pages. You may be asked for your gender, age, political leanings, religious views, hometown, phone number, mailing address, school name (current or past), sexual orientation, marital status, activities, favorite music — you name it. Enter only what you're comfortable sharing! Look for settings that enable you to control who can see this information; we recommend that you not specify your hometown (unless it's a big, big city), birth date, or other identifying information. In Facebook, you can also edit your notifications (when you want Facebook to e-mail you about events, like people adding you as a friend) by clicking Account and then Notifications.

5. **Take a look at your page.** In MySpace, click Home. In Facebook, click Profile. Make sure that you're comfortable with the entire world reading the information that's there — keeping in mind your boss, your minister, your kids, your parents, and that creep that you changed your phone number to get away from. (You get the idea.)

6. **Upload pictures, if you want to.** In MySpace, click Add/Edit Photos. In Facebook, click the Edit link in the Photos heading — you can create albums with hundreds of pictures that can vary from portrait shots, pictures taken at group outings, and other group activities. You can upload photos from your PC, organize them into albums, and add captions. You can also choose who can see them (everyone or just your friends). Facebook prompts you to click the individual faces in your photos and identify them, and then offers to e-mail the people in your pictures to let them know that you're online (very cool).

Finally, you have your own home page! At MySpace, the site's URL is `http://myspace.com/` followed by your username. Facebook is `www.facebook.com/profile.php?id=` followed by a number — a far less groovy Web address, but Facebook is still a pretty nice site.

Keeping your page current

Some people check their profiles once a week to see whether new comments or messages are posted online. Others feel the need to update and redesign their accounts daily. (Perhaps these people check their voice mail every hour, too.) It's all up to you — that's why they call it MySpace.

Updating pictures is an easy way to keep your page current. New photos change the look of your profile and allow users to comment ("Where were you and what were you doing?!" "New shirt?").

MySpace and Facebook enable you to add other elements to your profile, like a Weblog (blog) of your news and musings or posting notes on your and your friends' "walls" (a section of your Facebook page).

Making connections

The whole point of social networking sites is, believe it or not, social networking. Your MySpace or Facebook profile isn't complete until it includes links to lots of friends, preferably people you actually know. (Why add a stranger as your friend if he or she is a stranger?)

On Facebook, click Friends, and then click the Find Friends tab, as shown in Figure 17-4. If you store your friends' email addresses in your Yahoo Mail, Gmail (Google Mail), Hotmail, or AOL address book, Facebook offers to search your address book for the addresses of people who have Facebook accounts. (This works fine, but remember that if you use other Yahoo services, like Wallet, or other Windows Live services keyed to your Hotmail account, they use the same password as your e-mail account, so they're only as secure as Facebook is.) An equally scary feature (but we tried it anyway) was uploading the address book from our e-mail program (we use Thunderbird) so that Facebook could identify people with Facebook accounts that we might want to invite to be our Facebook friends. Click Friends, click Find Friends, click Email Application, and follow the instructions for users who use an e-mail client.

Or, you can search for classmates or co-workers from the networks you've joined. Click Networks and Search or Browse to see people in the networks you're in. Click Browse All Networks to find other networks to join.

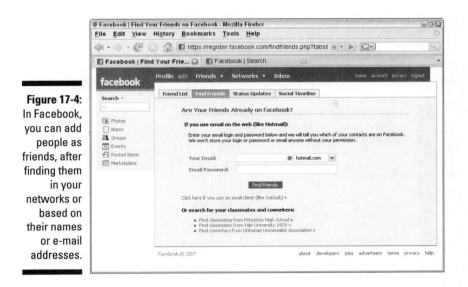

Figure 17-4:
In Facebook, you can add people as friends, after finding them in your networks or based on their names or e-mail addresses.

On MySpace, click Search and use the Find a Friend search box to find people by name, MySpace username, or e-mail address.

After you have friends, you can send them e-mail messages, look at their pages, look at their friends, look at their friends' pages, look at *their* friends, and so on, ad infinitum. On MySpace, you can click Post Bulletin to send out a news blast to all your MySpace friends. On Facebook, you can scroll down to The Wall (a section of a person's profile page) and "write on it" (leave a note) — it's a kind of personalized digital graffiti.

For more information about MySpace, get *MySpace For Dummies*, by Ryan Hupfer, Mitch Maxson, and Ryan Williams (Wiley Publishing, Inc.).

What's in a Blog?

A *Weblog*, usually abbrev'd as *blog*, is a public online diary where someone posts more or less regular updates. A blog uses software that makes it easy to post entries by using your Web browser — no additional software is needed.

Most blogs are updated frequently by one author and contain short, dated entries, like a diary, with the newest ones at the top. Other blogs are more complex, with multiple topics or pictures as well as (or instead of) words, but they retain the idea of relatively short entries, updated relatively often. Figure 17-5 shows the philosophical and religious blog of a friend of ours, Doug Muder (http://freeandresponsible.blogspot.com).

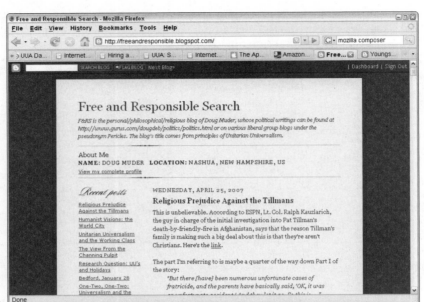

Figure 17-5:
A blog is like
an online
diary, and
its value
depends on
whether its
author has
anything
interesting
to say.

The best blogs offer cutting-edge journalism and commentary and brilliant, witty, sparkling writing, whereas the worst disprove the old cliché that a million monkeys at a million typewriters would eventually produce the works of Shakespeare. If you Google for the word *blog* or *weblog* and some topic words that are of interest to you, you'll invariably find someone blogging away at it. But keep reading to find out better ways to discover and organize the blogs you read.

As blogs have become more popular, many Web sites that weren't originally set up as blogs have become increasingly blogular. Just about every newspaper and magazine with a Web site have made it possible to treat their sites as blogs, or as collections of blogs — one for each section of the paper. My Yahoo (`http://my.yahoo.com`), the customizable Web page you can set up at Yahoo, has added more and more bloggish features so that you can now include anyone else's blog as part of your My Yahoo page, and you can use many of My Yahoo's own parts as blogs in collections you make elsewhere.

How to read a blog

Reading a blog is easy; blogs are just Web pages. Point your browser at the home page of the one you're interested in and read it. (Bet you thought it would be more complicated than that.) If you want to see more about a particular story, click the link in the story.

Reading one blog is like eating only one potato chip, which never happens. When you find one blog, it usually has links to other blogs. If you search for one blog, you find a dozen blogs, and before you know it, you're mired deep in the swamps of Blogistan, with far too many interesting blogs to keep track of.

Because blogs change frequently (at least they're supposed to), you might want to bookmark your favorite ones in your Web browser so that you can find them again. As you find more blogs, you soon find your bookmark folder and your brain exploding, from trying to keep track of them.

Luckily, you can subscribe to blogs so that you don't have to remember to return to each blog Web site to read the latest postings. When you subscribe to a blog, the new entries arrive on your computer automatically, so you don't have to check the blog Web site.

An *RSS feed* is the blogging feature that enables you to subscribe to the blog and receive new postings automagically. (*RSS* stands for Really Simple Syndication.) An RSS feed is a special Web address (URL) that usually ends with `.rss`. When you're reading a blog in your Web browser, look for a Subscribe or RSS link, which should display information about the site's RSS feed. Some blogs use a URL at `http://feeds.feedburner.com` for their feeds.

The system you use to subscribe is an *aggregator*, although almost no one uses the term. One type of aggregator is Web-based, a Web site that tracks and shows you all your favorite blogs. The other is desktop-based, a program that lets your computer track and show your favorite blogs.

Your favorite blogs

Here are three of our favorite aggregator Web sites, all free:

Bloglines
`www.bloglines.com`

Bloglines, shown in Figure 17-6, is the premier site for people who want to follow a whole lot of blogs. To get started at Bloglines, you set up a free account and then tell it to subscribe to the blogs you're interested in. If you know the RSS feed's URL, you can enter it directly, but it's usually easier to use the built-in search engine. Type a few words describing blogs you might like, and pick the likely-looking ones. Many blogs also have a Bloglines button you can click to take you to the Bloglines site and add that blog to your account.

For each blog, Bloglines tracks the items in the blog and remembers which ones you've looked at, reporting the number unread in parentheses after the name of each blog. That makes it easy to cruise by and catch up on what's new. You can mark stories of interest to add to your private clipping folder, and you can also publish a blog of clippings, optionally adding notes to each clipping. (Your clipping blog is a real blog with its own RSS feed, so your friends can read it and save entries, and their friends can read their clipping blogs, offering nearly theological blogs within blogs within blogs.)

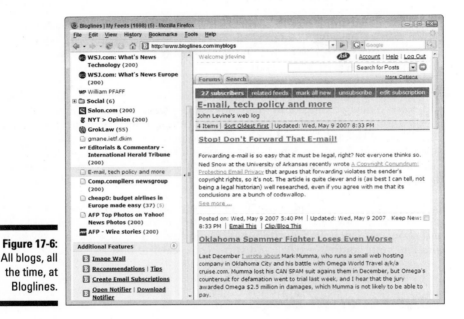

Figure 17-6:
All blogs, all
the time, at
Bloglines.

Google Reader

www.google.com/reader

After you log in with your free Google account, you can start subscribing to blogs. (This Google account works with all Google services; if you don't already have one, click the Create an Account Now link.) Google Reader offers bundles of popular feeds to get you started. To add a blog from Blogger (Blogspot), MySpace, Facebook, Flickr, LiveJournal, or several other popular blog sites, you can select the site and type the name of the blog. You can either click the Add Subscription link at any time to search for a blog by name or topic (this is Google, after all) or paste in an RSS feed.

My Yahoo

`http://my.yahoo.com`

If your goal is just to read blogs, My Yahoo isn't the best place to do it. But if you already use My Yahoo because of all the built-in content it offers, adding a few RSS feeds (or a lot of RSS feeds) is easy. When you click the Add Content link, you can enter an RSS feed's URL (there's a tiny link next to the Find button) or choose from its catalog of all the RSS feeds Yahoo knows about. When you add an RSS feed, My Yahoo makes it look just like Yahoo's built-in content.

Because Bloglines, Google Reader, and My Yahoo are so popular, many blogs offer a one-click way to add the blog to your subscriptions.

Other ways of subscribing to blogs

If you really want to get close to your blogs, you can set them up in a program right on your desktop. You can use our favorite Web browser, Mozilla Firefox, to display them as folders of bookmarks, or you can use our favorite e-mail program, Mozilla Thunderbird, to display your blogs as mail folders.

Reading blogs in Firefox

If you use Mozilla Firefox as your Web browser, as we suggest in Chapter 6, you're only a few clicks away from having all your favorite blogs as *live bookmarks,* which look like folders in the bookmark menu, containing all the blog's items as individual bookmarks. The "liveness" is that the folder's contents update automatically as the blog changes. Firefox live bookmarks are much easier to set up than Thunderbird blog folders (described in the next section), but after they're set up, they're not quite as useful unless you use the Sage extension, described in the following Tip paragraph.

Whenever you visit a Web page and click a link for an RSS feed, Firefox asks whether you want to subscribe to the page by using Live Bookmarks. To make a live bookmark for that page, just click the Subscribe Now button. Firefox displays the Add Live Bookmark dialog box; adjust where you want the bookmark to appear in your Bookmarks menu, and click OK.

To look at a feed, just find its bookmark on the Bookmark menu and click it to see a list of all the current items. Click any one of them to open it or, for a good time, click Open in Tabs at the bottom of the bookmark folder, and Firefox opens all the blog entries at once, with each in a separate tab in the browser.

Get the free Sage extension for Firefox at `http://sage.mozdev.org`, which turns Firefox into a first-rate blog reader. When you click the little leaf icon that Sage adds to your Firefox menu bar, the window splits into a three-panel format, like Thunderbird's, with a list of blogs, a list of messages in the blog, and the regular Firefox window, which can show summaries of the blog's entries (generated on the fly by Sage). You can click the summaries to see full entries, a blog entry or, of course, any other Web pages you click to, because it's still Firefox. Sage remembers which entries you've already seen so that you can skip to the new ones.

Reading blogs in Thunderbird

In Chapter 13, we encourage you to install Mozilla Thunderbird and use it as your regular e-mail program. If you do that, it's easy to tell Thunderbird to follow a few blogs and show them to you as though they were mail folders. If you follow a whole lot of blogs, T'bird probably isn't the best program to use. For watching a few as you check your mail, though, it's quite handy.

First, you have to tell Thunderbird to set up a blog folder:

1. **Choose Tools⇨Account Settings and click the Add Account button.**

   You see the Account Wizard's New Account Setup page.

2. **Select RSS News & Blogs and click Next a few times until you can click Finish.**

   Now you have an RSS folder, and you can add RSS feeds to it. The RSS folder appears in the list of accounts on the Account Settings page.

3. **Click the RSS folder and select Manage Subscriptions to open the RSS Subscriptions window, shown in Figure 17-7.**

   If you're looking at the regular Thunderbird window rather than the Account Settings window, the RSS folder appears in your list of folders, and you can right-click it and choose Manage Subscriptions.

4. **To add a blog, click Add to display the News Feed Properties dialog box, type or paste the URL of the blog's RSS feed into the Feed URL box, and then click OK.**

   Thunderbird offers no automated way to find RSS feed URLs, which is a pain. One approach is to open the blog in your browser, find the Subscribe, RSS, or XML link on the blog's page, right-click that link, and select Copy Link Location (in Firefox) or Copy Shortcut (in Internet Explorer) to put the link on the Windows clipboard. Then you can press Ctrl+V to paste the URL into the Feed URL box on the News Feed Properties dialog box in Thunderbird. Yes, this process is a pain, which is one of the reasons we don't recommend it for heavy blog users.

Figure 17-7: Thunderbird can show blog postings as well as e-mail.

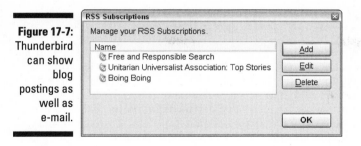

When your blogs are set up, each blog appears as a mail folder under News and Blogs. You can see the list of headlines and read the blog entries exactly the way you read mail messages. It remembers the ones you've seen, and you can delete the ones you've read. (They're not deleted from the blog itself, just from the Thunderbird folder.) You can save the ones you like in local folders, just like mail messages, and do everything you can do with mail messages except reply to them — blog entries don't have return addresses.

Writing Your Own Blog

Now that you've seen all the ways to read other people's blogs, how about starting your own? People read blogs for their brilliant, witty, sparkling content. Sparkling is hard, and sparkling regularly is exhausting. If you start your own blog, try blogging for a while on your own before telling all your friends about it. Otherwise: "It was okay at the beginning, but now, pee-yew."

Top five reasons not to start your own blog

Blog entries are usually short, so in that spirit we offer you a short list:

5. You work on your blog when you should be working on your day job, annoying your co-workers and boss, and you spend hours reading *other* blogs, looking for topics to comment on or borrow.

4. Every conversation or experience becomes a potential blog entry rather than part of your life (also known as novelist's syndrome).

3. You try to have strange conversations and experiences in order to have something to blog (bad novelist's syndrome).

2. Everything, no matter how trivial, takes on a deep bloggable meaning. ("Did you ever notice all the different ways that rain streaks the dirt on the side of a city bus?")

1. You realize that you have nothing to say.

We practice what we preach here. None of us has a personal blog, just work-related ones.

Finding where to put your blog

Running blog software is simple enough that there are probably 10,000 different places that you can host your blog. But many big blog sites let you blog away without having to install anything. Unless you have a friend who's dying to install some blogware on her Web site, use one of these. These sites offer a basic usable blog for free. Some also have extra-cost add-ons that they hope you'll use. For reasons that will shortly become apparent, if you read this entire section, we suggest that most of our users try Blogger.

Here are some popular blog-hosting sites:

Blogger

```
www.blogger.com
```

Also known as Blogspot, Blogger is now part of the Google empire, although Google hasn't Google-ized it, at least not yet. After you create an account, you can add and edit blog entries through the Web site, customize it in any of a zillion ways, and publish your blog. It also supports mobile blogs (moblogs) that let you post text and pictures from your mobile phone.

Blogger is remarkably uninterested in asking for your money. As far as we can figure out, its reason for existence is mostly to be a place for people to display Google ads. That's fine — it's a nice site, and the ads are entirely optional.

LiveJournal

```
www.livejournal.com
```

The cliché LiveJournal user is a college student who needs to provide too much information to his 100,000 closest friends on topics ranging from taste in music to short-term party plans to personal political philosophy. If this sounds like you, LiveJournal's the place. The basic blog is free, and a paid account can include extra features in your blog, such as polls and surveys.

Xanga

```
www.xanga.com
```

Xanga is a lot like LiveJournal except that the average user seems to be about five years younger. Unlike the other two sites, Xanga shows its ads on your blog unless you buy a premium account. Xanga also includes some social networking features, like MySpace and Facebook.

Yahoo 360°

`http://360.yahoo.com`

Yahoo supports every other known Web feature, so they added a blogging site too. It has social networking features, including linking to friends and groups.

You can also add a blog to your MySpace, Facebook, or other social networking site. See the section "Setting up your social site," earlier in this chapter.

Illustrating your blog

Text is so 20th century. (Actually, it's more 15th century, but who's counting?) If you find text constraining, just about every blog site, including the three we describe in the preceding section, lets you include pictures as part of your blog, often as a *moblog* (mobile blog) that lets you upload directly from your mobile phone.

Songs on the Net

If you're a storyteller or musician, or just have a lot to say, you can post your digital recordings on the Web as a *podcast*, which is an audio blog. You can upload any audio file that you created yourself, containing music, speech, or any sounds you like, and other people can subscribe to it, just like a blog. Chapter 9 describes how to find and subscribe to podcasts.

Several Web sites will host your podcast for free or for a small monthly fee. Here are a few:

- ✔ **PodBean,** at `www.podbean.com`, is free for the first 100MB of audio files. To store more files, you need to pay a modest monthly fee.

- ✔ **PodKive,** at `www.podkive.com`, gives you more control over the look of the Web site but doesn't offer free accounts.

- ✔ **SwitchPod,** at `www.switchpod.com`, offers a free account for the first 450MB of files, and a monthly fee after that.

After you have a podcast, be sure to submit it to the iTunes Store so that people who use iTunes can easily subscribe: Run the free iTunes program (which is useful even if you don't own an i-Anything), click Music Store, click Podcasts, and click Submit a Podcast. (See Chapter 9 to find out how to use iTunes.)

You can post and read blogs from your phone

Blogs are all well and good if you feel the need to let the world know the details of your life as it happens. But what if you're not always near your computer? How can you tell your friends right away that you found something great at the mall or that you're stuck in traffic? And how can you receive these vital messages from your friends when you're on the road? Sites such as Twitter (at www.twitter.com) and Jaiku (www.jaiku.com) are the answer.

When you create a free Twitter account, you create blog a with a difference: You can post to Twitter by text-messaging from your mobile phone. (By the time you read this, all the major blogging sites may have added this feature, but in 2007, it was pretty "rad.") Twitter has a special five-digit phone number — 40404 — that can be used only for text-messaging. (Google has one, too — it's 46645, which spells GOOGL, and you can use it to do Web searches by text message.) When you send a text message to this number, Twitter posts the message on your Twitter page and sends it out as a text message to the list of friends you designated. Twitter is free, although you'll probably be charged for sending and receiving messages, depending on your mobile plan.

Jaiku works the same way, giving you a Web site at *your-user-name*.jaiku.com. Because the company is in Finland, the phone number is way, way longer, though, and texting it may cost more.

If you want to post via text message to an existing blog at Blogger, MySpace, or a few other blogs, you can do so from http://letmeparty.com. This Web site is run by a student, so we hope that it's still around when you read this chapter.

Lights, action, podcast!

If you want to go the full multimedia route and you have a camera or phone that records video, www.vidblogs.com hosts video blogs. Because video files are large, only users with snappy broadband connections need apply. If you think that you can make brilliant, sparkling, witty one-minute movies, here's your chance.

Working Together on a Wiki

Whereas a blog is basically an exercise in personal vanity publishing, a *wiki* lets a group of people collaborate on a Web site. A wiki (named for the Hawaiian word *wiki-wiki*, which means "in a hurry" — no, really) can have an unlimited number of authors, all of whom can add and change pages within the wiki Web site. Unlike a blog, it doesn't have to be a chronological list of journal entries. Instead, you can organize your text any way you like, including making as many new, interlinked pages as you like.

If this process sounds potentially chaotic, it is, but most wikis have ground rules that keep the group moving in more or less the same direction. A wiki can work well if you have a group of people who trust each other to edit each other's writing. For example, a group of co-workers can make a wiki that contains information about a project they're working on. A church or club can make a wiki with committee meeting minutes, mission statements, plans, and schedules.

The biggest wiki of them all is Wikipedia (Figure 17-8), at `www.wikipedia.org`, a collaborative encyclopedia which, with almost 2 million entries, is well on its way to including all human knowledge.

Figure 17-8: The Wikipedia has articles on almost everything.

You can create your own wiki in one of two ways:

✔ **Set up a Web site and install wiki software.** The wiki program that Wikipedia uses is MediaWiki (at `www.mediawiki.org`). This method assumes that you know how to create a Web site and install a program, so this is probably not your best option.

✔ **Use a *wiki farm*, which is a Web server that already runs wiki software.** Wikipedia has a list of wiki farms — look up **wiki farm**. We've had good luck with Wikispaces at `www.wikispaces.com`.

When you sign up for a wiki at a wiki farm, you may need to pay a monthly or yearly fee, or you may have the option to run the wiki for free in return for displaying ads. After you create your account and name your wiki, you can invite your collaborators to use it, usually by typing or pasting their e-mail addresses into a form so that the system can send them invitations. Each user has a username and password so that only they can make changes to the wiki content.

Chapter 18

Making Web Sites with Your Bare Hands

Chapter 17 described eleventeen different ways to post material on the Web. However, each of these methods has its limitations — you're putting your text, pictures, sounds, or videos on pages controlled by the Web site that hosts them.

What if you want more control of your site? What if your ideas don't fit into the structure of the types of sites listed in Chapter 17? For example, if you want to make a Web page for your club, church, synagogue, mosque, or other group, the site might not be "create-able" by using a blog or wiki. Instead, you may need to roll up your sleeves and make the site with your bare hands.

This chapter covers two options for making a free-form site:

✔ **Use Google Page Creator** to make a Web site at `http://googlepages.com`. You don't have complete control over the format of the site, but you have lots more leeway than you have with any of the options in Chapter 17. You can make as many pages as you want, with links from one page to the next, and text and pictures on each page.

✔ **Use a Web page editor to upload pages to a Web server.** This method is truly the old-fashioned way to make a Web site, and it's the way that many larger sites are built. A Web page editor gives you complete control over how your Web site looks. You need to get a program or two (possibly requiring payment of actual money — not everything on the Web is free) and find out about Web page formatting.

This chapter describes both these options. If you're ready to make a Web site, read on!

Web Site Creation Concepts

Before we explain how to create a Web page, here's an introduction to Web site structure and the definitions of some terms you encounter.

Do you need a home page, or more?

Although any Web site can consist of many Web pages, the main page of a site is generally known as its *home page.* People have home pages, companies have home pages, and groups of highly talented authors and speakers have home pages. (You can check out John's at `www.johnlevine.com`, Margy's at `http://gurus.com/margy`, and Internet Gurus Central at `http://net.gurus.com`.)

If you have only one page of information to put on the Web, you can make a home page. If you have more to say, or information on several different topics, you should make more than just a home page. Your home page can be the front page from which people can find your other pages. For example, if you wrote an essay on the current political situation (and who hasn't?), collected pictures of your chickens, and created a killer recipe for Key lime pie, make four pages:

- ✔ Your home page, with links to the other three pages
- ✔ A page with your political essay
- ✔ A page with your chicken pictures
- ✔ A page with your Key lime pie recipe

Creating a Web page is pretty easy. Choosing what you put on your page, however, is harder. What is the page for? What kind of person do you want to see it? Is it for you and your family and friends and potential friends across the world, or are you advertising your business online? If your page is a personal page, don't include your home address or phone number unless you want random people who see the page potentially calling you up. If it's a business page, by all means include your address and phone number.

Be extremely careful about putting identifying information about your children on your Web page. We each have kids whom we love dearly, but you won't read anything about them on our home pages. Just knowing your hobbies and your kids' names and where they go to school may be enough for some no-goodnik to pose as a friend of the family and pick them up after school.

After you have an idea of which page or pages you might want to put on the Web, you need to know how Web pages and Web servers work.

Naming your page

As you create Web pages, the name of the file becomes part of the Web page's address, so choose a filename that makes sense. Filenames for Web pages end with the extension .html or .htm. For example, if you're making a page about your cats, name it something like mycats.html or cats.html. Don't use spaces, punctuation, or capital letters in your filenames — if you must, you can use underscores (_) or hyphens (-) to make them readable.

You should generally call your home page, the one you want people to see first, index.html. If someone goes to your Web address without specifying a filename, such as www.iecc.com/~elvis/, a universal convention is to display the page named index.html or index.htm. If you don't have a page by that name, some Web servers construct a page with a directory listing of the files in your site, and others display an error page.

Why you don't care (much) about HTML

Just so that you know what *HTML* is, in case someone asks, it stands for *HyperText Markup Language,* and it's the language used for formatting Web pages. Web pages are made up of text and pictures that are stuck together and formatted with HTML codes. Fortunately, you have waited until now to get started in creating a Web page, when clever programs are available that let you create your pages and write the HTML codes for you automatically, so you don't have to write the codes yourself.

If you want to write a lot of Web pages, you should eventually master some HTML. Although complex, interactive pages require a fair amount of programming, the basics aren't all that complicated. The HTML for **complicated** is <b>complicated</b> (that's <b> for bold type). In case you decide that you want to be in the Web-page creation business, entire books have been written about how to do it. Stick to recent titles because extensions to HTML are evolving at a furious pace, and the books go out of date in less than a year. We recommend *HTML 4 For Dummies,* Fifth Edition, written by Ed Tittel and Mary Burmeister (Wiley) for the basics, and *Web Design in a Nutshell,* Third Edition, by Jennifer Niederst (O'Reilly & Associates) for more advanced information.

Producing pictures for your site

Most Web pages contain graphics of some sort. Each picture that appears on a Web page is stored in a separate file. To add an image to a Web page, you add an HTML *tag* (command) that includes the name of the file that contains the picture, the size of the picture as it should appear on the screen, a caption for the visually impaired, and positioning information (whether you want the pictures to the left, center, or right and whether text should flow around it).

Where do pictures come from? You can draw them by using a paint program, scan in photographs, or use that fancy digital camera you got for Christmas. Then use Paint or a better graphics editor to crop your pictures, fix the red-eye, and generally spiff up your pix. Save your files as GIF or JPEG files, and resize them to be less than 500 pixels wide and smaller than 200KB in file size.

If you need graphics that you can't produce yourself, you can find lots of sources of graphical material:

✔ Plenty of freeware, shareware, and commercial clip art are available on the Net. Try the Clip Art page at our favorite Web directory, the Open Directory Project list, at www.dmoz.org/Computers/Graphics/ Clip_Art.

✔ If you see an image you want to use on a Web page, write to the page's owner and ask for permission to use it. More likely than not, the owner will let you use the image.

✔ Lots of regular old software programs totally unrelated to the Internet, such as paint and draw programs, presentation programs, and even word processors, come with clip art collections.

✔ You can subscribe to a clip art site. We use Clipart.com, which has subscriptions starting at $15.

Clip art, like any art, is protected by copyright laws. Whether it has already been used on a Web page or whether a copyright notice appears on or near the image doesn't matter. It's all copyrighted. If you use someone else's copyrighted art, you must get permission to do so. Whether your use is educational, personal, or noncommercial is irrelevant. If you fail to secure permission, you run the risk of anything from a crabby phone call from the owner's lawyer to winding up on the losing end of a lawsuit.

Most people are quite reasonable whenever you ask for permission to use something. If an image you want to use doesn't already come with permission to use it, check with the owner before you decide to add it to your own Web page.

Linking to other pages and sites

The *hyper* in hypertext is the thing that makes the Web so cool. A *hyperlink* (or just *link*) is the thing on the page that lets you "surf" the Web — go from page to page by just clicking the link. A Web page is hardly a page if it doesn't link somewhere else.

The immense richness of the Web comes from the links that Web page authors place on their pages. Contribute to this richness by including links to places you know of that the people who visit your page may also be interested in. Try to avoid including links to places that everyone already knows about and has in their bookmarks. For example, everyone knows were to find Google and Yahoo, so leave them off. If your home page mentions your interest in one of your hobbies, however, such as canoeing or volleyball or birding or your alma mater, include some links to related sites you know of that are interesting.

Cutting and Pasting a Web Site

Google Page Creator is another free and elegant Web-based product from Google. You can set up one or a set of Web pages, including text, pictures, and links to other pages. Your Web site will be at *username*.googlepages.com, where *username* is your Google account name.

Setting up your Google Pages site

In your Web browser, start at www.googlepages.com. To use Google Page Creator, you need a free Google account; sign in if you have one, or click the link to create a new account.

As of mid-2007, Google Page Creator was still in testing, and you needed a Gmail account, not just a Google account, to use it. You can sign up for a free Gmail account at www.gmail.com. We expect that by the time you read this chapter, Google Page Creator will be available for all Google account holders so that you can skip this step. Go to www.googlepages.com to see what the login instructions say.

You see a Google Page Creator Site Manager, as shown in Figure 18-1, with a list of your pages. Right now, you have only a home page, with no title and no content.

Editing a page

To edit a page shown on the Site Manager page, click the little box that represents the page. You see the Edit Page screen, shown in Figure 18-2. It has boxes into which you can type (or cut-and-paste) a page title, a subtitle, the main text of the page, and a page footer.

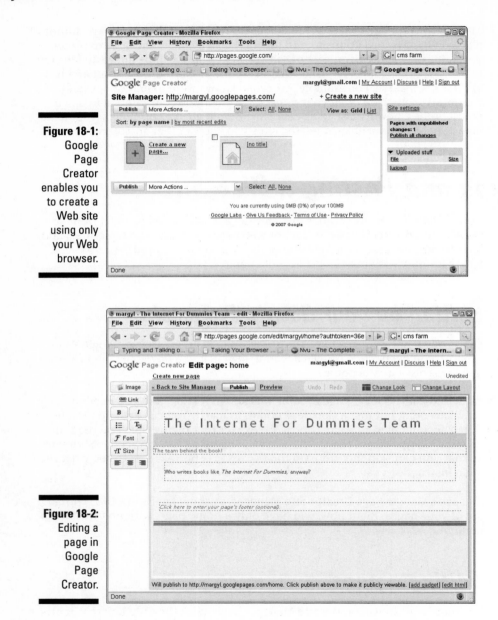

Figure 18-1:
Google
Page
Creator
enables you
to create a
Web site
using only
your Web
browser.

Figure 18-2:
Editing a
page in
Google
Page
Creator.

Here are other things you can do to control the format of the page:

✔ **Use the formatting buttons to the left of the page.** There are buttons for boldface, italics, bullets, font color, typeface, type size, and text alignment, just like a word processor. You can also format paragraphs as headings.

- ✔ **Click the Change Look link.** Google Page Creator comes with a preformatted set of page designs that will look familiar to users of Blogger. Choose a color scheme that you think will work with the content of your site, and Google Page Creator applies the formatting and returns to the page you're editing.

- ✔ **Click the Change Layout link.** You can choose the plain layout, shown in Figure 18-2, or go with a multicolumn layout.

- ✔ **Add pictures.** Move your cursor to the place on the page where you want to put a picture. Click the Image button and upload an image file from your PC. Or, you can specify the URL of an image that's already somewhere on the Web. (Get permission first, if the picture isn't yours!) Click the Add Image button and the image appears! If you put it in the wrong place, you can drag it around the page with your mouse.

- ✔ **Add links to other pages.** You can make any text or picture into a link. Select the text or image with your mouse and click the Link button. Choose whether you're linking to a page on your own site (you can create one if it doesn't exist yet), to a file you want to upload (perhaps a PDF file or other non-Web-page type of file), to a Web page that's not in your site, or to an e-mail address (so that when a visitor clicks the link, her e-mail program opens with a new message addressed to that address). Click OK to create the link.

- ✔ **Add other cool stuff.** Google provides a bunch of other things you can add to your pages by clicking the Add Gadget link. Gadgets include a clock, calendar, weather report, MP3 music player, maps, and videos. For example, you can include a map to your church or club's meeting location.

- ✔ **Edit the HTML.** As you make changes to your page, Google Page Creator writes the HTML to the formatting you ask for. If you're a glutton for punishment, or if you want to tweak the look of your page, Google Page Creator enables you to see and edit the HTML — click the Edit HTML link.

Publishing your first Web page!

When you like the look of your page, click the Publish button to save your changes. Click the View It on the Web or View Live link, or type **username. googlepages.com** (replace *username* with your Google account name) into your browser's address box, to see your site.

To add more pages, click the Back to Site Manager link, and then click the Create a New Page link. Be sure to create links among your pages so that your visitors have a way to see them (without requiring them to guess the page names and type them as part of the Web address).

Hand Me the Web Editor, Please

If you're an old-fashioned type of person and want to make a Web site from scratch, you can use the time-honored tools of our Web-site-making forebears — Web editors and file transfer programs. Making a Web site from scratch gives you full control over the layout of the site, and enables you to add data-base-driven or other advanced features. Here's a quick overview of how the process works:

1. **Sign up for Web server space.**

   Lots of Web hosting companies are out there, ready to charge $5 to $20 per month to store your Web pages on their *Web servers* — computers where Web pages live. We've used `pair.com`, `ipowerweb.com`, and `myhosting.com` but there are lots of good ones. Your Internet service provider (ISP) may include Web hosting in your Internet service, so you may already have Web server space. Your ISP or Web hosting company gives you a server name, username, and password so that you can upload your pages to its site.

2. **(Optional) Buy a domain name.**

   You don't have to have a domain name (that is, `something-or-other.com` or `.net` or `.org`) to have a Web site, but it's classier. Your ISP or Web hosting company can help you find out whether the domain name you want is already taken (all the good names are long gone) and can help you buy it. Domain names cost $7 to $20 per year. See the section "Be the Master of Your Domain," later in this chapter.

3. **Write some Web pages.**

   One page is plenty to start with. You can use any text editor or word processor, but spiffy Web-page authoring programs designed for this purpose are available @— and some are free — so you may as well use one. Dreamweaver is the most widely used Web editor, but it costs several hundred dollars. Nvu (pronounced "N-view") is an open-source Web editor that includes a file transfer (FTP) program; you can download it from `www.nvu.com`.

   Save the pages in files on your computer's hard drive, using the filename extension `.htm` or `.html`. You can see how the pages look by opening them in your browser, using the File⇨Open File command (or press Ctrl+O and browse to the file).

4. **Upload your Web pages to your Web server.**

   The rest of your world can't see Web pages that are stored on your disk. You have to copy them to your ISP's or Web hosting company's Web server. You can use an FTP program like FileZilla (from SourceForge, at `http://sourceforge.net/projects/filezilla`). Or, your Web editor may have a built-in FTP program (Nvu and Dreamweaver do).

Your Web server at your service

Many Web page editing programs have a Publish, Upload, or Remote Save command on the File menu that sends your creation to your Web server. If your program doesn't have this command, you can use File Transfer Protocol (FTP), a type of program we discuss in more detail on our Web page at http:// net.gurus.com/nettcr/ftpsw.html. In either case, you need to know these details:

✔ **The name of the computer to which you upload your files:** The name you use when uploading Web pages isn't always the same as the Web server name you use when viewing the pages in your browser. At one of our local ISPs, for example, the Web server is www.lightlink.com, whereas the FTP upload server is ftp.lightlink.com.

✔ **The username and password to use for FTP:** If you're using your ISP's Web server, this is the same as the name and password you use to connect in the first place and to pick up your e-mail.

✔ **The name of the folder (directory) on the server to which you upload the pages:** For example, it might be /www/*username*.

✔ **The filename to use for your home page:** Usually, this is index.html or index.htm. (You can name your Web pages anything you want, but this page is the one that people see first.)

✔ **The URL where your pages will appear:** It's usually www.*yourisp*.com/ ~*username* or www.*yourisp*.com/*username*.

You can usually find this info on your ISP's Web site or, in the worst case, you can call them or e-mail them and ask.

Choosing a Web editor: just say Nvu

The two general approaches to creating Web pages are the geek approach, in which you write all the HTML codes yourself, and the WYSIWYG approach, in which a program writes them for you. If you were an HTML geek, you wouldn't be reading this chapter, so we're not going to discuss that approach. The more normal approach is to use a WYSIWYG Web page editor.

WYSIWYG, pronounced "WHIZ-ee-wig," stands for *w*hat *y*ou *s*ee *i*s *w*hat *y*ou *g*et. In the case of Web editors, it means that as you create your page, rather than see seriously unattractive HTML codes, you see roughly what it will look like in a browser. HTML purists point out that WYSIWYG editors churn out less-than-elegant HTML code, but the pages they make generally look fine. If you're planning to create a large, complex Web site, WYSIWYG editors will run out of steam, but for a page or three, they're great. Google Page Creator, described earlier in this chapter, is a WYSIWYG editor.

A number of free and cheap Web page editors are available. You can choose one yourself: Start at www.download.com, click the Developer Tools link on the left, click Web Page Creation, and then click HTML Editors. Many editors have free demos, but to continue to use the program, you have to pay for it, which usually costs from $20 to $70 dollars, as shown in the Download.com listing.

Serious Web developers use more expensive programs, mainly Dreamweaver (from Macromedia, at www.adobe.com/products/dreamweaver). But before shelling out several hundred dollars, try a cheap (or free) program first.

In this chapter, we use Nvu, which is based on the Mozilla Composer program that used to come from the same people who created Firefox. Download Nvu from www.nvu.com/download.php and install it. (See Chapter 12 for how to download and install software from the Internet.) An Nvu tutorial is available at http://nvu.com/websitehelp.php. When Nvu starts up, it looks like a word processor, with lots of formatting buttons and menu options, with the addition of the Nvu Site Manager on the left side of the Nvu window — this is where you can see the list of Web pages in your site and choose which to edit (see Figure 18-3).

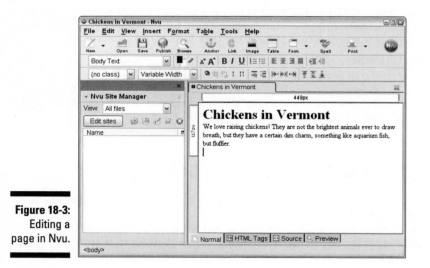

Figure 18-3: Editing a page in Nvu.

You probably already have a Web editor — your own word processor. Both Microsoft Word (versions 97 and later) and WordPerfect (versions 8 and later) have adequate Web-editing features built right in. Web page authoring tools are usually more convenient, have more advanced features, produce more efficient pages, and include a file transfer program to upload your pages to your Web server. Microsoft Word creates pages that contain large numbers of extra codes that make the pages take longer to download and view. If you use Microsoft Excel (a spreadsheet program) or Access (a database program), you can export reports as Web pages, too. Nvu is cheap, quick to download and install, and easy to use. Just get it!

Making Web Pages with Nvu

A Web page is a file — just like a word-processing document or a spreadsheet. You create it and save it, and then open it and edit it some more, just like any other document.

Picking up your pen

You begin by creating your Web pages directly on your hard disk. You can see how they look by telling your browser to view them from your hard disk. (Browsers are happy to accept filenames to display rather than URLs.) Edit and view the pages until you have something you like, and then upload them to your ISP to impress the world.

Here's our step-by-step approach to using Nvu. If you would rather use another program, feel free, although the commands are a little different.

Making your page

Before you start making pages, create a folder on your PC (or Mac) to store them in. You create pages on your computer and then upload them to the Web server so that you always have a backup copy.

1. **Run Nvu.**

   You see a window like the one shown earlier, in Figure 18-3. The Nvu Site Manager lists the file in your Web site (so it starts out blank), and the rest of the Nvu window (apart from a zillion formatting buttons) is the blank canvas on which you can paint your Web page.

   If you want to edit an existing Web page that you have stored on your hard disk, click Open, choose File➪Open File, or press Ctrl+O to open it), and then choose the file.

2. **Type text into the new Web page or edit the one you opened.**

   You're face to face with a big, empty page. Go ahead — make your page the same way you would in a word processor, by entering headings and paragraphs of text. Stuck for ideas and where to start? Make a page about your favorite hobby, author, or musician!

3. **Save your page by clicking Save, choosing File⇨Save, or pressing Ctrl+S.**

   When you've done enough work that you wouldn't want to have to start over from scratch if your computer suddenly crashed, save your work. In principle, when you're done with your page, you save it, but dismal experience has taught us to save early, save often.

   If you haven't given your page a title (the text that appears on the title bar of a visitor's browser, as well as in bookmarks and search engine results), Nvu prompts you for one now.

   The first time you save the page, Nvu asks for a filename. Nvu suggests the page's title as the filename. Don't take its suggestion! If you're creating your home page, name it `index.html`. Otherwise, choose a short filename with no spaces or punctuation, all lowercase, ending in `.html`. Then click Save.

That's all there is to creating a simple Web page!

Formatting pages with pictures in Nvu

Nvu has icons for boldface, italics, bullets, font color, typeface, type size, text alignment, and spell-checking, just like a word processor. Hover your mouse over an icon to see what it does.

Adding pictures

To add pictures, follow these steps:

1. **Prepare your picture for the Web.**

   In a graphics program (like Paint, which comes with Windows), make a version that's no more than 500 pixels wide (that's wide enough to stretch across your Web page). Save it as a GIF-, JPEG-, or PNG-formatted file so that all browsers can display it. Make sure that it's no larger than about 100KB so that it doesn't take too long to arrive in your visitor's browser. Save the image in the folder where you're storing your Web pages, using a filename that contains no space or punctuation, all lowercase.

2. **Choose where you want the picture.**

   Move your cursor to the place on the page where you want to put a picture.

3. **Click the Image icon.**

   You see the Image Properties dialog box.

4. **Click the Choose File button and choose an image file from your PC.**

5. **Type a caption in the Alternate Text box.**

6. **Format your picture on the page.**

   Click the Appearance tab if you want to add space around your picture or change the way it aligns with adjacent text.

7. **Click OK to finish adding your image.**

After you insert the picture, it may look terrible — it may be the wrong size or push the text out of the way in an unattractive manner. Delete the picture (by clicking in it and pressing Del), edit it with a graphics editor, and reinsert it. If the size is wrong, use Paint or some other program to resize it. In Paint, open the picture file by choosing File⇨Open, and then choose Image⇨Stretch and Skew (which sounds unnecessarily violent to us). Enter a percentage to shrink or expand the picture, using the same number for the Horizontal and Vertical percentages if you don't want to warp the picture.

You can control the way that text flows around a picture: Right-click the picture and choose Image Properties from the menu that appears. Click the Appearance tab and change the Align Text to Image setting — try different settings until you find one you like.

In JPEG files, you can adjust the "quality" level to a lower quality, which makes the file smaller. You can set the quality of Web images quite low with little effect on what appears on users' screens.

You can also take advantage of the cache that browsers use. The *cache* keeps copies of previously viewed pages and images. If any image on a page being downloaded is already in the browser's cache, that image isn't loaded again. When you use the same icon in several places on a page or on several pages visited in succession, the browser downloads the icon's file only once and reuses the same image on all the pages. When creating your Web pages, try to use the same icons from one page to the next, to give your pages a consistent style and speed up downloading.

Making links

To make a link on your Web page, highlight the text that you want to be a link and click the Link button on the toolbar. In the Link Properties dialog box, type the exact URL into the Link Location box, or click the Choose File button to choose another Web page you've created. (Rather than type a URL, consider cutting and pasting from the Address or Location box of your browser, to avoid typos.) Then click OK.

Nvu is a WYSIWYG editor, so it writes the HTML formatting codes for you. If you want to see the codes or tweak the look of your page, click the Source tab at the bottom of the Nvu window. Click the Normal tab to return to the WYSIWYG editor.

Making more pages

To create more pages, click New, choose File⇨New, or press Ctrl+N. You can have multiple pages open in Nvu — they appear on tabs, similar to the tabs in Firefox and IE7. If a dialog box pops up, asking what kind of document to create, choose A Blank Document.

Putting your pages on the Web

After you make some pages you're happy with (or happy enough with) and you're ready for other people to see them, you have to release your pages to the world. No two Web servers handle the uploading process in quite the same way.

If you create multiple pages, you can put links among your pages; be sure to upload all the pages.

To upload your files, you need an FTP program. Luckily, well-designed, convenient, and totally groovy Web design programs like Nvu have an FTP program built right in! First, tell Nvu about your Web server, and then upload your first page. Follow these steps:

1. **Click the Publish button on the toolbar.**

   You see the Publish Page dialog box, shown in Figure 18-4.

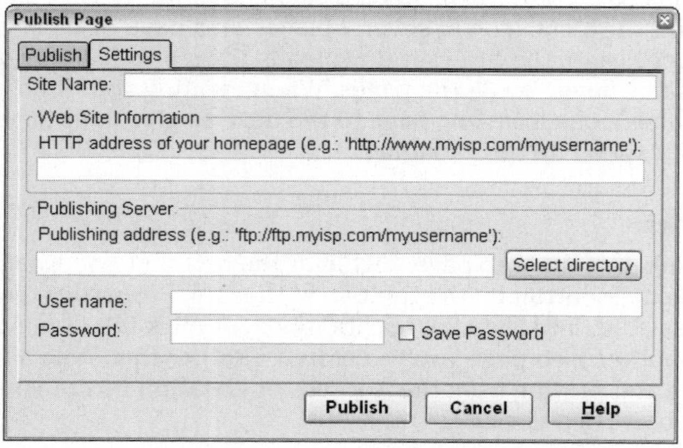

Figure 18-4:
When you click Publish, Nvu asks for information about how to upload your Web pages to a Web server.

Publish Page

Publish | Settings

Site Name:

Web Site Information
HTTP address of your homepage (e.g.: 'http://www.myisp.com/myusername'):

Publishing Server
Publishing address (e.g.: 'ftp://ftp.myisp.com/myusername'):
[Select directory]

User name:
Password: ☐ Save Password

[Publish] [Cancel] [Help]

2. **Complete the fields on the Settings tab.**

   Pick a site name to use when you edit these pages in the future, and then enter the publishing address, the FTP address your ISP gave you to upload your pages, and your username and password. (The HTTP address is optional.) Most of this information was diligently collected by you in the section "Your Web server at your service," earlier in this chapter. Select the Save Password check box unless you share your computer with unsavory characters.

3. **Next, click the Publish tab to enter information about this page.**

   Fill out the page title (the name that you want to appear on the title bar of the browser when your page is displayed) and the filename to use when uploading, usually the same as the filename you use on your own computer, to avoid confusion.

   Click the Publish button to start the upload. Nvu may display a window with the status of the page file and any image files that appear on the page, as shown in Figure 18-5. Click Close when it's done. (You can tell Nvu to display this window by choosing Tools⇨Preferences and choosing the option Always Show Publishing Dialog When Publishing Pages.)

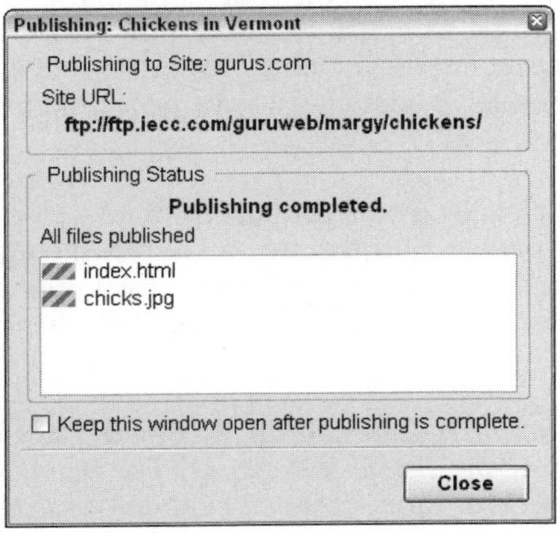

Figure 18-5: Publishing your Web page (and the picture on the page) to your Web server.

You can see and edit the site settings to which you publish pages by choosing Edit⇨Publish Site Settings to display the Publish Settings dialog box.

After you finish uploading, take a look in your browser! Use the Web address where your ISP or Web hosting company told you your pages would appear.

A few other Web page editors

If you don't like Nvu for Web editing, you have lots of other options. Here are two possibilities:

✔ **Dreamweaver** (www.adobe.com/products/dreamweaver): If you get serious about making a Web site, Dreamweaver is the serious Webweaver's program. It's not cheap, but it has lots of features, including built-in FTP, error-checking, an HTML reference, and code view.

✔ **CoffeeCup HTML Editor** (www.coffeecup.com): This Windows Web editor lets you choose page elements from a list so that you never have to see HTML codes. Your formatting options are limited, but it's a great way to get started. An FTP program is included for uploading your finished pages. This program is no longer free, but it's a good deal.

Testing your page

Be sure to check out how your page looks after it's on the Web. Inspect it from someone else's computer to make sure that it doesn't accidentally contain any references to graphics files stored on your own computer that you forgot to upload. If you want to be compulsive, check how it looks from various browsers — Firefox, Internet Explorer 6 and 7, Opera, Lynx, and AOL, to name a few. If you're not compulsive, just check your pages in Internet Explorer and Firefox.

Shortly after you upload your pages, you'll probably notice a glaring mistake. (We always do.) To update a page, edit the copy on your own computer and then upload it to your Web server, replacing the preceding version of the page. If you change some but not all of your pages, you don't have to upload pages that haven't changed.

See *Building a Web Site For Dummies,* 2nd Edition, by David A. Crowder (Wiley) or *Building Web Sites All-in-One Desk Reference For Dummies,* by Doug Sahlin and Claudia Snell (Wiley) for more detailed explanations of how to create a Web site, add pictures, make links among your pages and from your pages to other sites, and publicize your site.

Be the Master of Your Domain

A home page address like this one:

```
www.people.stratford-on-avon-internet.com/~shakespeare/
PrinceOfDenmark/index.html
```

just doesn't attract as many visitors as

```
www.hamlet.org
```

Getting your own domain name is a lot easier and cheaper than you might think. Follow these three steps:

1. **Choose a name.**

   Pick one that's easy to remember and to spell. Pick out a couple of alternative names in case the one you want is taken. Don't use a variation of a popular trademark like Coke or Sony (or Dummies) unless you like dealing with lawyers. Also be sure that the name isn't already taken; whoever you pick to register your domain will have a lookup service to see what's available.

2. **Ask your ISP or Web hosting company to host your name.**

   Hosting your name means that your ISP or Web hosting company (wherever you store your Web pages) breathes some incantations that tell the Internet where to go when someone types your personal Web address. Many ISPs charge a fee for this service, but a few do it for free. Your ISP may be able to handle the next step, registration, for you too.

3. **Register your name if your ISP doesn't.**

   Hundreds of registrars compete for business in the popular `.com`, `.net`, `.org`, and `.info` categories. The going rate is between $7 and $20 per year.

   If your ISP wants to charge you big bucks (more than $10 a month) to register your name and to host your pages, consider using a Web hosting service. Pair Networks at `http://pair.com` and MyHosting at `http://myhosting.com` are both reputable, reliable, and cheap.

Shout It Out: Getting Your Web Site Found

After your pages are online, you may want to get people to come and visit. Before you do any online publicity, make sure that your pages have two types of information that search engines and Web directories look for:

✓ **Page description:** You can store a one-sentence description of your page in the *metatags* (hidden codes) at the beginning of each Web page. Yahoo, Google, and other sites display this text when your page appears in their listings, and they use the text to determine how to categorize the page. In Nvu, you can add a page description by choosing Format⇨Page Title and Properties.

✔ **Keywords:** You can provide a list of key words and phrases that people might search for if they want to find your page. Nvu doesn't make it easy to add keywords to your page's metatags, but here's how: Choose View⇨ HTML Source to display the HTML codes that make up your page. Skim down until you find `</head>`. Just above that, add a tag like this:

```
<meta content="chickens, hens, eggs, poultry, domestic poultry"
      name="keywords">
```

Replace the list of chicken-related terms with your own. Then choose View⇨Normal Edit Mode to display your page the way it normally looks.

After your page description and keywords are in place, upload your pages again.

To publicize your site, visit your favorite Web directories and search engines, such as Google (`http://google.com`), Yahoo (`http://yahoo.com`), and the Open Directory Project (`http://dmoz.org`), and submit your URL (the name of your page) to add to their databases. All these sites have on their home pages an option for adding a new page — the option is usually labeled Suggest URL or Suggest a Site or Add Your Site. (Sometimes it's a teeny little link near the bottom of the page.) Automated indexes, like Google, add pages promptly, but manually maintained directories, like dmoz.org, may not accept them.

Don't pay to have your site included: Every respectable search engine and directory has an option for adding your noncommercial site for free, although it make take a while for your site to show up.

Getting lots of traffic to your site takes time. If your site offers something different that is of real interest to other folks, it can build a following of its own. Even we *For Dummies* authors have gotten into the action: A few of our home-grown sites that keep growing in popularity are Margy's Great Tapes for Kids site, at `www.greattapes.com`; John's Airline Information On-Line on the Internet site, at `http://airinfo.aero`, and Arnold Reinhold's Math in the Movies page, at `www.mathinthemovies.com`. Just imagine what you can come up with!

Chapter 19

Games and Worlds on the Web

*B*esides being useful, the Internet is also lots of fun, and enterprising designers have found myriad ways to use it for entertainment. In this chapter, we try to give you a sense of what games are out there on the Web as well as some practical tips for getting started.

Creating an Account

For many of the games described in this section, you need to create an *account,* which is simply an online identification that helps the site owners distinguish you from your neighbor. Creating an account generally involves these steps:

1. **Find either the Create Account or Register link and click it.**

   It's on the home page of the Web site. If you see a Sign In link, click it because it probably leads to a page with a link to register.

2. **Enter your information, including a username and password.**

   Make up a username that you can remember and that reflects the kind of character you want to be in the game. Choose a password that's not in the dictionary and that's not the same as any non-game passwords.

Don't choose the same password you use for online banking or making purchases!

3. **Check your e-mail for the activation code.**

   Generally, the Web site sends you an *activation code* that you must enter in order to activate your account. This system allows the Web site to confirm that your e-mail address is really yours.

4. **If the e-mail doesn't include your password, write it down somewhere or, better yet, type it in a message and e-mail it to yourself.**

5. **Play!**

What type of information do game Web sites ask for? Generally, they want your name, birth date, mailing address, phone number, and e-mail address. (Feel free to make up a birth date other than your real one. What business is it of theirs?) For games that cost money, you have to provide credit card information. This is never entirely without risk but, as we discuss elsewhere in this book, not nearly as dangerous as you might think.

A Solitaire-y Pastime

When people say "online gaming," we often assume that they mean multi-player games, and for good reason: The Internet is fundamentally a communication technology, and the biggest advantage to online games is the enormous pool of other players available at any time. If you're feeling antisocial, though, plenty of solitary games can be found. Here are some places to look:

✔ **Your ISP:** The site `http://games.aol.com`, for instance, has numerous solitaire games available to anyone willing to create a free account.

✔ **AddictingGames:** One of countless Web sites dedicated to solitary gaming is `www.addictinggames.com`, shown in Figure 19-1. A good search engine can help you find others, like *Miniclip* (`www.miniclip.com`).

✔ **Merchandising advertising**: Many corporations advertise their products through downloadable games. If you like Legos, try `www.lego.com/eng/bionicle/games.aspx`.

✔ **Neopets:** You can play action, puzzle, and word games to earn money at `www.neopets.com`. You earn money to buy things for your virtual pets. *Neopets* allows for some degree of interaction between players, but most activities are solo.

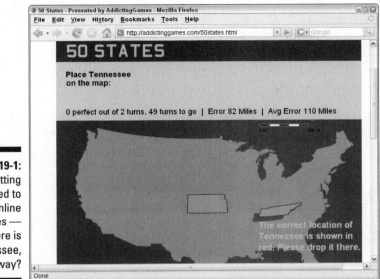

Figure 19-1:
Getting
addicted to
online
games —
where is
Tennessee,
anyway?

Plays Well with Others

Anyone who spends much time playing games on the Internet will probably eventually want to play with other people. Most of us simply find more thrill in facing off with another human being than with an electronic box.

When looking for a game to play online, don't think you need to sift through the overflowing shelves of the local video game store. An easy way to start is with games you already know.

A great many classic games have been adapted for online play, both proprietary ones, like Scrabble and Monopoly, and ancient ones, like chess and Go. Chances are that you're already comfortable playing at least one of them, so look for a free site on which to play. Here's what to do:

1. Choose a game — one you're comfortable with already. The field is wide open!

2. Consult with friends who play the game; they may recommend a Web site, or you may end up referring them to *your* choice.

3. If you have an AOL account (perhaps you use AIM), you'll find its game service (at `http://games.aol.com`) mostly free and easy to use. If not, try the MSN game site (`http://games.msn.com`).

4. Try typing **online game** in your favorite search engine. You can find many free, independent sites, like OKbridge (at `www.okbridge.com`) or Miniclip (`www.miniclip.com`).

Looking to become a bridge master? At certain sites, like the American Contract Bridge League (at `www.acbl.org`), you can earn master points by playing online.

MMORPGs Are More Fun than They Sound

MMORPGs (massively multiplayer online role-playing games) are one of the biggest online gaming industries, and something of a pop culture phenomenon. You may not have heard the term, but if you spend any time around gamers, you hear the names — *RuneScape, World of Warcraft,* and *EverQuest* among them.

What's all the fuss about? Read on, and we'll show you.

The general idea

MMO stands for *massively multiplayer online*, which just means that it's a big online game with lots of people playing together at one time. RPG stands for *role-playing game*, which may require more explanation. In a role-playing game, you invent a character, a fictitious personality who represents you in some fictional world and whose actions you control. You play the role of a fictitious personality while exploring an imaginary world.

Computer RPGs generally ask you to take on the role of a warrior or adventurer, and the main activities of your alter ego are fighting and treasure-hunting, although many MMORPGs also have possibilities for trading, crafting, nation-building, and more. These RPGs are as much about developing your character's abilities as his or her personality; as you fight, your character gains levels of skill and better equipment, with which you can fight more dangerous monsters and earn yet more levels and equipment.

One of the earliest commercially successful RPGs, the pen-and-paper game *Dungeons and Dragons,* has a fantasy setting, a tradition that many modern RPGs uphold. If elves and dwarves leave you cold, there are MMORPGs for you, like the franchise title *Star Wars Galaxies*.

Who's playing?

Many people think that MMORPGs are the exclusive playground of geeky, straight, white, male gamers. (Of course, we know that *you* don't hold that narrow-minded view!) Without getting into nature-versus-nurture debates, our experience suggests that there's some truth to this stereotype.

Whether it's a cause or an effect of their scarcity, minority gamers may sometimes feel less than welcome in the online world. Emboldened by anonymity and able to assume that other users are just like them, you may find that other players express offensive sentiments more freely than they might in person. Every game has anti-harassment policies, but many games are used by so many players that enforcement is sometimes patchy.

That said, MMORPGs are *not* purely white men's spaces, nor are they used only by stereotypical gamers. Most MMORPGs depend more on quick thinking than on quick reflexes, and are thus accessible to those without much video game experience.

If you feel like an outsider among gamers, you should know that there are alternative gaming communities in which you may feel more comfortable. Rather than be discouraged by the occasional bigoted remark, why not seek out a feminist mercenary guild, Chicano raiding team, or band of LGBT-friendly orcs? Believe us, they exist!

Choosing a server

After you choose an MMORPG to play, create an account, and provide your credit card information, you may need to choose a *server*. Large games may have tens of thousands of people playing simultaneously. To avoid overloading the system, the players are divided up over a number of servers. Each server is a separate computer system running a separate copy of the "world," to prevent it from getting too crowded. For the most part, all the servers are equally usable, but here are some thoughts to consider:

 ✔ **Location:** Servers located near you physically are less likely to lag, which is important if you have a slow machine. The amount of time it takes your command to get halfway around the world to a distant server may prove annoying.

- **RP:** Some designated "role-play" servers require users to speak with medieval affectations and eschew modern slang and game terms, forsooth.

- **PvP:** Some Servers are all about player-versus-player combat, whereas others forbid it.

- **Population:** On a smaller server, your connection is slightly faster, but it may be harder to find players to trade or fight with.

- **Friends:** If you know someone who plays, ask which server she's on and join that one.

Roaming around RuneScape

RuneScape is a popular fantasy MMORPG. Its chief claim to fame is its price tag: $0. *RuneScape* has a simplistic but serviceable combat engine and many nonviolent pastimes, such as mining, cooking, and other handicrafts (see Figure 19-2).

Figure 19-2:
RuneScape,
a world of
knights,
rangers,
orcs,
demons,
and
dwarves.

The advantages of *RuneScape* include:

- ✔ It's freely available online.
- ✔ It has manageable system requirements.
- ✔ It has useful guides and manuals, and may be less intimidating than some more advanced RPGs. Its tutorial explains how to play the game and gets you started easily.

However, *RuneScape* has some disadvantages:

- ✔ If you prefer gaming with adults, the low-price *RuneScape* attracts a younger population.
- ✔ Its graphics are less sophisticated than those in pricier games.
- ✔ It has less character customization than other RPGs. (All characters are human, for instance.)
- ✔ It isn't *completely* free. Some skills and areas are available to only those who pay for membership, which starts at $5 per month.

Want to try it out? Find it at www.runescape.com. After you make your account, we recommend jumping right in. The beginning of the game is a handy tutorial. After you play around a bit, you may want to go back and read the online manual, which makes more sense in context.

RuneScape isn't the only free online RPG. Many others are on the Web, including the two-dimensional *AdventureQuest* (www.battleon.com), the chess-based *Tactics Arena Online* (www.tacticsarena.com), and the text-adventure *Kingdom of Loathing* (www.kingdomofloathing.com).

Crafting war in World of Warcraft

World of Warcraft, Everquest, and *Final Fantasy XI* are examples of MMORPGs from mainstream game developers. These games have more content, more options, and snazzier graphics than free online games. They're also significantly more expensive.

Your first step, if you choose to play one of these games, is to acquire the software. Unlike the rest of the games in this chapter, which you can play in your Web browser, these fancier games require you to install special programs on your computer. For *World of Warcraft,* you probably make a pilgrimage to your local game shop to buy the game.

After you get it installed, you (as usual) set up an account, enter your credit card information, and decide how to pay for the game. Most of these games require a monthly fee, like a magazine subscription. Also like a magazine, they give you a bulk discount, and you can cancel at any time.

Rather than make a long-term commitment early, a better idea is to get a free trial of the game and then decide how to pay after your trial. Here are some ways to acquire a free trial:

- ✔ **Referrals:** Many games let current members give their friends free trial accounts.

- ✔ **Out of the box:** Often, you get a free trial when buying the game. These games are released and re-released frequently, so do some comparison shopping and make sure that the edition you buy gives you enough time to evaluate.

- ✔ **Demo disks:** We have gotten free software and trial periods through magazine promotions and the like.

- ✔ **Special offers:** As in any industry, there are often good deals for the persistent and discerning on the game Web sites.

After you're playing, *World of Warcraft* is similar to *RuneScape,* with a few additional wrinkles. You can pick a race (elf, orc, or catgirl, for example) and a class (fighter, wizard, healer) for your character. Choosing wisely is important — if you dislike your character, you generally have to start again from the beginning. However, the rulebooks don't tell what you'll enjoy, so we recommend trying a few different characters briefly before settling on one.

The basic activities of the game are killing monsters for levels and rare items, a process that can sometimes grow tedious. To liven it up and speed things along, consider working together with other players. Either arrange to play at the same time as your friends, or ask around online to find others looking for a group. Some classes are more popular in groups than others, something you might consider when designing your character.

After you've been playing for a while, you may want to consider joining a guild. *Guilds* are simply associations of like-minded players who cooperate to earn power, wealth, and prestige. The chief benefit is the ease with which you can recruit party members, but most games also offer mechanical incentives to join guilds. Of course, many people join more for the camaraderie and guild-marked clothing than for any material benefit.

One recent game that's quite different from those discussed here is Guild Wars, at www.guildwars.com. *Guild Wars* has no monthly fees. Joining a guild should be your first priority because the focus of the game is guild-on-guild combat. The monster-hunting, treasure-finding part of the game has been abridged and streamlined to let you jump into PvP (player versus player rather than player versus computer) action that much faster.

It's a Whole New World

Second Life is a game unlike any other, if it can even be accurately termed a game. It's a complex phenomenon that shares properties of MMORPGs and social networking sites like MySpace and Facebook (described in Chapter 17).

Second Life is essentially a simulation of the entire world. In *Second Life,* you can run a store, buy and sell clothes, visit nightclubs, or do practically anything else that some daring user has programmed. Although you create a character to represent you, as in an RPG, you don't fight monsters (unless that's what you really want to do) and you don't accumulate levels. Rather, the game attempts to simulate the real world in its entirety — or at least an alternative reality populated by 20-something hipsters and a smattering of dragons and talking raccoons.

Whom might you meet on *Second Life?* Almost anyone. The population skews slightly male and geekier than the average population, but it's certainly not used only by gamers and programmers. You find artists, stay-at-home moms, and presidential candidates as well (no joke!). A few corporations own islands in *Second Life* in which they hold virtual business meetings. You can even attend religious services in *Second Life*.

A day in the Second Life

The www.secondlife.com Web site is where you can acquire the free *Second Life* software. You must be at least 18 to play; minors 13 and above should check out http://teen.secondlife.com. Either way, the first thing you want to do is create an account and download the software.

The basic version of *Second Life* is free, although if you provide your credit card information, you get some free Linden Dollars, the currency of *Second Life*. We recommend that you do this. Providing your information now makes it easier for you to be tempted to spend money later, but you don't get far in *Second Life* without a few Linden Dollars.

You start off on Tutorial Island, shown in Figure 19-3. You learn how to create and dress your avatar, the *Second Life* version of you. The screen prompts walk you through walking, flying, picking up items, and looking around. At that point, you can head off to the mainland.

Figure 19-3:
Watching
Second Life
go by.

Absolutely the first thing you want to do is change your clothes. Tutorial Island gives you three stylish outfits to choose from; don't wear them. Seize the chance for a little self-expression and design something that doesn't mark you as so obviously new. Fashion snobbery is alive and well on the Internet, but you generally get an A for effort. As long as your attire reflects you, and not corporate homogeneity, you'll be fine. If not, you can change outfits instantly.

The easiest way is to right-click your character, choose Edit Appearance, and take off all your clothes. Then you can design new costume pieces one by one and click Save As Outfit to name them. Don't neglect the Create Skirt button, even if your character is male — with a few tweaks, it can be used to create coats, cloaks, and capes.

After you've done that, you can begin your *Second Life* journey. A few things you may be interested in doing are listed here:

  ✓ **Collect free stuff:** Search "freebies" or ask around for places with free clothes, tools, or animations.

  ✓ **Join a group:** Search for groups through the search engine or look in the profiles of interesting people you meet.

✔ **Shop:** Everywhere you go, you find things for you to spend your money on.

✔ **Build:** Search for a "sandbox" area where you can use the builder to construct more elaborate objects. This process takes a while to get good at, but can be very rewarding.

Who's Linden?

Linden Dollars are the currency of *Second Life.* As in the real world, you don't get far without them. Fortunately, you don't need to buy food or transportation, but you can still empty your virtual pocketbook in plenty of ways. Here are some uses for Linden Dollars:

✔ **Shopping:** If you don't want to create everything yourself, you want some Linden Dollars to decorate your character (and home, if you have one). You can buy better clothes than standard issue or items for your home, like furniture and trees.

✔ **Designing:** You must pay a small fee to upload objects and screen shots into *Second Life.* At this point, you can sell them, give them away, or trade them with other players.

✔ **Buy land:** You need a premium account to do this, but you can buy virtual property to use a house, club, clubhouse, store, or whatever strikes your fancy.

Hopefully, you already have a few Linden Dollars. If not, look into acquiring some. Here are a few ways to make money:

✔ **Sign-up bonus:** This is the money you get just for registering.

✔ **Direct purchase:** If you can afford it, you can simply exchange U.S. dollars for Linden bucks.

✔ **Stipend:** A more effective way to get money may be to shell out for a premium account. You pay a monthly fee but get a weekly stipend and the right to own land.

✔ **Sales:** Write scripts, design objects, write music, or take pictures, and you can sell them to other players. You need some money to get started because it costs a small number of Linden Dollars to upload your creations, but after that, it can be both fun and rewarding. You also retain real-world rights to your creations.

Part VI
The Part of Tens

The 5th Wave   By Rich Tennant

"I don't mean to hinder your quest for knowledge; however, it's not generally a good idea to try and download the entire Internet."

In this part . . .

We have lots of interesting odds and ends we want to tell you about, so (to provide the illusion of organization) we've grouped them into lists. By the strangest coincidence, each list consists of exactly *ten* facts. (*Note to the literal-minded:* You may have to cut off or glue on some fingers to make your version of ten match up with ours. Perhaps it would be easier just to take our word for it.) The glossary is back in this part of the book, too.

Chapter 20

Ten Problems and Ten Solutions

Gosh, using the Internet is exciting. But sometimes things get so fouled up that you want to push your computer out the window and go back to the communication methods our ancestors used, like newspapers, telephones, and smoke signals.

Don't give up just yet. This chapter offers up some common problems that many Internet users encounter, as well as some solutions to those problems.

My Computer Takes Forever to Boot Up, Pop-Up Ads Have Taken Over My Screen, and It's Really Slow

All these symptoms suggest that your computer is infested with *malware*, sneaky programs that do bad things to your computer, including spyware (which arrive via your Web browser), worms (which copy themselves over the Net into your computer), and viruses (which arrive via e-mail). A full-scale war is going on in cyberspace for control of the world's PCs, and your computer is likely a casualty. Chapter 2 describes both types of malware, Chapter 4 suggests strongly that you install virus-checker and anti-spyware programs, and Chapter 14 describes how to configure your virus checker. Make sure that you have downloaded the latest improvements to your Windows operating system, and check that your virus checker and spyware removers are up to date as well. And, if you still use Internet Explorer to browse the Web, consider trying a different browser, such as Firefox.

We like these anti-spyware programs, all three of which we use:

- Spybot Search & Destroy, from www.safer-networking.org (shareware)

- Ad-Aware, from Lavasoft, at www.lavasoftusa.com (shareware)

- Microsoft Windows Defender, at www.microsoft.com/athome/security/spyware/software (free, already included in Vista)

For all three programs, download, install, and run them, and be sure to download updates regularly.

The nuclear option

If you have installed and run antivirus and anti-spyware programs and you still have problems, it may be too late for band-aid remedies. Your computer may be so thoroughly infested that you have no choice but to blow everything away and start over.

Before you reinstall Windows, you *must* get a firewall to protect your computer. Most distributed versions of Windows are so insecure that you simply cannot install the program and all its security updates before you're reinfected with viruses and worms. (Installing and updating Windows and your application programs take a couple of hours. Infection takes perhaps 10 seconds.) The routers we mention in Chapter 5 that let you connect several computers to your Internet connection include adequate firewalls that are quite cheap. Even if you have only one computer, the $30 you spend for a router is well worth it.

Before you can reinstall Windows, be sure to make a copy of all your files. If you haven't been backing up regularly, make two copies, just to be safe. Back up at least one copy to more reliable CD-Rs or DVD-Rs rather than to rewritable media. Make sure that you have the installation CD or DVDs and all the registration codes, license codes, and key codes for all the applications you use.

Before reinstalling Windows, you may want to get a copy of *Windows For Dummies,* by Andy Rathbone (Wiley) or *Windows XP Home Edition: The Complete Reference,* or *Windows Vista: The Complete Reference.* (The latter two books were written by John and Margy and published by Osborne/McGraw-Hill.) These books contain more details about how to reinstall Windows than we have room for here. You need the original CDs that came with your computer or a new copy of Windows XP or later. Put the Windows CD or DVD in your CD or DVD drive and reboot. Follow the instructions to where it asks whether you want to rewrite or destroy all the information on your hard drive. You may need to select something like Advanced Options to find this. Take a deep breath and answer Yes and then Yes again to all the warnings indicating that all your files will be erased. They will — that's why we have you back them up — but they'll erase the worms, too.

When the reinstallation of Windows is complete, follow the on-screen instruction to reenter your Internet settings. Then go immediately to `http://windowsupdate.microsoft.com` (which works only with Internet Explorer — sigh) and download all the suggested updates to Windows, which takes quite a while. Load your antivirus and anti-spyware software, and get their latest updates. Then reinstall all your applications. Yes, this process is a real pain.

Next, place your data backup CD in the CD drive and have your antivirus program scan it. We recommend that you do not reinstall all your data files at first; just the ones you need to use. If you made two copies as we told you to, keep them in two different places, preferably in two different buildings.

Finally, create separate, password-protected accounts for everyone who will be using the computer, and make them all Limited rather than Administrator accounts unless they have a good reason to be installing their own programs. Have a talk with everyone about the risks of free downloads and online game sites. Suggest that, should you have to repeat this process, their use of your computer will be terminated. This is not the kind of problem you want to keep dealing with, as you have no doubt concluded if you just had to rebuild your system.

The switcheroo

Plan B is to consider getting an Apple Macintosh computer, even if only for your e-mail and Web surfing. As of this writing, there aren't any serious online threats to Apple's Mac OS X. This situation could change, but at least Apple has a head start over the hackers, rather than the other way around for Microsoft. You should still keep your Mac's operating system up to date and rebuild your PC if you still plan to use it. If you need certain programs for work, look for Mac equivalents or check out Boot Camp (`www.apple.com/macosx/bootcamp`), which lets you run your Windows system and programs on your Mac.

This Nice, Free Program Doesn't Run If I Turn Off the Ads

Lots of free programs are supported by advertising. That's the deal. You may be able to find equivalent programs that don't show ads, or you can pay to register the program and make the ads go away. Even if you're willing to trade ad-watching for free software, we do *not* recommend that you use any program that shows Web-based ads — *adware* — while other programs are running. (Ads displayed in the program itself rather than in your browser, like Eudora and Opera, are fine.) Adware companies swear up and down that it's not spyware and that they don't compile personal dossiers of all the Web sites you visit to decide which ads to send to your computer, but we don't trust them.

I Can't Send Large E-Mail Attachments

Some Internet service providers and some system administrators limit the size of files you can e-mail by using their mail servers. In the case of problems at work, the solution may be as simple as talking to the person in charge of your Internet access and asking for the limit to be changed. Your ISP might not be so accommodating. We have another way to move giant files from point A to point B.

For local file transfers, *sneakernet* (transferring files by walking them from one computer to another) has made a comeback in the form of USB flash drives. Flash drives work with recent versions of all major operating systems. They operate like removable disk drives but are about the size of your thumb (or smaller, especially if you have big thumbs) and have a shiny, rectangular plug at one end. Some geeks carry one on a lanyard around their necks or on their key chains. To use one, just plug it into a USB port on your computer. For very large files (many gigabytes), you can use an iPod as a portable USB hard drive. After you copy whatever files you want, you need to tell your operating system that you're done with the drive before you unplug it. Windows uses a tiny icon in the system tray that does this. On Macs, drag the disk's icon to the trash.

If your computer has a CD or DVD writer, you can also burn your files on a CD or DVD to give to your friend. It's not as cute and compact as a USB drive, but it's more durable. Your camera's memory card can also hold files.

I'm Worried about ID Theft

The U.S. Federal Trade Commission (www.ftc.gov/idtheft) offers this advice to prevent identity theft: First, look out for *phishing,* e-mail that claims to come from a bank or other online account, such as eBay, and claims that your account has a problem that you can clean up by clicking a link in the message. These messages are never real, but they're very dangerous. If your bank thinks there's a security problem, it doesn't tell you by e-mail. If you're not sure, contact the company by phone or type its Web address (for example, www.yourbank.com) into your browser by hand and look for the customer service section. See Chapter 2 for more about phishing.

The Internet isn't the only source of information about you. Keep bills and other documents that bear your account and Social Security numbers in a safe place, and tear up or shred old bank statements and credit card bills. Get a shredder that cross-cuts the paper into short strips rather than the cheaper shredders that make strips the length of the page; patient thieves can paste those together. Those offers for pre-approved credit cards are also dangerous if they fall into the wrong hands. Shred them or stop them altogether by calling 1-888-5OPTOUT or visiting www.optoutprescreen.com. If your driver's license still has your Social Security number on it, get a new license issued.

Get in the habit of scanning your bank and credit card statements when they arrive (or even earlier, online). Don't worry about the bank's arithmetic, but look for charges that you don't remember incurring. If you find any, contact your bank or credit card company immediately. After you verify any fraudulent charges, tell the bank that you want new accounts with new credit card numbers. You may need to file a police report, although in our experience, if you have fraudulent charges, the bank will issue new cards without hassle.

I Can't Remember All My Web Site Passwords

The standard advice is to construct passwords out of a mixture of letters, numbers, and special symbols; to have a different password for each account; to never write down passwords; and to change them every few months. Most Internet users who have dozens of accounts ignore this advice because only a truly unusual person can remember dozens of different random passwords and which account each one goes with.

We suggest a compromise. Make up one good password to use on all your low-risk accounts — accounts in which letting someone else gain access has little consequence, such as online newspaper subscriptions. Use different passwords for the accounts that really matter, such as online banking. If you feel that it's necessary, writing down those passwords and keeping them in a safe place is better than picking a password that's easy for someone to guess. Don't list your passwords in your desktop Rolodex or on a sticky note stuck to your computer's monitor. *Never, ever* choose a password that is a regular English word (a word that appears in a dictionary) or a common name.

Some decent programs are available for safely storing passwords on personal digital assistants (PDAs). We like the free, open-source *Keyring* for Palm PDAs and cellphones, available at `http://gnukeyring.sourceforge.net`. Be sure to pick a really strong master password and have a backup plan for when your PDA falls into the bathtub and dies. (Ink on paper has stood the test of time.)

I Get Messages Telling Me That E-Mail I Never Sent Is Undeliverable

There's not much you can do about this problem after it has happened. Many computer viruses spread by taking over someone's computer and sending copies of themselves to everyone in that computer's address book. The virus uses addresses it finds in the computer's address book as fake return addresses to trick people into thinking it's real mail. Most spammers use computers that have been taken over in this way to send spam, again using fake stolen return addresses. Make sure your computer is not the source of such unwanted messages by keeping its operating system and antivirus software up to date, using a router as your firewall (see Chapter 5), and by turning the computer (or at least its connection to the Internet) off when not in use.

People Seem to Know a Lot about Me

The rate at which we're all losing our privacy scares us, too. Here are a few tips:

Get rid of spyware that may be lurking on your machine

Spyware does just what it sounds like — it spies on you and your activities. You think your Internet activities are private, but unless you keep your PC spyware free, they're not. Browse one mortgage lender site and you'll hear from the universe of mortgage lenders. Buy from one pharmacy and you'll get solicitations for drugs you didn't even know existed from everyone else. Your inbox is full of names that closely resemble people you actually know — but not quite. If all this sounds familiar, chances are, software is recording your every keystroke. Get rid of it! (The software, not the keyboard.) When we use Internet Explorer (some folks still have Web sites that work only with Internet Explorer), we often have to clean our machines because worms and viruses often sneak through security holes in it. Because it's so widely used, it's targeted by hackers all over the world, which is why we use Firefox instead (see Chapter 6).

Don't be dumb

Don't put information on your Web page that you don't want everyone in the world to know. In particular, don't include your home address and phone number unless you want calls and visits. We know at least one person who received an unexpected phone call from someone she met on the Net and wasn't too pleased about it. Why would Net users need this information, anyway? They can send you e-mail!

Don't order stuff by using a public PC

Normally, ordering stuff over the Web or by e-mail is perfectly safe — at least as safe as handing your credit card to a waiter you've never met! However, some shopping sites store information about you (including a link to your mailing address and payment info) in a file on your computer. This works perfectly when you're ordering from your own computer — you don't have to type all that info when you visit the site the next time you order. But when you order stuff at the library or at a cybercafé, this personal information may be stored on that computer. This means that the next person who uses that computer and goes to that site has all your personal data available and may be able to use it to place an order. Better not chance it.

I Can't Get My Kids, Spouse, or Significant Other Off the Computer

Games and instant messaging are highly addictive and seem to be getting more so. Microsoft's Steve Ballmer brags about the addictive nature of the games his company sells and smiles as he says he wouldn't let *his* kid play them. That ought to give you a hint.

Set clear limits on computer usage and stick to them. Have a talk with your spouse or significant other about which kinds of online chatting are okay and which aren't. Also think about how much time *you* spend in front of a computer screen. Use some of your Internet time to make a list of outside activities you enjoy and stick it next to your computer screen. Promise yourself you'll do at least one fun off-computer activity every day. Internet addiction is serious — you may need professional help to quit the habit.

On the other hand, if it's your spouse, sometimes it makes more sense to squander $500 on a second computer (see Chapter 5 for hints on connecting you both to the Net by using a single account) than to squander your marriage.

When I Click a Link, My Browser Says "404 Page Not Found"

Web pages move about or disappear on the Internet. If you type a URL from a printed source, make sure that you type it exactly as it was printed, including capitalization. If you read a URL that's part of a sentence, watch out for the comma, period, or hyphen at the end. That comma, period, or hyphen may or may not be part of the URL — or it may be punctuation for the sentence.

If you clicked a hypertext link or you're sure that you typed the URL correctly and you still get this error message, the data on the site may have been reorganized. Try "walking up" the URL by deleting the portion to the right of the last slash character and trying again; then delete the portion after the next-to-last slash character; and so on. If you get a File Not Found message when you try entering this line, for example:

```
epicurious.com/cooking/menus/cooknow/omelettes.html
```

try these in order:

```
epicurious.com/cooking/menus/cooknow
epicurious.com/cooking/menus
epicurious.com/cooking
epicurious.com
```

At one of these levels, you may find a hint about where the file you seek can be found. Alternatively, go to your favorite search engine and search for it.

A page long gone may still be found on the Wayback Machine at www. archive.org, a free site that has attempted the daunting task of periodically saving snapshots of the whole World Wide Web.

1 Want to Include My E-Mail Address on My Web Page

Including your e-mail address in a Web page is a sure way to attract spam. Spammers have programs that crawl the Web looking for e-mail addresses to spam. You can thwart them by *describing* your e-mail address rather than just typing it out — "It's al at blahblah.com" — or use obscure HTML coding on the Web page. At the least, we suggest you set up a separate e-mail address for your Web site at a free site, such as Gmail.com, Hotmail.com, or Yahoo.com. If the flood of unwanted mail becomes too great, you can abandon that account and set up a new one.

One useful trick is to ask Web site visitors to include some special word in the subject line of their messages. For example, if your Web page is about belt buckle collecting, you can ask correspondents to include "buckles" in the subject line. You can use an e-mail filter to put just the messages that contain that word into a special folder and send the rest of the messages to the trash.

Chapter 21

Ten Fun or Worthwhile Things You Can Do Online

In This Chapter

▶ Taking film-free pictures for family and friends

▶ Checking out short movies and TV advertisements

▶ Playing games and touring the solar system

▶ Taking a look at webcams, diaries, and art museums around the globe

▶ Exploring space, curing cancer, building a jumbo jet, and changing children's lives

You can use the Internet in hundreds of ways for work and profit. In this chapter, we focus on fun. When you find new and fun things to do on the Net, let us know. Send e-mail to us at internet11@gurus.com.

Share Pictures with Your Friends and Family

E-mail attachments (see Chapter 15) are a great way to ship snapshots anywhere in the world for free. You don't even need a digital camera. Many film developing services will digitize your photos and deliver them to you online or on a CD-ROM (for a fee, of course). Other services, like Kodak's EasyShare Gallery (www.kodakgallery.com), develop your pictures and let you organize them into albums on its Web site. You can point your friends to your album by giving them the URL, and they can view the pictures online and order prints of the ones they especially like.

Online photography is even simpler if you buy a digital camera. These cameras have become more affordable, especially if you consider how much money you save on film and developing costs, and you can choose to print only the pictures you like. You can find out more about digital cameras and still digital photography at the following sites, all of which review digital cameras and equipment:

- ✔ Digital Camera Resource Page: www.dcresource.com
- ✔ Digital Photography Review: www.dpreview.com
- ✔ Megapixel.net: www.megapixel.net

Edit an Encyclopedia

Wikipedia (http://en.wikipedia.org) is not only a free encyclopedia, it also lets you edit its articles. If you feel knowledgeable about a topic, look it up in Wikipedia. If you find mistakes or have more to say, just set up a free account and then click the Edit This Page tab. If no article exists, Wikipedia offers to let you create one. Stop by Wikipedia's Village Pump (at http://en.wikipedia.org/wiki/WP:VP) for more information on how to get started and work within the wiki culture. See Chapter 17 for more about how groups can edit a Web site communally using a wiki.

Watch Short Movies and TV Ads

The Internet has created a new way for makers of short and experimental movies to find an audience. Many sites feature miniflicks that you can watch for free. The most popular is Google's YouTube at YouTube.com, whose users upload vast amounts of video, from the profound to the inane. Try looking for **airplane landings**.

IFILM (www.ifilm.com) has a good selection of commercial shorts. You can find a few movie sites at http://dmoz.org/Arts/Movies/Filmmaking/Online_Venues; click the subtopics listed. The quality of these films varies from dreadful to inspired to occasionally creepy, but you can occasionally find some real gems.

If for some reason you don't see as many ads on TV as you want, visit www.advertisementave.com, where you can catch up on all the ads you've missed. The excellent AdCritic (www.adcritic.com) also features the best current ads and classics, but now requires a paid subscription. Either way, now you can catch those great Super Bowl ads without the tedious football.

These film sites use a variety of video formats — QuickTime, RealMedia, and Windows Media Player — see Chapter 9 for how to watch videos on the Web.

Listen to Current and Classic Radio Programs

Have you ever turned on your radio, found yourself in the middle of a fascinating story, and wished you could have heard the beginning? National Public Radio in the U.S. keeps many of its past programs available online. If you want to hear the whole program, visit www.npr.org. You can also use the site's search feature to browse for stories that you missed completely.

Many NPR affiliates and other radio stations have live streaming audio of their programs, so you can listen live to stations all over the country — go to Google and search for the station call letters or the program name. (John recommends his local station at http://wrvo.fm, especially the old shows from the 1930s through 1950s, which they play in the evening.) Many other radio stations now let you listen to their live programs over the Internet, which is particularly handy in large office buildings with poor radio reception. You can listen to stations from around the world and get a taste of world music firsthand or hear the news from different perspectives.

Play Checkers

. . . or chess, poker, hearts, bridge, backgammon, cribbage, Go, or any other board game or card game. The classic games hold up well against the ever-more-bloody electronic games. Now you don't need to round up live friends to play with — you can find willing partners at any time, day or night, at sites like http://games.yahoo.com or http://zone.msn.com (Windows users only for MSN, of course).

True bridge aficionados like to think of bridge not as a card game but, rather, as a way of life. You can round up a bridge foursome at www.bridgeclublive.com and www.okbridge.com. Each charges $99 per year after a free trial period. Many free and fee sites are listed at www.greatbridgelinks.com. MSN (http://zone.msn.com) offers bridge for free.

See Chapter 19 for more elaborate games (and entire artificial worlds) on the Web.

Watch the World Go By

Webcams are live video cameras that you can access over the Internet. They let you see what's happening right now — wherever that camera is pointing. Watch wildlife, events of the day, a city street, a shopping mall, a highway interchange, Slovakia, or even someone's living room. The views are generally updated every few seconds. Go to OnlineCamera at `www.onlinecamera.com`, the ODP Webcam list at `http://dmoz.org/Computers/Internet/On_the_Web/Webcams` — or just search for **webcams** at `www.google.com` or `www.yahoo.com`.

Shoo any children out of the room before you connect to a webcam site, because you never know what you might see. Many will be for, um, adult viewing only. But the live Vegas weddings at `www.vivalasvegasweddings.com` (click Live Web Cam) are usually pretty tame.

Build Your Own Jumbo Jet

Even the staidest corporate sites have the occasional goodies tucked away. Airbus builds airplanes, including the very, very, very large A380 superjumbo. Normally, an A380 lists for $300 million, but if that's a little out of your price range, Airbus Goodies has some paper versions you can print, cut out, fold, and fly, at `www.airbus.com/en/myairbus/goodies`.

Journal Online with Blogs

Posting your diary on the Internet may seem as bizarre as having a webcam in your bedroom, but many people do it and enjoy getting feedback from other diarists. Some people post a series of articles about topics other than their personal lives — for example, about politics, spirituality, or cats. These online journals are *blogs*, and they're covered in the section "What's in a Blog?" in Chapter 17. Here are a few interesting blog sites:

- **Blogger**, at `www.blogger.com`, is owned by Google.
- **LiveJournal**, at `www.livejournal.com` is one of the most popular blog sites.
- **DiaryLand**, at `www.diaryland.com,` gives you a window into the mind of the young.

Some blog sites require you to register (for free) before you can read their articles.

Visit Art Museums around the World

Art museums are great places to spend a rainy afternoon. Now you can visit museums and galleries all over the world via your browser. Not all museum Web sites have online artwork, but many do. Our favorites include the Louvre in Paris (www.louvre.fr, click English in the upper right corner if you don't read French), Boston's Museum of Fine Arts (www.mfa.org), The Metropolitan Museum of Art in New York (www.metmuseum.org), and the State Hermitage Museum in Russia (www.hermitagemuseum.org). Check out the spectacular color photographs from Tsarist Russia by Sergei Prokudin-Gorskii, digitally reconstructed by the Library of Congress, at www.loc.gov/exhibits/empire, and the amazing American Memory collection of historical photos at http://memory.loc.gov. You can find a wide selection of other museums at http://dir.yahoo.com/Arts/Museums__Galleries__and_Centers.

Build Your Own World

Virtual worlds are electronic places you can visit on the Web — kind of like 3-D chat rooms. Rather than create a screen name, you create a personal action figure, or *avatar,* that walks, talks, and emotes (but doesn't make a mess on your floor). When you're in one of these worlds, your avatar interacts with the avatars of other people who are logged on in surroundings that range from quite realistic to truly fantastic. In some virtual worlds, you can even build your own places: a room, a house, a park, a city — whatever you can imagine. Other worlds let you make money, gain status, and battle complete strangers. People who enjoy role-playing games can disappear into online games for hours, days, or months at a time.

Most virtual worlds require you to download a plug-in or special software. Some are free, whereas others require a monthly or annual subscription.

Here are some places where you can enter or create virtual worlds:

- **Second Life, at http://secondlife.com**, lets you can create your own part of a shared online world, including spending real world money.
- **EverQuest, at http://eqlive.station.sony.com**, is a world of monsters, cities, wilderness, creatures, and deities.
- **RuneScape, at www.runescape.com**, is a medieval-style world.

Web-based online worlds are an outgrowth of MUDs (which stands for Multi-User Dimensions, Multi-User Dungeons, or various other names, depending on whom you ask), which were text-based virtual online worlds long before there was a Web.

Tour the Earth

The modestly named Google Earth at `http://earth.google.com` is a downloadable program that lets you fly around the earth and zoom in and out. After you get fairly close to the ground, you find links to pictures contributed by users (including some impressively remote places — try looking for South Georgia), links to Wikipedia, and enough to keep you busy for hours, days, or even months, if you're not careful.

Tour the Solar System

The last half of the 20th century will go down in history as the time when humans began to explore outer space. Probes visited several comets and asteroids and every planet but Pluto. (For a song about planetary exploration, see `www.christinelavin.com/planetx.html`.) The probes sent back amazing pictures: storms on Jupiter, oceans on Europa, mudslides on Mars, and the Earth at night.

Which generation will actually get to play tourist in the solar system remains to be seen; here are some great space sites:

- You can follow the adventures of the Mars rovers, at `http://marsrovers.jpl.nasa.gov`, and virtual tours are available now at sites such as `http://sse.jpl.nasa.gov`.

- Be sure to bookmark the astronomy picture of the day at `http://antwrp.gsfc.nasa.gov/apod/astropix.html`.

- Above all, don't miss NASA's incredible montage of human civilization at `http://antwrp.gsfc.nasa.gov/apod/image/0011/earthlights_dmsp_big.jpg`.

Search for Extraterrestrial Life or Cure Cancer

SETI@home (`http://setiweb.ssl.berkeley.edu`) is a scientific experiment that uses Internet-connected home and office computers to search for *extraterrestrial intelligence* (SETI). The idea is to have thousands of otherwise idle PCs and Macs perform the massive calculations needed to extract the radio signals of other civilizations from intergalactic noise. You can participate by running a free program that downloads and analyzes data collected at the Arecibo radio telescope in Puerto Rico.

If eavesdropping on space aliens seems a bit far out, you may enjoy lending your computer's idle time to solving problems in cryptography and mathematics. Distributed.net (`www.distributed.net`) manages several projects. (Feel free to join the Internet Gurus team there.) When you sign up to help a project at Distributed.net, you agree to run its program on your computer when the computer isn't otherwise occupied, and your donation of computer time helps achieve the goal of the project.

If math and cryptography don't ring your chimes, consider joining the Folding at Home project at `http://folding.stanford.edu`. This project studies how proteins get their three-dimensional shapes, an important question in medical research. By signing up to run its program, you're helping with basic research that may help find a cure for "Alzheimer's, Mad Cow (BSE), CJD, ALS, Huntington's, Parkinson's disease, and many cancers and cancer-related syndromes."

Adopt a Kid

Do you surf the Web for hours each day? Maybe your life needs more meaning. Adopting a kid is more of a commitment than upgrading to the latest Microsoft operating system, but at least kids grow up eventually and you don't have to reinstall them to get rid of viruses. Here are two excellent Web sites that list special children in need of homes: `www.rainbowkids.com` and `www.capbook.org`. It can't hurt to look.

Glossary

....

404 Not Found: An error message your Web browser frequently displays when it can't find the page you requested. Caused by mistyping a URL (your fault) or clicking a broken link (not your fault).

ActiveX: A Microsoft scheme for downloading little programs, sometimes known as objects. Internet Explorer supports ActiveX. Unfortunately, these little programs may contain spyware.

address: Internet users encounter two important types of addresses: e-mail addresses (for sending e-mail to someone; e-mail addresses almost always contain an @ symbol) and Web page addresses (more properly called *URLs*).

AIM (AOL Instant Messenger): A free instant messaging program that you can use whether or not you have an AOL account.

America Online (AOL): A value-added, online service that provides many services in addition to Internet access, including access to popular chat groups. Go to www.aol.com for more information. AOL offers free accounts at http://free.aol.com.

applet: A small computer program written in the Java programming language. You can download applets by using a Web browser. Applets run in a special way that makes it difficult for them to do damage to your computer.

archive: A single file containing a group of files that have been compressed and glommed together for efficient storage. You have to use a program such as WinZip, PKZIP, tar, or StuffIt to get the original files back out.

attachment: A computer file electronically stapled to an e-mail message and sent along with it.

BCC (blind carbon copy): A way to send a copy of your e-mail to someone without other recipients knowing about it. *See also* CC.

binary file: A file that contains information other than text. A binary file might contain an archive, a picture, sounds, a spreadsheet, or a word processing document that includes formatting codes in addition to text characters.

bit: The smallest unit of measurement for computer data. Bits can be *on* or *off* (symbolized by 1 or 0, respectively) and are used in various combinations to represent different types of information.

bitmap: Little dots put together in a grid to make a picture.

BitTorrent: A method for transmitting large files over the Internet that spreads the load among many cooperating computers.

biz: Last part of an Internet domain name (such as example.biz) to indicate that the host computer is run by a commercial organization that couldn't get the .com address it really wanted.

blog: Short for Web log, which is a personal diary on the Internet. Any fool can publish a blog, and many fools do.

bookmark: The address of a Web page to which you may want to return, stored in your browser. Firefox lets you maintain a list of bookmarks to make it easy to go back to your favorite Web pages. Also called *favorites*.

bounce: To return e-mail as undeliverable. If you e-mail a message to a bad address, it bounces back to your mailbox.

broadband: A fast, permanent connection to the Internet, such as one provided by DSL, cable modem, or satellite. *See also* DSL.

browser: A program that lets you read information on the Web. Some all-singing, all-dancing browsers can do e-mail and other things, too.

byte: A group of eight bits, enough to represent a character. Computer memory and disk space are usually measured in bytes.

cable modem: A box that connects your computer to your cable TV company's wiring. Needed for a cable Internet account.

CC (carbon copy): A type of address in which addressees get a copy of your e-mail, and other recipients are informed of it if they bother to read the message header. *See also* BCC.

certificate: Cryptographic data that identifies one computer or person to another.

chat: To talk (or type) live to other network users from any and all parts of the world. To chat on the Internet, you use an instant message program (like AOL Instant Messenger, Yahoo Messenger, or Windows Messenger) or an Internet Relay Chat (IRC) program like mIRC, or you chat via a Web site.

client: A computer that uses the services of another computer or a server (such as e-mail, FTP, or the Web). If you dial in to another system, your computer becomes a client of the system you dial in to (unless you're using X Windows — don't ask). *See also* server.

com: Last part of an Internet domain name (in `http://net.gurus.com`, for example) to indicate that the host computer is run by a commercial organization.

cookie: A small text file stored on your computer by a Web site you have visited; used to remind that site about you the next time you visit it.

cyber-: A prefix meaning the use of the computers and networks that comprise the Internet, as in *cyberspace, cybersex,* or *cybercop.* Used by itself, it's short for *cybersex,* referring to licentious online conversations.

default: Information that a program uses unless you specify otherwise.

DHCP (Dynamic Host Configuration Protocol): A system that assigns IP addresses for a local-area network (LAN) or a broadband system that doesn't require individual logins. *See also* PPPoE.

dial-up connection or dial-up networking: The built-in Internet communication program in Windows that connects over an ordinary telephone line.

digest: A compilation of the messages that have been posted to a mailing list recently.

domain: Part of the official name of a computer on the Internet — for example, `gurus.com`. Microsoft also calls groups of computers on a LAN controlled by a Windows server a *domain.*

domain name server (DNS): A computer on the Internet that translates between Internet domain names, such as `xuxa.iecc.com`, and numeric IP addresses, such as `208.31.42.42`. Sometimes just called *name server.*

download: To copy a file from a remote computer "down" to your computer.

DRM (Digital Rights Management): Technology that attempts to restrict what you can do with material you find on the Internet.

DSL (Digital Subscriber Line): A technology that lets you transmit data over phone lines at high speed, as much as 7 million bps. Nice if you can get it — ask your phone company.

DSL modem: A box that connects your computer to a DSL line.

dummies: People who don't know everything but are smart enough to seek help. Used ironically.

eBay: The original and most successful Web-based auction site, at `www.ebay.com`.

edu: Last part of an Internet domain name (in `www.middlebury.edu`, for example) to indicate that the host computer is run by an educational institution, usually a college or university.

e-commerce: Electronic commerce; mainly buying and selling goods and services over the Internet.

e-mail: Electronic messages sent via the Internet.

emoticon: A combination of punctuation or punctuation and letters intended to communicate emotion on the part of the writer, especially in e-mail, chat, or instant messages. Emoticons include smileys (see later in this glossary) and combinations like <g> for "grin."

Facebook: Social networking Web site.

FAQ (Frequently Asked Questions): An article that answers questions that come up often. Many mailing lists and Usenet newsgroups have FAQs that are posted regularly. To read the FAQs for all newsgroups, go to `www.faqs.org`.

favorites: A list of files or Web pages you plan to use frequently. Internet Explorer lets you maintain a list of your favorite items to make it easy to see them again. Same idea as *bookmarks*.

Firefox: A popular, free browser from the Mozilla Foundation that competes with Internet Explorer and has fewer safety issues.

firewall: Security software, often running in a router or a user's computer, that connects a local network to the Internet and, for security reasons, lets only certain kinds of messages in and out.

flame: To post angry, inflammatory, or insulting messages. Don't do it! Too much flaming between two or more individuals is a *flame war*.

Flash: *See* Shockwave Flash.

FTP (File Transfer Protocol): A method of transferring files from one computer to the other over the Net.

gateway: A computer that connects one network with another, where the two networks use different protocols.

GIF (Graphics Interchange Format): A patented type of graphics file originally defined by CompuServe and now found all over the Net. Files in this format end in `.gif` and are called *GIF files* or just *GIFs*. Pronounced "jif" unless you prefer to say "gif."

giga-: A prefix meaning 1 billion (1,000,000,000).

Gmail: Google's free Web mail service, at `http://gmail.com`.

Google: A search engine used for finding things on the Web, with extra smarts to look for the most useful pages. It's on the Web at `www.google.com`.

gov: Last part of an Internet domain name (in `http://cu.nih.gov`, for example) to indicate that the host computer is run by some government body in the U.S., probably the federal government.

header: The beginning of an e-mail message containing To and From addresses, subject, date, and other gobbledygook important to the programs that handle your mail.

home page: The entry page, or main page, of a Web site. If you have a home page, it's the main page about you. A home page usually contains links to other Web pages.

hostname: The name of a computer (or *host*) on the Internet (`http://net.gurus.com`, for example).

HTML (HyperText Markup Language): The language used to write pages for the Web. This language lets the text include codes that define fonts, layout, embedded graphics, and hypertext links. Web pages are stored in files that usually have the extension `.htm` or `.html`. Don't worry: You don't have to know anything about HTML to use the Web.

HTML mail: E-mail messages formatted with HTML codes. Not all e-mail programs can properly display them.

HTTP (HyperText Transfer Protocol): The way in which Web pages are transferred over the Net. URLs for Web pages start with `http://`, although you almost never have to type it.

HTTPS: A variant of HTTP that encrypts data for security.

hypertext: A system of writing and displaying text that enables the text to contain *links* to related documents. Hypermedia extends the concept to images and audio. The Web uses both hypertext and hypermedia.

IM (instant message): A message sent from one person to another that appears immediately on the recipient's computer, allowing a text conversation.

IMAP (Internet Message Access Protocol): A method used for storing and delivering Internet e-mail that lets you see the same view of your mailbox no matter what computer you check it from.

info: Last part of an Internet domain name, such as `mta.info`, to indicate (supposedly) useful information. Sometimes it even is.

Internet: All the computers that are connected into an amazingly huge global network so that they can talk to each other. When you connect your puny little computer to your Internet service provider, your computer becomes part of that network.

Internet Connection Sharing (ICS): A Windows feature that allows a computer to share its Internet connection with other computers on a LAN.

Internet Explorer: A Web browser vigorously promoted by Microsoft that comes in Windows, and (arguably) UNIX flavors. The Mac version is no longer being upgraded. *See also* Firefox, *and* Safari.

Internet Relay Chat (IRC): A system that enables Internet folks to talk to each other in real time (rather than after a delay, as with e-mail messages).

intranet: A private version of the Internet that lets people within an organization exchange data by using popular Internet tools, such as browsers.

IP (Internet Protocol): The scheme used to route packets of data through the Net, often used with TCP as TCP/IP. A newer version, IPv6, allows many more addresses. *See also* TCP.

IP address: A four-part number, such as 208.31.42.252, that identifies a host on the Internet.

iPod: Apple's line of personal music players.

ISP (Internet service provider): The folks who bring the Internet to you — via dial-up, DSL, or cable modem, including folks like AOL, Comcast, and MSN.

iTunes: Apple's music software and online music store.

Java: A computer language invented by Sun Microsystems. Because Java programs can run on many different kinds of computers, and most Web browsers can run chunks of Java code called *applets,* Java makes it easier to deliver application programs over the Internet. JavaScript is a different language that also is widely used on Web pages.

JPEG: A type of still-image file found all over the Net. Files in this format end in .jpg or .jpeg and are called *JPEG* (pronounced "jay-peg") files. Stands for Joint Photographic Experts Group.

K, KB, or Kbyte: 1,024 bytes, kilobyte. Usually used as a measure of a computer's memory or hard drive storage, or as a measure of file size.

kilo-: Prefix meaning one thousand (1,000) or often, with computers, 1,024.

LAN (local-area network): Computers in one building or campus connected by cables so that they can share files, printers, or an Internet connection.

link: A hypertext connection that can take you to another document or another part of the same document. On the Web, links appear as highlighted text or pictures. To follow a link, you click the highlighted material.

Linux: A version of UNIX; an operating system that runs on a wide variety of computers, including PCs. Many Internet servers run UNIX or Linux.

list server: An e-mail mailing list management program; a program that maintains a subscriber list and distributes list postings to those subscribers. Common list servers include ListProc, LISTSERV, and Majordomo. The names of mailing lists maintained by LISTSERV often end with -L.

lurk: To read a mailing list or chat group without posting any messages. Someone who lurks is a *lurker*. Lurking is okay and is much better than flaming.

mailbomb: To send someone vast amounts of unwanted e-mail.

mailbox: A file on your incoming (POP or IMAP) mail server where your e-mail messages are stored until you download them to your e-mail program. Some e-mail programs also call the files in which you store messages *mailboxes*.

mailing list: A special type of e-mail address that remails all incoming mail to a list of subscribers to the mailing list. Each mailing list has a specific topic, so you subscribe to the ones that interest you. Often managed by using LISTSERV, Majordomo, Mailman, or another list server program.

mega-: Prefix meaning one million.

mil: Last part of an Internet domain name, like `www.army.mil`, to indicate that the host computer is run by some part of the U.S. military.

MIME (Multipurpose Internet Mail Extensions): The scheme used to send pictures, word processing files, and other nontext information through e-mail.

mirror: An FTP or Web server that provides copies of the same files as another server. Mirrors spread out the load for more popular FTP and Web sites.

mobi: Last part of an Internet domain name, such as `amtrak.mobi` or `giggle.mobi`, used for Web sites intended to be viewed on mobile phones.

modem: A gizmo that lets your computer talk on the phone or on cable TV. Short for *modulator/demodulator*.

moderator: The person who looks at the messages posted to a mailing list, newsgroup, or chat forum. The moderator can nix messages that are stupid, redundant, off the topic, or offensive.

Mozilla: The foundation (at `www.mozilla.com`) that supports and enhances open source software originally from Netscape. The foundation distributes the Firefox browser and the Thunderbird mail program.

MP3: A music file format available on the Net.

MPEG: A type of video file found on the Net. Files in this format end in `.mpg` or `.mpeg`. Stands for Moving Picture Experts Group.

MSN: Microsoft Network, Microsoft's Internet provider. It also offers MSN Explorer, which you can use to browse the Web with your MSN account, and MSN Messenger, Microsoft's instant messaging program.

MSN TV: Formerly WebTV; an online Internet service that includes hardware (an Internet terminal and remote control) that you connect to your TV. No computer needed.

MySpace: Social networking Web site used primarily by teenagers and music groups.

Napster: An online music source that charges a flat monthly fee for all you can listen to.

net: A network, or (when capitalized) the Internet itself. When these letters appear as the last part of an address (in `www.abuse.net`, for example), they indicate that the host computer is run by a networking organization.

.NET: Microsoft's platform for Web services, which allows applications to communicate and share data over the Internet. No relation to `.net` addresses.

network: Computers that are connected together. Those in the same or nearby buildings are in a *local-area network;* those that are farther away are in a *wide-area network;* and when you interconnect networks all over the world, you get the Internet!

newsgroup: A topic area in the Usenet news system. (See the Web page `http://net.gurus.com/usenet` for a description of Usenet newsgroups.)

org: Last part of an Internet domain name (in `www.uua.org`, for example) to indicate that the host computer is probably run by a noncommercial organization.

Outlook: An e-mail program (among other things) that is part of Microsoft Office. Powerful, flexible, and notoriously susceptible to worms and viruses.

Outlook Express: The e-mail program that comes with Microsoft Windows XP. Utterly unrelated to Outlook and not quite as susceptible to worms and viruses. The Vista version is Windows Mail.

page: *See* Web page.

password: A secret code used to keep things private. Be sure to pick one that's hard to guess, preferably two randomly chosen words separated by a number or special character.

PayPal: A Web-based service through which you can make and receive payments by e-mail or from links on Web sites. Owned by eBay.

PDF file: A method for distributing formatted documents over the Net. Windows and Linux users need the special reader program Acrobat. Get it at www.adobe.com/products/acrobat.

phishing: Using e-mail or IM to trick people into revealing personal information, such as credit card numbers.

ping: To send a short message to which another computer automatically responds. If you can't ping the other computer, you probably can't talk to it any other way, either.

plug-in: A computer program you add to your browser to help it handle a special type of file.

podcasting: A system for distributing audio files with timely content that is meant to be heard on personal music players, such as the Apple iPod.

POP (Post Office Protocol): A system by which a mail server on the Net lets you pick up your mail and download it to your PC or Mac. A POP server is the computer from which you pick up your mail. The most recent version is POP3.

POP server: A server that stores your incoming e-mail messages until you download them to your e-mail program.

pop-up: A new, usually annoying, window that appears in response to some action you took. Pop-ups are often used for advertising.

port number: An identifying number assigned to each program that is chatting on the Net. You hardly ever have to know these numbers — the Internet programs work this stuff out among themselves.

portal: A Web site designed to be a starting point for people using the Web.

PPP (Point-to-Point Protocol): The most common way a computer communicates with the Internet over a phone line.

PPPoE (PPP over Ethernet): The way you log in to a broadband account that requires an account and password. *See also* DHCP.

protocol: The agreed-on rules that computers rely on to talk among themselves. A protocol is a set of signals that mean "go ahead," "got it," "didn't get it, please resend," or "all done," for example.

proxy server: A program that translates between a LAN and the Internet.

QuickTime: A video and multimedia file format invented by Apple Computer and widely used on the Net. You can download it from `www.apple.com/quicktime`.

RealPlayer: the program that plays RealAudio streams, available from `www.real.com`.

router: A device that connects two or more networks. Can be a separate piece of equipment or software running on a PC.

RSS (Really Simple Syndication): A Web technology that lets you track multiple information sources, with automatic notification of new content.

Safari: The Web browser that comes with Mac OS X.

search engine: A program used to search for information on the Web. Google is a fairly popular one.

secure server: A Web server that uses encryption to prevent others from reading messages to or from your browser. Web-based shopping sites often use secure servers so that others cannot intercept your ordering information.

server: A computer that provides a service — such as e-mail, Web data, Usenet, or FTP — to other computers (known as *clients*) on a network.

shareware: Computer programs that are easily available for you to try with the understanding that you will pay for them if you keep using them. A great deal of good stuff is available, and people's voluntary compliance makes it viable.

Shockwave Flash: A program for viewing interactive multimedia on the Web. For more information about Flash and for a copy of the program's plug-in for your browser, go to `www.shockwave.com`.

skin: The arrangement of buttons, menus, and other items displayed by a program. Some programs (such as Opera and Firefox) let you choose among several skins.

Skype: A software product for making free or low-cost long-distance and international telephone calls. Owned by eBay.

smiley: A combination of special characters that portray emotions, such as :-) or :-(. Although hundreds have been invented, only a few are widely used, and all are silly. A smiley is a type of emoticon.

SMS (Short Message System): A system to send short text messages to and from mobile phones.

SMTP (Simple Mail Transfer Protocol): The optimistically named method by which Internet mail is delivered from one computer to another.

SMTP server: A server that accepts e-mail messages for delivery to local users or the rest of the Internet.

social networking site: A Web site where people can create online profiles, photo albums, and blogs, and can link to their friends' pages. See Chapter 17.

spam: Messages sent to large numbers of people who didn't ask for them. It's antisocial, ineffective, and often illegal. To fight spam, see www.cauce.org.

spyware: Software that sends information about you and how you use your computer to other people without your permission.

SSL (Secure Socket Layer): A Web-based technology that lets one computer verify another's identity and allow secure connections; used by secure Web servers. A newer version is known as *TLS*.

stationery: Formatted e-mail that you can use when composing messages to send to recipients by using graphical e-mail programs. (Not everyone's e-mail program can display formatted e-mail.)

streaming audio or video: A system for sending sound or video files over the Net that begins playing the file before it finishes downloading, letting you listen or watch with minimal delay. RealAudio (www.real.com) is the most popular streaming format.

StuffIt: A file-compression program that runs on Macs. StuffIt creates a SIT file that contains compressed versions of one or more files. To restore these files to their former size and shape, you use UnStuffIt.

surf: To wander around the World Wide Web and look for interesting stuff.

T1: A telecommunications standard that carries 24 voice calls or data at 1.544 million bps over a pair of telephone lines.

TCP (Transmission Control Protocol): The system that two computers use to synchronize data. Usually used with IP as TCP/IP to manage connections over the Net. *See also* IP.

telnet: A program that lets you log in to some other computers on the Net. Many prefer the more secure program ssh. See `http://net.gurus.com/telnet`.

tera-: A prefix meaning trillion (1,000,000,000,000).

text file: A file that contains only textual characters, with no special formatting, graphical information, sound clips, video, or what-have-you.

thread: A message posted to a mailing list or newsgroup, together with all the follow-up messages, the follow-ups to follow-ups, and so on.

Thunderbird: A popular e-mail client from the Mozilla Foundation. See Chapter 13.

top-level domain (TLD): The last part of an Internet domain or hostname. If the TLD is two letters long, it's the *country code* in which the organization that owns the domain is (usually) located. If the TLD is three letters or longer, it's a code indicating the type of organization that runs the domain.

UNIX: A geeky operating system originally developed at Bell Labs. Used on many servers on the Net. *Linux* is now the most popular version.

upload: To copy your stuff to somebody else's computer.

URL (Uniform Resource Locator): A standardized way of naming network resources, used for linking pages on the World Wide Web.

Usenet: A system of thousands of newsgroups. You read the messages by using a newsreader. (See the Web page `http://net.gurus.com/usenet` for a description of Usenet newsgroups.)

viewer: A program to show you files that contain stuff other than text.

virus: A self-replicating program that piggybacks on e-mail messages or other programs, frequently with destructive side effects. *See also* worm.

virus checker: A program that intercepts and destroys viruses as they arrive on your computer.

VoIP (Voice over Internet Protocol): A method for sending telephone calls via the Net. Go to `http://net.gurus.com/phone` for more information.

watermark: A message hidden in a music, image, or video file designed to detect copyright violations. *See also* DRM.

WAV: A popular Windows format for sound files (`.wav` files) found on the Net.

Web Folder: A Windows XP feature that enables you to use Windows Explorer to see, download from, and upload to an FTP or Web server.

Web page: A document available on the World Wide Web.

Web page editor: A program for editing files in HTML for use as Web pages.

Web server: A program that stores Web pages and responds to requests from Web browsers.

Web site: A collection of Web pages stored on a Web server. The Web pages belong to a particular person or organization.

Weblog: *See* blog.

webcam: A digital video camera that attaches to your computer and transmits video over the Internet. The video can appear on a Web page or as part of a chat or conference.

WEP (Wired Equivalent Privacy): A broken security system for WiFi. Use WPA instead.

WiFi: The most popular kind of wireless network. Also known as 802.11b/g, after the number of the standard that defines it.

Wiki: Short for *wikiwiki,* which is Hawaiian for *fast.* A technology that lets you rapidly create and edit Web pages by using your Web browser.

Wikipedia: The open source, Web-based encyclopedia at `http://wikipedia.org`.

WiMax: A wireless broadband access technology that hopes to provide an alternative to cable and DSL.

wireless network: A network that uses radio waves rather than cables.

World Wide Web: A hypermedia system that lets you browse through lots of interesting information. The Web has become the central repository of humanity's information in the 21st century.

worm: A malicious program that spreads directly from computer to computer.

WPA (WiFi Protected Access): A well-regarded security system for WiFi.

XML (eXtensible Markup Language): A markup language and set of related technologies that can be used to make information on the Internet sharable by different types of programs, not just Web browsers.

Yahoo: A Web site (at `www.yahoo.com`) that provides a subject-oriented guide to the World Wide Web and many other kinds of information.

YouTube: A video-sharing Web site owned by Google.

ZIP file: A file with the extension `.zip` that has been compressed with ZipMagic, WinZip, or a compatible program. Windows calls it *Compressed Folder.*

Index

Forbes Limited-Time Offer

Choose 2 years of FORBES — it's like getting

Now!

36 ISSUES FREE

and get all Special Issues and coverage includ

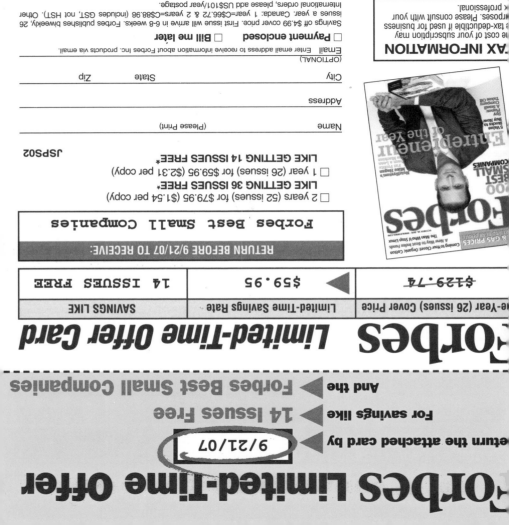

BUSINESS, CAREERS & PERSONAL FINANCE

0-7645-9847-3

0-7645-2431-3

Also available:
- Business Plans Kit For Dummies
0-7645-9794-9
- Economics For Dummies
0-7645-5726-2
- Grant Writing For Dummies
0-7645-8416-2
- Home Buying For Dummies
0-7645-5331-3
- Managing For Dummies
0-7645-1771-6
- Marketing For Dummies
0-7645-5600-2

- Personal Finance For Dummies
0-7645-2590-5*
- Resumes For Dummies
0-7645-5471-9
- Selling For Dummies
0-7645-5363-1
- Six Sigma For Dummies
0-7645-6798-5
- Small Business Kit For Dummies
0-7645-5984-2
- Starting an eBay Business For Dummies
0-7645-6924-4
- Your Dream Career For Dummies
0-7645-9795-7

HOME & BUSINESS COMPUTER BASICS

0-470-05432-8

0-471-75421-8

Also available:
- Cleaning Windows Vista For Dummies
0-471-78293-9
- Excel 2007 For Dummies
0-470-03737-7
- Mac OS X Tiger For Dummies
0-7645-7675-5
- MacBook For Dummies
0-470-04859-X
- Macs For Dummies
0-470-04849-2
- Office 2007 For Dummies
0-470-00923-3

- Outlook 2007 For Dummies
0-470-03830-6
- PCs For Dummies
0-7645-8958-X
- Salesforce.com For Dummies
0-470-04893-X
- Upgrading & Fixing Laptops For Dummies
0-7645-8959-8
- Word 2007 For Dummies
0-470-03658-3
- Quicken 2007 For Dummies
0-470-04600-7

FOOD, HOME, GARDEN, HOBBIES, MUSIC & PETS

0-7645-8404-9

0-7645-9904-6

Also available:
- Candy Making For Dummies
0-7645-9734-5
- Card Games For Dummies
0-7645-9910-0
- Crocheting For Dummies
0-7645-4151-X
- Dog Training For Dummies
0-7645-8418-9
- Healthy Carb Cookbook For Dummies
0-7645-8476-6
- Home Maintenance For Dummies
0-7645-5215-5

- Horses For Dummies
0-7645-9797-3
- Jewelry Making & Beading For Dummies
0-7645-2571-9
- Orchids For Dummies
0-7645-6759-4
- Puppies For Dummies
0-7645-5255-4
- Rock Guitar For Dummies
0-7645-5356-9
- Sewing For Dummies
0-7645-6847-7
- Singing For Dummies
0-7645-2475-5

INTERNET & DIGITAL MEDIA

0-470-04529-9

0-470-04894-8

Also available:
- Blogging For Dummies
0-471-77084-1
- Digital Photography For Dummies
0-7645-9802-3
- Digital Photography All-in-One Desk Reference For Dummies
0-470-03743-1
- Digital SLR Cameras and Photography For Dummies
0-7645-9803-1
- eBay Business All-in-One Desk Reference For Dummies
0-7645-8438-3
- HDTV For Dummies
0-470-09673-X

- Home Entertainment PCs For Dummies
0-470-05523-5
- MySpace For Dummies
0-470-09529-6
- Search Engine Optimization For Dummies
0-471-97998-8
- Skype For Dummies
0-470-04891-3
- The Internet For Dummies
0-7645-8996-2
- Wiring Your Digital Home For Dummies
0-471-91830-X

* Separate Canadian edition also available
† Separate U.K. edition also available

SPORTS, FITNESS, PARENTING, RELIGION & SPIRITUALITY

0-471-76871-5

0-7645-7841-3

Also available:
- Catholicism For Dummies
  0-7645-5391-7
- Exercise Balls For Dummies
  0-7645-5623-1
- Fitness For Dummies
  0-7645-7851-0
- Football For Dummies
  0-7645-3936-1
- Judaism For Dummies
  0-7645-5299-6
- Potty Training For Dummies
  0-7645-5417-4
- Buddhism For Dummies
  0-7645-5359-3

- Pregnancy For Dummies
  0-7645-4483-7 †
- Ten Minute Tone-Ups For Dummies
  0-7645-7207-5
- NASCAR For Dummies
  0-7645-7681-X
- Religion For Dummies
  0-7645-5264-3
- Soccer For Dummies
  0-7645-5229-5
- Women in the Bible For Dummies
  0-7645-8475-8

TRAVEL

0-7645-7749-2

0-7645-6945-7

Also available:
- Alaska For Dummies
  0-7645-7746-8
- Cruise Vacations For Dummies
  0-7645-6941-4
- England For Dummies
  0-7645-4276-1
- Europe For Dummies
  0-7645-7529-5
- Germany For Dummies
  0-7645-7823-5
- Hawaii For Dummies
  0-7645-7402-7

- Italy For Dummies
  0-7645-7386-1
- Las Vegas For Dummies
  0-7645-7382-9
- London For Dummies
  0-7645-4277-X
- Paris For Dummies
  0-7645-7630-5
- RV Vacations For Dummies
  0-7645-4442-X
- Walt Disney World & Orlando
  For Dummies
  0-7645-9660-8

GRAPHICS, DESIGN & WEB DEVELOPMENT

0-7645-8815-X

0-7645-9571-7

Also available:
- 3D Game Animation For Dummies
  0-7645-8789-7
- AutoCAD 2006 For Dummies
  0-7645-8925-3
- Building a Web Site For Dummies
  0-7645-7144-3
- Creating Web Pages For Dummies
  0-470-08030-2
- Creating Web Pages All-in-One Desk
  Reference For Dummies
  0-7645-4345-8
- Dreamweaver 8 For Dummies
  0-7645-9649-7

- InDesign CS2 For Dummies
  0-7645-9572-5
- Macromedia Flash 8 For Dummies
  0-7645-9691-8
- Photoshop CS2 and Digital
  Photography For Dummies
  0-7645-9580-6
- Photoshop Elements 4 For Dummies
  0-471-77483-9
- Syndicating Web Sites with RSS Feeds
  For Dummies
  0-7645-8848-6
- Yahoo! SiteBuilder For Dummies
  0-7645-9800-7

NETWORKING, SECURITY, PROGRAMMING & DATABASES

0-7645-7728-X

0-471-74940-0

Also available:
- Access 2007 For Dummies
  0-470-04612-0
- ASP.NET 2 For Dummies
  0-7645-7907-X
- C# 2005 For Dummies
  0-7645-9704-3
- Hacking For Dummies
  0-470-05235-X
- Hacking Wireless Networks
  For Dummies
  0-7645-9730-2
- Java For Dummies
  0-470-08716-1

- Microsoft SQL Server 2005 For Dummies
  0-7645-7755-7
- Networking All-in-One Desk Reference
  For Dummies
  0-7645-9939-9
- Preventing Identity Theft For Dummies
  0-7645-7336-5
- Telecom For Dummies
  0-471-77085-X
- Visual Studio 2005 All-in-One Desk
  Reference For Dummies
  0-7645-9775-2
- XML For Dummies
  0-7645-8845-1